MULTI-SIDED MUSIC PLATFORMS AND THE LAW

Multi-Sided Music Platforms and the Law explores the legal and regulatory frameworks surrounding copyright protection, competition and privacy concerns arising from the way multi-sided platforms use copyright-protected content in digital advertising.

This book suggests how stakeholders in Africa, and their advisors, may ingenuously reform and apply various legal and regulatory frameworks to address these issues which arise from the manner in which multi-sided platforms use copyright-protected content in digital advertising. The book critically engages with the regulatory efforts in other jurisdictions, particularly the EU, with a view to bringing an African perspective to the debate and practice. It undertakes a consideration of this issue by asking how multi-sided platforms may be deployed in a manner that continues innovative uses of copyright content while protecting the economic freedom of African copyright owners as small businesses.

Providing the first pro-Africa approach to the regulation of multi-sided platforms, particularly with reference to music, this book focuses on key aspects of digital commercial activity and highlights the main challenges and opportunities for its regulation. It will be of interest to lawyers, policymakers and students across Nigeria, South Africa and internationally among the African Union, European Union and beyond.

Dr. Chijioke Ifeoma Okorie is currently the inaugural postdoctoral research fellow under the South African Research Chair in intellectual property, innovation and development at the University of Cape Town, South Africa. She also runs a copyright, internet and technology law consultancy in Nigeria – Penguide Advisory (penguideng.com) – and is a valued alumna of one of Nigeria's leading commercial law firms. She is the Africa Correspondent for the IPKat (most popular intellectual property law blog of all time), contributing blogs which monitor, report on and comment on various intellectual property–related issues in and around Africa.

CONTEMPORARY COMMERCIAL LAW

Maritime Law in China
Emerging Issues and Future Developments
Edited by Johanna Hjalmarsson and Jenny Jingbo Zhang

Illegality in Marine Insurance Law
Feng Wang

Insurance Law Implications of Delay in Maritime Transport
Ayşegül Buğra

Online Arbitration
Faye Fangfei Wang

Double Insurance and Contribution
Nisha Mohamed

The Law and Autonomous Vehicles
Matthew Channon, Lucy McCormick and Kyriaki Noussia

FIDIC Yellow Book
A Commentary
Ben Beaumont

The Contract of Carriage
Multimodal Transport and Unimodal Regulation
Paula Bäckdén

FIDIC Red Book
A Commentary
Ben Beaumont

Blockchain Technology and the Law
Opportunities and Risks
Muharem Kianieff

Third Party Protection in Shipping
Carlo Corcione

Multi-sided Music Platforms and the Law
Copyright, Law and Policy in Africa
Chijioke Ifeoma Okorie

For more information about this series, please visit:
www.routledge.com/Contemporary-Commercial-Law/book-series/CCL

MULTI-SIDED MUSIC PLATFORMS AND THE LAW

COPYRIGHT, LAW AND POLICY IN AFRICA

CHIJIOKE IFEOMA OKORIE

informa law
from Routledge

First published 2020
by Informa Law from Routledge
2 Park Square, Milton Park, Abingdon, Oxon OX14 4RN

and by Informa Law from Routledge
52 Vanderbilt Avenue, New York, NY 10017

Informa Law from Routledge is an imprint of the Taylor & Francis Group, an informa business

First issued in paperback 2021

British Library Cataloguing-in-Publication Data
A catalogue record for this book is available from the British Library

Library of Congress Cataloging-in-Publication Data
Names: Okorie, Chijioke Ifeoma, author.
Title: Multi-sided music platforms and the law : copyright, law and policy in Africa / Chijioke Ifeoma Okorie.
Description: Abingdon, Oxon ; New York, NY : Informa Law from Routledge, 2019. | Based on author's thesis (doctoral - University of Cape Town, 2018) issued under title: Open and freemium music business models in Africa : copyright and competition consequences. | Includes bibliographical references and index.
Identifiers: LCCN 2019032824 (print) | LCCN 2019032825 (ebook) | ISBN 9780367137366 (hardback) | ISBN 9780429028380 (ebook)
Subjects: LCSH: Copyright—Music—South Africa. | Copyright—Music—Nigeria. | Music trade—Law and legislation—South Africa. | Music trade—Law and legislation—Nigeria. | Advertising—Music—South Africa. | Advertising—Music—Nigeria. | Multi-sided platform businesses—South Africa. | Multi-sided platform businesses—Nigeria. | Digital rights management—South Africa. | Digital rights management—Nigeria.
Classification: LCC KQC375 .O46 2019 (print) | LCC KQC375 (ebook) | DDC 346.0482—dc23
LC record available at https://lccn.loc.gov/2019032824
LC ebook record available at https://lccn.loc.gov/2019032825

ISBN: 978-0-367-13736-6 (hbk)
ISBN: 978-1-03-208601-9 (pbk)
ISBN: 978-0-429-02838-0 (ebk)

Typeset in Times New Roman
by Apex CoVantage, LLC

To Chinonyerem, Enyichi, Chifumnanya and Akunna –
onyinye Chukwu nyelu m.

CONTENTS

DETAILED CONTENTS

ACKNOWLEDGEMENTS

This book would not be possible without the continuous outpouring of God's love and favour, which I have received. This outpouring of love and favour extends to the humans whose efforts brought this book into existence.

Special thanks to my husband and partner, Ikenna, for all the ways he has walked and worked with me. I am ever so grateful to my parents, Mr. and Mrs. Benjamin and Felicia Okoli for their prayers, support and encouragement in all my pursuits. My siblings Obianuju, Chinedu, Ogechukwu and Chidera are the stuff of (sibling) dreams. I am thankful for their support and encouragement and all-round help. My mother-in-law, Mrs Salome Okorie, deserves special mention for the gift of her prayers and presence that enabled me take the needed time to complete this book.

Professor Caroline Ncube, South African Research Chair in Intellectual Property, Innovation and Development, supervised my doctoral thesis, which culminated in this book and has not stopped showering me with the gift of her support and experience, which was the hallmark of my PhD journey.

I have been blessed to receive support and encouragement from friends too numerous to mention. In particular, I would like to thank Suzzana Harvey, Uchenna Ogwo, Uche Nwokeafor, Desmond Oriakhogba, Chidinma Ndubuisi, Onyinye Onungwa and Dotun Kazeem for being friends in need and friends indeed. Hanani Hlomani also deserves special mention for coming to my rescue and revising my bibliography. Thanks too go to Dr. Omogbai Omo-Eboh for consistently giving me the benefit of his experience and encouragement.

I am grateful to the renowned Professor Jeremy Philips for bringing me on to the Afro-IP blog team. Thanks to my activity as a blogger for the Afro-IP blog, I met the fantastic Dr. Eleonora Rosati, who alongside other *PermaKats* brought me on to the IPKat blog team as Africa Correspondent. Indeed, it was a guest post for the IPKat blog that caught the attention of Amy Jones, editor at Informa Law from Routledge leading to the commissioning of this book.

I am grateful to Amy Jones and Senior Editorial Assistant Caroline Church for all their support and understanding in getting this book from conception to production. Their superb editorial assistance has worked magic on the manuscript that birthed this book.

This book is based on the research supported in part by the National Research Foundation (NRF) of South Africa. Any opinion, finding and conclusion or recommendation expressed in this book is entirely mine.

FOREWORD

Multi-sided Music Platforms and the Law: Copyright, Law and Policy in Africa by Chijioke Okorie, PhD is an important and timely contribution to the discussion of music platforms. It comes at a time when the global scholarly and legal practice communities are still coming to grips with the import of the EU Directive on Copyright in the Digital Single Market for these platforms. It takes the reader on an in-depth exploration of multi-sided platforms from the vantage point of South African and Nigerian legal systems. Specifically, it considers copyright, competition and privacy regulation. Under copyright, the book focuses on infringement concerns arising from the applicable copyright access and usage terms. It also examines the meaning and extent of the copyright holder's rights including the right to communicate the work to the public. This is juxtaposed with a discussion of the relevance of safe harbour regimes and the value gap proposal. In relation to competition, Okorie canvasses restrictive agreements and abuse of dominance by copyright holders and platform firms. The privacy aspects considered include an examination of how platform terms of use comply with relevant privacy regulation which is found in dedicated privacy legislation and other sources, such as consumer protection legislation.

Okorie's consideration of these legal aspects within the context of prevailing business models is one of the major strengths of this work. Its classification of the most common models for the monetisation of copyright-protected music content and its detailed overview of how multi-sided platforms are designed and operate lends credence to the legal analysis that follows.

To my knowledge, this is the first work that considers multi-sided platforms from the above perspectives under South African and Nigerian law. As such, Okorie has broken new ground and opened an important discussion.

Caroline B. Ncube
DST/NRF SARChI Research Chair in Intellectual Property, Innovation and Development
University of Cape Town

PREFACE

With the advent of the internet and the development of information and communication technologies (ICTs), online platforms have become a veritable tool for the distribution of diverse content and information including copyright-protected content. Music content is one of such content protected by copyright law.

This book explores the application of copyright law, privacy law in addition to competition law to regulate multi-sided music platforms – firms that use copyright-protected music content in digital advertising. The jurisdictional focus is on Nigeria and South Africa.

For so long, the legal discourse on the use of music (and other copyright-protected) content in advertising has largely been on platform users and their actions in reproducing the protected content. Copyright scholars and litigants have sought to respectively explain and litigate such uses as indirectly authorised or induced by the owners of the platforms. However, a different and emerging approach consists in looking at the platform firm's actions and the implications of such actions. The use of copyright-protected music content in advertising affects the revenue that may accrue to the copyright owner by virtue of copyright protection and may also affect the uses of copyright-protected music content that may be outside the scope of copyright protection. So, rather than focus solely on the activities of platform users and how such may have been induced or authorised by the platform firm, this book proceeds on the premise that it is equally important to examine multi-sided music platforms from the perspective of the actions or activities of the platform firms (as copyright users) instead. This is especially so given that the money flow comes from the activities of the platform firms even though undertaken to attract the attention of potential and actual users of the platform.

A similar approach is adopted in considering the privacy protection regime's right of access and right to seek redress as the relevant rights of copyright owners as data subjects in the context of multi-sided music platforms. Using cases from several jurisdictions, particularly at the Court of Justice of the European Union (CJEU) and in the US, the book provides a vivid description of copyright and privacy terms prevalent in multi-sided music platforms.

It is hoped that the contributions in this book will be particularly helpful for those who are interested in the legal and policy issues related to the digital economy, copyright, competition law and privacy law, particularly in Africa, be they academics, practitioners, lawyers or students of the law.

TABLE OF CASES

South Africa

Nigeria

Other jurisdictions

TABLE OF STATUTES

South Africa

Nigeria

International instruments

CHAPTER 1

Introduction to multi-sided music platforms

Background

1.1 A platform is a place (physical or virtual) that enables interaction between various market participants such as sellers, buyers, suppliers, advertisers etc. Within a platform, sellers have a forum to sell their products or provide services to customers and consumers.[1] For instance, a store, a digital download website, a streaming website and even a concert stage are all platforms because they enable various kinds of sellers, service providers, customers, suppliers and other market participants to interact. With the advent of the internet and the development of information and communication technologies (ICTs), online platforms have become a veritable tool for the distribution of diverse content and information. For instance, streaming and download sites have supplanted traditional platforms (e.g. music CD stores) for the distribution of music.[2]

1.2 This book focuses on one of these online platforms deployed in the distribution of music content – the multi-sided music platforms.[3] In the multi-sided music platforms, firms which own and operate online platforms (platform firms) offer music content on the internet to the general public free of charge or at zero price, either on a revenue-based licence or based on a *gratis* licence, to create, deliver and capture value by providing advertising services.[4] The best-known global examples of multi-sided music platforms are YouTube, Facebook and SoundCloud[5] where music content may be 'streamed' free of charge.[6] Within the African continent, multi-sided

1 See Evans DS, 'Multisided platforms, dynamic competition, and the assessment of market power for internet-based firms' [2016] 10(2) *Competition Policy International Journal* 6.

2 Streaming is the transmission of audio in real time over the internet. See Kopp SW and Suter TA, 'Developments in copyright policy and network technologies: The First Generation' [1998] 17(2) *Journal of Public Policy & Marketing* 306.

3 For examples of music platforms especially in the digital scene, see Bourreau M, Moreau F and Gensollen M, *The Digitization of the Recorded Music Industry: Impact on Business Models and Scenarios of Evolution* (Department of Economics and Social Sciences Telecom Paris 2008) 14.

4 There is no universally accepted definition of multi-sided platforms. However, the definition adopted here corresponds with descriptions provided in key literature. See Osterwalder A and others, *Business Model Generation* (John Wiley & Sons 2010).

5 See Fouché JA, *Crafting the Commons: Modern Approaches to Music as Product* (Masters, University of Cape Town 2005).

6 For the purpose of this book, 'free' in relation to music content or copyright works is used to identify music content or copyright works provided without charging any monetary price.

music platforms such as NotJustOk.com, TooXclusive.com, 360nobs.com etc. are quite well known.[7] Basically, platform firms in this context use copyright-protected music content as a tool to generate profits and increase the number of platform users for their advertising service.[8] Generally, users of the platform can access and consume music without the requirement or expectation of payment. The music consumption comes with specialised functions and services such as an unlimited music catalogue, advertisements alongside the music, and extended search features.

1.3 This book explores the legal and regulatory frameworks surrounding copyright protection, privacy, and competition concerns arising from the way multi-sided music platforms use copyright-protected music content in digital advertising. Platform firms are primarily users of music content protected by copyright law and authored and/or produced by others. Therefore, although this book considers the use of the music content by producers and uploaders[9] of music content, its principal focus is *inter alia* on the significance of how the music content is used by the platform firms in generating revenue from advertising. A by-product of using copyright-protected music content in advertising is the acquisition and processing of data regulated by privacy laws. Accordingly, this book also discusses privacy regime in South Africa and Nigeria as it concerns the activities of multi-sided music platforms. As shown in this book, these platform firms are said to operate multi-sided platforms because they create value by enabling interactions between two or more customer segments.[10] In this regard, the primary legal and regulatory frameworks explored are those of copyright, privacy and competition laws.

1.4 In promoting competition, copyright law strives to maintain a balance between the rights of copyright owners[11] and those of users[12] of copyright works.[13]

7 Schultz AJ, 'IP and African music industries: An interview with Phil Chard – Part 4' (*Afro-IP*, 2 September 2016), http://afro-ip.blogspot.com/2016/09/ip-and-african-music-industries_2.html (accessed 22 June 2019).

8 See Evans 2016 supra at 7.

9 To 'upload' means 'to transfer (data, files, etc.) from a computer to the memory of another device (such as a larger or remote computer)'. An uploader would be a person who carries out such action. See Merriam-Webster, 'Definition of upload' (*Merriam-webster.com*, 2019), www.merriam-webster.com/dictionary/upload (accessed 22 June 2019).

10 See Evans 2016 supra at 6. On the regulatory implications of multi-sided platforms, see Gürkaynak G, İnanılır Ö, Diniz S and Yaşar AG, 'Multisided markets and the challenge of incorporating multisided considerations into competition law analysis' [2017] 5(1) *Journal of Antitrust Enforcement* 100–129.

11 'Copyright owners' in this book refers to the person or entity who holds/owns the copyright, and may unless otherwise indicated, include not only authors such as artists), but also intermediaries or entities who have acquired rights from the authors.

12 'Users', 'users of copyright products' or 'copyright users' are used interchangeably to include any person or entity, other than the copyright owner who may need the copyright work for any purpose. Accordingly, it envisages persons or entity that merely 'consume' or enjoy the copyright work. However, the more appropriate term 'consumer' is used where the relevant person or entity is merely enjoying or listening to the music, without more. See, e.g., Elkin-Koren N, 'Copyright in a digital ecosystem: A user rights approach', in Ruth Okediji (ed), *Copyright Law in an Age of Limitations and Exceptions* (Cambridge University Press 2017).

13 'Copyright work' generally refers to any work eligible for copyright. See Section 1(1) of the Copyright Act, Cap. C28, Laws of the Federation of Nigeria, 2004 (Nigerian Copyright Act);

In regulating economic activities including those that involve the dissemination of copyright-protected content and the processing of data, competition law complements both copyright law and privacy law.

Multi-sided platforms

1.5 When a platform is multi-sided, it provides an avenue or means for several market participants to interact with themselves and derives revenue from providing that avenue for interaction. Market participants in a multi-sided platform occupy different 'sides' on the platform and they use the platform for different reasons related to their needs. While a two-sided platform provides goods or services to two distinct groups of customers who need each other in some way and who rely on the platform to facilitate transactions between them, a multi-sided platform would serve more than two sides.[14] They differ fundamentally from single-sided platforms that typically make or procure products, which they sell directly to customers. These operate along a linear supply chain and are single-sided because they do not have customers with interdependent demands.

1.6 Multi-sided platforms were in existence in ancient Greece in the form of insurance exchanges, which existed to connect shippers who needed insurance and financing with people who had the money and were willing to lend.[15] In the same period, many societies had matchmakers who informally connected bachelors with spinsters for the possibility of marriage. However, efforts to study multi-sided platforms as species of businesses became popular following the work of economists Rochet and Tirole, published around 2000.[16] The early studies focused on two-sided platforms that generate profits primarily from connecting two distinct groups of customers who need each other in some way and who rely on the platform to facilitate transactions between them.[17] However, with more developments in ICTs, platforms started to have several customer segments as opposed to one or two customer segments.[18] First, there were multi-sided platforms developed by software companies such as Microsoft and Linux. These platforms brought together users, application developers and hardware makers. With the development of the commercial internet in the mid-1990s came a new set of multi-sided platforms used for advertising (Google and Yahoo), transactions (eBay and Amazon), social networking (Facebook and MySpace) and many

Section 2(1) and 3(1)(a) and (b) of the Copyright Act, 1978 (Act No. 98 of 1978) (South African Copyright Act).

14 See Evans DS, 'The antitrust economics of two-sided markets' [2003] 20 *Yale Journal on Regulation* 325.

15 Evans DS, 'Some empirical aspects of multi-sided platform industries' [2003] 2 *Review of Network Economics* 191.

16 Ibid.

17 See Rochet JC and Tirole J, 'Two-sided markets: A progress report' [2006] 37 *RAND Journal of Economics* 645.

18 Even though multi-sided platforms became recognised as a category of business around 2000, multi-sided platforms have been around for ages. See Rochet JC and Tirole J, 'Platform competition in two-sided markets' [2003] 1(4) *Journal of the European Economic Association*, 990–1029.

others. These new generations of multi-sided platforms rely heavily on the internet and technology.[19]

Features of multi-sided platforms

1.7 Three features of multi-sided platforms set them apart from many other platforms deployed by firms: network effects, the 'chicken-and-egg problem' and the use of 'free' content or product. These features also affect how the law may be applied to the core activities of platform firms.

1.8 At inception, platform firms must resolve the 'chicken-and-egg problem': one customer segment will not participate on the platform without the participation of another customer segment.[20] A typical example is YouTube. Viewers will not come to the platform unless there are uploaded videos to watch. And, if there are no viewers on the platform, advertisers will not pay to advertise their products and/or services on the platform. To solve this 'chicken-and-egg' problem, platform firms have to adopt a marketing strategy that will attract the desired customer segments to the platform.[21]

1.9 Indeed, an increasingly common marketing strategy is to grant access to uploaders and viewers to upload and view content on the platform free of charge. Free products ('content') are often used in multi-sided platforms to attract the desired customer segments.[22] The free content may be music, film, news items, games and other entertainment products. Owing to the availability of free content and free access to the platforms themselves, many platform firms have attracted millions of users to the platforms. For example, Facebook, which started in 2004, currently has more than 2.2 billion active users worldwide,[23] and had advertising revenue in 2018 of more than $55 billion.[24] YouTube, which started in 2005, currently has over 1 billion active users worldwide,[25] and reportedly paid over $1.8 billion to artists and record companies in 2018.[26]

---

19 See generally Ghaziani A and Ventresca MJ, 'Keywords and cultural change: Frame analysis of business model public talk, 1975–2000' [2005] 20(4) *Sociological Forum* 523–559; Yip GS, 'Using strategy to change your business model' [2004] 15(2) *London Business School Review* 17–24.

20 See Evans 2016 supra at 7.

21 Ibid.

22 Ibid.

23 Barr S, 'The story of how Facebook was created in a Harvard dorm room' (*The Independent*, 23 August 2018), www.independent.co.uk/life-style/gadgets-and-tech/facebook-when-started-how-mark-zuckerberg-history-harvard-eduardo-saverin-a8505151.html (accessed 22 June 2019).

24 'Facebook: Annual Revenue 2018 | Statistic' (*Statista*, 4 February 2019), www.statista.com/statistics/268604/annual-revenue-of-facebook/ (accessed 22 June 2019).

25 Dickey MR, 'The 22 key turning points in the history of YouTube' (*Business Insider*, 15 February 2013), www.businessinsider.com/key-turning-points-history-of-youtube-2013-2?IR=T#youtube-launches-its-beta-site-in-may-2005–2. See also, www.businessinsider.co.za/youtube-user-statistics-2018-5?r=US&IR=T (accessed 22 June 2019).

26 Sanchez D, 'What Streaming Music Services Pay (Updated For 2018)' (*Digital Music News*, 16 January 2018), www.digitalmusicnews.com/2018/01/16/streaming-music-services-pay-2018/ (accessed 22 June 2019).

1.10 Linked to using free products to address the chicken-and-egg problem is the presence of 'indirect network effects'. As a concept, network effects occur where a product or service gains additional value for one customer segment as more people or other customer segments use it.[27] For instance, YouTube is more valuable to advertisers as more people view music videos uploaded to the platform. YouTube equally becomes more valuable to uploaders as more people view their music content on the platform. Facebook may become more valuable to a music artist because of the number of views the artist's music may have generated on the platform.

Multi-sided music platforms

1.11 In a narrower sense, a multi-sided music platform is like every other multi-sided platform, but the focus is on the music content used as (one of) the free products deployed to increase network effects and indirectly attract other customer segments. Within the multi-sided music platform, one class of users offers their own music content to the public at no cost (i.e. free of charge). These users seek to promote and widely disseminate their music content and the platforms offer a cost-effective avenue to do so. Other users upload music content belonging to other copyright owners. Platforms rely on both categories of users to attract other classes of users such as consumers and advertisers. The consumers come to the platforms to listen to and enjoy music content free of charge. The advertisers come to the platform to advertise their products and services to the teeming users available on the platform and attracted to the platform by either the opportunity to freely share their music content or the opportunity to access shared content. Because these platforms enable interactions between these categories of users, they are often collectively identified as 'multi-sided platforms'.[28] And because music content is the rallying point for the users of these platforms (at least from the perspective of this book), the platforms are referred to as 'multi-sided music platforms' in this book.

Music content in multi-sided music platforms

1.12 Since the Berne Convention in 1979, music has always been part of creative content protected by copyright law.[29] Copyright law grants copyright holders and authors an exclusive bundle of rights in their works upon fulfilment of specified criteria depending on the nature of the work.[30] For music, several categories

27 See Katz A, 'A network effects perspective on software piracy' [2005] 55(2) *University of Toronto Law Journal*, 164. On the regulatory implications of network effects, see Lemley MA and McGowan D, 'Legal implications of network economic effects' [1998] 86 *Calif L Rev* 479; Gal MS and Rubinfeld DL, 'The hidden costs of free goods: implications for antitrust enforcement' [2016] 80 *Antitrust Law Journal* 521.

28 See Evans 2016 supra at 6.

29 See art 2, Berne Convention for the Protection of Literary and Artistic Works, 1979.

30 The expression of the idea encompassing the work must be original and the work must be in a fixed medium. The author of the work must also be eligible for protection in that country as a citizen or person domiciled in that country. Section 1(2)(a) and (b) and 2(1)(i) and (ii) of the Nigerian Copyright Act, and Section 2(1) and 3(1)(a) and (b) of the South African Copyright Act, respectively.

of copyright works may be protectable: the lyrics of the song (eligible for protection as 'literary work'), the music composition or the music of the song (eligible for protection as 'musical work'), the sound recording embodied in a CD or other format and containing a reproduction of the musical work (eligible for protection as 'sound recording'), the photographs and images used as cover art[31] (eligible for protection as 'artistic work') and the music videos and DVDs containing a reproduction of the sound recording and moving images (eligible for protection as 'cinematograph film').[32] 'Music' or 'music content' is used in this book to mean a collective of these categories of protected work and the rights accruing to them under the applicable copyright laws.

1.13 Depending on the copyright work, copyright law defines an author to mean 'the creator of the work' and 'the person who made arrangements for the making of the work or in whose name the work was made'.[33] The copyright holders, authors or assignees of music content (collectively, 'copyright owners') enjoy the exclusive right to reproduce the work, perform the work in public, publish the work, make a cinematograph film or a record in respect of the work, distribute the work for commercial purposes and communicate or broadcast the work to the public.[34] Any person intending to exploit any of these rights must first obtain the licence or permission of the relevant copyright owner.

1.14 The multiplicity of rights and categories and owners inherent in a single unit of music content[35] in comparison to other categories of copyright products has combined well with the easy content dissemination and social production enabled by the internet to turn music content into the one of the most popular products for multi-sided platforms.[36] These attributes in turn attract legal scrutiny as new uses test the boundaries of statutory and regulatory frameworks.

1.15 The same platform may 'host' all kinds of content: music, film, news items, games and other entertainment goods. Despite this, certain differences in industry calibrations result in equally different legal implications.[37] Put

---

31 Cover art may be described as an artwork or photograph on the outside of a music single or album which is used to promote the music content it is displayed on. See Jones S and Sorger M, 'Steve Jones And Martin Sorger: Covering Music: A brief history and analysis of album cover design' [1999] 11(1) *Journal of Popular Music Studies* 68–102.

32 See Section 1(a), (b) and (e) as well as Section 51 of the Nigerian Copyright Act. See also Section 2(1)(a), (b) and (e) and Section 1 of the South African Copyright Act.

33 See Section 51(1) of the Nigerian Copyright Act; Section 1(1) of the South African Copyright Act.

34 For a delineation of each of the exclusive rights available for the mentioned categories of copyright works, see Sections 6, 7 and 8 of the Nigerian Copyright Act; Section 6(1)(a)-(g) South African Copyright Act. Each music content comes with those categories and number of copyright owners. See Rae-Hunter C, 'Better mousetraps: Licensing, access, and innovation in the new music marketplace' [2012] 7 *J Bus & Tech L* 45–46.

35 See Rae-Hunter 2012 supra at 39–40.

36 Telegraph Reporters, 'Top 10 most watched YouTube videos of all time' (*The Telegraph*, 4 August 2017), www.telegraph.co.uk/technology/0/most-watched-youtube-videos-of-all-time/ (accessed 22 June 2019).

37 See Elkin-Koren N, 'Creative Commons: A skeptical view of a worthy pursuit', in Hugenholtz B and Guibault L (eds), *The Future of the Public Domain* (Kluwer Law International 2006).

differently, the nature of each type of content will significantly determine the applicable legal implications.[38] For instance, while books, journals, software and the like[39] may be protected as literary work under copyright law,[40] the stakes are different, as players in each sector may want different things. Unlike software that requires regular updates flowing from/connected to the original software, music may not require such update. Accordingly, multi-sided platforms that allow free use of software and music may face different demands from software developers and music artists.[41] For this reason, this book is written on the premise that a general analysis of multi-sided platforms and the law is likely to be untenable and unwieldy. As such, the focus is on multi-sided platforms where music is (one of) the free products used to increase network effects and indirectly attract the advertisers.

How multi-sided music platforms operate

The design of the platform

1.16 Platform firms begin by developing a user-friendly, multi-sided music platform that is capable of hosting or storing a large catalogue of music content (and other copyright-protected and non-protected content), which users of the platform may upload thereon.[42] Members of the public may access the uploaded music content free of charge and in such cases may either download or stream music content depending on the specific platform.[43] The platform firms optimise the consumer-experience through tags, search features and automatic playlists based on the direction of the consumer and the like.[44] The platform also comes

38 The way the multi-sided music platform operates in the copyright industry depends on the nature of the copyright-protected product. See Russi G, 'Creative Commons, CC-plus and hybrid intermediaries: A stakeholders' perspective' [2011] *International Law and Management Review* 170; Klebanow A, 'Is music the next eBooks – An antitrust analysis of Apple's conduct in the music industry' (2015) 39 *Colum JL & Arts* 128.

39 Books are protected as literary works, software as computer programs and artwork as artistic works. See s 51(1) of the Nigerian Copyright Act.

40 South Africa protects software as computer programs under a specific category. See s 2(1)(i) of the South African Copyright Act.

41 For example, GNU General Public Licence. The GNU General Public License is a free, copyleft license for software and other kinds of works. See 'The GNU General Public License V3.0 – GNU Project – Free Software Foundation' (*Gnu.org*, 29 June 2007), www.gnu.org/licenses/gpl-3.0.en.html (accessed 22 June 2019).

42 See para. 6.1 of the Particulars of Claim in *PRS v SoundCloud* which SoundCloud admitted in paras 10, 17, 19, 20 of its Statement of Defence. *Performing Rights Society v SoundCloud*, Claim number 2015–903033, before the High Court of Justice, Chancery Division, Intellectual property (*PRS v SoundCloud*). See also *Viacom International, Inc. v YouTube, Inc.* 676 F.3d 19, United States Court of Appeals, Second Circuit, decision of 5 April 2012, para. 22.

43 See paras 4, 5 and 6.4 of the Particulars of Claim in *PRS v SoundCloud.* See also Schultz AJ, 'IP and African music industries: An interview with Phil Chard – Part 4' (*Afro-IP*, 2 September 2016), http://afro-ip.blogspot.com/2016/09/ip-and-african-music-industries_2.html (accessed 22 June 2019).

44 See Perel M and Elkin-Koren N, 'Accountability in algorithmic copyright enforcement' [2015] 19 *Stan Tech L Rev* 485. Also, see para. 8 of the Particulars of Claim and paras 37 and 70 of the Statement of Defence in *PRS v SoundCloud.*

with the creation and operation of registration or some entry requirement that keeps an index of users' activities and/or interaction with the music content ('views' or 'download' counts), which helps advertisers appreciate the number of consumers ('eyeballs') that may potentially view their product advertisements. For example, YouTube channels provide the number of views for each uploaded content. NotJustOk.com provides the number of downloads and streams for each uploaded content.

1.17 These activities involving the music content, in particular the operation of registration or entry requirement, involve the collection and processing of personal data (names, email addresses, telephone numbers, name of the content creator, date of creating the content etc.) regulated by privacy law. There is also an interface that can serve advertisements to users and other platform visitors in such a manner as not to detract from the user-friendly experience.

1.18 The platform is designed to enable all these market participants to interact, and the 'endgame' is to ensure profit for the platform firms.[45]

Terms of use

1.19 Beyond designing the platform, platform firms present all users of the platform with a 'unilateral' contract in the form of terms of use and privacy policies.[46] Terms of use and privacy policies are documents to which registered users assent to or are presumed to have assented to upon using the platform or uploading content thereon.[47] These documents particularly stipulate the nature of the platform firm's service and the representations and warranties obtained from the registered users.[48] In most cases, the terms of use stipulate the representations and warranties provided by registered users regarding copyright ownership and processing of users' data obtained from their registration and participation on the platform.

1.20 With respect to copyright ownership, the terms of use address the issue of supply of the music content, revenue generation as well as access to the music content.[49] The terms of use, which concern copyright ownership, function as a way to recognise the private interests of the copyright owner in revenue generation and the public interests of users and consumers in accessing the music

45 See Pujol 2010 supra at 1; Ritala S, 'Pandora & Spotify: Legal issues and licensing requirements for interactive and non-interactive internet radio broadcasters' [2013] 54 IDEA 42–43; Alex Solo, 'The role of copyright in an age of online music distribution' [2014] 19 *Media and Arts Law Review* 184–187.

46 Unilateral contracts lack mutuality given that the offeree or promisee is not bound to perform the requested act or forbearance. Examples include click-wrap contracts, browse-wrap contracts. See Clark D, 'Revocation and the unilateral contract: A reappraisal' [2000] NZL Rev 35.

47 See paras 19, 20 and 73 of the Statement of Defence in *PRS v SoundCloud*.

48 See Elkin-Koren N, 'Tailoring copyright to social production' [2011] 12(1) *Theoretical Inquiries in Law* 329; para. 88.2 of the Statement of Defence in *PRS v SoundCloud*.

49 By continuing to use the platform, the user is deemed to accept the terms stipulated by the platform firm. See Derclaye E and Favale M, 'Copyright and contract law: regulating user contracts: The state of the art and a research agenda' [2010] 18 *J Intell Prop L* 65, 100.

content. These terms – copyright terms – indicate the various ways in which the copyright-protected music content available on their platforms may be used and accessed. These copyright terms also function as a framework to legitimise the platform firm's use of the music content, as they need to be able to show compliance with extant copyright laws. Also, the copyright terms serve as a tool for the platform firms to enhance their competitiveness given that the terms explain the ways in which the music content is used. Further, users of the platform are guided by these copyright terms to also enable compliance with copyright laws. Without these terms as a guide, platform firms run the (greater) risk of copyright infringement liability and infraction of competition statutes.

1.21 The aforementioned copyright terms are of three main types: licensing terms and access and usage terms.[50] The specific content of these typical copyright terms may vary from one platform firm to the other, making it difficult to describe them with exactitude.[51] Nevertheless, the licensing, access and usage terms play a significant role as they function as constraints on the relevant stakeholders. From a policy perspective, they are important as the choice of relevant terms and their implementation by any stakeholder directly reflect the standards of competition within the copyright law framework.

1.22 With respect to user data, the terms of use (in particular, the privacy policy) address the issue of information or data, which platform firms collect from the platform users. Most platform firms require users to undergo some sort of registration process before uploading music content to the platform. Such registration usually involves the provision of personal data such as names, addresses, email address, telephone numbers etc. These 'privacy terms' also indicate the reason why such information is collected, how they are used and how users may stop the platform firms from continued use of such information. They function to legitimise the platform firm's use of such personal data, as they need to be able to show compliance with extant privacy laws.

1.23 Privacy terms vary across multi-sided platforms, and some platform firms do not have a formal privacy policy even though there are patterns that may be observed from their processing of data or business activities generally.[52] For purposes of this book, the key privacy terms are those relating to the rights of copyright owners and uploaders of music content to the user data held and processed by platform firms. In this regard, the right of access and the right to seek redress are the most relevant as they particularly relate to the copyright-protected music content. As discussed in Chapter 4, the protection available to copyright

50 See, e.g., para. 5 of YouTube's terms of service. See also Perel and Elkin-Koren 2015 supra at 473.

51 Indeed, users of the platform may sometimes find it difficult to clearly identify which of the copyright terms apply to their actions. For instance, the Creative Commons licences as a platform for the deployment of the open music business model have been criticised on the grounds that it misunderstands some key aspects of copyright law. See Susan Corbett, 'Creative Commons licences, the copyright regime and the online community: Is there a fatal disconnect?' [2011] 74(4) *Modern Law Review* 518.

52 Cf. 'Google Privacy Policy' (*Policies.google.com*, 22 January 2019), https://policies.google.com/privacy?hl=en-US (accessed 22 June 2019); NotJustOk.com.

owners, uploaders and other platform users in any jurisdiction usually depends on the available and applicable laws.

Multi-sided music platforms through the lens of the law

1.24 As a corollary to the foregoing, it can be said that the process of deploying multi-sided music platforms is largely unilateral as it is mostly directed by the platform firms. For one, the uploading of the music content presumes that the uploader owns or has acquired copyright in the music content uploaded.[53] The consent or licence of the copyright owner is therefore implied in the case where it is not the uploader. As evident from Box 1.1, several platforms direct copyright owners to request a takedown of music content where the copyright owner was not the uploader and/or where the copyright owner objects to the uploaded music content.

1.25 Furthermore, many platform users (including copyright owners) are also attracted by the availability of the platform free of charge to store and help distribute their music content. From this perspective, some copyright owners elect to accept the terms of use and consider the platforms to be a popular way of showcasing and promoting their music content. Whatever the case, the terms of use are set unilaterally by the platform firms.

Box 1.1 Takedown policies

Take down[54]

If you want to make a complaint about any of our online services or if you think your or someone else's intellectual property or other rights have been infringed by our online services you can do so by submitting full details by sending your email to *dcma@tooxclusive.com.*

(TooXclusive.com's takedown policy)

Submit a copyright takedown notice[55]

If your *copyright-protected* work was posted on YouTube without authorization, you may submit a copyright infringement notification. Be sure to consider whether *fair use*, fair dealing, or a similar exception to copyright

53 See paras 3, 4, 26, 27, 52, 54 and 73.2 of the Statement of Defence in *PRS v SoundCloud*.

54 'Terms Of Use Tooxclusive' (*tooXclusive*, 2019), https://tooxclusive.com/terms-of-use/ (accessed 2 July 2019).

55 'Submit a Copyright Takedown Notice – YouTube Help' (*Support.google.com*, 2019), https://support.google.com/youtube/answer/2807622?hl=en (accessed 2 July 2019). See also 'A Guide to YouTube Removals' (*Electronic Frontier Foundation*, 2019), www.eff.org/issues/intellectual-property/guide-to-youtube-removals (accessed 2 July 2019).

applies before you submit. These requests should only be sent in by the copyright owner or an agent authorized to act on the owner's behalf.

The fastest and simplest way to submit a copyright takedown notice is through our webform. You'll find this easier on a desktop or laptop computer than on a mobile device or tablet.

(YouTube's takedown policy)

1.26 The use of unilateral processes in multi-sided music platforms has grown rapidly and consistently as a mechanism for distributing music content in South Africa and Nigeria. This process represents the most common approach to deploying multi-sided music platforms globally on the internet. In the context of copyright law, unilateral processes are faster and less formal than bilateral processes. This is because unilateral processes do not necessarily require the prior agreement of the copyright owner, and therefore there may be no lengthy negotiation process.[56]

1.27 These characteristics of unilateral processes, at the same time, may be contrary to the policy approach of copyright law. There may be concerns for compliance with copyright law where platform firms, which obtain revenue based on the use of the music content, control and direct the deployment of the multi-sided music platform, without the prior involvement of the copyright owner.[57]

1.28 In general, platforms firms provide users with a forum for interaction (e.g. content uploads and consumption), a standard set of contractual terms (as exemplified by the terms of use) and a secure method of payment for advertising/advertisers. They do not themselves create content, nor do they directly upload content on to the platform in question. They typically provide a platform to facilitate exchanges and charge people or firms who wish to advertise their products on the platform. This ad-based model is not unique: television, newspapers and radio pioneered it in the pre-1990s and sold advertising time and/or space as their viewership or readership increased.[58] However, the provision of third party content and leveraging on the content for advertising revenue is more complex than when a firm produces and distributes its own content in the form of broadcasts; content may be protected by copyright law, and free access to the platform can enable abuse of power enhanced by network effects.

1.29 Multi-sided platforms therefore ask users to upload their content and to offer the platform firms a free, non-exclusive and worldwide licence to use the uploaded content. Nevertheless, the rapid expansion of platforms like YouTube

56 See Heald PJ, 'How notice-and-takedown regimes create markets for music on YouTube: An empirical study' [2014] 83 *UMKC L Rev* 318.

57 See Ginsburg J, 'The role of the author in copyright', in Okediji R (ed), *Copyright Law in an Age of Limitations and Exceptions* (Cambridge University Press 2017).

58 See Picard RG, 'Shifts in newspaper advertising expenditures and their implications for the future of newspapers' [2008] 9(5) *Journalism Studies*, 704–716; Rohe B, 'Huffpost is now a part of Oath' (*Huffpost.com*, 10 October 2010), www.huffpost.com/entry/journalism-needs-a-new-business-model-and-its-based_b_59d62025e4b0666ad0c3cafd (accessed 22 June 2019).

and Facebook has generated enormous controversy. Well-publicised cases of copyright infringement and anti-competitive practices against platform firms suggest that the platforms' *gratis* licences and business models may never be wholly acceptable. Controversies have also arisen from the platforms' proprietary control over consumer data. Facebook for instance, has been accused of restricting other firms' access to its user data – data to which those firms need access to in order to compete.[59] Google has been alleged to abuse its dominant position by denying other firms' access to data that would work to increase those firms' bottom lines.[60]

1.30 But multi-sided platforms are also understood to have broader impacts: recently, the activities of Facebook and Cambridge Analytica in using data obtained from consumers' preferences in influencing elections and polls in many countries have engendered massive demands for stricter privacy regimes.[61] Governments in some jurisdictions (US and the EU especially) have attempted to regulate and address the activities of multi-sided platforms. But these firms' technological infrastructure, standard contract and choice of law provisions have in some cases allowed them to circumvent conventional regulatory frameworks, generating debates about the merits of these regimes.[62] Indeed, authors and owners of copyright works are clamouring for due recognition and reward and remuneration for their creative efforts; users crave more access and freedom to make transformative and collaborative uses of creative content.[63] These ideals challenge legal regimes that regulate business activities as well as exploitation of creative content. Both copyright owners and platform firms ought to be certain as to permissible and impermissible conduct as well as licensable and unlicensed uses.[64] Obviously, these challenges – and potential responses to them – are multi-faceted and multi-jurisdictional. These are discussed in greater detail in subsequent chapters through the lens of copyright, privacy and competition laws.

The stakes at issue in the music copyright industry

1.31 One of the key policy questions is whether the restrictions imposed on platform users and those obligatory for platform firms to put up are permissible

59 Solon O and Farivar C, 'Inside bikini-photo startup Six4three's scrappy battle to put Facebook on trial' (*NBC News*, 16 April 2019), www.nbcnews.com/tech/social-media/inside-bikini-photo-startup-six4three-s-scrappy-battle-put-facebook-n995016 (accessed 22 June 2019).

60 See, e.g., the case of Attrakt against Google where Google's arbitrary termination of contract and withdrawal/denial of access annihilated the business of Attrakt. *Attrakt S.R.L. v Google Ireland Ltd*, General Case List no. 86198/2013. Available on www.attrakt.com (*Attrakt v Google*). The judgment delivered in the case is available in Appendix II.

61 Cadwalladr C, 'Google, democracy and the truth about internet search' (*The Guardian*, 4 December 2016), www.theguardian.com/technology/2016/dec/04/google-democracy-truth-internet-search-facebook (accessed 22 June 2019).

62 See Gal and Rubinfeld 2016 supra.

63 This is most exemplified in the 'value gap' debate. See International Federation of the Phonographic Industry (IFPI), 'Global Music Report 2017: Annual state of the industry' (2017), www.ifpi.org/downloads/GMR2017.pdf (accessed 22 June 2019).

64 See Quinn A, 'Are online music platforms undermining the principles of copyright law?' [2017] 13(1) *Journal of Intellectual Property Law & Practice* 49–60.

within the scope of rights available to the copyright owner. A related question is whether platform firms may be compelled to grant copyright owners access to user data within the scope of rights permissible under privacy laws. In this regard, it is important to recognise the relationships and interests between the market players in the music industry in the context of multi-sided music platforms.[65] This is especially so as the focus of this book is on the use music content in multi-sided music platforms.

1.32 On the one side, there are the authors and owners of copyright in the music content which are strategic for the profitable operation of the multi-sided music platforms in terms of advertising, which can include individual artists, composers and companies predominantly involved in music recording, production, publishing and distribution. Three major record companies dominate the global music industry. These are Sony Music Entertainment, Universal Music Group and Warner Music Group. These record companies are large-sized conglomerates with branches in many countries. They also have a significant music distribution network with a large artist roster housing some of the world's biggest music artists. These companies control many smaller record labels and may exercise oligopolistic powers, which may influence prices of music content and thus directly affect the position of competitors.[66] Every other record company outside these three global majors are usually referred to as 'independent' record labels. In South Africa, Universal Music Group and Sony Music Entertainment also operate as the major record labels, while Warner Music Group is represented by Gallo Records.[67] In the case of Nigeria, these three major record labels are not active as the major record labels. While Sony Music Entertainment began operations in Nigeria in 2016,[68] Universal Music Group only commenced operations in Nigeria in 2017.[69] Warner Music Group is yet to establish operations in Nigeria but recently in 2019 entered into a distribution agreement with a Nigerian company, Chocolate City Music Group.[70] The situation is the same on the publishing side.

1.33 In essence, independent record labels and music publishers populate the music industry in South Africa and Nigeria. As copyright owners, these independents qualify as small and medium-sized enterprises (SMEs) due to their small size and small market share.[71] Small businesses are separate and distinct business

65 See Elkin-Koren 2011 supra at 311.

66 See Garcia KA, 'Penalty default licenses: A case for uncertainty' [2014] 89 NYUL Rev 1117.

67 See Matzukis N, *South African Music Law, Contracts and Business* (3rd edn, Academy of Sound Engineering 2013); Fouché 2015 supra at 34–38.

68 'Nigeria: Sony Music Entertainment opens office in Nigeria' (*allAfrica*, 26 February 2016), http://allafrica.com/stories/201602250349.html (accessed 22 June 2019).

69 Aroture B, 'Copyright Society of Nigeria welcomes Universal Music Group to Nigeria' (*Nigerian Law Intellectual Property Watch Inc*., 19 January 2017), https://nlipw.com/copyright-society-nigeria-welcomes-universal-music-group-nigeria/ (accessed 22 June 2019).

70 Eggertsen C, 'Warner Music Group announces partnership with Nigerian label Chocolate City' (*Billboard*, 2019), www.billboard.com/articles/business/8504493/warner-music-group-chocolate-city-nigerian-label-partnership (accessed 22 June 2019).

71 Abor J and Quartey P, 'Issues in SME development in Ghana and South Africa' [2010] 39(6) *International Research Journal of Finance and Economics* 219.

entities managed by one or more owners and are usually characterised according to industry, number of employees, total turnover and total asset value.[72] In South Africa, the National Small Business Act categorises small businesses into microenterprises, very small enterprises, small enterprises and medium enterprises. As SMEs, these copyright owners do not have the resources and market power of the major record companies or any large-sized firm. Accordingly, they need consistent growth in terms of revenue to lower the risk of financial failure and market exit.[73] The aim pursued by this group is to maximise the revenue originating from licensing their music copyright out, with the purpose either to reinvest or simply to make profits out of their assets.[74]

1.34 To achieve their aim of generating revenue and/or making profits, copyright owners also need data or information regarding public reception of their music content as well as proper accounting of the payments made by those who use and/or access their music content.[75] Indeed, as argued in Chapter 5, the greater the revenue, the better their chances of staying in the market. This correlates with their status as small business.[76]

1.35 On the other hand, there are those players who (may) need a licence to use the music content protected by copyright, to legally implement their communication of the music content in the course of advertising. The aim pursued by this second group of firms is to either obtain a *gratis* licence or to pay the lowest possible amount as royalties and to obtain fair licensing terms. This is expected to enable them enhance their competitiveness and recoup their investments in designing the platform and its features. These market players do not wish to be compelled to undertake onerous filtering and monitoring measures to check copyright infringement. Further, they do not wish to be compelled to disclose or grant access to certain user data as a way to comply with privacy law requirements.

1.36 Finally, also a third category of market player operates within the context of multi-sided music platforms, namely the creative users who may apply the music content to producing new creative outputs. For creative users, there is some room within copyright limitations and exceptions and subject matter restrictions that should enable them make certain creative uses of music content.[77] Users of music content in the digital environment generally are looking for unrestricted access for transformative use; interaction; and absence of contractual and technical restrictions as well as absence of constraints that may prevent them from

72 See s 1(xv) National Small Business Act (102 of 1996).

73 Okpara JO, 'Factors constraining the growth and survival of SMEs in Nigeria: Implications for poverty alleviation' [2011] 34(2) *Management Research Review* 156–171.

74 See Elkin-Koren 2017 supra at 135–137.

75 See Rethink Music, 'Fair Music: Transparency and payment flows in the music industry' (Berklee Institute of Creative Entrepreneurship 2015), www.berklee.edu/sites/default/files/Fair%20Music%20-%20Transparency%20and%20Payment%20Flows%20in%20the%20Music%20Industry.pdf (accessed 22 June 2019).

76 Ibid.

77 See Carroll MW, 'Creative commons as conversational copyright' [2007] *Public Policy Research Paper* 530.

engaging with the music content, transforming and remixing it.[78] Accordingly, certain restrictions in their access to the music content and the platform itself may frustrate the aim of this category of users in investing in further creative efforts. Such will be to the detriment of the copyright market.

1.37 Beyond users who propose to apply the copyright-protected music content to further creative activities, there are consumers who need to be able to access the music content for the purposes of consumption and consequent interaction with the copyright owner.[79] For this category, it is important to them that their quest to enjoy the music content does not engender copyright infringement liability for them.[80]

1.38 As shifts in business models occur in the wake of digitisation and information technologies, the copyright owner, like every business entity, relies more and more on virtual or digital platforms to distribute copyright content and generate revenue therefrom. Put differently, copyright owners usually rely on the assistance of digital platforms and firms who operate such platforms to realise the economic interests from exploiting their exclusive rights through business models. If platform firms were to exclude paid licensing from their terms of use, there may be fewer firms investing in the creative outputs in copyright markets. It should be recalled that copyright owners are usually incentivised in investing resources in creativity if they get rewarded for their economic efforts. Rewards may consist either in the payment of royalties or in sharing of revenue realised from business activities ancillary to the dissemination of music content.[81] Copyright owners thus have the need to be able to exert control over their creative outputs,[82] access data relating to their music content and reduce the cost of licensing and monitoring use of their creative outputs.[83] Exclusion of paid licensing from multi-sided music platforms and in some cases restriction of access to user data may therefore result in less creativity and less competition within the music copyright industry. In other words, the immediate consequence could be a reduced number of professional creative outputs.[84] The ultimate effect could be detrimental to competition as well as the welfare of consumers, and may impact negatively on their consumption levels.

1.39 A slightly different position has been adopted by Elkin-Koren, who has argued that the music content is experiential and demand is dependent on

78 See Elkin-Koren 2016 supra at 4, 12–14, 19–20. Users producing user-generated content (UGC) are looking for attribution, online reputation, autonomy that can restrict unacceptable commercialisation and autonomy over use of purchases.

79 See Dusollier S, 'The master's tools v. the master's house: Creative commons v. copyright' (2006) 29 *Columbia Journal of Law & Arts* 290.

80 Ibid.

81 See Carroll 2007 supra at page 530; Kim M, 'The Creative Commons and copyright protection in the digital era: uses of Creative Commons licenses' (2007) 13(1) *Journal of Computer-Mediated Communication* 187–209.

82 Dusollier 2006 supra at 280.

83 Perel and Elkin-Koren 2015 supra at 477.

84 It should be noted that the impact of this may not be as strong as it may be in the context of books and scholarly articles, a distinction recognised by Ginsburg. See Ginsburg 2017 supra at 69.

individual perception.[85] Nevertheless, there is significant consensus in the literature and in industry reports that copyright is considered a tool for revenue generation and whether it is directly (as in the case of assignment or licensing) or indirectly applied (as in the case of brand sponsorships and licensing of personality rights), the expectation of revenue persists.[86] Indeed, even in the case of the Creative Commons and other business models that allow free use of copyright-protected content, actions for copyright infringement results in damages once the work is used outside the dictates of the licence.[87] Further, as Elkin-Koren points out, even though user-generated content is not produced for profit, it is increasingly shaped by market forces and can be distributed in a commercial setting and may, in fact, generate revenues.[88]

1.40 On the other side of the spectrum, it is to be noted that platform firms as a category of copyright users invest considerably in creating and operating platforms.[89] The platform firms offer several economic incentives: monetising activities through advertisements, charging subscription fees and using free distribution to market artists by cashing in on the online reputation. Platform firms generate revenue from social motivation and sometimes share advertising revenue with copyright owners who may also be platform users.[90] They facilitate trade and increase economic efficiency by making it easier for copyright owners to interact with their customers and people who value their music content and creative outputs.[91] For example, a person who loves the artist Flavour's '*Nwa Baby*' can listen to the song on YouTube or on NotJustOk.com at no charge. In turn, Flavour or the copyright owner can see on YouTube the number of views to gauge consumer reaction to the song. Especially in low-income economies like Nigeria and South Africa, platforms and platform firms can help achieve wider revenue-based distribution and allow copyright owners to concentrate on creating better music content.[92]

1.41 However, platform firms need a large music catalogue that will attract both platform users and advertisers to their platform. As stated in the Particulars of Claim filed in the suit between PRS and SoundCloud in the UK,[93] such user-friendly service centred around availability of music content may include provision of categorised and easily searchable music content,[94] making recommendations to users based on their indicated preferences, pushing and

85 Elkin-Koren 2011 supra at 312, 326.

86 Booth N and Matic JA, 'Mapping and leveraging influencers in social media to shape corporate brand perceptions' [2011] 16(3) *Corporate Communications: An International Journal*, 184–191.

87 *Jacobsen v Katzer*, 2008 U.S. App. LEXIS 17161 (Fed. Cir. 2008).

88 See Elkin-Koren 2010 supra at 22–23.

89 Perel and Elkin-Koren 2015 supra at 518–520.

90 See Elkin-Koren 2011 supra at 323–324.

91 See Evans 2016 supra at 6. See also Koscik M and Savelka J, 'Dangers of over-enthusiasm in licensing under Creative Commons' [2013] 7 *Masaryk UJL & Tech* 218; Elkin-Koren 2011 supra 5 at 343, 345; Perel and Elkin-Koren 2015 supra at 485.

92 See Rethink Music 2015 supra at 5.

93 See Appendix I (*PRS v SoundCloud* – Originating Processes).

94 For example, paras 40–41 of the Defence filed in *PRS v SoundCloud.*

promoting particular music content to users, and providing facilities for users to follow, like and share particular music content.[95] Platform firms therefore incur costs of maintenance and updates, online marketing, managing the online community and protection against potential legal liability, and they need ways to recoup these costs. They therefore adopt different business models (such as advertising) to recoup costs.[96] Their services are provided with a view to generating revenue therefrom.[97] Hence, by coordinating technology and by enabling the growth of music distribution, platform firms stand in a crucial position in relation to balancing the so-called private-public interest inherent in copyright law.[98]

1.42 Advertisers have also become key stakeholders in the music copyright industry. Given that the revenue flow is from advertising services, the availability of music (and other popular) content is crucial to the platform firm's success. In each case, the relevant platform firm aggregates a large music catalogue, thereby increasing the likelihood that music consumers will be attracted to the site and companies seeking to advertise their products would pay a fee to access the advertising audience. In the circumstances, there is the question whether platform firms should be compelled to share advertisement revenue with copyright owners, bearing in mind that the availability of the platform can create revenue streams from brand sponsorships and live performances for copyright owners.[99] Platform firms generally pursue the aim of working outside the exclusive rights framework to obviate any need for licensing obligations.

1.43 Therefore, while economic and social benefits stimulated by the way copyright-protected music content is used on multi-sided music business platforms are widely recognised by scholars and regulatory institutions, it is also true that the market players in that context present diverse interests which are crucial to the promotion of competition in the music copyright industry.

Jurisdictional focus

1.44 The discussion in this book is limited in its jurisdictional scope. Africa is a continent with over 50 countries. Each country has its own set of laws and legal system. It would therefore be unwieldy if not impossible to undertake the issues discussed in this book from the perspective of all the countries in Africa. Such undertaking would be inappropriate, as each country's regulatory framework, socio-economic status, developmental goals and business practices must be considered.

---

95 See para. 8 of the Particulars of Claim and para. 70 of the Defence filed in *PRS v SoundCloud*.

96 See Elkin-Koren 2010 supra at 11.

97 See para. 52 of the Defence filed in *PRS v SoundCloud*; Elkin-Koren 2010 supra at 8–10.

98 Elkin-Koren 2011 supra at 319; Elkin-Koren 2017 supra at 133–135; Russi 2011 supra at 109–110.

99 See Evans 2016 supra at 7; Heald 2014 supra at 318.

1.45 In relation to the foregoing, the jurisdictional focus is on South Africa and Nigeria. This choice is based on several compelling factors. Both countries are somewhat large developing countries within the African region. South Africa is a predominant force in the Southern Africa region (specifically the Southern African Development Community, or SADC), while Nigeria occupies a similar position within the Western Africa and the Economic Organisation of West African States (ECOWAS). There are also similarities in the socio-economic measures within the two countries. High levels of poverty, unemployment and inequality exist within the two countries. Accordingly, both countries can serve as credible representatives as they present features reflective of most countries within the African continent.

1.46 Further, Nigeria's copyright law shares a common heritage with the South African copyright regime. The two copyright law regimes were adapted from the UK's Imperial Copyright Act of 1916. Also, both countries are currently at different stages of the process of amending their respective copyright statutes and the proposed amendments have not detracted from the commonality which the two copyright regimes share.[100] These similarities may allow for some interesting convergence in the regulatory behaviour of the two countries. Notwithstanding these similarities, there are some material differences between the two countries. Institutionally, South Africa has a more advanced copyright legislative framework than Nigeria. For instance, while South Africa joined the developed economies in recognising the need to protect internet intermediaries from copyright infringement liability given the nature of their services and the way in which the internet operates, Nigeria is yet to do so.[101] In this regard, South Africa's Electronic Communications Transactions Act exempts hosting, caching, linking and conduit intermediaries from copyright infringement liability upon fulfilment of stated conditions.[102] These differences should reveal some pertinent variation in the regulatory behaviour of the two countries.

1.47 In terms of the economy, the 2017 gross domestic product (GDP) per capita (adjusted for purchasing power parity) ranking by the World Bank, South Africa's GDP of $12.8 million is quite ahead of Nigeria's GDP of $5.9 million.[103] In terms of the state of the music market, South Africa's music industry is more

100 See Appendix 3 for the Draft Copyright Bill 2015 prepared by the Nigerian Copyright Commission. For South Africa, see Appendix 4 for the Copyright Amendment Bill 2017 presented to the National Assembly through the Minister of Trade and Industry. A comparison of the two bills shows that their central objective is to make the law more suited to the digital age.

101 The proposed amendment to the Copyright Act now provides for the safe harbour regime. See ss 47–54 of the bill.

102 In this regard, South Africa's Electronic Communications Transactions Act 2002 exempts hosting, caching, linking and conduit intermediaries from copyright infringement liability upon fulfilment of stated conditions. See Chapter XI, ss 70–79.

103 South Africa's GDP per capita of $5,273.6 million is quite ahead of Nigeria's GDP of $2,178 million. See 'GDP Per Capita (Current US$) | Data' (*Data.worldbank.org*, 2019), https://data.worldbank.org/indicator/NY.GDP.PCAP.CD?locations=ZA&name_desc=false (accessed 22 June 2019).

developed than its Nigerian counterpart.[104] Also, South Africa has features of both developed and developing economies especially in terms of institutional development, as evidenced by its membership of the economic bloc comprising Brazil, Russia, India, China and South Africa (BRICS) and its accepting developed nation status during negotiations for the World Trade Organization (WTO) agreements.[105] On the other hand, Nigeria has the characteristics of developing and least developed countries due to the state of its institutions and the income level of its citizens. Least developed countries (LDCs) are based on the United Nations (UN) classification looking at indexes such as population, markets, institutions, infrastructure, GDP, life expectancy and the like. Generally, markets in LDCs have weaker institutional support in terms of political and financial stability and lower levels of protection for property rights.[106] While Nigeria does not fall under the UN classification of LDCs, it does possess LDC features such as lack of political and financial stability affecting markets, high population growth and environmental degradation, amongst other similarities.[107] This mix of developed, developing and least developed nation status represents the economic status of the countries within the African continent. Such a mix makes it permissible to make some suggestions that may influence the regulatory approach of other African countries.

1.48 It is to be noted that whilst this book's primary focus is Nigeria and South Africa, it also considers the position in the EU, the United Kingdom (UK) and the US. Both the UK and the US represent the leading music markets in the world.[108] Moreover, the copyright laws of both Nigeria and South Africa were derived from the UK's Copyright Act and the two jurisdictions share features of common law jurisdictions. This makes the consideration of the UK approach and the EU approach, given the UK's prior membership of the EU[109] and its consequent harmonisation of the EU Copyright Directive, particularly persuasive for Nigeria and South Africa.[110] Such consideration may be particularly useful if there are no music content-related cases in the two jurisdictions, and if the UK and EU

104 See International Federation of the Phonographic Industry (IFPI), 'Digital Music Report 2014: Lighting up new markets' (International Federation of the Phonographic Industry (IFPI) 2014), www.ifpi.org/downloads/Digital-Music-Report-2014.pdf (accessed 22 June 2019).

105 Fasan O, *Compliance with WTO Law in Developing Countries: A Study of South Africa and Nigeria* (PhD, London School of Economics and Political Science, United Kingdom 2007).

106 See Makino S, Beamish PW, and Zhao NB, 'The characteristics and performance of Japanese FDI in less developed and developed countries' [2004] 39 *Journal of World Business* 4, 378.

107 See United Nations Industrial Development Organization, 'Industrialization in Africa and least developed countries: Boosting growth, creating jobs, promoting inclusiveness and sustainability' (United Nations Industrial Development Organization (UNIDO) 2016), www.unido.org/sites/default/files/2016-09/G20_new_UNIDO_report_industrialization_in_Africa_and_LDCs_0.pdf (accessed 22 June 2019).

108 See generally 'BPI response to the digital copyright exchange call for evidence' (*Webarchive.nationalarchives.gov.uk*, 2011), https://webarchive.nationalarchives.gov.uk/20140603125239/www.ipo.gov.uk/dce-c4e-bpi.pdf (accessed 22 June 2019); IFPI 2017 supra.

109 Britain voted to leave the EU but the departure process is yet to be concluded.

110 The copyright law in both South Africa and Nigeria has its roots in the English copyright legal system. See Ola K, 'Evolution and future trends of copyright in Nigeria' [2014] 2 *Journal of Open Access to Law* 1, 7–8 (Ola 2014); Schönwetter T, *Safeguarding a Fair Copyright*

cases provide an indication on how such issues may be addressed in the two countries.[111] In terms of competition law, the EU and the US represent the oldest competition law jurisdictions in the world, and accordingly, they lead the way in the application of competition law to the analysis of issues related to businesses based on the concept of 'free', such as the platform firms that operate multi-sided music platforms.

Balance – Contemporary Challenges in a Changing World: Lessons to be Learnt from a Developing Country Perspective (PhD, University of Cape Town 2009) (Schönwetter 2009).

111 See *Adetoun Oladeji Nig Ltd v NB Plc* (2007) 5 NWLR Pt 1027 p 415 at 443–444 paragraphs H-F.

CHAPTER 2

Multi-sided music platforms and key regulatory frameworks

Introduction

2.1 Before delving into the main parts of this book, it is important to provide background as to the interaction between the various regulatory frameworks applicable to multi-sided music platforms. This will aid the readers' understanding of the rest of this book.

2.2 This chapter identifies the objectives of copyright law by looking at the interface between copyright and income generation, and between copyright's limitations and exceptions and how they help to promote competition in copyright markets. The focus is on the music industry and the link between copyright and income generation. Also, the chapter provides an evaluation of other aspects of copyright law (in South Africa and Nigeria) that aim to promote competition. Similarly, the chapter examines the body of rights available to data subjects (i.e. persons whose data are being collected and/or processed) and how they help to advance competition also in music copyright industry. The chapter further considers the objectives of copyright law, privacy law and competition law in the context of multi-sided music platforms, showing the role that competition law plays in complementing and serving the objectives of both copyright law and privacy law.

Key regulatory frameworks

2.3 Platform firms use or apply copyright-protected music content and information gathered from consumers and consumer activities (including information from or about copyright owners) to generate profit. From the way the platform is designed, to the way uploaders and listeners (consumers) are attracted to the platform, it is evident that the aim of the platform firm is to get their (key) customer – advertisers – to pay.

2.4 For platform firms, the use of these tools of the trade – music content and user data – enables them to stay competitive and retain the interest of consumers. Competition is a struggle or battle for superiority.[1] It is a process in which firms strive with other firms through strategies and economic activities aimed

1 Whish R and Bailey D, *Competition Law* (9th edn, Oxford University Press 2018).

at satisfying the needs of customers and capturing value or revenue therefrom.[2] In this regard, firms which are efficient and which have a business model with the appropriate value proposition are able to rise above their competitors and dominate the marketplace in satisfying consumer needs. Accordingly, the process of competition can lead to a firm becoming the most preferred by the consumers because of its business model, efficiency, innovative products, quality of its goods and/or lower prices.[3] As stated in the Draft Competition and Consumer Policy Paper prepared by the Nigerian government, 'through competition among suppliers, consumers have access to the widest possible range of choice of goods and services at the lowest possible prices and highest possible quality'.[4] Hence, competition between firms may be considered as a necessary instrument for the promotion of efficiency and consumer welfare in the marketplace.

2.5 The law does not set out specific or detailed business models for firms (platform firms inclusive) to deploy in competing in the marketplace. Instead, the law provides a legal and regulatory framework to ensure that economic activities do not stifle or restrict competition by illegitimate acquisition and/or undue exercise of market power. Several legal regimes such as competition law, copyright law, privacy law, consumer protection law, property law, contract law and bankruptcy law, amongst others, are considered as one of the regulatory frameworks to promote and/or protect competition between firms and for enhancing efficiency in the marketplace.[5] However, while competition law provides a general overarching framework to protect competition across a wide range of economic activities, each of the other regulatory frameworks applies to regulate competition in a specific sector or industry. Copyright law, for instance, provides a regulatory tool for the protection and promotion of competition in the copyright sector.[6] Privacy and data protection laws, on the other hand, serve to protect the interests of consumers and natural (and sometimes legal) persons in their data or personal information and may prohibit misuse and/or abuse of information about natural and legal persons.

2 See UK Competition Commission, 'Merger References: Competition Commission Guidelines' (Competition Commission and the Office of Fair Trading 2010), https://assets.publishing.service.gov.uk/government/uploads/system/uploads/attachment_data/file/284449/OFT1254.pdf (accessed 25 June 2019); UK Competition Commission, 'Guidelines for Market Investigations: Their Role, Procedures, Assessment and Remedies' (Competition Commission 2013), https://assets.publishing.service.gov.uk/government/uploads/system/uploads/attachment_data/file/284390/cc3_revised.pdf (accessed 25 June 2019).

3 Whish and Bailey 2018 supra at 19–21.

4 Federal Government of Nigeria, 'Draft Competition and Consumer Protection Policy' (2014). Other governments have expressed similar views. See UK Department of Trade and Industry, 'White Paper, Productivity and Enterprise: A World Class Competition Regime' (2002), www.gov.uk/government/publications/a-world-class-competition-regime (accessed 25 June 2019).

5 Maskus KE and Lahouel M, 'Competition policy and intellectual property rights in developing countries' [2000] 23 *World Economy* 596–600.

6 Stadler SK, 'Copyright as trade regulation' [2007] University of Pennsylvania Law Review 899–960; Katz A, 'Copyright and competition policy', in Towse R and Handke C (eds), *Handbook on the Digital Creative Economy* (Edward Elgar 2013).

2.6 The key regulatory frameworks that are most important for the purposes of this book are copyright law, competition law and laws regulating privacy and the use of data. The rest of this chapter discusses the nature of the relationship between these fields of law and explains how these regulatory frameworks apply to the key activities of multi-sided music platforms.

2.7 In South Africa and Nigeria, the Copyright Act of 1978 and the Copyright Act of 2004 are the principal statutes that regulate copyright and the use of copyright-protected products, respectively. While South Africa has had a Competition Act since 1998,[7] Nigeria only enacted a competition statute in 2019: the Federal Competition and Consumer Protection Act.[8] These statutes provide a general framework to protect competition across a wide range of economic activities. With respect to privacy protection, South Africa has the Protection of Personal Information Act 2013. Nigeria's president has declined assent to the Digital Rights and Freedoms Bill 2016 which was passed by the Nigerian Senate and House of Representatives.[9] Nevertheless, the National Information Technology Development Agency (NITDA) issued the Nigerian Data Protection Regulation 2019, which is considered the first comprehensive legislation on data protection and privacy legislation in Nigeria.[10]

Copyright and the promotion of competition

2.8 Copyright protection is a tool used to promote competition and the public interest from two distinct but interconnected perspectives. From an *ex ante* point of view, prior to making investments in creative works, copyright law promotes competition and rivalry as firms are incentivised to compete to enjoy the benefits of copyright protection. From an *ex post* perspective, copyright protection comes with constraints and limitations on the exclusive rights of copyright owners to encourage greater creativity,[11] access to and dissemination of copyright-protect content.

2.9 Several aspects of copyright law in the context of South Africa and Nigeria explain and conceptualise how copyright law promotes competition principles.[12] In recognising the link between copyright law and competition, one of

7 Competition Act 89 of 1998.

8 This is not for want of trying. Between 2003 and 2007, three different Draft Competition Bills were prepared but none has been signed into law till date. See Dimgba N, *Introduction to Competition Law: A Sine Qua Non to a Liberalised Economy* (Rules Watch: Competition Legislation & the New World Order, Lagos, 2006).

9 See Ekwealor V, 'Nigeria's president refused to sign its Digital Rights Bill, what happens now?' (*Techpoint.Africa*, 27 March 2019), https://techpoint.africa/2019/03/27/nigerian-president-declines-digital-rights-bill-assent/ (accessed 8 July 2019).

10 Nigerian Data Protection Regulation 2019.

11 See Fishman JP, 'Creating around copyright, (2014) 128 *Harv L Rev* 1333.

12 The same goes for copyright law in other jurisdictions. See for instance Cotter TF, 'The pro-competitive interest in intellectual property law' [2006] 48 *Wm & Mary L Rev* 483; Katz 2013 supra; Samuelson P, 'Justifications for copyright limitations & exceptions', in Okediji R (ed), *Copyright Law in an Age of Limitations and Exceptions* (Cambridge University Press 2017) (Samuelson

the central questions relates to the underlying meaning and purpose of copyright protection. The various approaches to copyright protection render the concept capable of being designed and interpreted to address a variety of issues.[13] Two main justification theories stand out: utilitarianism and the natural rights theory.[14]

Main theories and justification for copyright protection

2.10 The first theory, utilitarianism, posits that copyright-protected materials possess the non-exclusivity and non-excludability nature of public goods.[15] In other words, the use of copyright-protected materials by one person does not reduce another person's use (non-exclusivity), nor would it be easy or possible to prevent someone else's use (non-excludability).[16] As a result, it may be difficult, in the absence of regulation, to recoup the investments and cost of producing such public goods. In other words, the utilitarian theory highlights the role and utility of copyright in incentivising copyright owners to invest in the creation of further copyright works.[17] The rationale here is that the exclusive nature of copyright protection enables monetary or economic gains and that in the absence of copyright protection and the resultant economic gains, there would be little or no incentive to create.[18] This would explain the monopolistic nature of copyright.

2.11 The second theory, usually referred to as the natural rights theory, is grounded on the author's natural property rights in his work and his entitlement to reap the reward of his creative labour.[19] From a historical perspective, this view emanates from John Locke's Second Treatise of Government, written in 1690.[20] Locke's argument is that every person is entitled to the natural property rights resulting from their own labour, but such rights are limited by the rights of others

2017). See also Katz A and Veel PE, 'Beyond refusal to deal: a cross-Atlantic view of copyright, competition, and innovation policies' [2013] 79(1) *Antitrust Law Journal* 141–142 (Katz and Veel).

13 Giblin R and Weatherall K, 'If we redesigned copyright from scratch, what might it look like?' in *What If We Could Reimagine Copyright?* (Australia National University Press 2017).

14 Other justifications include 'personality rights' theory and 'democratic right' theory, the 'cultural argument', the 'freedom of expression' argument and the like. See Schönwetter 2009 supra at p. 30; Fisher W, 'Theories of intellectual property', in Munzer SR (ed), *New Essays in the Legal and Political Theory of Property* (Cambridge University Press 2001); Zemer L, 'On the value of copyright theory' [2006] 1 IPQ 55.

15 Rizk N, 'Stories from Egypt's music industry: De facto commons as alternatives to copyright' in *Access to Knowledge in Egypt*, p. 172.

16 Ibid.

17 For a seminal work on the utilitarian theory for copyright, see Landes WM and Posner R, 'An economic analysis of copyright law' [1989] 18(2) *Journal of Legal Studies* 325.

18 Cohen JE, Loren LP, Okediji R and O'Rourke MA, *Copyright in a Global Information Economy* (Wolters Kluwer Law & Business 2015); Hugenholtz PGB, *International Copyright. Principles, Law, and Practice* (3rd edn, Oxford University Press 2013); Harms LTC, *The Enforcement of Intellectual Property Rights: A Case Book* (3rd edn, World Intellectual Property 2012).

19 See Craig CJ, 'Locke, labour, and limiting the author's right: A warning against a Lockean approach to copyright law' [2002] 28(1) *Queen's Law Journal*, 18–20; Hughes J, 'The philosophy of intellectual property' [1988] 78 *Geo LJ* 287; Ginsburg J, 'The role of the author in copyright', in Okediji R (ed), *Copyright Law in an Age of Limitations and Exceptions* (Cambridge University Press 2017).

20 See Schönwetter 2009 supra at p. 32.

to the 'common stock of property'.[21] In this regard, copyright protection is to be seen as a reward for labour. Natural rights theory differs from the utilitarian theory in that it prioritises the property rights of the author to reap the fruits of their creation[22] and satisfy the innate need to create.[23]

2.12 Even without deeper reflection, a cursory examination of these theories shows that they are inextricably interwoven and ultimately explain the import and desirability of copyright for the society. Indeed, it is now well established from a variety of studies that the differences between so-called utilitarian-oriented copyright systems and the natural law–based jurisdictions have become blurred in the wake of globalisation and current international copyright treaties such as the Berne Convention, the 1994 Agreement on the Trade Related Aspects of Intellectual Property (TRIPS Agreement), the WIPO Copyright Treaty (WCT) and the WIPO Performances and Phonograms Treaty.[24]

2.13 The preamble to the WCT, which incorporates the elements of the Berne Convention and the TRIPS Agreement, is instructive:

> The Contracting Parties . . . desiring to develop and maintain the protection of the rights of authors in their literary and artistic works in a manner as effective and uniform as possible, emphasizing the outstanding significance of copyright protection as an incentive for literary and artistic creation,
>
> [and]
>
> . . . recognizing the need to maintain a balance between the rights of authors and the larger public interest, particularly education, research and access to information, as reflected in the Berne Convention.[25]

2.14 This notwithstanding, various objections have been raised against copyright justifications. One of the foremost criticisms contends that there is no proof that the exclusivity of copyright results in more creativity or incentivises further creation of new products.[26] Some argue that other non-exclusionary systems may provide incentives to create, and as such consider the exclusivity of copyright protection as a threat to the public interests and outside what should be the fundamental objectives of copyright.[27] Furthermore, the distribution of copyright works using open business models[28] has been presented as evidence

21 See, e.g., Gordon WJ, 'A property right in self-expression: Equality and individualism in the natural law of intellectual property' [1993] 102(7) *Yale Law Journal*, 1533.

22 Craig 2002 supra at 20–21.

23 See Schönwetter 2009 supra at p. 33. Also Bently L and Sherman B, *Intellectual Property Law* (Oxford University Press 2014), 36–38.

24 See Schönwetter 2009 supra at p. 37; Senftleben M, *Copyright, Limitations, and the Three-Step Test: An Analysis of the Three-Step Test in International and EC Copyright Law* (Vol. 13, Kluwer Law International BV 2004); Harms 2012 supra at p. 19.

25 Preamble to the WIPO Copyright Treaty, 20 December 1996, WIPO Doc. CRNR/DC/94, available at www.wipo.int/wipolex/en/treaties/text.jsp?file_id=295157.

26 See, e.g., Vaver D, 'Some agnostic observations on intellectual property' [1994] 1 Intellectual Property Rights 238; Zimmerman DL, 'Copyrights as incentives: Did we just imagine that?' [2011] 12(1) *Theoretical Inquiries in Law* 38–40. Also Bently and Sherman 2014 supra.

27 Gürel B, 'An external method for establishing the balance in intellectual property rights' scope: Article 102 of the TFEU' [2009] 10 *Global Antitrust Review*, 53.

28 On the concept of open business models, see paragraphs 2.30 to 2.37, below.

that monetary or economic incentive is not required for the creation or availability of copyright works in the marketplace.[29] As an example, these commentators point out the (relative) success of open source software projects such as Linux, the Mozilla internet browser, Google Android and the like, in which copyright owners participate in the development and creation of software whilst offering a *gratis* licence of their copyright in the software.[30] Another argument put forward against copyright protection is that it inhibits competition and wider distribution of copyright-protected materials, all of which may not be in the public interest.[31]

2.15 While these criticisms may hold in certain respects, they are not of general application. Copyright protection has clearly been used as a leverage to receive economic rewards even when creation and distribution have taken place outside economic negotiations. This is particularly applicable in the open business model deployed by authors and copyright owners.[32] Within such business models, the protected work is given away for free using an express or implied licence, and revenue is derived albeit indirectly from the 'enhanced reputation and market share' which the copyright owner enjoys from giving out the work for free.[33] Further, copyright protection has a significant impact on the willingness to engage in creative and productive activities for the enjoyment of the public.[34] Freemium business models, for instance, operate on the basis of a strong fixation on advertising revenue made possible by the same enhanced reputation and market share.[35] The US Federal Circuit Court recognised this position in *Jacobsen v Katzer*, where it held that the fact that a copyright owner elects to waive some of his rights does not obviate the economic interests in the copyright work.[36]

2.16 In any event, no copyright theory is without criticisms and differences in theories, and national approaches to copyright protection may be more a question of emphasis than outcomes.[37] Further, even in jurisdictions that are said to share similar approaches or justification, there are still significant differences between their copyright laws and/or their application.[38] The debate on the justifications for copyright protection inevitably applies to the scope of copyright protection

---

29 See 'What We Do – Creative Commons' (*Creative Commons*, 2019), http://creativecommons.org/about (accessed 26 June 2019). Also Rizk 2010 supra at 124–127.

30 See generally Lessig L, *Remix: Making Art and Commerce Thrive in the Hybrid Economy* (Penguin 2008); Stallman R, *Free Software, Free Society: Selected Essays of Richard M. Stallman* (Free Software Foundation Inc. 2002); Boldrin M and Levine D, 'The case against intellectual property' [2002] 92(2) *American Economic Review* 209–212.

31 See Davies G, *Copyright and the Public Interest* (2nd edn, Sweet & Maxwell 2002), 250.

32 See Shagall Y, '*Jacobsen v. Katzer*: Federal Circuit affirms economic interest of open source copyright holder' (*Harvard Journal of Law & Technology*, 23 August 2008), http://jolt.law.harvard.edu/digest/jacobsen-v-katzer (accessed 26 June 2019).

33 Ibid.

34 Waelde C, Kheria S, Cornwell J and Brown A, *Contemporary Intellectual Property Law and Policy* (4th edn, Oxford University Press 2016).

35 See paras 2.39–2.42.

36 2008 U.S. App. LEXIS 17161 (Fed. Cir. 2008).

37 See Goldstein P, *International Copyright: Principles, Law, and Practice* (Oxford University Press, 2001), 10. See also Cornish J, 'Sound recordings and copyright' [1993] 24 *International Review of Intellectual Property and Competition Law* 306 at 307.

38 Schönwetter 2009 supra at 30.

and highlights the need for set boundaries. In this context, policymakers need to ensure that the protection of the interests of the copyright owner does not adversely affect the public interests.[39] On the one hand, there is need to incentivise the author to create and the copyright owner to invest in the production of copyright works by providing effective legal protection. On the other hand, it must be ensured that the public has access to these products. Put differently, it is essential to guarantee that the public is ultimately able to access creative outputs. Where such access does not exist or is unduly constrained, the society would not be able to benefit from the creative nature of copyright works.

2.17 To reach a reasonable balance between public and private interests,[40] provisions are made for the duration of copyright protection (resulting in the notion of the 'public domain')[41] and for limitations and exceptions to copyright protection.[42] Such provisions are geared towards ensuring that the much-sought balance between the interests of copyright owners and that of users of copyright works can be maintained. This 'internal mechanism' has contributed to defining the boundaries of the scope of copyright and the markets for copyright-protected materials.[43]

Exclusive rights and competition

2.18 As stated earlier, copyright law grants copyright owners rights in exclusivity meaning that other persons cannot exercise those rights in relation to the copyright work without their permission or licence. The exclusive rights common to the categories of works protected under copyright law in respect of music content include the right to reproduce the work, perform the work in public, publish the work, make a cinematograph film or a record in respect of the work, distribute the work for commercial purposes and communicate or broadcast the work to the public.[44] The exclusive nature of these rights enables income generation by necessitating requests for prior authorisation (licence) from the relevant copyright owner from any person wishing to exercise any of the rights. The request for license may result in payment of license fees while failure to obtain a license for uses outside those statutorily permitted, may result in the payment of damages for copyright infringement.[45] In other words, these rights are secured

39 Cross J and Yu P, 'Competition law and copyright misuse' (2007) 56 *Drake L Rev* 433 (Cross and Yu 2007).

40 Ibid.

41 Corbett S, 'Creative Commons licences, the copyright regime and the online community: Is there a fatal disconnect?' [2011] 74(4) *Modern Law Review* 528 (Corbett 2011).

42 Cross and Yu 2007 supra at 429. Sections 12, 13 and 14 of the South African Copyright Act create certain exceptions to copyright protection including using the work for the purpose of criticism or review.

43 Katz 2013 supra.

44 For a full description of each of the exclusive rights available for the mentioned categories of copyright works, see Sections 6, 7 and 8 of the Nigerian Copyright Act; Section 6(1)(a)–(g) of the South African Copyright Act.

45 See sections 16 to 18 of the Nigerian Copyright Act; see also section 24 of the South African Copyright Act; Olubiyi IA, 'A comparative analysis of copyright enforcement provisions in Nigeria: Maximising the current legal regime' [2014] 5 *Nnamdi Azikiwe University Journal of*

through the provisions for appropriate remedies where they are exercised without the licence of the copyright owners. Most copyright law cases relate to the application of copyright infringement rules. This is typically due to the fact that copyright infringement rules envisage the possibility of the copyright owner generating revenue from exclusively exercising his rights to reproduce, distribute and/or license its copyrighted works.[46]

2.19 These rights together with the possibility of obtaining monetary remedies for their infringement form the basis for the design and deployment of business models in the copyright marketplace.[47] Even in so-called pure open business models, where licence to use the protected work is granted for free, the economic rights are activated once the licensee operates outside the terms of licence. Further, at the heart of the copyright infringement suits against platform firms that use copyright-protected content in advertising is the question of who is entitled to what share of the advertising revenue from using such content.[48] As such, from the moment the copyright work is created, the author or the right holder may be perceived as an entrepreneur or firm who has a 'product' to sell or license for revenue generation.[49]

Monetisation of copyright-protected music content

2.20 From a copyright law perspective, the revenue received from sale of music CDs and DVDs, licences for the streaming of music, digital downloads and the like is said to be directly attributable to the exercise and enforcement of the statutorily protected reproduction rights and rights ancillary thereto.[50] Accordingly, copyright law requires the authorisation of the person or entity who owns the reproduction right in the music content before the right may be exercised or exploited in any manner.[51] The exploitation by the copyright owner or the implied

International Law and Jurisprudence 90 (Olubiyi 2014); Angelopoulos C, *European Intermediary Liability in Copyright: A Tort-Based Analysis: A Tort-Based Analysis* (Kluwer Law International BV, 2016), 14.

46 Olubiyi 2014 supra at 89; Ouma M, 'Copyright and the music industry in Africa' [2004] 7(6) *Journal of World Intellectual Property*, 921; Ginsburg 2017 supra at 81–82.

47 See Coetzer BL, *A Business Model for the Digital Distribution of Music in the South African Context* (Masters, University of Pretoria 2009), p. 41. Also see Rethink Music, 'Fair music: transparency and payment flows in the music industry' (Berklee Institute of Creative Entrepreneurship 2015), www.berklee.edu/sites/default/files/Fair%20Music%20-%20Transparency%20and%20Payment%20Flows%20in%20the%20Music%20Industry.pdf (accessed 22 June 2019).

48 Ginsburg 2017 supra at 81–82.

49 Ibid.

50 Kretschmer M, 'Artists' earnings and copyright: A review of British and German music industry data in the context of digital technologies' [2005] 10(1) *First Monday*, 3. See also Future of Music Coalition (FMC) Report on music industry revenue streams. FMC refers to this income stream as 'songwriter and composer revenue'. 'Artist Revenue Streams' (*Money.futureofmusic.org*, 2012), http://money.futureofmusic.org/wordpress/wp-content/uploads/2012/01/revenue-streams-handoutlist.pdf (accessed 26 June 2019).

51 As earlier stated, the exception to this rule may be 'fair dealing' under Nigerian and South African copyright regimes, with the music content. Licensing obligations may not exist when the music content is either in the public domain or not eligible for copyright due to subsistence challenges or for private enjoyment or use of a small portion of the work. Also see para. 2.45.

or express authorisation of the exploitation of the reproduction right and/or other ancillary right is reflected in the business model.[52] However, the law does not set out the specifics or details of business models for the use and exploitation of copyright products. Rather, copyright law provides the regulatory framework within which business models consisting of the exercise of and control of the exclusive rights can be designed and deployed.[53]

2.21 The monetisation of music content has historically rested on two primary economic rights – (1) the performing right and (2) the reproduction right – with the capacity of having 'something to sell or license' or to monetise each of these rights being driven by technology. Prior to any significant technological development, revenue or value could only be generated from the performance of music by assembling people at a specific place and time to listen to the music being performed *at that time*. When the music performance ended, there was no way to monetise or create value from the music thereafter, except to arrange for another music performance. Reproducing music, prior to the Gutenberg press in 1454, was done by copying music on a sheet ('sheet music') and distributing the sheet music for a fee. This was, of course, a laborious and time-consuming process with relatively low output. With the arrival of the Gutenberg press, the capacity to reproduce music into copies was greatly enhanced as the 'reproduced' sheet music was available and accessible to anyone who could or wished to learn a musical instrument, at a time of their choosing, and with the sheet music at hand, the music could be performed.[54]

2.22 With more technological advancements, the reproduction right migrated from generating revenue through sheet music to generating revenue through piano rolls, acetates and then vinyl, then on to tapes to cassettes[55] to CDs, and now to digital files and streaming. These mediums represented the means of exploiting the reproduction right to generate revenue. Similarly, technological advancements ensured that revenue could be generated from performing rights without the requirement of assembling the audience in one place and at a specific time. Instead, revenue was generated from the performing right through the public performance, the broadcast, the transmission through diffusion services and the communication to the public[56] of the music content. In this regard and leveraging on the statutory provision that reproduction of any copyright work

52 See Towse R, 'Copyright and music publishing in the UK', in *The Artful Economist* (Springer 2016) 135.

53 See Stadler 2007 supra at p. 910; Newman J, 'Copyright freeconomics' [2013] 66 *Vand L Rev* 1451–1456.

54 See Coetzer 2009 supra at 14–19; Towse R, 'The economic effects of digitization on the administration of musical copyrights' [2013] 10(2) *Review of Economic Research on Copyright Issues*, 55–67; Towse 2016a supra.

55 The piano roll, acetates, vinyl and cassettes were the old ways of listening to recorded music. The piano roll, for instance, is a music storage medium used to operate a player piano, piano player or reproducing piano. See Barnet RD and Burriss LL, *Controversies of the music industry* (Greenwood Publishing Group 2001).

56 See section 9(e) of the South African Copyright Act. This right is not applicable in Nigeria presently. It is, however, provided for in the current Copyright Amendment Bill 2015.

can be 'in any manner or form',[57] digitisation and technology have necessitated the expansion of the exercise of the reproduction right to include performance[58] of the reproduced work through 'broadcast' rights, 'transmission through a diffusion service' rights and 'communication to the public' rights, and have also evolved to include the 'publishing' rights and 'adaptation' rights.[59] Accordingly, apart from public performance in a live format, the reproduction right became the most recognised value metric or revenue generator for the recorded music copyright sector because it involved the many ways in which music content may be perceived.

2.23 In providing for these exclusive rights, copyright is therefore one of the essential institutional mechanisms which has helped facilitate the creation and dissemination of cultural and creative works through business models, by providing a framework to manage the need for the public to have access to copyright-protected materials.[60] As such, it is much more than a mechanism for protecting the revenue or royalties derived from an intellectual resource; it is part of the institutional framework that helps define a marketable product as well as reliable income flows (through royalties and related income).[61]

2.24 In a related manner, copyright law, by necessitating the prior license of the copyright owner before exercising any of the exclusive bundle of rights, protects the right holder from others taking over and reaping the rewards from his or her intellectual efforts, that is, from free riding on these efforts through the copying of another's expression (imitation). By prohibiting the use of copyright works without the permission of the copyright owner, copyright law 'excludes competition by imitation' and 'forces the investors in creative production to rely on their own creativity, or the creativity of people they employ, to come up with different products that may please consumers'.[62] Therefore, the exclusivity of copyright is to be interpreted as encouraging competition by substitution in the long-term benefit of the consumers.[63]

57 See ss 6(d), 8(1)(c) and 9(c) of the South African Copyright Act.

58 See the following provisions of the South African Copyright Act: ss 6(d), 8(1)(c) and 9(c) for broadcast rights; ss 6(e), 7(d) and 8(1)(d) for the transmission through a diffusion service rights; s 9(e) for the communication to the public rights. Apart from the right of communication to the public, corresponding provisions in the Nigerian Copyright Act may be found in ss 6, 7 and 9.

59 'Publishing', in the context of music content involves the acquisition of musical compositions from composers and songwriters, the subsequent transformation of the musical composition from manuscript to performance, recording and subsequent uses. See Towse R, 'Economics of music publishing: copyright and the market' [2017] 41(4) *Journal of Cultural Economics*, 404–405.

60 See Drexl 2013 supra at 5–6.

61 Andersen B, Kozul-Wright Z and Kozul-Wright R, *Copyrights, Competition and Development*. No. 145 (UNCTAD Discussion Paper, 2000).

62 See Drexl 2013 supra at p. 39. See the case of *Mandla-Matla Publishing (Pty) Ltd* v *Independent Newspapers (Pty) Ltd* (48/CR/Jun04) [2006] ZACT 84 (6 November 2006), para. 54 (Mandla-Matla Publishing). See also Fishman 2014; Burk DL, 'The creating around paradox: Responding to Joseph P. Fishman, Creating around copyright, 128 Harv. L. Rev. 1333' [2015] 128 *Harv L Rev* 118.

63 See 'Antitrust guidelines for the licensing of intellectual property' (*Justice.gov*, 12 January 2017), www.justice.gov/atr/IPguidelines/download (accessed 26 June 2019).

2.25 Due to the exclusive nature of the rights conferred by copyright law, the copyright owner may now possess 'something to sell or license' to generate revenue.[64] In this regard, copyright owners design and deploy business models based on these exclusive rights.[65] Therefore, copyright law is said to encourage firms to compete in the kind of works they create so as to enjoy copyright protection. Furthermore, since copyright protection and exploitation is expected to yield sales and/or licensing revenue, the provision of remedies for the unlicensed exercise or exploitation of those exclusive rights promotes competition and enables firms to obtain and retain competitive advantage.

2.26 Accordingly, by creating rights that may help to guarantee returns on creative investments, copyright law encourages competition amongst potential authors to create new works.[66] Indeed, the promotion of competition through the grant of exclusive rights is so sacrosanct that courts are quite reluctant to interfere with such rights even under the guise of competition law. In this regard, the application of competition law to the exercise of this right is said to be *prima facie* prohibited and may only be undertaken 'in exceptional circumstances'.[67]

Copyright driving business models

2.27 The advent of today's knowledge-based economy has increased the importance of copyright and made it more significant in the strategies and processes of many firms. Several firms have started to design and deploy new uses and new approaches to the use of copyright and have begun to market same, exclusively focusing on such new uses to fuel their core business.[68] Platform firms are increasingly interested in generating profits from new, innovative ways of using music content rather than from traditional ways of selling or licensing music content.[69] Seen in that light, platform firms may be considered as key partners to copyright owners as they have the capability to provide a means for artists, music publishers and record companies to connect more with fans and customers.[70] Through their multi-sided music platforms, platform firms also enable social interaction amongst other copyright users and also provide a means for 'social production'.[71]

---

64 See Kretschmer 2010 supra at 144. Also see Corbett 2011 supra at 433, referring to copyright as 'a commodity'; Andersen and others 2000 supra at 6, 23.

65 Towse 2016a supra at 135–138; Rajan MTS, 'Creative Commons: America's moral rights' (2010) 21 *Fordham Intell Prop Media & Ent LJ* 931–932 (Rajan 2010); Drexl 2013 supra at 5.

66 See Van Aswegen PF, 'The right to exclude others from using claimed intellectual property: A perspective from competition law' (2003) 14 *Stellenbosch L Rev* 125–126.

67 See Drexl 2013 supra at 36. Also Van Aswegen 2003 supra at 125–126.

68 See Towse 2017 supra at 415–416.

69 Ibid. See also Dörr J, Wagner DV, Benlian A and Hess T, 'Music as a service as an alternative to music piracy?' (2013) 5(6) *Business & Information Systems Engineering* 385.

70 See Rajan 2010 supra at 929. See also Rethink Music 2015 supra at 4; 'PRS For Music and SoundCloud reach licensing agreement' (*Prsformusic.com*, 21 December 2015), www.prsformusic.com/press/2015/prs-for-music-and-soundcloud-reach-a-multi-territory-licensing-agreement-ending-legal-proceedings (accessed 26 June 2019).

71 Social production is a major type of content production facilitated by social media platforms, both commercial and nonprofit, where individuals are playing a more significant role in the

2.28 The crucial function of multi-sided music platforms and platform firms in this context has also been recognised in many countries including South Africa and Nigeria, where the umbrella body for the recorded music industry, the International Federation of the Phonographic Industry (IFPI), noted the steady rise in the number of such platforms in the two countries.[72] Indeed, everyone nowadays seems to be familiar with these digital platforms, from the most basic to the most sophisticated.[73] The majority of these platforms are multinational internet companies with footprints across many jurisdictions in the light of the global reach of the internet.[74]

2.29 In a context of increasing attention towards new ways of using and assessing copyright-protected content, the business model of platform firms have generated much interest.[75] Specifically, the business model deployed by platform firms is considered as 'open' and 'freemium' and relates to the policy question of whether compelling platform firms to obtain a paid licence for the music content may benefit the music copyright industry as well as the users and final consumers of music content. The concept and debate surrounding the open and freemium music business models are discussed in the next section.[76]

Open business models

2.30 A business model explains the processes and strategies adopted by a business entity (firm) to generate revenue in the business environment.[77] It is widely recognised that business models are tools with which firms compete with other firms to gain competitive advantage. Defined as a representation or description of the rationale of how a firm 'creates, delivers and captures value',[78]

production of content outside the usual organisational structure of the content industry. See Elkin-Koren N, 'Tailoring copyright to social production' [2011] 12(1) *Theoretical Inquiries in Law*, 311–313.

72 See International Federation of the Phonographic Industry (IFPI), 'Digital Music Report 2014: Lighting up new markets' (International Federation of the Phonographic Industry (IFPI) 2014), www.ifpi.org/downloads/Digital-Music-Report-2014.pdf (accessed 22 June 2019). See also Heald PJ, 'How notice-and-takedown regimes create markets for music on YouTube: An empirical study' [2014] 83 *UMKC L Rev* 313.

73 YouTube.com and Facebook.com rank as the second and third top sites globally. In Nigeria, the two platforms rank fourth and fifth top sites, while in South Africa they rank as third and fourth, respectively. See 'Top Sites in South Africa – Alexa – Alexa' (*Alexa.com*, 2019), www.alexa.com/topsites/countries/ZA (accessed 26 June 2019).

74 For example, YouTube is headquartered in the US with offices in the UK, Nigeria and many other jurisdictions.

75 See Solo A, 'The role of copyright in an age of online music distribution' [2014] 19 *Media and Arts Law Review* 183.

76 See Solo 2014 supra at 183. Newman 2013 supra at 1407.

77 See Weill P, Malone T and Apel T, 'The business models investors prefer' [2011] 52(4) *MIT Sloan Management Review* 17–19.

78 See Osterwalder A and Pigneur Y, *Business Model Generation: A Handbook for Visionaries, Game Changers, and Challengers* (John Wiley & Sons 2010) 19 (Osterwalder and Pigneur). Value may involve what a firm delivers to the customer or the needs of the customer which the firm seeks to satisfy. Value may be created through offering new products, customisation, price reduction etc. See p. 25.

business models constitute a fundamental component of trading and economic behaviour.[79] Economic behaviour is exhibited in the creation, production, distribution, provision and use of goods and services.

2.31 Usually, business models are better explained from the context of a specific firm or enterprise operating in a stated industry. In other words, as conceptual blueprints, business models identify the customers and value propositions[80] of a particular firm and are tools for a firm to convert plans and strategies into operations.[81] However, the notions of 'open and freemium' business models are not identified in the business model literature as pertaining to any specific industry or sector. Instead, within the business model literature, open and freemium business models are prototypes of a category of activities that may be undertaken by any organisation in the creation and delivery of value.[82] These prototypes are distinct from the product, organisation, industry, sector or network. As prototypes, the description of the open and freemium business models may not be centred on a focal organisation but their boundaries are determined by those of the firm deploying the business model as well as the economic activities within the industry or sector in which they are deployed.[83] The 'open business model' and the 'freemium business model' are expressions used in the adjectival sense to explain how organisations create and deliver their value proposition as well as how they generate revenue.[84]

Open vs. proprietary

2.32 The business model literature distinguishes between proprietary and non-proprietary business models and between open and closed business models. However, there is some debate as to whether the notions of 'proprietary' and 'open' are compatible – whether it is possible to have both a proprietary and open business model.[85] In other cases, there are arguments that proprietary business

79 See Teece DJ, 'Business models, business strategy and innovation' [2010] 43(2) *Long Range Planning* 172–194.

80 Magretta J, 'Why business models matter' [2002] 80(5) *Harvard Business Review* 87.

81 Pateli A and Giaglis GM, 'A framework for understanding and analysing ebusiness models', *Bled 2003 Proceedings*. Available at: https://domino.fov.uni-mb.si/proceedings.nsf/Proceedings/4C84233423603AD0C1256EA1002D1A29/$File/25Pateli.pdf, 337 (accessed 19 November 2017).

82 See Zott C, Amit R and Massa L, 'The business model: recent developments and future research' (2011) 37(4) *Journal of Management* 1025.

83 See Preston M and Zurer R, 'Open content and the search for a better intellectual property model: Lessons from open source' (*Cs.duke.edu*, 11 December 2013), www.cs.duke.edu/courses/cps182s/compsci342s/cps182s/spring05/assign/project/fall03/raz3_1/opencontent.pdf (accessed 26 June 2019).

84 Several authors aptly demonstrate this. For instance, Chesbrough in his book explains how organisations can adopt and maintain an 'open' or 'more open' business model. H Chesbrough, *Open Business Models: How to Thrive in the New Innovation Landscape* (Harvard Business School Press 2006). Also, Osterwalder and Pigneur explain 'open' and 'freemium' as each having 'specific patterns', 'similar characteristics, similar arrangements of business model Building Blocks, or similar behaviors'. These patterns form the basis of such business models. See Osterwalder and Pigneur supra at 49. See also Chesbrough HW, 'The era of open innovation' [2006] 127(3) *Managing Innovation and Change* 34–41.

85 Müller RM, Kijl B and Martens JK, 'A comparison of inter-organizational business models of mobile app stores: There is more than open vs. closed' [2011] 6(2) *Journal of Theoretical and Applied*

models are usually closed, as they require access to the copyright owner or firm's intellectual property rights (e.g. copyright). Consequently, such arguments link the notion of openness only to business models that do not restrict access to such intellectual property rights.[86]

2.33 In relation to business models that pertain to music and/or music content, the notion of 'open' could be defined in the context of whether the proprietary rights in copyright are retained or waived. In such instance, the business models would be described as proprietary when the use of the music content requires access to and the right to use or exercise the exclusive bundle of rights provided by copyright law.[87] Accordingly, a firm or copyright owner that reserves and exercises the entire exclusive rights provided by copyright law and requires a (paid) licence or exclusive assignment before legitimate use can be made may be said to be deploying a proprietary business model.[88] For example, record companies that sell their music CDs in stores and/or on the Apple Music website and would legally resist unlicensed use of their music may be said to operate a proprietary business model.

2.34 On the other hand, when the business model is open or non-proprietary, it would not be necessary to negotiate a licensing agreement or pay for the purchase or download of music content or request permission to use or modify the music content. The relevant copyright owner would have obliterated this need by providing a licence and indicating terms which permit many uses of the music content. For instance, a copyright owner may provide a Creative Commons[89] licence such as the 'Attribution'[90] and 'Attribution-Share Alike'[91] licences with respect to the use of his copyright-protected music content. The Attribution licence permits other persons to distribute, remix, tweak and build upon existing work, even commercially, provided that such person credits the copyright owner for the original creation.[92] Music content may also be distributed under the 'open

Electronic Commerce Research 63–76; Trott P and Hartmann DAP, 'Why 'open innovation' is old wine in new bottles' [2009] 13(4) *International Journal of Innovation Management* 715–736.

86 Chesbrough H, 'The logic of open innovation: managing intellectual property' [2003] 45(3) *California Management Review* 33–58.

87 Ibid. See also Osterwalder and Pigneur 2010 supra at 49.

88 Ibid. See also Chesbrough 2003 supra at 35.

89 Creative Commons is an organisation established for the purpose of increasing the availability of creative works which the public may legally access and build upon. Towards this commitment, the Creative Commons has designed a range of licences available to the public free of charge and which may be used to permit different level of access for users of creative works. See 'What We Do – Creative Commons' (*Creative Commons*, 2019), http://creativecommons.org/about (accessed 26 June 2019). See also Dusollier S, 'The master's tools v. the master's house: Creative commons v. copyright' [2006] 29 *Columbia Journal of Law & Arts* 274; Elkin-Koren N, 'What contracts cannot do: The limits of private ordering in facilitating a creative commons' [2005] 74 *Fordham L Rev* 383.

90 See Corbett 2011 supra at 512; Dusollier 2006 supra at p. 275.

91 This license permits others to remix, tweak, and build upon existing work even for commercial purposes, as long as they credit the copyright owner and also license their new creations under the identical terms. See Corbett 2011 supra at 512; Dusollier 2006 supra at 275.

92 Ibid.

music archive' system, which permits the use of music held in common by a group as a whole.[93]

2.35 Further, the notion of open and freemium music business models may be considered from some other perspectives: access to the creative process and access to the music content once created or produced.[94] First, the creative process refers to the development and approval of the music content by the relevant copyright owner.[95] Access to the creative process may then be interpreted as being open when (a) interested persons or firms are not restricted from using the music content and the rights inherent in them, to create new (copyright-protected) products;[96] and/or (b) there is collaboration (inviting external persons or firms or using their protected subject matter) in the creation of a firm's music content.[97] These elements are significant.[98] For instance, Osterwalder and Pigneur describe open business models as business models that:

> can be used by companies to create and capture value by systematically collaborating with outside partners. This may happen from the 'outside-in' by exploiting external ideas within the firm, or from the 'inside-out' by providing external parties with ideas or assets lying idle within the firm.[99]

2.36 From the foregoing, it can be seen that the underlying principle of 'openness' may be expressed through external collaborations and through explicit or implicit licences.[100] The copyright owner as an entity may collaborate with persons outside the firm in carrying out its key activities,[101] especially in the creation or development of the music content. Within such an open music business model, the exclusive rights belonging to the copyright owner ('internal properties') and/

93 According to the open music archive website, '[T]he Open Music Archive concerns itself with the public domain and creative works which are not owned by any one individual and are held in common by society as a whole'. See 'Open Music Archive – About' (*Openmusicarchive.org*, 2005), www.openmusicarchive.org/about.php (accessed 26 June 2019).

94 Okoli C and Carillo K, 'Beyond open source software: An introduction to researching open content: A framework, implications, and directions for researching open content' [2013] SSRN Electronic Journal 2–3. See also Domb Krauskopf AE, '"Fire, Lights, Everything!": Exploring symbolic capital in the Tecnobrega dance scene' (Master of Science in Comparative Media Studies, Massachusetts Institute of Technology 2009); Russi G, 'Creative Commons, CC-plus and hybrid intermediaries: A stakeholders' perspective' [2012] *International Law and Management Review* 110. See also Jarvenpaa S and Lang K, 'Boundary management in online communities: Case studies of the Nine Inch Nails and ccMixter music remix sites' [2012] 44 *Long Range Planning* 440–457.

95 Ibid.

96 This may involve express or tacit permission of cover versions or mash-ups of music content. See Rimmer M, 'The grey album: copyright law and digital sampling' [2005] 114(1) *Media International Australia Incorporating Culture and Policy* 40–53. Elkin-Koren 2017 supra at 142–143.

97 Rimmer 2005 supra.

98 Okoli and Carillo 2013 supra at 5; Preston and Zurer 2003 supra; Elkin-Koren N, 'The new frontiers of user rights' [2016] 32 *Am U Int'l L Rev* 1; Santos A, 'Nurturing creative industries in the developing world: The case of alternative systems of music production and distribution' [2013] 21 *Mich St U Coll L Int'l L Rev* 601.

99 Osterwalder and Pigneur 2010 supra at 80.

100 See Okoli and Carillo 2013 supra at 5.

101 Key activities include creation/production of key resources, establishing and maintaining channels of distribution and customer relationships, delivering the value proposition and solving customer problems. The specific key activities will differ with each business model, each industry and each organisation. See Osterwalder and Pigneur 2010 supra at 39.

or the exclusive rights belonging to another copyright owner who has waived all or some of the rights ('external properties') are utilised in creating the music content that is distributed to users and consumers. Likewise, the copyright owner may also grant an explicit licence or permission to the public in respect of its copyright in a given music content. Such licences specify the uses to which the copyright may be put and is meant for users who need access to the music content to create new music content. The creative process of the music content and the resultant product are expected to be enhanced or unaffected by the uses to which the copyright may be put. In other words, the author may create a better received or new product based on ideas resulting from 'inviting' others to participate in the use of its copyright. The copyright owner and any external key partner, whom the copyright owner may use or rely upon, usually set the 'some rights reserved' licence and the implementation of collaborative creative process.

2.37 Secondly, the concept of openness may be appraised based on the access to the music content once created or produced. In this context, the copyright owner retains the entire exclusive rights granted by copyright law but refrains from or waives the right to exploit or monetise those rights. Instead, the copyright owner explores alternative means of revenue generation, which may be attributable to the waiver of the rights in the first place. In this context, further differentiation may be made. It is possible to distinguish between access for use of the music content in some other creative endeavour or for distribution and access for consumption of the music content. While access for use refers to the ability of distributors, digital platforms and firms to use the music content in the operation of their distribution, music subscription or other services, access for consumption involves persons who require the music content for their listening and personal enjoyment only.[102] Because copyright law demands that access for the purposes of using the music content requires the licence of the relevant copyright owner,[103] and also access for consumption purposes demands a sale and purchase arrangement,[104] access for use without paid licence and access for consumption free of charge may still be considered as deploying the open business model.

Freemium

2.38 Apart from business model patterns described as 'open', the business model literature also describes some business models as based on the concept of 'free'.[105] Here, the relevant firm creates and captures value by offering a

102 Stazi A, 'Digital copyright and consumer/user protection: moving toward a new framework?' [2012] 2 *Queen Mary Journal of Intellectual Property* 158–174; Ritala S, 'Pandora & Spotify: Legal issues and licensing requirements for interactive and non-interactive internet radio broadcasters' [2013] 54 *IDEA* 23; Richardson J, 'The Spotify paradox: How the creation of a compulsory license scheme for streaming on-demand music services can save the music industry' [2014] 22 *UCLA Ent L Rev* 45.

103 See Heald 2014 supra at 313; Perel M and Elkin-Koren N, 'Accountability in algorithmic copyright enforcement' [2015] 19 *Stan Tech L Rev* 473.

104 See Derclaye E and Favale M, 'Copyright and contract law: Regulating user contracts: The state of the art and a research agenda' [2010] 18 *J Intell Prop L* 92–95.

105 Osterwalder and Pigneur 2010 supra at 67.

product free of charge and generating revenue through other means or sale of other products. In this regard, the concept of 'free' may translate into an advertisement-based free offer, a subscription-based free offer and/or a free offer based on a 'bait and hook' pattern where the free offer is used to attract customers to a paid offer.[106] 'Freemium' provides a veritable example of business models based on the notion of 'free' or 'zero price'.

2.39 To be able to offer the music content free of charge to the consumers, a firm may provide 'freemium' services to consumers – either offer subscription services to a category of consumers ('subscription-based freemium') and/or offer adver tising services to firms that may wish to advertise their products to the consumers on the platform ('ad-based freemium').[107] Subscription-based freemium enables users of the platform to access certain music consumption features free of charge and requires users to pay a subscription fee or some similar fee (usually referred to as a 'premium') to enjoy specialised functions and services such as an unlimited music catalogue, ad-free listening, offline access and extended search features.[108] The process here involves the platform firms themselves uploading the music content onto their platforms. As a result, there is the requirement to obtain the licence of the relevant copyright owner of the music content, which may be an individual, a record company, a collective management organisation (CMO) and/or a music publisher.[109] Such licensing terms are usually set by agreement between the platform firm and the copyright owner and would represent terms of access to the music content.[110] The agreement would also stipulate how the subscription fees received from subscribers may be shared and also stipulate whether the music content is to be available to the free or non-subscribing customers.[111] In many cases, most platform firms that deploy a subscription-based freemium business model combine such with ad-based freemium. In such instance, the agreement

106 Ibid.

107 Mounier P, 'Freemium as a sustainable economic model for open access electronic publishing in humanities and social sciences' [2011] 31(3–4) *Information Services & Use* 230; Halmenschlager C and Waelbroeck P, 'Fighting free with free: Freemium vs. piracy' [2014] *SSRN Electronic Journal*. Available at https://ssrn.com/abstract=2475641, 2–3 (accessed 7 August 2016).

108 Bekkelund KJ, 'Succeeding with freemium: Exploring why companies have succeeded and failed with freemium' [2011] 4350 *Innovation and Entrepreneurship, Specialization Project* 6–7. Examples in the music industry include Spotify, Deezer and Spinlet. See generally 'Music for everyone' (*Spotify.com*, 2015), www.spotify.com/us/about-us/contact/ (accessed 26 June 2019); 'Spinlet' (*Spinlet*, 2015), https://spinlet.com/faq-african-musicians-and-more (accessed 26 June 2019); Pujol N, 'Freemium: attributes of an emerging business model' [2010] SSRN Electronic Journal, https://doi.org/10.2139/ssrn.1718663 (accessed 19 July 2016).

109 Ritala 2013 supra at 42–43.

110 Ibid. See also Solo 2014 supra at 184–187.

111 For example, popular US artist Taylor Swift had at some point withdrawn her music content from the Spotify platform because she did not want her music offered for free. See Dredge S, 'Taylor Swift still has bad blood with Spotify over streaming music dispute' (*The Guardian*, 4 August 2015), www.theguardian.com/technology/2015/aug/04/taylor-swift-bad-blood-spotify-streaming-music (accessed 26 June 2019). See also Sawer P, 'Spotify must change its free music service, says Universal Records' (*Telegraph.co.uk*, 21 March 2015), www.telegraph.co.uk/culture/music/music-news/11487187/Spotify-must-change-its-free-music-service-says-Universal-records.html (accessed 26 June 2019).

usually addresses the issue of whether and how to share the subscription fees and/or the advertisement fees received from subscribers and advertisers, respectively.[112] In this regard, the terms of the agreement are expressly stated in line with the copyright law regulatory framework.[113]

2.40 On the other side of the spectrum are platform firms, which deploy an ad-based freemium service where rather than the platform firm it is the users of the platform that upload the music content onto the platform. Within this spectrum, there are also firms that upload the music content onto the platforms following submission from users. In either case, any member of the public may then access the music content free of charge. As a result of this, a lot of users are attracted to the platform both for the purpose of consuming the music content and for the purpose of uploading or submitting music content onto the platform. Advertisers, in turn, pay an advertising fee to the platform firms to use the platform to advertise their product and services to the teeming users of the platform.[114] The challenge in terms of the copyright law lies in ad-based freemium where there may be no explicit licensing agreement between the copyright owner and the platform firm or where the platform firm is able to 'force' the issuance of a *gratis* licence.[115]

Concluding remarks on open and freemium music business models classification

2.41 From the foregoing, it is evident that there is no straightforward answer in defining an open music business model. On the one hand, the notion of open access to the creative process does not seem to raise many questions in terms of acceptance as an 'open' business model. On the other hand, the issue regarding open access to the use and consumption of the music content has been at the core of some serious debate. While some platform firms collaborate with copyright owners to provide open access to the consumption of music content without any discussion as to revenue or revenue share,[116] other platform firms enter into terms with the copyright owner to receive and share the subscription fees and/or the advertisement fees received from subscribers and advertisers, respectively.[117] The major reservation, therefore, is whether music business models can be interpreted as open even when they are based on the use of copyright-protected works, which are not licensed for free but under terms that only provide free access for music consumption. The answer may be relevant for copyright owners who have a policy interest in deploying proprietary music business models (hence, covered by exploitable copyright-protected works) while maintaining some form of openness. However, the significance of the debate is not only connected to the import

112 See Ginsburg 2017 supra at 74.

113 See Derclaye and Favale 2010 supra at 110.

114 See Maurer G, 'YouTube Business Model' (*prezi.com*, 2 June 2015), https://prezi.com/puvz-26rl2cbg/youtube-business-model/ (accessed 26 June 2019).

115 See Chapter 3.

116 For instance, NotJustOk.com.

117 See Ginsburg 2017 supra at 74; Heald 2015 supra at 318. See also YouTube's Content ID, discussed in Chapter 3.

of openness as such. Rather, the different arguments made by the literature focus on a much more relevant issue, which calls into question the relationship between the platform firm's interests and the copyright terms applicable to multi-sided music platforms. For policymakers in particular, the issue pertains to the need to, in the context of multi-sided music platforms, align the public interests in the use of the copyright products with the private interests of the copyright owners in being rewarded for their creative efforts.

2.42 More importantly, for the purposes of this book, it is worth noting that the various theories and interpretations developed for open and freemium business models suffer from lack of uniform terminology. However, the discussion in this section has been provided to explain the main classifications in an attempt to shed some light on the issue and address possible misconstructions.

2.43 From the discussion on the design of the platform in Chapter 1,[118] it can be seen that multi-sided music platforms operate an open and freemium music business model based on a combination of selected features of the prototypes as described earlier. The possibility of uploading and accessing the music content free of charge falls within the 'open' description, while the possibility of collecting advertising payments from some other customer segment falls within the 'freemium' description. In these contexts, the business model of multi-sided music platforms is 'open' in the sense of being free of charge to the consumer and 'freemium' in the sense of receiving a premium in terms of an advertising fee. Platform firms such as YouTube, SoundCloud, and Facebook and local companies such as NotJustOk.com discussed in this book exemplify this business model.[119]

Other ways copyright law promotes competition

2.44 Apart from the role of exclusive copyright protection in promoting competition in copyright markets, copyright law contains other provisions and adopts other doctrines to encourage competition in the copyright market. These provisions aim at providing a balance between the exclusive rights and control of copyright owners and the rights of access by copyright users. Further, such provisions may also constitute the basis for designing and deploying business models that aid increased access to copyright products, as exemplified in the case of Google Books (developed on the basis of the US fair use exception).[120]

2.45 Provision for a limited term of copyright protection resulting in the notion of 'public domain',[121] the fair dealing provision, and other provisions for limitations and exceptions to copyright protection,[122] the originality requirement and

118 See para. 1.16.

119 These platforms are also referred to as 'user-upload' platforms. See International Federation of the Phonographic Industry (IFPI), 'Global Music Report 2017: Annual State of the Industry' (2017), www.ifpi.org/downloads/GMR2017.pdf (accessed 22 June 2019).

120 See Stadler 2007 supra at 903; *Authors Guild v Google, Inc.*, No. 13–4829 (2d Cir. 2015).

121 Corbett 2011 supra at 528.

122 Cross and Yu 2007 supra at 429. Sections 12, 13 and 14 of South African Copyright Act.

the idea-expression dichotomy[123] all help in different ways to prevent copyright owners from restricting the public from finding satisfactory market substitutes.

2.46 In the case of the originality requirement, copyright protects only original expressions and does not protect ideas, procedures and the like. By protecting only original expressions, copyright protection will by implication be unavailable to works that do not measure up to such standards. Copyright owners may therefore be incentivised to create quality original works to be sure to enjoy the benefit of copyright protection. Users are, by extension, able to have access to quality copyright products.

2.47 Copyright protection does not exist in perpetuity. Rather, the protection lasts for a stated period. In the case of Nigeria, the term of copyright protection in a musical work is life of the author plus 70 years.[124] Upon the expiration of the term of protection, the protected work is said to enter the public domain.[125] The limited term of copyright serves to increase the chances that the work in the public domain will generate more competitive pricing for similar works that still enjoy copyright protection.[126] Limited term also serves to reduce the cost of future works that seeks to build on existing works.[127] Likewise, to successfully compete with works and attract higher prices, new works have to offer something better, or at least different, than the said works.[128] It must be noted that the benefits of a limited term of protection may have been substantially whittled down by the length of the term of protection. The initial 14-year term provided for in the Statute of Anne has now given way to protection for the life of the author plus 70 years.[129] As Katz rightly notes, 'the public benefit arising from current copyright terms that can easily exceed a century is highly doubtful'.[130]

2.48 While copyright owners may exercise their exclusive rights to encourage competition by substitution, copyright users can also rely on the previously stated provisions or 'internal safeguards'[131] to compete by creating copyright-protected materials which may act as substitutes for other protected materials. Each of these provisions may also serve as defences to copyright infringement and are more fully discussed in Chapter 3 of this book.

2.49 Apart from the internal mechanisms within copyright law, other factors such as the application of competition law may play a significant role in

---

123 See Cross and Yu 2007 supra at 429. Also Katz 2013 supra at 212.

124 See Section 2(2) and the First Schedule to the Nigerian Copyright Act. The duration of protection in the case of South Africa is 50 years. See section 3(2) of the South African Copyright Act.

125 Corbett 2011 supra at 518.

126 Katz 2013 supra at 211–212.

127 Erickson K and others, 'Copyright and the Value of the Public Domain: An Empirical Assessment' (Intellectual Property Office 2015), www.gov.uk/government/uploads/system/uploads/attachment_data/file/561543/Copyright-and-the-public-domain.pdf (accessed 11 June 2019).

128 Katz A, 'Substitution and Schumpeterian effects over the life cycle of copyrighted works' [2009] *Jurimetrics* 113–153. See also Elkin-Koren 2005 supra at 376–377.

129 For a discussion on the expansion of copyright protection and the history of open licensing, see Frosio G, *Open Access Publishing: A Literature Review* (Centre for Copyright and New Business Models in the Creative Economy 2014) 1.

130 Katz 2013 supra at 212.

131 Cross and Yu 2007 supra at 429.

achieving the objective of promoting competition in copyright markets. The next section now looks at the role of competition law in copyright policy.

Protection of consumer data and privacy

2.50 Platform firms design multi-sided music platforms to obtain information about users/consumers from the users/consumers themselves. These users include copyright owners who upload their music content on the platforms. In *PRS v SoundCloud*, SoundCloud admitted that it transcoded the music files,[132] operated automated indexing and search facilities[133] and provided automated content recommendations.[134] These functionalities were enabled by the information provided by consumers and users of the platform. Most platforms use information supplied by users and consumers to provide categorised and easily searchable music content,[135] make recommendations to users based on their indicated preferences, push and promote specific music content to users.

2.51 Apart from the use of consumer data to optimise the value of the music content, multi-sided music platforms leverage on consumer demand for free music content to obtain consumers' data or information (direct personal information such as names, age, address, email addresses and information relating to users such as their preferences), which they in turn use to deliver targeted ads to those consumers. Such information or data may also inform the creation of new products for consumers.

2.52 Privacy law grants certain rights to data subjects to protect their privacy and individual liberties. Under privacy laws, individuals have the following rights: the right to access data collected from them or data relating to them, the right to request the erasure or rectification of their data, the right to consent to the use and processing of their personal data etc.[136] By granting these rights to data subjects and stipulating compliance with regulations that indicate how data may be processed, privacy law directs the activities of firms and individuals in the marketplace that deal with and/or control data. By extension, privacy laws protect competition between firms for the purpose of ensuring that control of and activities in relation to data are not anti-competitive. Given that the control of data is largely in the hands of few dominant market players,[137] the focus of pri-

---

132 Paragraph 35 Statement of Defence.

133 Paragraph 40 and 41 Statement of Defence.

134 Paragraph 47 Statement of Defence.

135 Example, paras 40–41 of the Defence filed in *PRS v SoundCloud.*

136 OECD Guidelines Organisation for Economic Co-operation and Development, '*OECD Guidelines on the Protection of Privacy and Transborder Flows of Personal Data – OECD*' (oecd.org, 2013), www.oecd.org/internet/ieconomy/oecdguidelinesontheprotectionofprivacyandtransborderflowsofpersonaldata.htm (accessed 8 July 2019).

137 According to Forbes, platform firms such as Google (owners of YouTube) and Facebook currently epitomise a duopoly in the US in terms of digital advertising fuelled by data. See Dani A, 'The state of digital advertising: The Google, Facebook duopoly tightens its grip' (*Forbes.com*, 19 March 2017), www.forbes.com/sites/avidan/2017/03/19/the-state-of-digital-advertising-the-google-facebook-duopoly-increases-its-grip/#7fddaab47eae (accessed 6 July 2019).

vacy laws on the data processing practices of firms serves to protect and promote competition.

The role of competition law

2.53 As already stated, competition law provides a general regulatory framework to ensure the promotion and protection of competition in the marketplace. Competition law prohibits concerted conduct in terms of agreements that have the effect of substantially preventing, or lessening, competition in a market ('restrictive agreements'). It also prohibits unilateral conduct by firms in dominant market position where such unilateral conduct affects competition in the market place ('unilateral conduct').

2.54 In doing these, competition law may act as a complementary framework to guarantee that copyright owners are able to get the expected returns for investments made in creativity. Competition law may also complement copyright law by ensuring that neither concerted nor unilateral conduct restricts the wider distribution of copyright-protected products. In achieving this purpose, competition law is applied to the creation of a fair and competitive market for creative works.[138] Similarly, the application of competition law against the unilateral abusive exercise of market power may complement privacy law by ensuring that the use and processing of data (particularly those of or those relating to copyright owners) are not undertaken to the detriment of competition and consumer welfare.[139]

2.55 Competition law complements copyright law by creating and protecting competitive and efficient distribution markets for copyright-protected products. Its prohibition of restrictive agreements and abuse of dominance serve as tools that help to ensure the proper functioning of copyright markets. In recognition of this point, Drexl opined:[140]

> Copyright law is designed to provide the author of works with fair remuneration for his or her creative work. Yet it is not the exclusive right in itself that produces such income but the willingness of consumers to pay. This requires that consumers actually have access to works they prefer. Hence, copyright law essentially depends on the functioning of the distribution channels and of copyright-related markets on different levels of distribution. If these markets for authorised use do not work properly, consumers will even be incited to switch from legal copies to illegal ones. Competition law plays a crucial role in creating and maintaining competitive and efficient distribution markets. . . . Competition law practice is abundant with regard to distribution cases. This is mostly due to the fact that, while works are usually highly diverse and have the potential to compete most effectively for consumers, copyright-related markets often have to rely on the bundling of works in the form of

138 Cross and Yu 2007 supra at 429 and 434. It must be noted that competition law serves other purposes which may not be apposite to the discourse in this book. One example is the regulation of mergers.

139 Lynskey O, 'At the crossroads of data protection and competition law: time to take stock' (2018) 8(3) *International Data Privacy Law* 179–180.

140 Drexl 2013 supra at 5–6.

> attractive repertoires and the use of centralised platforms for licensing and distribution. Both needs produce the tendency of market power in the hands of the intermediaries that control such repertoires and platforms. . . . competition law should not at all be understood as the 'enemy' of copyright law but rather as a most important tool of a modern, more holistic copyright policy on the national and international level.

2.56 Competition law may apply its prohibition against restrictive agreements and abuse of dominance to prevent firms that control the distribution of copyright products from anticompetitive conduct. Such anticompetitive conduct may derail the dissemination of copyright products or adversely affect the economic freedom of small businesses such as copyright owners by unduly preventing them from generating revenue from the distribution of their works.

2.57 When competition law is applied to the conduct of platform firms in using copyright-protected content, competition law complements the role of copyright law in incentivising creativity and encouraging the wider dissemination of copyright works.[141] In this regard, competition law is not applied to restrict the exercise of copyright but rather, competition law uses its legal tools in a complementary manner to serve the same goals of incentivising creativity and enhancing consumer welfare.[142]

2.58 Copyright law encourages creativity by granting the copyright owner an exclusive bundle of rights for a limited period.[143] Exclusive rights safeguard the creative efforts and the investments of the copyright owner by restricting imitation (copying), which may reduce the commercial value of the copyright work. In a case where the commercial value of a copyright work is reduced by copying, the copyright owner is unable to recoup his investments and may be discouraged from further creativity – ultimately affecting the consumers. Consumer welfare or public interest is further enhanced by provisions that permit limited and specific uses of a copyright work during its term of protection without the consent of the copyright owner, provision of a limited term of protection during which the exclusive rights of the owner may be exercised and the use of copyright-inspired tools such as collecting societies and blanket licensing[144] to ensure wider opportunities for the availability and dissemination of copyright works. In the same vein, competition law promotes creativity and enhances consumer welfare

141 See Santos 2013 supra at 623.

142 Consumer Focus 2011 supra at 2, 18. Also Russi 2011 supra at 170; Polverino F, 'Hunting the wild geese: Competition analysis in a world of 'free' [2012] 1 *Concorrenza e Mercato*, 1; Newman 2013 supra at 1443; Santos 2013 supra at 624; Gal MS and Rubinfeld DL, 'The hidden costs of free goods: Implications for antitrust enforcement' [2016] 80 *Antitrust Law Journal* 521.

143 See 'Antitrust guidelines for the licensing of intellectual property' (*Justice.gov*, 12 January 2017), www.justice.gov/atr/IPguidelines/download (accessed 26 June 2019) (US Antitrust Guidelines 2017).

144 Blanket licensing provides licensees with a licence and a flat fee is charged for a variety of approved uses of a music catalogue rather than billing for each music based on specific uses. See Towse R, 'Economics of copyright collecting societies and digital rights: Is there a case for a centralised digital copyright exchange?' [2012] 9(2) *Review of Economic Research on Copyright Issues* 16.

by prohibiting concerted and/or unilateral conduct where it may distort or harm competition in the (copyright) marketplace.[145]

2.59 Following this approach, the competition law assessment of the conduct of the copyright owner in the copyright marketplace may involve checking whether such conduct accomplishes or prevents the achievement of the objectives of incentivising creativity and enhancing consumer welfare.[146] Usually, such checks do not apply the same parameters as copyright law.[147] Indeed, the conduct of the copyright owner in exercising exclusive rights may ordinarily appear restrictive of competition, but is encouraged on the grounds that the pro-competitive effects of such conduct outweighs the anti-competitive effects.[148] For example, the exercise of copyright may be anti-competitive in that it restricts competition by preventing competitors from competing with the copyright owner in respect of his rights. The same exercise of copyright can be pro-competitive in the sense that it forces competitors to create their own works and compete on the basis of their works rather than compete by imitating or copying another's creative efforts.[149] Kolstad explains this in economic terms:

> But the key issue is not to maximise static and dynamic efficiency, respectively, but to maximise the sum of both static and dynamic efficiency. If the overriding goal is an efficient use of society's scarce resources, the task is to find the interpretation of Articles 81 and 82[150] that gives the best overall result. . . . The challenge is to develop an analytical framework that includes the effects on dynamic competition and dynamic efficiency in the analysis of conduct alleged to be contrary to articles 81 and 82. This is especially important for the analysis of conduct based on IPRs. IPRs promote innovations and technological progress, and if this is not recognised in competition analysis one risks prohibiting conduct that may have a positive effect on dynamic efficiency. When assessing whether conduct based on IPRs is contrary to Articles 81 and 82, the effects of the conduct on both static and dynamic efficiency must be taken into account. Only if the sum is negative is the conduct contrary to the efficiency goal of Articles 81 and 82.[151]

2.60 This application of competition law extends to conduct by persons or entities other than the copyright owner. In the case of provision of music content 'free of charge' to consumers, there may be real benefits to consumers and as such may be considered pro-competitive.[152] However, this is not always so. Depending on the modalities of providing the music content free of charge, there may be

145 US Antitrust Guidelines 2017 supra at 2; Van Aswegen 2003 supra at 118–119.

146 Anderson (2008) supra at 457; Solo 2014 supra at 183.

147 See Drexl 2013 supra at 39–44; Katz 2013 supra at 217–221.

148 Polverino 2012 supra at 19–20; Haunss S, 'The changing role of collecting societies in the internet' [2013] 1 *Internet Policy Review*, http://ssrn.com/abstract=2339950 (accessed 4 November 2015) (Haunss 2013); Klebanow and Wu 2015 supra at 34–35.

149 See Russi 2011 supra at 146–147; Haunss 2013 supra at 4.

150 Articles 81 and 82 (now Articles 101 and 102) of the Treaty on the Functioning of the European Union (TFEU) are the two fundamental provisions on European competition law.

151 Kolstad O, 'Competition law and intellectual property rights – Outline of an economics-based approach', in Drexl J (ed), *Research Handbook on Intellectual Property and Competition Law* (Edward Elgar 2008), p. 5.

152 Gal and Rubinfeld 2015 supra at 3 and 13.

significant anti-competitive effects.[153] Indeed, despite the fact that the consumer does not pay a direct price for free music content, there are indirect 'prices' (free music content reducing the ability of at least some firms to provide competing works, possibility of abuse of private information, etc.) that reflect the opportunity cost associated with the consumption of free music content. Despite this opportunity cost, the provision of free music content can improve consumer welfare. Given these considerations, competition law advocates the consideration of both the pro- and anti-competitive effects of such uses of copyright-protected content.[154]

2.61 Accordingly, given the importance of copyright protection for the larger copyright market and the way in which competition law prohibits both anti-competitive concerted and unilateral conduct, it becomes clear that competition law may play a significant role in relation to the use of copyright-protected content in the course of economic activities. Where the conduct of any person or entity involved in the deployment of copyright-based business models harms or distorts the functioning of copyright markets, such conduct is opposed to the very objectives of copyright law. In such case, competition law may also be applied to maintain the proper functioning of such copyright market.[155] Competition law will apply to treat any conduct that harms the functioning of copyright markets, regardless of whether such conduct is initiated by copyright owners, and/or distributors of copyright products. Especially when initiated by distributors, the harm to competition is highlighted by the fact that such conduct may encourage or increase the chances of piracy and/or copyright infringement.[156] Further, piracy and copyright infringement may dislodge copyright owners who are small businesses from participating in the market for the production and distribution of copyright products. A lack of authors, entrepreneurs, and SMEs who churn out creative products will be to the detriment of consumers, as there is reduced availability of creative products. Competition law can protect the economic freedom of market participants in the interest of the competitive process.

2.62 In the case of privacy protection, competition law may apply to address anti-competitive conduct. Specifically, competition agencies have the competence to examine markets and mergers and ensure that dominant firms do not abuse their dominance in a manner that excludes other efficient firms or consumer welfare.[157] As earlier stated, consumer welfare and competition are goals pursued by privacy law, albeit from a different perspective. While competition law adopts economic tools to assess the state of consumer welfare and market efficiency; privacy law uses a human rights perspective in giving consumers control over their personal information.[158]

---

153 Ibid. at 3, 14 and 15.

154 Anderson 2008 supra at 451. See also Santos 2013 supra at 602 and 610.

155 See Drexl 2013 supra at 40–41.

156 Drexl 2013 supra at 44.

157 Lynskey 2018 supra at 180.

158 Volmar MN and Helmdach KO, 'Protecting consumers and their data through competition law? Rethinking abuse of dominance in light of the Federal Cartel Office's Facebook investigation' [2018] 14(2–3) *European Competition Journal* 195–215.

2.63 Emerging cases in Europe reveal that multi-sided platforms may apply privacy policies in an anti-competitive manner. For instance, a US company, Six4Three Inc. sued Facebook in 2015 for restricting its (Six4Three) access to the user data that its app and other apps relied on to function. Facebook had restricted access on the claims that it needed to address user privacy concerns. Six4Three claimed instead that Facebook's access restriction was targeted at reducing its (Six4Three's) ability to compete. While there are questions regarding the appropriate balance between privacy law obligations and the need to protect and promote competition especially in multi-sided music platforms and platforms generally,[159] competition law does offer some solutions.

2.64 Nevertheless, the existence of other complementary paradigms for incentivising creativity does not mean that copyright should be jettisoned. Rather, copyright is complemented with these regimes so that they can co-exist.[160] The US IP Licensing Guidelines 2017[161] and the EU Technology Transfer Guidelines of 2014[162] make a similar suggestion.[163] Notably, the recent US IP Licensing Guidelines issued in 2017 reiterates similar provisions as the 1995 version.[164] Likewise, similar provisions are made in the revised EU Technology Transfer Guidelines of 2014.[165] The same position applies to privacy protection. Privacy laws should not jettisoned but may rather be complemented by the application of competition law.[166]

Conclusion

2.65 This chapter discussed the relationship between copyright law, privacy law and competition. It explored some of the ways through which copyright law itself works to advance competition policy goals. It showed that the grant of exclusive rights promotes competition, as firms are incentivised to compete by substitution rather than by imitation or copying. It also showed how the exclusive rights provide a framework, consisting of revenue generation as a product of the response to the access and consumption needs of users and consumers, can explain some key elements of the law, and provide guidance in its further

159 For some discussion of privacy issues, see Gal and Rubinfeld 2016 supra. Also Cadwalladr C, 'Google, democracy and the truth about internet search' (*The Guardian*, 4 December 2016), www.theguardian.com/technology/2016/dec/04/google-democracy-truth-internet-search-facebook (accessed 22 June 2019).

160 See Santos 2013 supra at 624, 628.

161 US Antitrust Guidelines 1995 supra at 2.

162 'Commission Notice: Guidelines on the Application of Article 101 of the Treaty on the Functioning of the European Union to Technology Transfer Agreements OJ No. 2014/C 89/03' (2014), https://eur-lex.europa.eu/legal-content/EN/ALL/?uri=CELEX%3A52014XC0328%2801%29 (accessed 26 June 2019), para. 7 (EC Technology Transfer Guidelines).

163 See also Anderson R, 'Competition policy and intellectual property in the WTO: More guidance needed?' in Drexl J (ed), *Research Handbook on Intellectual Property and Competition Law* (Edward Elgar 2008), 451 (Anderson 2008).

164 US Antitrust Guidelines 2017 supra at 2.

165 EC Technology Transfer Guidelines 2014 supra at para. 7.

166 Lynskey 2018 supra at 180.

development. The chapter also demonstrated how the limited term of copyright, limitations on subject matter, fair dealing and other limitations and exceptions to copyright protection apply to ensure that the copyright protection may not unduly constrict the interests of copyright users in accessing and enjoying copyright products.

2.66 The principle under which copyright protection generates competition as firms strive to create more to obtain the benefit of copyright protection may also be applied to the context of multi-sided music platforms. Beyond creating value, multi-sided music platforms are designed to capture value through revenue generation from business activities and processes. Revenue generation furnish the main incentive for rights holders to distribute and/or control the dissemination of their music products. But, in the case of multi-sided music platforms, the use of the copyright-protected music content may generate revenue for platform firms exclusively as they take advantage of the copyright-protected music content in deploying their platforms. This raises the question of how this conduct may be assessed. Questions arise regarding whether such conduct should form the basis of a claim in competition within the copyright system or whether it should be seen as the legitimate exercise of the platform owner's control over its platform.

2.67 In the case of privacy law, the chapter drew a nexus between its objectives and those pursued by competition law albeit from a different perspective. Two of the most controversial issues relating to multi-sided music platforms and their use of personal (or even third party company) data, are how such data is processed and whether privacy rights are being respected. By granting rights to data subjects, privacy law may protect competition and consumer welfare.

2.68 Extending the analysis to competition law, the chapter showed that the application of competition rules prohibiting as anti-competitive; conduct which derail the functioning of copyright markets can complement the 'efforts' of copyright law. The chapter further highlights an attractive feature of using competition law to complement the achievement of the goals of copyright law particularly in relation to the distribution of copyright products. The value of this approach lies principally in its ability to reframe the demands for financial incentives as a reality rather than an ideal for copyright owners. Further, it reframes public demands for access to copyright products as valid statutorily recognised entitlements similar to those accorded to copyright owners. Such language shift can help to restructure legal norms and negotiating strategies. Indeed, such a reframing encourages copyright reform advocates to engage with international competition law forums to clarify ambiguous treaty texts and evaluate copyright laws and policies from a competition-based perspective.

2.69 As will be further explained in the next chapters, the deployment of copyright and consumer data to gain competitive advantage is central to the functioning of multi-sided music platforms, whose main aim is to generate revenue from advertising fuelled by unique uses of copyright-protected content and consumer data. The provision of an avenue for legitimate access to music content is central in the deployment of multi-sided music platforms, given that platform firms deal with products protected by copyright law.[167] Consent of and remuneration for the copyright owner constitute a significant basis of the legitimacy of the access provided by the platform firms. A similar situation applies to the use of consumer data (including those of copyright owners), which is regulated by privacy protection laws as complemented by competition law.

2.70 The rest of this book builds on this chapter by examining the conduct of the platform firms through the lens of copyright law, privacy law and competition law in South Africa and Nigeria.

167 See Joshi D, 'You wouldn't stream a car – What Netflix's refusal to bow to pirates means for digital piracy' (*SpicyIP*, 13 May 2017), https://spicyip.com/2017/05/you-wouldnt-stream-a-car-what-netflixs-refusal-to-bow-to-pirates-means-for-digital-piracy.html (accessed 26 June 2019).

CHAPTER 3

Copyright infringement

Introduction

3.1 The introductory chapter highlighted the processes and copyright terms regarding the music content used in the context of multi-sided music platforms. That chapter also showed how copyright law influenced the establishment and implementation of the terms that determine the conduct of platform firms, copyright owners and users of the platform in relation to the music content.

3.2 The copyright system is built around both private and public interests. It seeks to protect the private interests of copyright owners and provide a mechanism that helps to incentivise and reward them for their creative efforts and investments. The system protects the public interests of copyright users by providing limitations to copyright protection to ensure both creative and consumptive access to music content for users. However, the establishment and implementation of the copyright terms involved in multi-sided music platforms may create concerns for the incentives expected by the copyright owners both in terms of licensing revenue and in terms of the potential for success in obtaining damages for infringement. Some of these concerns relate to the concepts of 'value gap' and 'scraping'[1] said to be perpetuated by the copyright terms within these platforms. There are also concerns regarding the ability of users of copyright works to lawfully access and use the music content in every manner outside the protected uses guaranteed by the copyright framework. While copyright users expect to use the music content for a wide variety of purposes given the limitations and exceptions to copyright, the copyright terms may present some restrictions on those expectations.

3.3 This chapter focuses on copyright ownership and infringement in the context of the activities on multi-sided music platforms. It will:

- Highlight the copyright terms applied in multi-sided music platforms;
- Explain the exclusive rights under the copyright framework that apply specifically to the activities on multi-sided music platforms;

1 Scraping is usually described as an automated process that firms can use to efficiently collect amounts of targeted data from different websites hosted by another company. See Goldfein S and Keyte J, 'Big data, web 'scraping' and competition law: The debate continues' [2017] 258(49) *New York Law Journal* 1. In the context of multi-sided music platforms, 'scraping' occurs when a platform firm 'scraps' or applies a copyright owner's music content in generating profits without any payment to or licence from the copyright owner.

- Explain how copyright infringement can occur in multi-sided music platforms;
- Identify available and possible defences;
- Highlight basic jurisdictional aspects of a claim for copyright infringement (particularly in Nigeria).

Copyright terms applied in multi-sided music platforms

3.4 Platform firms stipulate 'copyright terms', which indicate the various ways in which the copyright-protected music content available on their platforms may be used and accessed. As stated in Chapter 1 of this book, the copyright terms address the issue of licensing of the music content, access to the music content and use of the music content.[2] These are discussed below.

Licensing terms

3.5 As noted earlier, a licence is required where any person other than the relevant copyright owner wishes to exercise or exploit any of the exclusive rights granted under copyright law. By extension, licensing arrangements determine the money flow to the copyright owner as well as the extent of use of the copyright-protected content by the licensee.

3.6 Within multi-sided music platforms, platform firms stipulate licensing terms, which require registered users of the platform who upload music content thereon to grant a non-exclusive, worldwide, royalty-free licence to the platform firm with respect to the uploaded music content.[3] Box 3.1 and Box 3.2 provide examples of these licensing terms in the case of YouTube and Facebook.

Box 3.1 YouTube's terms of use[4]

Rights you licence

8.1 When you upload or post Content to YouTube, you grant:

A to YouTube, a worldwide, non-exclusive, royalty-free, transferable licence (with right to sub-licence) to use, reproduce, distribute, prepare derivative works of, display, and perform that Content in connection with the provision of the Service and otherwise in

2 See, e.g., para. 5 of YouTube's terms of service. 'Terms of Service – YouTube' (*YouTube.com*, 25 May 2018), www.youtube.com/static?template=terms (accessed 27 June 2019). See also Perel and Elkin-Koren 2015 supra at 473; Elkin-Koren 2016 supra at 3–7.

3 See para. 6.2 of the Particulars of Claim and paras 28–31 of the Statement of Defence in *PRS v SoundCloud*. See also para. 6(c) of YouTube's terms of service.

4 'Terms Of Service – YouTube' (*YouTube.com*, 25 May 2018), www.youtube.com/static?template=terms (accessed 27 June 2019).

connection with the provision of the Service and YouTube's business, including without limitation for promoting and redistributing part or all of the Service (and derivative works thereof) in any media formats and through any media channels; and

B to each user of the Service, a worldwide, non-exclusive, royalty-free licence to access your Content through the Service, and to use, reproduce, distribute, prepare derivative works of, display and perform such Content to the extent permitted by the functionality of the Service and under these Terms.

3.7 Uploaders may be able to, in the case of certain platforms specify whether or not the music content is to be available to all platform users and whether download should be enabled.

Box 3.2 Facebook's terms of service[5]

The permissions you give us

We need certain permissions from you to provide our services:

1 Permission to use content that you create and share: You own the content that you create and share on Facebook and the other Facebook Products you use, and nothing in these Terms takes away the rights that you have to your own content. You are free to share your content with anyone else, wherever you want. To provide our services, however, we need you to give us some legal permissions to use this content.

Specifically, when you share, post or upload content that is covered by intellectual property rights (e.g. photos or videos) on or in connection with our Products, you grant us a non-exclusive, transferable, sub-licensable, royalty-free and worldwide licence to host, use, distribute, modify, run, copy, publicly perform or display, translate and create derivative works of your content (consistent with your privacy and application settings). This means, for example, that if you share a photo on Facebook, you give us permission to store, copy and share it with others (again, consistent with your settings) such as service providers that support our service or other Facebook Products that you use.

3.8 Furthermore, to address cases where the royalty-free licence was invalidly given (that is, in cases where the 'uploader-licensor' is not the copyright owner

5 'Terms of Service' (*Facebook*, 19 April 2018), www.facebook.com/terms.php (accessed 27 June 2019).

or does not have the licence/authorisation of the copyright owner), the licensing terms further provide for the relevant copyright owner to notify the platform firm to takedown infringing music content.[6] Such notification may be made using designated forms provided by the platform firm for that purpose, by email or by post. This is the case, for instance with platforms such as YouTube.com, SoundCloud.com, NotJustOk.com and TooXclusive.com.

3.9 Notice and takedown procedures are part of the unilateral contract (in that there was no negotiation of the terms with the copyright owner) widely used by platform firms in the multi-sided music platform context.[7] Under such procedure, platform firms undertake to act expeditiously to remove or disable access to infringing music content to be exempted from copyright infringement liability.[8] Notice and takedown procedures may be implemented in two different ways. First, the platform firm may make the music content available on its platform by itself following submissions from users. In this regard, the platform firm may procure the music content from different sources and then directly upload the music content to the platform. The platform firm further indicates its willingness to respond promptly to any request from the relevant copyright owner to take down such content. Such platform firms understand that copyright likely subsists in the music content, which it makes available on its platform.[9] However, they operate on the presumption that silence on the part of the relevant copyright owner is tantamount to consent or implied authorisation.[10] This presumption may be risky, as the act of uploading music content without the consent of the relevant copyright owners may expose the platform firms to liability for copyright infringement.[11] Such platform firms are prevalent in Nigeria. In this regard, NotJustOk.com,[12] tooXclusive.com[13] and 360nobs.com[14] are typical examples.

3.10 A second approach to implementing notice and takedown procedures involves the platform firm providing an enabling environment for copyright owners, users and consumers to make the music content available on that platform.[15] Similar to the first approach, there is recognition that copyright may subsist in

6 See Heald 2014 supra at 313.

7 See Perel and Elkin-Koren 2015 supra at 477.

8 Ibid. See also Lee Y, 'Copyright and freedom of expression: A literature review' (*Zenodo.org*, 2015), https://zenodo.org/record/18132/files/CREATe-Working-Paper-2015-04.pdf (accessed 21 October 2016).

9 See, e.g., Box 1.1.

10 See Schultz 2016 supra; NotjustOk.com, 'About NotJustOk' (NotJust*Ok*, 2016), https://notjustok.com/about/ (accessed 14 March 2018).

11 As the relevant copyright statutes provide, copyright is infringed when there is a reproduction of the work without the authorisation of the relevant rights holder. See, e.g., Section 15(1)(a) of the Nigerian Copyright Act.

12 See NotJustOk (2016). *About Us – NotJustOk*. Available at http://notjustok.com/about/ [Accessed 14 Mar. 2016]

13 *See* tooXclusive (2017). *Contact Us – tooXclusive*. Available at http://tooxclusive.com/contact-us/ (accessed 21 November 2017).

14 360Nobs.com (2017). *About 360NoBS.com | 360Nobs.com*. Available at www.360nobs.com/about/ (accessed 21 November 2017).

15 See Heald 2015 supra at 313.

music content available on its platform. But the assumption is that the copyright owner is either the person uploading the music content or it authorised the upload. However, it is to be noted that a copyright owner may not in fact have authorised the upload and may also rightfully decline to use the notification avenues provided by the platform firm. Such copyright owner may instead sue the platform firm for copyright infringement, as occurred in the *PRS v SoundCloud*[16] case.

Revenue sharing in multi-sided music platforms

3.11 Apart from the *gratis* licence issued by uploaders to the platform firms in respect of the music content uploaded to the platform, some platform firms also set licensing terms that could result in payments to copyright owners.[17] These payments may be received directly from the platform firms or from aggregators selected by copyright owners due to the aggregator's relationship with the platform firm.[18] Such payments are based on advertising revenue arising in connection with the use of the music content on the platform. Examples include YouTube's Content ID system, Facebook's Rights Manager and the like.

3.12 The Content ID for the copyright community developed by YouTube operates very much like both a payment system and a decision-making system regarding the copyright-protected music content. As a payment system, it operates between the copyright owner and YouTube to signal whether revenue is to be expected in relation to specific music content through YouTube's AdSense program.[19] In this context, the copyright owner from YouTube's perspective may be the actual copyright owner or an aggregator (based on YouTube's 'Multi-Channel Network' system) having the authority of a multiplicity of actual copyright owners to deal with YouTube on their behalf.[20] As a decision-making system, Content ID offers a mechanism for automatic detection of uploaded music content that was put up without the consent and/or authorisation of the copyright owner.[21] The system creates an ID file for music content and stores it in a database. This reference content comes mostly from several pre-selected partners – an arrangement that naturally leaves some blind spots when it comes to independent musicians and other rights holders.[22] The Content ID system is only available to copyright

16 See Appendix I, particularly paras 61–63 of the Statement of Defence in *PRS v SoundCloud*.

17 See Heald 2015 supra at 313.

18 See paras 3.12–14.

19 See Perel and Elkin-Koren 2015 supra at 513–514.

20 See Google.com, 'Multi-Channel Network (MCN) overview for YouTube Creators' (*YouTube Help*, 2018), https://support.google.com/youtube/answer/2737059?hl=en (accessed 29 January 2018). Multi-channel Networks raise some issues around privacy law highlighted in para 4.69, below.

21 See Heald 2014 supra at 313; Official Google Blog (2007). *Latest content ID tool for YouTube*. Available at https://googleblog.blogspot.co.za/2007/10/latest-content-id-tool-for-youtube.html (accessed 21 November 2017).

22 See Perel and Elkin-Koren 2015 supra at 513–514.

owners who meet specific criteria specified by Google, the owners of YouTube.[23] One of such criteria is that a Content ID applicant must have exclusive rights to a fairly large music catalogue sought to be uploaded.

3.13 When another platform user uploads music content (in the form of a video), it is checked against the database, and the Content ID system flags the video as a copyright violation if such content matches music content previously uploaded by a Content ID partner/copyright owner.[24] When this occurs, the copyright owner has the choice of muting the audio of a video file, blocking the video to make it unavailable, permitting continued reproduction while monitoring the viewing statistics of the video, or adding advertisements to the video.[25] Unless the copyright owner accepts the displaying of advertisements alongside its music content, using the Content ID system, no revenue can accrue to such copyright owner.

3.14 To be able to receive the revenue accruing from his decision to include advertisements alongside his music content on YouTube, the copyright owner is required to operate a 'Google AdSense' account.[26] The Google AdSense account may only be established and operated based on an AdSense Agreement – a standard contract unilaterally drafted by Google.[27] Under the AdSense arrangement, if Google were to serve advertisements alongside or simultaneously with the music content, the payment made to Google by the company whose advertisement is served would be split between the copyright owner and Google. Advertising fees become the revenue stream – it serves implicitly as the new value metric available to the copyright owner in an environment where exploitation of reproduction rights previously held sway. In this context, the copyright work may be reproduced and distributed repeatedly without a single payment made to the copyright owner. Payment is only made to the copyright owner when the consumer takes interest in the advertisement running on the copyright content and if the copyright owner is part of the AdSense program. So, for example, music content uploaded by an AdSense partner may show advertisement of a new baby monitor before, during and/or at the end of communicating the music content to the consumer. But the revenue paid to the copyright owner would only accrue because the advertisement of the baby monitor was served to the consumer. This would be the case because the consumer is presumed to have indicated that his attention was first drawn to the music content – even if he ends up seeing the music content *and* the baby monitor advertisement. Access to the consumer is procured through his interest in the copyright-protected music content. Accordingly, the AdSense account and the AdSense relationship enable payment of revenue for the application of advertisement on the music content. Without Content ID, a copyright

23 Ibid.

24 See Perel and Elkin-Koren 2015 supra at 477–479.

25 Ibid. at 504–507, 515. See also Heald 2014 supra at 313.

26 See, e.g., the case of *Attrakt v Google* supra, where Google's arbitrary termination of contract and withdrawal/denial of access annihilated the business of Attrakt.

27 Ibid.

owner would be ratcheting up streams with no revenue to show for it. Indeed, Content ID accounts for over a third of the monetised views on YouTube.[28]

Terms relating to access ('access terms')

3.15 Access terms impose on the consumers to use the music content in accordance with the dictates of the platform firms and in respect for the copyright protection inherent in the music content. Like the licensing terms, access terms are established by platform firms with the intention of limiting copyright infringement and generally to protect the respective economic interests of the copyright owners and enhance the competitiveness of the platform firms.

3.16 Typically, the access terms concern the use of technological protection measures with respect to the music content. Music content can be accessed for free, but beyond that nothing much may be done with the music content. In some platforms such as YouTube and Facebook, users may not be permitted to download music content and may only stream such content.[29] To access the music content, the terms and conditions for such access are stated on the platform's terms of use and privacy policy.[30] Again, terms of use such as the Content ID and AdSense systems and other similar systems such as Facebook's Rights Manager offer good examples.

3.17 Beyond providing a system that has the potential to generate some advertising revenue for the copyright owner, the Content ID and AdSense systems and other similar systems such as Facebook's Rights Manager also serve to provide a mechanism for platform firms to determine the level of access, which the platform users may enjoy with respect to the music content.[31] In this regard, the platform firm may restrict or prevent the upload of music content based on prior arrangement with 'participating right holders' as shown from the Content ID example. Once a given music content is uploaded to the reference file by a copyright owner, others may be precluded from uploading or making available any music content found by the system to be a match with the uploaded music content.[32] Such music content may not be allowed on the platform – if uploaded, the music content would be blocked, removed or deleted. This is achieved through the operation of the same automated surveillance system that permits some (but not each) copyright owner to upload their music content in a reference file and specify what action may be taken when a non-participating uploader attempts

28 See Perel and Elkin-Koren 2015 supra at 477–479.

29 See for instance, YouTube's Terms of service. Specifically, clause 5.1(3) stipulates that 'YouTube hereby grants you permission to access and use the Service, subject to the following express conditions, and you agree that your failure to adhere to any of these conditions shall constitute a breach of these Terms on your part: you agree not to access Content through any technology or means other than the video playback pages of the Website itself, the YouTube Player, or such other means as YouTube may explicitly designate for this purpose'.

30 See Derclaye and Favale 2010 supra at 110–112. See also Elkin-Koren 2011 supra at 329.

31 Perel and Elkin-Koren 2015 supra at 476–477.

32 See Perel and Elkin-Koren 2015 supra at 510. See also Elkin-Koren 2017 supra at 132, 138.

to upload music content matching the former music content.[33] In taking down or refusing access of music content to the platform, the platform firm is able to influence the decision of consumers regarding each specific music content as well as whether the relevant copyright owner may receive a share of the advertising revenue. As Perel and Elkin-Koren noted, 'from an economic perspective, control over what information becomes available may shape the preferences of consumers, creating demand for particular content, while diminishing demand for other types of content'.[34]

3.18 Terms relating to access can also embody the openness that responds to the universal access objective of copyright law. They can offer copyright owners (performers and artists, particularly) the popularity and promotion that brings them more live performance opportunities, more brand sponsorships and more personality right licensing opportunities. Due to the fact that consumers are able to access the platform free of charge, the copyright owner enjoys instant access to millions of consumers to whom it may communicate and showcase its music content.[35] NotJustOk.com is a typical example, as it provides a platform for copyright owners to openly and freely share their music with fans and interested parties. The terms of use direct artists to share their music with friends, fans and followers. In terms of its 'mission statement',[36]

> *NotJustOk.com* offers a platform where Nigerian Music lovers around the world can access, listen, stream and give their opinions on Nigerian music content anywhere and anytime. Our music content is accessible at any time to our audience in all time zones. Furthermore, artists find our platform a useful source of direct feedback from their fans and a way to gain insight into what their fans respond to.[37]

3.19 However, there is the question of whether such exposure constitutes adequate consideration for the music content provided through a *gratis* licence.[38]

3.20 Apart from the potential benefit to copyright owners, terms relating to access form the foundation of revenue for platform firms. NotJustOk.com embodies this philosophy of generating revenue from advertising enabled by the availability and accessibility of music content.[39] As a firm, the operators of NotJustOk.com attract a lot of advertising revenue due to the platform's popularity as the

33 Ibid. at 478. See para. 6.19, 7 of the *PRS v SoundCloud* Particulars of Claim. See Rightsmanager.fb.com (2017). *Copyright Management | Facebook*. Available at https://rightsmanager.fb.com (accessed 23 November 2017); Elkin-Koren 2017 supra.

34 Perel and Elkin-Koren 2015 supra at 491–492.

35 See Schultz 2016 supra.

36 Ibid.

37 NotJustOk.com, 'About NotJustOk' (NotJust*Ok*, 2016), https://notjustok.com/about/ (accessed 14 March 2019).

38 See Rajan 2010 supra at 929. See also, Rosch T, 'Regarding Google's search practices – In the matter of Google Inc.' (*Ftc.gov*, 2017), www.ftc.gov/sites/default/files/documents/public_statements/concurring-and-dissenting-statement-commissioner-j.thomas-rosch-regarding-googles-search-practices/130103googlesearchstmt.pdf (accessed 22 November 2017); Lamadrid A, 'More on Google: is scraping anticompetitive?' (*Chillin' Competition*, 14 February 2013), https://chillingcompetition.com/2013/02/14/more-on-google-is-scraping-anticompetitive/ (accessed 22 November 2018).

39 Similar systems are in place as evident from Facebook, tooXclusive.com and SoundCloud.

go-to place for free music content in Nigeria. In fact, NotJustOk.com recognises the shift to access to the customer and the customer's data as the new value metric. It recognises that by being the most-visited music platform, revenue does not come from reproduction of the music content per se but from its amassing of millions of 'page views'. It is observed that this acquisition of page views – the foundation of its existence – may not be focused on the copyright owner or on the reproduction of its work. Rather, its objective is to attract the consumer's 'eye' – the only thing that an advertising company will pay for.[40] It is akin to the purpose of advertising in communicating a firm's message to the public in a medium/form where such message is most likely to be received.[41]

3.21 Furthermore, some access terms are crafted in a manner as to limit or increase a platform firm's interaction with consumers of music content ostensibly to mitigate the risk of both primary and secondary copyright infringement. Elkin-Koren in particular has noted that most platforms' terms of use and related documents are crafted to please powerful corporate copyright owners and may ordinarily be unconscionable.[42] Where the platform firm is actively involved with the consumer's activities in respect of the platform, such may affect its ability to successfully rely on the safe harbour regime to escape copyright infringement liability[43] (so-called safe harbour protection), discussed later in this chapter.

3.22 According to the foregoing, consumers and platform users accept that their use of and access to the music content can be removed or restricted if the platform firm so decides or where the alleged copyright owner requests such restriction.[44] In these circumstances, as more fully discussed later in this chapter, access terms that restrict such uses may conflict with statutory limitations and exceptions to copyright[45] as well as the statutory scope of copyright protection.[46] At the same time, too 'minor' restrictions may also be considered problematic for platform firms as they risk copyright infringement liability.[47]

40 Zeff RL and Aronson B, *Advertising on the Internet* (John Wiley & Sons Inc. 1999).

41 Ibid.

42 See Elkin-Koren N, 'User-generated platforms' In Dreyfuss RC, Zimmerman DL and First H (eds), *Working within the Boundaries of Intellectual Property* (Oxford University Press 2010), 111–136.

43 See Rosati E, 'Why a reform of hosting providers' safe harbour is unnecessary under EU copyright law' (2016) CREATe Working Paper 2016/11, https://papers.ssrn.com/sol3/papers.cfm?abstract_id=2830440 (accessed 6 September 2018).

44 See Perel and Elkin-Koren 2015 supra at 478.

45 See Grondal L, 'DRM and contract terms' [2006] 2 *Indicare* 3; S Bechtold, 'Digital rights management in the United States and Europe' [2004] 52(2) *American Journal of Comparative Law* 323–382.

46 See Elkin-Koren N, 'Copyright policy and the limits of freedom of contract' [1997] 12(1) *Berkeley Technology Law Journal* 106–113; Dreier T, 'Contracting out of copyright in the information society: The impact on freedom of expression', in Griffiths J and Suthersanen U (eds), *Copyright and Free Speech: Comparative and International Analyses* (Oxford University Press, 2005), 390–391; Noguchi Y, 'Freedom override by Digital Rights Management technologies: Causes in market mechanisms and possible legal options to keep a better balance' [2006] 11 *Intell Prop L Bull* 7–8; Moffat V, 'Super-copyright: contracts, preemption, and the structure of copyright policymaking' [2007] 41 *UC Davis L Rev* 55; Akester P, 'The new challenges of striking the right balance between copyright protection and access to knowledge, information and culture' [2010] 32(8) *EIPR* 375–376.

47 Rosati 2016 supra at 13–14.

3.23 Furthermore, access terms may impose on copyright owners that the music content and by extension, their access to revenue generation may be removed or suspended, where the relevant platform firm so decides.[48] The timing of such removal or suspension may affect revenue generation. There are both practical and policy reasons why this may be so. For one, the number of 'views' or 'streams' of the music content may serve as an index of the copyright owner's reputation and popularity.[49] Such popularity is the basis upon which advertisement fees are generated and shared. It may also provide or attract revenue from alternative sources such as invitations for concert performance,[50] brand endorsements and the like.[51] Accordingly, removal of the music content after such index has been amassed may affect the effectiveness of the alternative income streams.[52] Second, the effective enforcement of the copyright owners' rights to revenue lies largely in the hands of the platform firms because the platform firm regulates access to the music content and access of the music content itself to the platform.[53]

Terms relating to usage of the music content ('usage terms')

3.24 Usage terms are closely related to the terms regarding access. In this regard, usage terms determine what users of the platform and members of the public may do in relation to the music content. Members of the public may 'like' and 'repost' available music content. 'Like', 'share', and 'repost' are some of the buttons available on multi-sided music platforms. Users of these platforms may click any such button to express their feelings regarding the relevant content on the platform. As Robbins argues, clicking 'like' or 'share' may be construed as speech.[54]

3.25 Users may also share the music content on other platforms using the facilities provided by the platform firms. The use of the music content by members of the public is mostly experiential and collaborative.[55] Such collaboration may be at several levels depending on the extent of the commitment required of users. In this regard, the users of the platform may be restricted only to consumption or may be permitted to use the music content in other creative endeavours.[56]

48 See Perel and Elkin-Koren 2015 supra at 512–513.

49 See Elkin-Koren 2011 supra at 323–324.

50 Rizk 2010 supra at 114–117.

51 See Hu C, 'Understanding a data-driven music industry culture – Lessons from Fast Forward' (*Fastforward,* 24 February 2017), www.hypebot.com/hypebot/2017/03/fastforward-understanding-a-data-driven-music-industry-culture.html (accessed 23 November 2017); Booth N and Matic JA, 'Mapping and leveraging influencers in social media to shape corporate brand perceptions' [2011] 16(3) *Corporate Communications: An International Journal* 184.

52 Perel and Elkin-Koren 2015 supra at 483. See also *Attrakt v Google* supra.

53 See Perel and Elkin-Koren 2015 supra at 479–480.

54 See Robbins I, 'What is the meaning of "like": The First Amendment implications of social media expression' [2014] 7 *Fed Cts L Rev* 123, 140–142.

55 See, e.g., paras. 6.7 and 8 of the Statement of Claim and para 46 of the Statement of Defence in *PRS v SoundCloud.* See also Elkin-Koren 2011 supra at 312; Elkin-Koren 2010 supra at 8–9, 17–18.

56 See Elkin-Koren 2011 supra at 327–328.

The design of the platform often determines the nature of the collaboration and the nature of the relationships among users.[57]

3.26 Platform firms also utilise the tags[58] and title provided by the uploaders (using features provided on the platform) to offer search facilities and recommendations[59] related to the music content to users.[60] User preferences in terms of music content are used to rank popular music content such that other users can identify and view popular music content.[61] More generally, the music content is used to provide a 'webcast' for users of the platform. In this regard, the platform firm automatically selects continuous, successive music content for the user's listening pleasure once the user has selected specific music content.[62] For instance, if a user selects Casper Nyovest's (a South African artist) 'Move for Me', the platform will provide an automatic playlist of Casper Nyovest's songs as well as other songs from the same music genre as 'Move for Me'.

3.27 The music content is also used to provide a popularity index that enables uploaders to gauge public engagement with its uploaded music content.[63] Specific music content may be selected and promoted to registered users through various means such as on the platform, via email and also on social media platforms.[64] In some cases, platform firms also publicise and promote the availability of and available music content on its platform, thereby encouraging more user engagement with the platform and its services.[65]

3.28 The remainder of this chapter examines the relevant exclusive rights granted under copyright law vis-à-vis these copyright terms (licensing terms, access and usage terms) as well as the relevant limitations and exceptions to copyright protection in relation to the copyright terms.[66]

---

57 Ibid. at 328–329.

58 A tag is a 'word, phrase, or name used to identify digital content such as blog and social media posts as belonging to a particular category or concerning a particular person or topic'. See 'Tag' (2017). In *Oxford Dictionaries*. Oxford University Press. Available at: https://en.oxforddictionaries.com/definition/tag (accessed 22 November 2017).

59 Paras. 6.10–6.13 of the Particulars of Claim and para 47 Statement of Defence in *PRS v SoundCloud.*

60 See Elkin-Koren 2010 supra at 8–9, 17–18. See also paras 6.1,6.5 of the Particulars of Claim in *PRS v SoundCloud.*

61 Ibid. For the description of the various features offered by the platform firm, see paras 40–41 of the Statement of Defence in *PRS v SoundCloud.* Para. 41 specifically links the search facility to Google search engine.

62 See generally Heald PJ, 'How copyright keeps works disappeared' [2014] 11(4) *Journal of Empirical Legal Studies* 829–866 (Heald 2014b). See also para. 48 of the Statement of Defence in *PRS v SoundCloud.*

63 See Rajan 2010 supra at 929. See also Elkin-Koren 2011 supra at 332; paras 49–50 of the Statement of Defence in *PRS v SoundCloud.*

64 Ibid. See also para. 52 of the Statement of Defence in *PRS v SoundCloud.*

65 For instance, see NotJustOk.com; tooXclusive (2017). *Contact Us – tooXclusive*. Available at http://tooxclusive.com/contact-us/ (accessed 21 November 2017). See also SoundCloud's admission in paras 51–52, 54 of its Statement of Defence in *PRS v SoundCloud.*

66 The establishment and implementation of the copyright terms stem from the platform firm's interpretation of the copyright law system.

Copyright infringement claim in multi-sided music platforms: essential elements

3.29 Before discussing copyright infringement claims in detail, it will be useful to explore some fundamental questions that should be addressed before instituting a claim for copyright infringement in the context of multi-sided music platforms. Often, issues such as whether claimants/plaintiffs have the standing to sue and what they need to prove to commence a suit go to the question of jurisdiction of the court to even entertain their suit.[67] It is also essential to know what claimants need to prove in order to succeed in an action for copyright infringement. These fundamental questions are dealt with in the succeeding paragraphs.

Who can sue

3.30 The general rule with regard to bringing copyright infringement claims is that the owner of copyright (who may either be a natural person, juristic person or the state) must be a 'qualified person' to be entitled to sue for copyright infringement.[68] However, depending on the relevant copyright statute, copyright infringement claims can also be brought by:

- An assignee of copyright;[69]
- An exclusive licensee of copyright;[70]
- A (duly licensed) collecting society or collective management organisation;
- The federal or state government where it has commissioned the making of a work.[71]

3.31 Collecting societies are associations of copyright or neighbouring right owners, established with the key objective of negotiating and granting licences as well as collecting and distributing royalties for the benefit of their members. Section 39(8) of the Nigerian Copyright Act defines a collecting society to mean 'an association of copyright owners which has as its principal objectives the negotiating and granting of licences, collecting and distributing of royalties in respect of copyright works'. In that capacity, they may play a significant role in liaising with platform firms to obtain royalty payments for the platform firms' use of music content. In the international scene, the PRS for

---

67 See *Ajao v Popoola* (1986) 5 NWLR (Pt 45) 802 (Nigeria); *Apleni v African Process Solutions (Pty) Ltd and Another* (15211/17) [2018] ZAWCHC 160 (27 November 2018) (South Africa).

68 'Subject to the provisions of this Act, infringements of copyright shall be actionable at the suit of the owner of the copyright'. See Section 24(1) South African Copyright Act.

69 Section 11 of the Nigerian Copyright Act. See also *Adenuga v Ilesanmi Press & Sons (Nig.) Ltd* (1999) 5 NWLR (Pt. 189) 82 CA (Nigeria). To be effective, all assignments must be in writing. It must be noted that an assignment need not cover the entire world and may be restricted to the exercise or exploitation of a specific right. For example, an assignment may only cover the right to make an adaptation of the work or cover only Nigeria.

70 For example, s 24(1C) South African Copyright Act.

71 Section 4 Nigerian Copyright Act; Section 5 South African Copyright Act.

Music (a UK collecting society) and German collecting society Gesellschaft für musikalische Aufführungs- und mechanische Vervielfältigungsrechte (GEMA) have been at the forefront of copyright infringement suits against platform firms.[72] In Nigeria and South Africa, there have been significant activities by the Copyright Society of Nigeria (COSON) and Musical Copyright Society of Nigeria and the South African Music Rights Organisation (SAMRO) in ensuring mechanical royalty payments from firms deploying a subscription-based business model.[73] As explained in Chapter 2, the subscription-based freemium business model involves uploads by platform firms themselves, the procurement of licences by the platform firms and the receipt of subscription fees from users.[74] These activities may likely extend to the multi-sided music platforms described in this book.

3.32 It must be noted that in Nigeria, by virtue of section 17 of the Copyright Act, a collecting society must be licensed as such by the Nigerian Copyright Commission (NCC) in order to have standing (*locus standi*) to sue for copyright infringement. However, whether this requirement will 'disqualify' an unlicensed collecting society from instituting a copyright infringement action, has been rendered doubtful by recent decisions from the Nigerian Supreme Court. Currently, South Africa does not operate a licensing scheme for collecting societies even though such provisions have been made under the Copyright Amendment Bill presently awaiting presidential assent.[75]

3.33 In *Adeokin Records and another v Musical Copyright Society of Nigeria Limited (MCSN)*,[76] the Nigerian Supreme Court held that even though MCSN was an unlicensed collecting society, it had the capacity (*locus standi*) to institute the suit as owner, assignee and exclusive licensee of copyright. The court's decision was on the grounds *inter alia*, that in considering issues of *locus standi*, only the statement of claim may be considered and extraneous documents outside the statement of claim cannot be considered.[77] Given the fact that Adeokin Records did not challenge MCSN's averment in its statement of claim that it was 'owner, assignee and exclusive licensee of copyright', the court took the issue as established.

---

72 See for instance, *GEMA v YouTube*, District Court of Munich (Landgericht (District Court) Munich I, 30 June 2015, 33 O 9639/14); Court of Appeal of Hamburg (Oberlandesgericht (Court of Appeal) Hamburg, 1 July 2015, 5 U 87/12), Higher Regional Court of Munich Judgment of 28 January 2016 – Case Ref.: 29 U 2798/15.

73 For instance, in 2016, COSON instituted a suit against MTN Nigeria for infringement of copyright by virtue of MTN's use of music content in its subscription-based streaming service without obtaining relevant mechanical licence from COSON. See *COSON v MTN Nigeria,* Suit No. FHC/L/CS/619/2016. See also, '7Digital Announce Pan-African Licensing Agreement Through CAPASSO | 7Digital L Global B2B Music Services' (*7digital.com*, 2015), www.7digital.com/news/7digital-announce-pan-african-licensing-agreement-through-capasso (accessed 2 July 2019).

74 See s 1.3.

75 See Clause 22B of the Bill.

76 Appeal number SC/336/2008.

77 The Court also held that the requirement for operating licence for collecting societies was not in existence at the time the cause of action in the suit arose. See pages 30–32 of the decision.

3.34 Also, in *Musical Copyright Society of Nigeria Limited (MCSN) v Compact Disc Technology Limited and 2 Others*,[78] the Supreme Court held that MCSN had the capacity (*locus standi*) to institute the suit as owner, assignee and exclusive licensee of copyright. The court relied on its earlier judgment in *Adeokin Records & another v MCSN*.

3.35 As a result of these decisions, some scholars have argued that unlicensed collecting societies in Nigeria would have locus to sue for copyright infringement if they describe themselves as 'owners, assignees and exclusive licensees of copyright'.[79] This argument may be countered by the fact that *locus standi* is an issue of jurisdiction and as such may be raised at any stage of court proceedings.[80] If it is raised during trial or at the time of filing of written addresses, a defendant may rely on evidence adduced as to absence of the requisite licence to raise the failure of the unlicensed collecting society to comply with condition precedent to the institution of the action.[81]

Courts with jurisdiction and applicable law

3.36 As noted earlier, majority of platform firms are multinational online companies with footprints across many jurisdictions in the light of the global reach of the internet.[82] Usually, these platform firms indicate the applicable law and choose relevant court to which disputes may be brought.[83] For example, Paragraph 14.6 of YouTube's Terms of Use indicates that:

> The Terms, and your relationship with YouTube under the Terms, shall be governed by English law. You and YouTube agree to submit to the exclusive jurisdiction of the courts of England to resolve any legal matter arising from the Terms. Notwithstanding this, you agree that YouTube shall still be allowed to apply for injunctive remedies (or other equivalent types of urgent legal remedy) in any jurisdiction.

3.37 However, this does not mean that Nigerian or South African law will not apply to the platform firms. It is Nigerian and South African copyright laws that dictate copyright in the music content as discussed in this book.[84] In such circumstances, a copyright owner who did not upload or authorise the uploading

78 Appeal number SC.425/2010.

79 Oriakhogba DO, 'Copyright collective management organizations in Nigeria: the locus standi conundrum resolved?' [2018] 14(2) *Journal of Intellectual Property Law & Practice* 127–135; Oriakhogba DO and Erhagbe EO, 'How the Nigerian Supreme Court finally resolved the copyright collective management organizations' locus standi conundrum' [2019] *Journal of Intellectual Property Law & Practice*.

80 Okorie C, 'Nigerian Supreme Court issues guidance on locus standi of collecting societies' [2018] 13(12) *Journal of Intellectual Property Law & Practice* 931–933.

81 Ibid.

82 For example, YouTube is headquartered in the US with offices in the UK, Nigeria and many other jurisdictions.

83 See Van Eechoud MM, *Choice of law in copyright and related rights: alternatives to the lex protectionis* (Vol. 12, Kluwer Law 2002). Examples of choice of law provisions.

84 According to s 44(1) of the South African Copyright Act, 'no copyright or right in the nature of copyright shall subsist otherwise than by virtue of this Act or some other enactment in that behalf'.

of music content on the platform is not bound by the terms of use and may validly sue the relevant platform firm in Nigeria or South Africa. The *PRS v SoundCloud* suit discussed in different parts of this book is a typical example of this possibility. The institution of the suit was justified as 'the works are made available from the UK and/or are targeted at members of the public in the UK'.[85] As the PRS averred in its particulars of claim, the copyright owners allegedly damaged by SoundCloud's conduct obtained copyright protection on the basis of UK copyright law.[86] Hence, action against SoundCloud before the UK courts was considered appropriate. This is the correct approach because, even in the face of choice of law provisions, music content on digital platforms would still be subject to the copyright laws of the conferring country.[87]

3.38 It is important to note the court system in Nigeria with respect to copyright infringement suits. By virtue of the combined provisions of section 251(1)(f) of the Constitution of the Federal Republic of Nigeria 1999 as amended and section 46 of the (Nigerian) Copyright Act, the Federal High Court has exclusive jurisdiction to entertain matters relating to copyright.[88] This means that copyright infringement claims can only be brought before that court otherwise the suit may be struck out for want of jurisdiction.

When is copyright infringed?

3.39 Both South Africa and Nigeria provide for circumstances in which copyright may be infringed. By virtue of section 23(1) of the South African Copyright Act, 'copyright shall be infringed by any person, not being the owner of the copyright, who, without the licence of such owner, does or causes any other person to do, in the Republic, any act which the owner has the exclusive rights to do or to authorize'. Section 15 of the Nigerian Copyright Act contains a similar provision.

3.40 It is easy to envision the concept of copyright infringement when it is expressed as the unauthorised exercise of any of the exclusive rights of the copyright owner. However, to appreciate the concept of copyright infringement in relation to the activities of multi-sided music platforms, it is necessary to understand the basic elements of a cause of action in copyright infringement. In this regard, it is helpful to breakdown the tort into key elements using the statutory provisions quoted earlier.

85 See para. 13.2.3 of the *PRS v SoundCloud* Particulars of Claim.

86 See paras 1 and 2 of the *PRS v SoundCloud* Particulars of Claim.

87 See *Viacom v YouTube* supra; *GEMA v YouTube* supra. In these cases, the suits were validly instituted in the relevant jurisdictions despite the choice of laws chosen by the platform firms.

88 According to s 251(1)(F), 'Notwithstanding anything to the contained in this Constitution and in addition to such other jurisdiction as may be conferred upon it by an Act of the National Assembly, the Federal High Court shall have and exercise jurisdiction to the exclusion of any other court in civil causes and matters: any Federal enactment relating to copyright, patent, designs, trade marks and passing-off, industrial designs and merchandise marks, business names, commercial and industrial monopolies, combines and trusts, standards of goods and commodities and industrial standards'.

Key 'elements' of a copyright infringement claim

3.41 A claimant in an action for copyright infringement must prove that:

- He/she/it owns or acquired copyright in the infringed work;
- The infringing act complained of is one he/she/it has exclusive right to do or authorise;
- The defendant himself/herself/itself did the infringing act or the defendant authorised or caused another person to undertake the infringing act.

3.42 However, even where the aforementioned elements are present, it may be that the individual or firm alleged to have infringed the claimant's copyright has a defence open to them. The main defences open to a defendant are:

- Fair dealing (i.e. that the defendant's actions amounted to fair dealing with the work);
- The use is such that the relevant copyright statute permits a compulsory and/or statutory licence;
- Other statutory limitations and exceptions to copyright protection apply;
- Copyright does not subsist in the work;
- The defendant's activities in relation to the work are not covered by or are exempt from the scope of any of the exclusive rights.

3.43 Where the defendant cannot or does not put forward a defence or the defence is unsuccessful, the claimant will be entitled to recover damages and/or other reliefs.[89]

Copyright subsistence

Claimant is the copyright owner

3.44 Copyright is a non-registrable right and is therefore acquired without proof of registration. Copyright is held in the first instance by the authors or person who made arrangements for the work.[90] Accordingly, the claimant in an action for copyright infringement must draw a nexus between him and the work alleged to have been infringed. In most cases, the claimant would make an averment in the statement or particulars of claim stating that it owns the copyright in the subject work by virtue of being the author of the work, the exclusive licensee of the work or the assignee of the work.

3.45 The claimant would also need to show that he/she/it is a 'qualified person' or that the work was first published or made in the relevant country. In the case of qualified persons, the requirement is that the author is a citizen of

89 Note that the sum awarded by the court may depend on the behaviour of the parties or the flagrancy of the infringement. See, e.g., s 24(3) of the South African Copyright Act; s 16(4) of the Nigerian Copyright Act.

90 Section 21(1) of the South African Copyright Act.

or a person domiciled in the relevant country (e.g. South Africa or Nigeria). According to section 2(1) of the Nigeria Copyright Act, copyright shall be conveyed on every work eligible for copyright of which the author, or in the case of a work of joint authorship, any of the authors is, at the time when the work was made, an individual who is a citizen or domiciled in Nigeria ('qualified person').[91] A similar provision is stipulated in section 3 of the South African Copyright Act.

3.46 As held in the case of *Okoyo and Another v Prompter Quality Services (Nigeria) Limited and another*,[92] what is material once a given work is eligible for copyright protection is that the author is a citizen of Nigeria. Formal education, while desirable, is not a condition precedent for an author who is a Nigerian citizen to enjoy copyright protection.[93]

3.47 In the event that the claimant is not a qualified person, the claimant may proceed by showing that the work in question was first published or made in the relevant country.[94] Accordingly, ownership of works made by non-Nigerians/South Africans or persons not domiciled in Nigeria or South Africa would vest in their authors if the works were first published or made in Nigeria or South Africa.

3.48 A copyright owner can assign his rights to a collecting society to administer and manage the stated rights on behalf of such owner. Collecting societies fall into the same category as assignees of copyright. Where the collecting society is instituting the action for copyright infringement, it would aver to such fact in its statement of claim.

Exclusive rights

3.49 The activities, which are covered within the bundle of exclusive rights available to the copyright owner, have been indicated in Chapter 2. To reiterate, the copyright owner has the exclusive right to reproduce the work, communicate the work to the public, make an adaptation of the work, perform the work in public, publish the work, make a cinematograph film or a record in respect of the work, distribute the work for commercial purposes and communicate or broadcast the work to the public.[95] Accordingly, engaging in or authorising engagement in such activities without the authorisation of the copyright owner would amount to copyright infringement.

Rights of particular application to multi-sided music platforms

3.50 The application of copyright law to multi-sided music platforms focuses on the interpretation of the copyright terms implemented on the platforms

91 See also *Maurice Ukaoha v Broadbased Mortgage Finance Ltd & Another* (1997) FHCL 477 at 485.

92 (1996) FHCR 814.

93 Ibid. at 822.

94 See s 3(1) Nigerian Copyright Act; s 4 South African Copyright Act.

95 For a delineation of each of the exclusive rights available for the mentioned categories of copyright works, see ss 6, 7 and 8 of the Nigerian Copyright Act; s 6(1)(a)–(g) South African Copyright Act.

vis-à-vis the scope of the exclusive rights framework and of course, any limitations and exceptions to those rights. The most relevant rights for copyright owners in the online context in which the multi-sided music platforms operate, are[96]

- The right of reproduction;
- The right to communicate the work to the public.

3.51 The other economic rights recognised by the international copyright treaties (and by extension, Nigerian and South African copyright statutes), are either generally understood to be limited to tangible copies or more relevant in the physical space and are accordingly not relevant to the online context in which multi-sided music platforms operate.

Right to reproduce the work

Position under the international copyright regime

3.52 Before focusing on the South African and/or Nigerian copyright framework, it is important to first consider the various international copyright instruments that address the exercise of copyright. National regulation of copyright has largely taken its cue from existing international instruments and in particular the Berne Convention, the TRIPS Agreement and the WIPO Copyright Treaty (WCT). It is to be noted that despite the similarities that may arise from using the same legislative 'template',[97] the ratification approach specific to each jurisdiction as well as the promise of an eventual regulatory cumulative body of interpretative material as constructed by the courts are factors that result in national differences.[98] Consequently, the analysis here provides a brief description of any guidance that can be gleaned from this international 'template', before moving on to the consideration of the South African and Nigerian respective regulatory experiences.

3.53 As indicated in Chapter 2, the reproduction right has been the oldest and most prevalent value metric for the exploitation of music content. Article 9(1) of the Berne Convention to which both South Africa and Nigeria are signatories secures the right of reproduction in relation to copyright works. According to that provision, 'authors of literary and artistic works protected by this Convention shall have the exclusive right of authorizing the reproduction of these works, in any manner or form'. Further, art 9(3) clarifies that sound and video recordings are to be considered as reproductions.

3.54 Neither the TRIPS Agreement nor the WCT replicates these provisions. However, both art 9(1) of the TRIPS Agreement and art 1(4) of the WCT require

96 See Angelopoulos 2016 supra at 13; Harms 2012 supra at 217.

97 See Hugenholtz PB, Van Eechoud M, Gompel SV and Helberger N, *The recasting of copyright and related rights for the knowledge economy* (Vancouver 2012), 31.

98 Depreeuw S, *The Variable scope of the exclusive economic rights in copyright* (Wolters Kluwer 2014), 487; Reid L, 'The judge as law maker' [1972] 12 *J Soc'y Pub Tchrs ns* 22.

Contracting Parties to comply with them. As an 'internet treaty', which seeks to address the challenges posed by internet technology for the copyright ecosystem,[99] the Agreed Statement on art 1(4) of the WCT is apposite for the activities on multi-sided music platforms. The Agreed Statement provides that

> The reproduction right, as set out in Article 9 of the Berne Convention, and the exceptions permitted thereunder, fully apply in the digital environment, in particular to the use of works in digital form. It is understood that the storage of a protected work in digital form in an electronic medium constitutes a reproduction within the meaning of Article 9 of the Berne Convention.

3.55 Given that the storage of a protected work in digital form in an electronic medium such as a digital platform is recognised as a reproduction of that work, it will be immaterial that the form of the relevant copyright work was significantly modified during the process of copying. In this way, the digitisation of a given copyright work would still be considered as a reproduction of that work. This would mean that the reproduction right applies to every use of the work in the online context, no matter how ephemeral or economically irrelevant they might be. This approach has led to the suggestion that the level of copyright protection in the online context may be unduly higher than the physical environment given that the nature of the internet generally necessitates reproducing the work, even if temporarily.[100]

3.56 To avoid such unwholesome interpretation, legislators in many jurisdictions sought to provide exemptions ('safe harbour') to individuals and firms who only engage in acts of reproduction of copyright works in situations necessitated by the very nature of internet use or at the behest of users of the services provided by such individuals or firms.[101] These attempts led to the enactment of section 512 of the US Digital Millennium Copyright Act (DMCA) 1998 and the E-Commerce Directive in the EU, which are the two main global models for the safe harbour regime. The safe harbour regime is discussed under defences to copyright infringement.

Right to communicate the work to the public

Position under the international copyright regime

3.57 The international copyright instruments (Berne Convention, the TRIPS Agreement and the WCT) when analysed individually offer both guidance and

99 WIPO, 'WIPO Internet Treaties' (*Wipo.int*, 2017), www.wipo.int/copyright/en/activities/internet_treaties.html (accessed 31 January 2017).

100 See Hugenholtz and others 2012 supra at 116–118.

101 For historical context, see Pollack W, 'Tuning in: The future of copyright protection for online music in the digital millennium' [1999] 68 *Fordham L Rev* 2445; Traphagen M, 'The unfinished business of copyright: A look forward from the Digital Millennium Copyright Act' [2002] 63(7) *Int'l Intell Prop L & Pol'y* 1; Urban JM and Quilter L, 'Efficient process or chilling effects – Takedown notices under Section 512 of the Digital Millennium Copyright Act' [2005] 22 *Santa Clara Computer & High Tech LJ* 621; Rosati 2016 supra.

certain leeway to Member States in the construction and scope of the right of communication to the public, particularly in the digital era.

3.58 According to the Berne Convention, the authors of literary and artistic works shall have the exclusive right to authorise the communication of their works to the public.[102] The Convention does not explicitly define the right of communication to the public. However, that provision appears to restrict the application of the right to places where without being in the same place and at the same time where the transmission or communication is taking place, the recipients of the communication would not be able to perceive the work.[103] According to Ficsor, communication to the public within the meaning of the Berne Convention is restricted to

> A transmission by wire or wireless means, of images or sounds, or both, making it possible for the images and/or sounds to be perceived by persons outside the normal circle of a family and the closest social acquaintances or the family, at a place or places the distance of which from the place where the transmission is started is such that, without the transmission, the images or sounds, or both, would not be perceivable at the said place or places, irrespective of whether the said persons can perceive the images and/or sounds at the same place and at the same time, or at different places and at different times.[104]

3.59 Given that the Berne Convention predates the emergence of the internet and new media, it is unsurprising that the scope of the right under the Convention appears to be narrowly defined as to exclude those means of communication.

3.60 Article 9(1) of the TRIPS Agreement require Contracting States to recognise the right of communication to the public as provided in the Berne Convention. Nevertheless, art 8 of the WCT expands the scope of the right of communication to the public to include the 'making available to the public of works in such a way that members of the public may access them from a place and at a time individually chosen by them'.[105] While no explicit definition is provided for the right of communication to the public under the treaty, the inclusion of the 'making available' ambit clearly accommodates communication on the internet and new media in which each person determines when and where to access a given copyright-protected content. However, notwithstanding this broad inclusion, the 'Agreed Statement concerning art 8' in indicating that 'the mere provision of physical facilities for enabling or making a communication does not in itself amount to communication within the meaning of [the WCT] or the Berne Convention', appears to have reduced the scope of art 8 in relation to the internet.

---

102 See Berne Convention, Articles 11, 11bis, 11ter, 14(1)(ii) and 14bis(1). Also Dreier T, 'Berne Convention for the protection of literary and artistic works' In Dreier T and Hugenholtz PB (eds), *Concise European Copyright Law* (Vol. 2, Kluwer Law 2006), 49.

103 See Berne Convention, Article 11bis (1).

104 See Ficsor M, *Guide to the Copyright and Related Rights Treaties Administered by WIPO: And Glossary of Copyright and Related Rights and Terms* (WIPO, 2003), 275.

105 Angelopoulos C, 'Creative Commons and related rights in sound recordings: Are the two systems compatible?' in Guibault L and Angelopoulos C (eds.), *Open Content Licensing: From Theory to Practice* (Amsterdam University Press 2011), 247–248.

In this regard, it may be argued that as far as the right of communication to the public is concerned, the person or firm who did not create, but merely facilitated the dissemination of infringing content, will not be construed as communicating the work to the public.[106]

3.61 In these circumstances, mere facilitation of the distribution of music content may be outside the scope of the protected use involved in the right of communication to the public.[107] However, there is no definition of what kind of activity would qualify as a 'mere provision of physical facilities' under the treaty. Applying the literal rule of interpretation[108] would suggest that only the provision of hardware is excluded and that acts of installation of the physical facilities or of the provision of services that use them may fall within protected use. However, it is possible to argue that the services in the nature of digital facilities that enable distribution of protected content are excluded from the scope of protected use.[109] This may be particularly so when the activities in question are restricted to enabling distribution only. Significantly, it is to be noted that the Agreed Statement is limited to the act of communication to the public and there is no mention of the reproduction of copyright protected works. Accordingly, where the same act constitutes both reproduction and communication to the public, it appears that the Agreed Statement may not exempt the platform firm from liability for the act of reproduction.[110]

Interpretation of the exclusive rights in other jurisdictions

3.62 As evidenced from the foregoing analysis of the international copyright instruments, the international copyright instruments (Berne Convention, the TRIPS Agreement and the WCT) when analysed individually offers both guidance and certain leeway to Member States in the construction and scope of the right of communication to the public, particularly in the digital era. The EU, for instance takes advantage of this. In the case of the EU, the Copyright Directive[111] adopts the WCT approach providing a broad discretion to EU Member States in making their domestic laws. Like the WCT, art 3(1) of the Copyright Directive does not define the concept of 'communication to the public'. In the absence of

106 International Bureau of WIPO (1997). *WIPO National Seminar on Digital Technology and the New WIPO Treaties* (WIPO/CNR/SEL/97/1).

107 Ibid.

108 The Literal Rule requires that where the statutory provisions appear to be clear and unambiguous, they should be interpreted according to their literal meaning or in their usual grammatical sense. See *Nabhan v Nabhan* [1967] 1 All NLR 47 at 54; Faturoti B, 'Re-importing the concept of 'authorisation' of copyright infringement to Nigeria from the UK and Australia' [2017] 31(1) *International Review of Law, Computers & Technology* 4, 7.

109 Koelman K and Hugenholtz P, 'Online service provider liability for copyright infringement, Workshop on service provider liability' (*Pure.uva.nl*, 1999), https://pure.uva.nl/ws/files/3363649/6027_wipo99.pdf (accessed 8 February 2015).

110 See Angelopoulos 2016 supra at 139.

111 Directive 2001/29/EC of the European Parliament and of the Council of 22 May 2001 on the harmonisation of certain aspects of copyright and related rights in the information society; Official Journal L 167, 22/06/2001 P. 0010–0019.

an explicit definition, the CJEU has relied on the stated objectives of the Copyright Directive, which includes ensuring a high level of protection of intellectual property and for authors, to define the scope of the right of communication.[112] Further, in a long line of cases on the construction of the right of communication to the public,[113] the CJEU has consistently identified that the essential components of the right of communication to the public are an act of communication', which is directed to a 'public'.[114] Where the act of communication consists in making the work available to the public, the CJEU has also identified other relevant prerequisites.[115] These include considerations such as the indispensable intervention of the person or firm making the communication and the knowledge and awareness[116] of the maker of the communication regarding the consequences of his/its communication or intervention.[117]

3.63 In *Stichting Brein v Jack Frederik Wullems*,[118] the CJEU held that the notion of 'communication to the public' would include the sale of a multimedia player on which there are pre-installed add-ons, available on the internet, containing hyperlinks to freely accessible websites on which copyright works have been made available to the public without the authorisation of the copyright

---

112 See Recital 24 of the Copyright Directive.

113 See the following cases: *Sociedad General de Autores y Editores de España (SGAE) v Rafael Hoteles SA*, C-306/05, EU:C:2006:479 ('SGAE'); *Organismos Sillogikis Diacheirisis Dimiourgon Theatrikon kai Optikoakoustikon Ergon v Divani Akropolis Anonimi Xenodocheiaki kai Touristiki Etaireia*, C-136/09, EU:C:2010:151 ('Organismos Sillogikis Diacheirisis'); *Circul Globus Bucures ti (Circ & Variete Globus Bucures ti) v Uniunea Compozitorilor s i Muzicologilor din România – Asocia& ia pentru Drepturi de Autor (UCMR – ADA)*, C-283/10, EU:C:2011:772 ('Circul Globus Bucures ti'); *Football Association Premier League Ltd and Others v QC Leisure and Others (C-403/08) and Karen Murphy v Media Protection Services Ltd* (C-429/08), EU:C:2011:631 ('FAPL'); *Airfield NV and Canal Digitaal BV v Belgische Vereniging van Auteurs, Componisten en Uitgevers CVBA* (Sabam) (C-431/09) and *Airfield NV v Agicoa Belgium BVBA* (C-432/09), EU:C:2011:648 ('Airfield'); *Società Consortile Fonografici (SCF) v Marco Del Corso*, C-135/10, EU:C:2012:140 ('SCF'); *Phonographic Performance (Ireland) Limited v Ireland and Attorney General*, C-162/10, EU:C:2012:141 ('PPI'); *ITV Broadcasting Ltd and Others v TV Catch Up Ltd*, C-607/11, EU:C:2013:147 ('TV Catch Up'); *Nils Svensson and Others v Retriever Sverige AB*, C-466/12 ('Svensson'), EU:C:2014:76; *OSA – Ochranný* svaz autorský pro práva k dílů m hudebním os v Léč ebné lázně Mariánské Lázně as, C-351/12, EU:C:2014:110 ('OSA'); *BestWater International v Mebes and Potsch*, C-348/13, EU:C:2014:2315 ('BestWater'); *C More Entertainment AB v Linus Sandberg*, C-279/13, EU:C:2015:199; *Sociedade Portuguesa de Autores CRL v Ministério Público and Others*, C-151/15, EU:C:2015:468 ('Sociedade Portuguesa de Autores'); *SBS Belgium NV v Belgische Vereniging van Auteurs, Componisten en Uitgevers (SABAM)*, C-325/14, EU:C:2015:764 ('SBS Belgium'); *Reha Training Gesellschaft für* Sport- und Unfallrehabilitation mbH v Gesellschaft für musikalische Aufführungs- und mechanische Vervielfältigungsrechte (GEMA), C-117/15, EU:C:2016:379 ('Reha Training'); *GS Media BV v Sanoma Media Netherlands BV and Others*, C-160/15, EU:C:2016:644 ('GS Media'); *Stichting Brein v Jack Frederik Wullems, also trading under the name Filmspeler*, C-527/15, EU:C:2017:300 ('Filmspeler'); *Zürs*.net Staatlich genehmigte Gesellschaft der Autoren, Komponisten und Musikverlegerregistrierte Genossenschaft mbH (AKM) v *Zürs*.net Betriebs GmbH, C-138/16, EU:C:2017:218 ('Zürs.net'); and *The Pirate Bay* supra.

114 Rosati E, 'The CJEU Pirate Bay judgment and its impact on the liability of online platforms' [2017] *European Intellectual Property Review*, https://ssrn.com/abstract=3006591 (accessed 6 September 2017), 3.

115 Ibid. at 5.

116 Rosati 2017 supra at 11–12.

117 Ibid. at 3.

118 *Filmspeler*, para. 31.

owners. The Court took the view that an intervention like the one of the providers of a multimedia player is to be regarded as enabling access to unlicensed content that would be otherwise more challenging to find. As such, an intervention of this kind falls within the scope of art 3(1) of the Copyright Directive on the making of communication to the public.[119]

3.64 Regarding the 'public' to which the work is being communicated or made available in the online context, such would include any unspecified number of people such as the users of the platform (including advertisers)[120] as held in *Stichting Brein v Ziggo BV and XS4All Internet BV ('The Pirate Bay' or 'Pirate Bay')*, either where the copyright owner was not the one who uploaded or authorised the uploading of his work.[121] *The Pirate Bay* is particularly notable in that it dealt with a situation where the communication to the public is construed as being made by a platform firm. Accordingly, it is particularly apposite to the activities of the platform firm and the question of whether such may be construed as communicating the music content to the public. This differs from the safe harbour regime and the consequent value gap proposal where the platform firm may be considered liable for copyright infringement because of the actions of the platform users themselves. In other words, the safe harbour protection is particularly applicable in secondary liability cases where the platform users have to be primary or direct infringers.[122]

3.65 In *The Pirate Bay*, the Dutch Supreme Court sought guidance from the CJEU on the question of whether the operators of a website like the Pirate Bay, which operated a system that indexed and categorised protected works for users, are to be regarded as making acts of communication to the public within the meaning of art 3(1) of the Copyright Directive. While the CJEU decision has several implications particularly for the notions of primary and secondary liability,[123] the focus here lies on the CJEU's interpretation of the activities of the Pirate Bay (as a platform firm) vis-à-vis the act of communication to the public. The CJEU held *inter alia* that the right has two key components – (1) an 'act of communication' (2) directed to a 'public'.[124] The act of communication need not involve actual transmission of the protected work. Mere making available of the work suffices. According to the CJEU, the right also involves other inter-related,[125] complementary criteria, which include the indispensable role played by the platform firm[126] ('indispensability') and the profit-making nature of the communication

119 Ibid. at paras 31 and 37.

120 *The Pirate Bay* para. 37.

121 See *The Pirate Bay* paras 39 and 45.

122 See Rosati 2017 supra at 13; Riordan J, *The liability of internet intermediaries* (Oxford University Press, 2016), para. 12.11.

123 For instance, by requiring knowledge (actual or constructive) on the part of the platform firm before primary liability may be imposed, the *Pirate Bay* seems to have conflated the requirements for primary and secondary liability. See Rosati 2017 supra at 11.

124 *The Pirate Bay* supra at para. 24.

125 *The Pirate Bay* supra at para. 25.

126 *The Pirate Bay*, para. 26.

at hand ('profit-making').[127] Specifically, while the interpretation of the act of communication to the public will depend on the facts of each case, 'as a rule, any act by which a user, with full knowledge of the relevant facts, provides its clients with access to protected works is liable to constitute an 'act of communication' for the purposes of art 3(1) of Directive 2001/29'.[128] This follows the CJEU decision in cases such as *Svensson, BestWater, GS Media*[129] and *Filmspeler*.[130]

3.66 More importantly (for the purposes of this book), the CJEU held that a platform firm would be making an act of communication where it provides and manages a platform that provides users with access to the works concerned. In such circumstances, the platform firm satisfies the indispensability requirement and may be regarded as playing a crucial role in making the works available.[131] In the case of *The Pirate Bay*, this was satisfied by its indexing of torrent files to allow users of its platform to locate and share the protected works.[132] Further, the actions of a platform firm in indexing, categorising, deleting or filtering user-uploaded protected work constituted more than 'mere provision of physical facilities'.[133] Such actions were held to constitute an 'intervention' by the operators of the Pirate Bay. It was immaterial that these activities were undertaken automatically or using algorithms.[134]

3.67 Given that the protected works were uploaded by platform users (and in some cases, copyright owners themselves), it was required that the primary liability of the platform firm depended on its communication being directed to a 'new public', that is, a public not in the contemplation of the copyright owners when they authorised the initial communication. The CJEU held that a platform firm would satisfy this requirement where it is informed that its platform provides access to works published without the relevant copyright owner's consent.[135] This 'new public' requirement is also met where given the sheer number of protected works shared on the platform and the fact that the platform was operated for the purpose of making profit, the platform firm is presumed to be not unaware of the absence of the copyright owners' consent in some of the works published.[136] In this case, advertising revenue was held to satisfy the 'profit-making' intention.[137] Again, this follows the CJEU's reasoning in the cases of *GS Media* and *Filmspeler*.

---

127 *The Pirate Bay*, para. 29.
128 *The Pirate Bay*, para. 34.
129 *The Pirate Bay*, para. 32.
130 *The Pirate Bay*, para. 33.
131 *The Pirate Bay*, para. 37.
132 *The Pirate Bay*, para. 36.
133 *The Pirate Bay*, para. 38.
134 Rosati 2017 supra at 11.
135 *The Pirate Bay*, para. 45.
136 Ibid.
137 *The Pirate Bay*, paras 46 and 47.

Copyright terms and the South African copyright system

Right to reproduce the work (South Africa)

3.68 Under the South African Copyright Act, the reproduction right applies to all the categories of works and consists of the vesting of the exclusive right to reproduce or to authorise the reproduction of the applicable work 'in any manner or form'.[138] Section 1(1) of the Act provides some clarification regarding the scope of the reproduction right. 'Reproduction' in the Act is defined thus:

> 'Reproduction' in relation to – (a) a literary or musical work or a broadcast, includes a reproduction in the form of a record or a cinematograph film; (b) An artistic work, includes a version produced by converting the work into a three-dimensional form or, if it is in three dimensions, by converting it into a two-dimensional form; (c) any work, includes a reproduction made from a reproduction of that work; and references to 'reproduce' and 'reproducing' shall be construed accordingly.

3.69 In this regard, reproduction essentially means copying of a work either in the same medium or in some other form such as record, cinematograph film or three-dimensional form. Another indication of the scope of the reproduction may be found in the definition, which the Act ascribes to 'infringing copy' as a copy of the work infringed.[139]

3.70 The granting of the exclusive right of reproduction 'in any manner or form' has been suggested to mean that the right covers both digital and analogue reproductions.[140] Indeed, in the case of *Pastel Software (Pty) Ltd v Pink Software (Pty) Ltd*,[141] the court recognised that reproduction may take place electronically even if such reproduction was short-lived. The broad reach of the right is in line with the regulatory approach to copyright protection in South Africa, as stated in the preamble to the Copyright Act. Also, in keeping with the broad range of the reproduction right, the concept of 'material form' has a wide meaning by virtue of section 2(2) of the Act, where reference is made to a work being written down, recorded, represented, in digital data or signals or otherwise reduced to material form. In this way, the Act is aligned with the WCT in recognising that the digitisation of a work constitutes a reproduction of said work. According to Dean,

> The wide meaning given to 'reproduction' is of considerable significance in the electronic age and in e-commerce. Examples of what would constitute reproduction, whether in a material form or otherwise, for purposes of the Act include loading software and data into a computer; operating a computer program, (this entails a reproduction of the program being made internally in the computer); downloading material from the Internet; displaying material on a computer screen, including material sourced from the Internet; and incorporating material in a website. Electronic

138 In respect of the South African Copyright Act, see s 6(a) regarding literary or musical work, s 7(a) regarding artistic works, s 8(a) regarding cinematograph films, s 9(a) regarding the 'making directly or indirectly, a record embodying the sound recording'. See also ss 10(a) and 11B(a) regarding broadcasts and computer programs respectively.

139 See s 1(1) of the Act. See also Harms 2012 supra at 218.

140 See Dean 2006 supra at 39.

141 399 JOC (T).

> communications and the Internet bring about new situations with which copyright law must deal. It is necessary to adapt or extend classical copyright concepts so as to cater for these new situations, which have arisen in the electronic age.[142]

3.71 Furthermore, the use of the expression 'includes' in delineating the scope of the reproduction right highlights section 1(1)'s intention of defining the right of reproduction expansively to include different uses of the copyright-protected content. This non-exhaustive approach suggests that the storage of music content by platform firms in the context of multi-sided music platforms would fall within the scope of the exercise of the right of reproduction, which is exclusive to the copyright owner. Similarly, given that partial copies of a work are also covered by the reproduction right irrespective of the weight or size of the copied portion, the indexing and tagging of music content whether by an automated process is likely to qualify as a protected use under this interpretation. However, there is presently no court decision in South Africa regarding the import of indexing or storage in the digital context. But the safe harbour regime may absolve the platform firms from this liability.

Proposed amendments relating to the right to reproduce the work (South Africa)

3.72 South Africa is yet to ratify the WCT. However, the Copyright Amendment Bill 2017,[143] in proposing the introduction of a mandatory exception to the reproduction right in the case of temporary copies, may apply to ameliorate the strictness of such interpretation. Clause 13 of the Amendment Bill includes a new section 12C, which provides:

> 12C. (1) Any person may make transient or incidental copies or adaptation of a work, including reformatting, where such copies or adaptations are an integral and essential part of a technical process and the purpose of those copies or adaptations is – (a) to enable the transmission of the work in a network between third parties by an intermediary or any other lawful use of the work; or (b) to adapt the work to allow use on different technological devices, such as mobile devices, as long as there is no independent economic significance to these acts.[144]

3.73 This provision of the bill, if passed into law, may likely absolve access providers from direct liability for proxy caching for the sake of network efficiency or the transient copying necessary for the operation of search engines. The services of host providers, on the other hand, may not be covered by the exception, because the indexing and storage involved in hosting services may not be temporary or transient. As a result, hosting providers may still be liable for direct copyright infringements of the works they store.[145]

---

142 See Dean 2006 supra at 40; Harms 2012 supra at 218.

143 See Appendix 4.

144 This provision bears strong resemblance to art 5(1) of the EU's Copyright Directive.

145 See *Public Relations Consultants Association Ltd v Newspaper Licensing Agency Ltd and Others*, CJEU, C-360/13, 5 June 2014. See also Sag M, 'Copyright and copy-reliant technology' [2009] 103 *Nw UL Rev* 1607 (Sag 2009); Sag M, 'Inside Views: Lessons from South Africa: Protecting non-expressive uses in copyright reform' (*Intellectual Property Watch*, 11 July 2017), www.

Right to communicate the work to the public (South Africa)

3.74 With respect to the right of communication to the public, such is currently provided only for sound recordings. Section 9(e) of the Act provides that 'copyright in a sound recording vests the exclusive right to do or to authorise the doing of any of the following acts in the Republic: communicating the sound recording to the public'. Apart from sound recordings, communicating literary works, musical works and other categories of protected work to the public is not included within the scope of the exclusive rights under the Act. Further, the concepts of 'communication' and 'public' are not defined in the Act. This is unlike the EU where the WCT approach is adopted in art 3(1) of the Copyright Directive. Accordingly, in the absence of explicit statutory provision, clear statutory definition and/or judicial interpretation, it is uncertain whether the following constitutes the exercise of the right of communication to the public:

1 Communication to a public not present at the place where the communication originates; or whether local communications, such as public performance, recitation and display, are excluded.[146] This is different from Recital 23 of the EU Copyright Directive, which involves a broad interpretation of the right of communication to the public as to cover all communication to a public not present at the place where the communication originates. Indeed, what is pertinent is whether the public to which the communication is transmitted in a different place from where the communication originates.[147]

2 Mere provision of physical facilities for the distribution of the sound recording. This differs from Recital 27 of the EU Copyright Directive, which repeats the Agreed Statement on art 8 almost verbatim, thus introducing the WCT's deference for the mere provision of physical facilities to the EU legal landscape.

3 Making available to the public the sound recording in such manner that once completed, members of the public are able to access the sound recording from a place and at a time individually chosen by them (i.e. on demand). This is unlike the approach of the WCT.

4 Services that involve the provision of the sound recording to a user in circumstances that the user has no control over when and where to access the sound recording (so-called non-interactive services). Examples of

ip-watch.org/2017/07/11/lessons-south-africa-protecting-non-expressive-uses-copyright-reform (accessed 13 November 2017).

146 See Riby-Smith M, 'South African copyright law – the good, the bad and the Copyright Amendment Bill' [2017] 12(3) *Journal of Intellectual Property Law & Practice* 216, 218–219.

147 See Bechtold S, 'Directive on the harmonisation of certain aspects of copyright and related rights in the information society', in Dreier T and Hugenholtz PB (eds), *Concise European Copyright Law* (Vol. 2, Kluwer Law 2006), 360.

such non-interactive services include regular television and radio transmissions, webcasting and internet radio services.

5 Services that involve the provision of sound recording to a user in circumstances that the user may control when and where she accesses the sound recording (so-called interactive services). For instance, offers to download a work from a public website or online streaming services, which allow the consumer to access the work at her convenience.

Proposed amendments relating to the right to communicate the work to the public (South Africa)

3.75 Again, like the case of the right of reproduction, the Copyright Amendment Bill 2017 seeks *inter alia* to provide for a right of communication to the public in terms of the WCT. In this regard, clause 4 of the Amendment Bill seeks to amend section 6 of the principal Act which concerns copyright in a literary or musical work to include in sub-section (eA) the right to communicate 'the work to the public, by wire or wireless means, including by means of internet access and the making of the work available to the public in such a way that any member of the public may access the work from a place and at a time chosen by that person, whether interactively or non interactively'. The same right is provided for in the case of artistic works by amending section 7 of the principal Act,[148] cinematograph film by amending section 8 of the principal Act,[149] and sound recording by amending section 9(e) of the principal Act.[150]

3.76 However, until these provisions are enacted into law through the amendment of the Copyright Act, the right of communication to the public as stipulated in the Berne Convention and the WCT remains external to the South African copyright system.

Copyright terms and the Nigerian copyright system

Right to reproduce the work (Nigeria)

3.77 With respect to the creation of a reproduction right that applies to all the categories of works and consists of the vesting of the exclusive right to reproduce or to authorise the reproduction of the applicable work 'in any manner or form', the Nigerian Copyright Act is quite similar to its South African counterpart.[151] Further similarities exist with respect to the definition of 'reproduction' and the wide scope of the reproduction right itself. Section 52(1) of the Nigerian Copyright Act defines 'reproduction' to mean 'the making of one or more copies of a

148 See Clause 6 of the Amendment Bill.

149 See Clause 8 of the Amendment Bill.

150 Clause 10 of the Amendment Bill. This amendment clarifies the boundaries of the right of communicating the sound recording to the public, which is part of the current 1978 Act.

151 See ss 6, 7 and 8 of the Copyright Act.

literary, musical or artistic work, cinematograph film or sound recording'.[152] This definition has been confirmed in several cases such as *Oladipo Yemitan v The Daily Times (Nigeria) Ltd and Another*[153] and the case of *Peter Obe v Grapevine Communication Limited*,[154] where the Nigerian courts accepted that verbatim reproduction or copying of a protected work was the exclusive preserve of the copyright owner and as such amounted to infringement when undertaken without the consent of the copyright owner.

3.78 Regarding the scope of the right of reproduction, the Nigerian Copyright Act also uses the expression 'in any manner or form', which suggests that the right extends to both digital and non-digital reproductions of a protected work.[155] Furthermore, the fact that section 51(1) defines the reproduction right to mean the making of one or more copies of the work indicates that that the storage of music content by platform firms in the context of multi-sided music platforms would fall within the scope of the exercise of the right of reproduction. Similarly, the indexing of music content is likely to qualify as a protected use given that use of the expression 'in any manner or form' indicates that partial copies of a work, irrespective of the weight or size of the copied portion, are covered by the reproduction right.

Proposed amendments relating to the right to reproduce the work (Nigeria)

3.79 To further constrain the expansive boundaries of the reproduction right, the Copyright Bill 2015, like its South African counterpart, seeks *inter alia* to introduce an exception to the reproduction right in the case of temporary copies. Section 20(1) of the Copyright Bill provides thus:

> The rights conferred in respect of a work by sections 8 to 12 of this Act do not include the right to control –
>
> (p) temporary acts of reproduction which are transient or incidental and an integral and essential part of a technological process and whose sole purpose is to enable a transmission in a network between third parties by an intermediary; or for other lawful use, where such use has no independent economic significance.

3.80 Again, like its South African counterpart, this provision bears strong resemblance to art 5(1) of the EU's Copyright Directive. Further, while this provision may protect access providers from direct liability, it may not avail service providers engaged in the act of permanent copying for the purpose of indexing and storage of protected content. Instead, such activities may be safe from the boundaries of protected use by virtue of section 51 of the Copyright Amendment Bill, which offers safe harbour to hosting providers, similar its South African

152 See s 51(1) of the Copyright Act.

153 Unreported Suit No: FHC/L/1/1980.

154 Unreported Suit No. FHC/L/CS/1244/97.

155 See Ola K, 'Evolution and future trends of copyright in Nigeria' [2014] 2(1) *Journal of Open Access to Law* 1, 20–21 (Ola 2014).

counterpart. A close reading of this provision shows that like the case of South Africa, it is similar to art 14 of the EU E-Commerce Directive and section 512(c) of the US DMCA.[156] However, until the Copyright Amendment Bill is enacted into law, the position remains that temporary and permanent copies and indeed reproduction in any manner or form would fall within the boundaries of the reproduction right. Similarly, no safe harbour regime is available to hosting service providers unless section 51 of the Copyright Amendment Bill is enacted into law.

Right to communicate the work to the public (Nigeria)

3.81 Regarding the right of communicating the work to the public, such is presently is restricted to communication 'by a loud speaker or any other similar device' in the case of a literary or musical work[157] and is associated with the reproduction of the work in the case of a sound recording. Section 6(1) of the Act provides that, 'copyright in a sound recording shall be exclusive right to control in Nigeria – *(a)* the direct or indirect reproduction, broadcasting or communication to the public of the whole or a substantial part of the recording either in its original form or in any form recognisably derived from the original'.

3.82 Further, the notion of 'communication to the public' is given a non-exhaustive meaning in that the Act defines it to 'include, in addition to any live performance or delivery, any mode of visual or acoustic presentation, but does not include a broadcast or re-broadcast'.[158] However, similar to the case of South Africa, it is uncertain whether in the absence of clear statutory definition and/or judicial interpretation, linear and non-linear services, interactive and/or non-interactive services are within or outside the scope of the right.

Proposed amendments relating to the right to communicate
the work to the public (Nigeria)

3.83 The Copyright Bill does not provide authors with the exclusive right of communication to the public in the manner provided by the WCT. Instead, Art 15 of the WIPO Performances Phonograms Treaty (WPPT) is adopted to provide for remuneration for exercising the 'making available' right. In this regard, section 14(7) of the Bill provides that 'sound recordings made available to the public by wire or wireless means in such a way that members of the public may access them from a place and at a time individually chosen by them shall be considered as if they had been published for commercial purposes'. Publishing for commercial purposes entails the payment of 'a single equitable remuneration for the direct or indirect use of sound recordings'.[159] Performers and producers of sound recordings are entitled to such payment through their collecting societies.

156 See Aganga O, *The Indirect Liability of Mobile Service Providers in South Africa: A Comparative Study* (Masters, University of Pretoria 2013), 9–10.

157 Section 6(1)(a)(vii) of the Copyright Act.

158 Section 51(1) of the Copyright Act.

159 See s 14(1) of the Bill.

3.84 In providing for the making available right in terms of commercial purposes, the Copyright Bill 2015 offers potential for the adoption of a compulsory licensing scheme that would apply to activities related to the copyright terms. Such approach aligns favourably with a revenue-based licensing terms used by some platform firms.[160] However, by placing collecting societies at the centre of revenue collection[161] and performers and producers at the centre of revenue negotiation,[162] it appears the implementation of section 14(7) may be quite problematic given the potential for monopolistic abuses on the part of collecting societies.[163] Also, it is possible that the platform firms may still be able to procure a *gratis* licence leaving the collecting societies with no payment to enforce. In *VG Media Gesellschaft zur Verwertung der Urheber- und Leistungsschutzrechte von Medienunternehmen mbH v Google Inc. ('German Press Publishers')*, the press publishers represented by its collecting society, VG Media, instituted an antitrust complaint before the German competition regulator, *Bundeskartellamt*, against Google arguing that Google's market power enabled it to successfully procure a *gratis* licence despite the objective of the ancillary copyright, which was to provide revenue for press publishers.[164]

3.85 Consequently, even if the Bill is adopted in its current form, the lacuna created by the dichotomy between the personnel for revenue negotiation and that for revenue collection persists. In any event, it remains to be seen what provisions of the Bill would make it into the substantive Copyright Act.

The defendant's infringing activities

3.86 It has been explained in the previous sections of this chapter the meaning of the pertinent exclusive rights in the online context of multi-sided music platforms. This section looks at the activities in multi-sided music platforms (including the copyright terms) vis-à-vis the exclusive rights framework.

3.87 For copyright infringement liability to attach to a prospective defendant in the context of multi-sided music platforms, they must have undertaken a reproduction and/or communication of the music content to the public. This may be referred to as primary infringement. A prospective defendant may also be liable

160 See Ritala S, 'Pandora & Spotify: Legal issues and licensing requirements for interactive and non-interactive internet radio broadcasters' [2013] 54 *IDEA* 23, 42–43; Teague J, 'Saving the Spotify revolution: Recalibrating the power imbalance in digital copyright' [2012] *ExpressO* 27–28, http://works.bepress.com/jordan_teague/1/ (accessed 4 February 2019).

161 See s 14(5).

162 See s 14(3).

163 On the monopolistic abuse by collecting societies, see generally Jiang F and Gervais D, 'Collective management organizations in China: Practice, problems and possible solutions' [2012] 15(3) *Journal of World Intellectual Property* 221; Schroff S and Street J, 'The politics of the Digital Single Market: culture vs. competition vs. copyright' [2017] *Information, Communication & Society* 1; Von Lewinski S, 'EU challenges and solutions in the field of collective management of copyright and related Rights' [2014] 1 *Soc Persp.-J Legal Theory & Prac* 104.

164 Van Loon S, 'The power of Google: First mover advantage or abuse of a dominant position?' [2012] 22(9) *Google and the Law: Empirical Approaches to Legal Aspects of Knowledge-Economy Business Models* 34.

where they authorised other persons to undertake a reproduction and/or communication of the music content to the public. Infringement as a result of authorisation is usually referred to as secondary infringement. To succeed in an action for copyright infringement in the context of multi-sided music platforms, the platform firm must have by itself undertaken or authorised other persons to undertake a reproduction and/or communication of the music content to the public.

Primary or direct infringement

3.88 The members of the public are permitted to upload or submit music content on the platforms. Given that the storage and upload of a protected work in an electronic medium such as a digital platform is recognised as a reproduction of that work, uploaders may be directly infringing if they are neither the copyright owner nor persons authorised by the copyright owner.

3.89 Therefore, it is straightforward to show that the uploaders have directly infringed copyright in music content where such uploaders uploaded music content on to the platform without authorisation or licence. Such upload may be interpreted as reproduction of the music content. Similarly, where the platform firm uploads the music content to the platform by itself or following submissions from platform users (e.g. NotJustOk.com, TooXclusive.com, etc.), such platform firm may be liable for infringing the reproduction and/or communication to the public right if the upload is unauthorised.

3.90 As identified in Chapter 1, apart from providing a platform for user uploads of music content and storing music content at the direction of users, the platform firm's activities in relation to the music content and in the implementation of the licensing terms involve indexing, categorisation, deletion and filtering of music content as a way of attracting and retaining customers to the platform. In reality, the crux of the copyright terms established for multi-sided music platforms as evident from earlier paragraphs in this chapter hinges on access to the consumer, consumer's data and consumer's attention.[165] The payments and accounting are based on advertising revenue, which is hinged on consumer reach or access.

3.91 The copyright terms serve the purpose of gaining access to the copyright owners' consumers, consumers' data in terms of their likes and dislikes/tastes, and promotion for the artist (copyright owner). Outside user uploads, it is the indexing, storage and optimisation of user uploads and the provision of access to customer for the purposes of advertising that generates economic value in the context of multi-sided music platforms.

3.92 This may be directly infringing if it falls within the scope of the exclusive rights and if undertaken without the consent or authorisation of the relevant copyright owner. Where the copyright owner made the upload to the platform, it is taken that the copyright owner consented to the indexing, categorisation and

165 See also Chapter 2.

tagging of the music content under the relevant terms of use. However, where the copyright owner neither uploaded nor authorised the upload, the platform firm may be directly infringing. Of course, this depends on whether the activities on multi-sided music platforms fall within the scope of the exclusive rights conferred on the copyright owner in the relevant copyright statute.

3.93 Activities consisting of indexing, categorising, filtering and deleting relevant music files containing copyright content could be regarded as engaging in an act of communication to the public.[166] Further, and secondly, the indexing of the music files, compilation of view count, generating playlists, to enable users of the platform to locate the music content supports both the *gratis* licensing system and the revenue-based licensing system. According to the CJEU in *The Pirate Bay*:

> it is clear from the observations submitted to the Court that, in addition to a search engine, the online sharing platform TPB offers an index classifying the works under different categories, based on the type of the works, their genre or their popularity, within which the works made available are divided, with the platform's operators checking to ensure that a work has been placed in the appropriate category. In addition, those operators delete obsolete or faulty torrent files and actively filter some content. In the light of the foregoing, the making available and management of an online sharing platform, such as that at issue in the main proceedings, must be considered to be an act of communication for the purposes of Article 3(1) of Directive 2001/29.[167]

3.94 In the case of multi-sided music platforms, the licensing terms are formulated to address the fact that the platform firm is taking further independent steps to communicate the music content to the public and in making the work available to the public.[168] Indeed, it appears that this interpretation of the copyright terms is similar to the legal approach adopted by the PRS in its analysis of SoundCloud's behaviour in *PRS v SoundCloud*.[169] In this context, the PRS seems to have considered SoundCloud's conduct as infringing in the absence of a PRS licence for the relevant music content.

3.95 In the course of 2015, the PRS sent a letter to SoundCloud stating that given the nature of its activities on the SoundCloud.com website, the latter required a licence from the PRS to continue to undertake the specified activities.[170] Through this formal step, the copyright owner (that is, the PRS) indicates the copyright content made available without its licence. The requirements for this sort of letter under the notice and takedown procedure and/or the safe harbour regime are strict and specific. However, copyright owners whose copyright has been infringed directly and primarily by platform firms may proceed to sue for copyright infringement against the platform firm and may not be obliged to

166 Rosati 2017 supra at 9–11.

167 See paras 38 and 39.

168 Rosati 2017 supra at 10.

169 See para. 3.4.

170 See Greenstein N, 'Striking the right chord: A theoretical approach to balancing artists' intellectual property rights on remix audio-sharing platforms' [2016] 102 *Cornell L Rev* 211, 212–213.

request a takedown *per se*. In this regard, the PRS provided a list of works to which it owned copyright, and which were made available on the SoundCloud platform. Negotiations, which were commenced between the two organisations eventually, broke down leading to the commencement of the suit. However, the parties still picked up negotiations in the course of the suit, leading to an out-of-court settlement in 2016. A complete history of the case is well beyond the scope of this section, as the purpose is to address the facts relevant to the present discourse. Here, the focus is on the main legal features emerging from the case, to show its link with the *Pirate Bay* case and how both may apply to the South African and/or Nigerian regulatory framework.[171]

3.96 The legal features emanating from the *PRS v SoundCloud* case concerned the conduct of SoundCloud in relation to the exclusive rights of the PRS including whether such conduct infringed on PRS' copyright, the alleged existence of a duty to seek/obtain licence and the reliefs sought. The next paragraphs will focus on the analysis of PRS' line of reasoning. Due to the settlement reached by the PRS and SoundCloud in 2016 and given that the terms of settlement were not disclosed, the analysis of the parties' reasoning will be based mainly on the arguments emerging from the originating processes and the outcome of the announced settlement. Also, the appropriateness or otherwise of the court settlement reached in this case will not be addressed as the analysis is only relevant for the purpose of highlighting the potential of the copyright law regulatory framework for multi-sided music platforms in relation to South Africa and Nigeria.

3.97 One of the pertinent issues deserving due attention concerned PRS' rights protected by copyright law and implicated in the context of the suit against SoundCloud. PRS, it was contended, is an exclusive assignee of copyright in over six million songs (music content) and had the right *inter alia* to communicate the said music content to the public within the meaning of the UK Copyright Act.

3.98 The claimant/ PRS had alleged that SoundCloud had implemented an infringing behaviour aimed at denying PRS the proceeds of exploitation of PRS' exclusive rights.[172] Such conduct consisted *inter alia* in engaging in unauthorised acts of communication to the public. It was alleged that after the upload of the music content and its acceptance by the over 160 million SoundCloud user community, SoundCloud interacted and dealt with the content in such manner as to highlight its 'compatibility' with other content and to highlight 'compatible' artists as per its 'explore' section.[173] By these acts, SoundCloud was alleged to have infringed on PRS' exclusive right of communicating the relevant music content to the public.[174]

171 In the absence of case precedent, both South Africa and Nigeria may rely on foreign precedent for clarification. See the Nigerian case of *Adetoun Oladeji Nig Ltd v NB Plc* supra; *Moneyweb (Pty) Limited v Media 24 Limited and Another* supra at para. 103.

172 Two of the PRS claims were for damages and an account of profit. See page 17 of the Particulars of Claim in *PRS v SoundCloud*; Ginsburg 2017 supra at 81–85. See also Olubiyi 2014 supra at 93 on the import of the remedies available for copyright infringement.

173 See particularly, para. 6.6 of the Particulars of Claim.

174 See particularly, para. 13.1 of the Particulars of Claim.

3.99 In support of its allegation that SoundCloud was engaged in acts of communication to the public, PRS highlighted the primary goal pursued by SoundCloud. SoundCloud had a policy of open music, promoting those freely available to the public and uploaded by its users who are expected to be copyright owners or who have the requisite authority to upload such music. By its own admission, SoundCloud transcoded the music files,[175] operated automated indexing and search facilities[176]and also provided automated content recommendations.[177] However, it argued that these activities do not amount to using the music content in any manner pertaining to the exclusive rights of the copyright owner and as such, it had no obligation to seek a licence.

3.100 While there is no judicial precedent emanating from this case given the out-of-court settlement, the fact of the settlement and the fact that the parties have entered into and maintained formal licensing arrangement post-settlement supports the conclusion that the platform firms have a hand in the exploitation of the exclusive right. By extension, the licence of the copyright owner is required and a share of realised revenue, expected. However, the acceptance of the interpretation of the activities as one requiring a licence and affecting the copyright owners' exclusive rights depends on the specific legal framework. In the *PRS v SoundCloud* case, the right of communication to the public under UK's Copyright Act was allegedly infringed by the activities of SoundCloud itself. This raises the question of the availability and potential of the right of communication to the public under South African and Nigerian copyright law.

3.101 Presently, the right of communication to the public as stipulated in the Berne Convention and also the WCT and available under UK copyright law remains external to both the South African and Nigerian copyright system. A properly clarified right of communication to the public would need to be established in order to hold platform firms liable for primary infringement.

3.102 From the analysis of the *Pirate Bay* and the suit in *PRS v SoundCloud*, the indexing, tagging and optimising of music content based on users' preferences in the context of multi-sided music platforms may constitute acts of communication to the public which may require the relevant copyright owner's consent. While libraries are increasingly involved in similar conduct of indexing and tagging of protected works to aid their digital public lending services, they procure and reproduce the works themselves as against the case of the platform firms that rely on user uploads to index and tag protected content. Particularly, the ability to participate and actual participation of libraries in digital public lending has been subject of debate in many jurisdictions particularly in the EU and within the EU Member States.[178] Indeed, there have been concerns regarding the role of libraries as custodians and distributors of creative products, the economic

175 Paragraph 35 Statement of Defence.

176 Paragraph 40 and 41 Statement of Defence.

177 Paragraph 47 Statement of Defence.

178 Sganga C, 'Public e-lending and the CJEU: Chronicle of a missed revolution foretold' [2016] *Opinio Juris in Comparatione* 1, 7.

interests of authors as distinct from those of publishers, the legal categorisation of public lending practices and the appropriate regulatory approach to the issue of e-lending or public lending of digital books.[179] There is however significant consensus on the need for regulation of public lending practices and the undesirability of continued self-regulation in that field.[180] This debate and the increasing demand for access to e-books appear to have brought the indexing and search optimisation by libraries closer to the issues expressed for multi-sided music platforms. This is especially so when the import of the platform firms' activities is considered. However, the import of such indexing and related activities differ from that undertaken by libraries because of the background of the platform firm as advertising firms rather than authors and due to the profit-making nature to the communication in question as evidenced by the receipt of advertising revenue.[181] This means that providing a *gratis* licence in the context of the licensing terms is likely to result in loss of revenue that would have accrued to the copyright owner.[182] Without adequately remunerating these copyright owners (especially when they are SMEs), the implementation of the copyright terms may lead to revenue losses and anticompetitive effects on the copyright marketplace.[183]

3.103 Again, the availability of such remedies depends on the availability of the right, which must have been infringed. By extension, the availability and application of the right in the case of South Africa and Nigeria depends on their respective copyright laws, which have been examined in the previous paragraphs.

3.104 But in its current form, neither the relevant copyright statutes in both South Africa and Nigeria nor the Copyright Amendment Bill in both countries, provide for a properly clarified right of communication to the public. In the case of South Africa's Copyright Amendment Bill, it merely provides for the right without any clarification regarding key concepts such as what constitutes communication, definition of 'public' and the import of profit-making intention. In effect, such approach encourages innovators with new technologies to enter the copyright sector but results in the adoption of copyright terms that delivers value to platform firms at the expense of copyright owners and even other copyright users.[184]

Secondary or indirect infringement

3.105 As stated earlier, apart from engaging in unauthorised exercise of the exclusive rights conferred on the copyright owner, copyright may also be

179 Ibid. at 6–7, 10–11.

180 Ibid. at 12–13.

181 Rosati 2017 supra at 5.

182 See Ginsburg 2017 supra at 74.

183 The anticompetitive effects of inadequate or no remuneration for SMEs is discussed in Chapter 5.

184 Rens A, 'Department repeats mistakes of others in bid to alter copyright law' (*Business Day*, 13 October 2017), www.businesslive.co.za/bd/national/2017-10-13-department-repeats-mistakes-of-others-in-bid-to-alter-copyright-law/ (accessed 16 October 2017).

infringed by a person who authorised or induced another to engage in an infringing act. This is known as secondary or indirect infringement.[185]

3.106 In the case of multi-sided music platforms, attention appear to have largely focused on the activities of platform users and how such may have been induced or authorised by the platform firm within the context of the European Union (EU) and the United States (US) laws.[186] Because such reproduction of music content is undertaken by a large number of anonymous and possibly indigent users, who are usually spread across multiple jurisdictions outside the easy reach of the copyright owner, it is difficult to enforce the reproduction rights against them. Accordingly, the copyright owners attempt to enforce the reproduction right against platform firms on the grounds that they (the platform firms) authorised or induced the unlicensed reproduction by their users. In this regard, the argument or cause of action seems to be that the business model of platform firms is based on users' actions *per se*.[187]

3.107 Section 23 of the South African Copyright Act provides that 'copyright shall be infringed by any person, not being the owner of the copyright, who, without the licence of such owner, does or causes any other person to do, in the Republic, any act which the owner has the exclusive rights to do or to authorize'.

3.108 Similar provision is stipulated in section 15 of the Nigerian Copyright Act, which provides that 'copyright is infringed by any person who without the licence or authorization of the owner of the copyright (a) does, or causes any other person to do an act, the doing of which is controlled by copyright'. However, there has been no (clear) judicial interpretation of the expression 'causes any other person to do' in both South African and Nigerian courts.

3.109 In the absence of a clear judicial pronouncement on the meaning and factors for the court to consider in finding liability for 'causes any other person to do', it is doubtful whether the activities of platform firms in the context of multi-sided music platforms may be construed as causing users to infringe. For instance, it is not clear what relationship must exist between the platform firms (as secondary infringers) and the actual primary infringer. By extension, it is not clear whether there needs to be a relationship of authority or whether mere facilitation (or inducement) will suffice to affix liability.

3.110 Some scholars have suggested that the expression (i.e. causes any person to do) be given a 'purposive interpretation' that is not too broad as to encompass acts like 'facilitation, inducement, permission, aid and abet, persuasion, incitement and procurement' and not too narrow as to require 'perceived authority' between primary and secondary infringer.[188] In any event, the safe harbour regime,[189] which relies on the activities of platform users as a foundation for

185 Faturoti 2017 supra.

186 Ibid. See also Aganga 2013 supra.

187 See *Viacom v YouTube* supra; *GEMA v YouTube* supra.

188 Faturoti 2017 supra at 19.

189 Lemley M and Reese R, 'Reducing digital copyright infringement without restricting innovation' [2004] 56(6) *Stanford Law Review* 1345, 1367.

establishing the role of the platform firms, and which in certain circumstances exempts or limits the liability of platform firms for the activities of the said users of their platform, is a popular defence to secondary infringement claims.

Defences

Safe harbour regime

3.111 As stated earlier in this chapter,[190] platform firms sometimes have notice and takedown procedures where they undertake to remove ('take down') infringing content when notified by the relevant copyright owner. In this context, the platform firm does not upload the music content on the platform and is not directly responsible in the event that the uploaded content is found to be infringing. Rather, the notice and takedown procedure is stipulated to enable the platform firms enjoy the exemption or limitation of liability available under the statutory regime commonly referred to as the 'safe harbour' regime.

3.112 As described earlier, the safe harbour regime provides a limitation of liability framework, which protects providers of hosting (and other internet-related) services from liability for their users' reproduction of copyright-protected content unless they received actual notice or became aware of facts or circumstances indicating infringing content or activity.

3.113 In the context of multi-sided music platforms, platform firms are exempt from liability for copyright infringement resulting from the actions of their users in uploading and streaming the music content.[191] Such exemption applies in specified instances and in most cases the exemptions apply insofar as the platform firms act expeditiously to remove or disable access to infringing content upon notification. Usually, because most platform firms are established in Europe or in the US, the platform firms adopt the safe harbour regime applicable in either regime, as part of their licensing terms.[192] Accordingly, the safe harbour regime statutorily provided for under section 512(c) of the US Digital Millennium Copyright Act, 1998 (DMCA) and Arts 12 to 14 of the EU E-Commerce Directive provides one of the pillars of the copyright terms in the context of multi-sided music platforms.[193] Under section 512(c) of the DMCA, anyone who stored music content 'at the direction of a user' on a 'system or network controlled by or operated by the service provider' would ordinarily incur copyright infringement liability unless such person or entity falls within any of the criteria (safe harbour) provided under the statute. These criteria include that such person or entity:

> (A) (i) does not have actual knowledge that the material or an activity using the material on the system or network is infringing;
>
> (ii) in the absence of such actual knowledge, is not aware of facts or circumstances from which infringing activity is apparent; or

190 See para. 3.9.
191 See Lemley and Reese 2004 supra at 1367–1368.
192 Examples include YouTube, SoundCloud, Facebook.
193 See Perel and Elkin-Koren 2015 supra at 477.

(iii) upon obtaining such knowledge or awareness, acts expeditiously to remove, or disable access to, the material;

(B) does not receive a financial benefit directly attributable to the infringing activity, in a case in which the service provider has the right and ability to control such activity; and

(C) upon notification of claimed infringement as described in paragraph (3), responds expeditiously to remove, or disable access to, the material that is claimed to be infringing or to be the subject of infringing activity.

3.114 While the EU E-Commerce Directive is different in that it provides for all forms of online content including copyright-protected content, it makes quite similar safe harbour provisions.[194] For instance, art 14 provides that:

> Where an information society service is provided that consists of the storage of information provided by a recipient of the service, Member States shall ensure that the service provider is not liable for the information stored at the request of a recipient of the service, on condition that:
>
> (a) the provider does not have actual knowledge of illegal activity or information and, as regards claims for damages, is not aware of facts or circumstances from which the activity or information is apparent; or
>
> (b) the provider, upon obtaining such knowledge or awareness, acts expeditiously to remove or to disable access to the information.[195]

3.115 Efficient takedown procedures enable the platform firms to meet the requirements for safe harbour protection and avoid liability for 'authorising', 'enabling' or 'directing' the infringement of their registered users. Indeed, the efficacy or validity of the takedown procedures to exempt the platform firms from liability for the infringement of their users has been challenged without much success in several suits in the US and within the EU.

3.116 In *Viacom v YouTube*,[196] Viacom argued *inter alia* that YouTube was generally aware that the reproduction of music content on its platform was infringing and, for that reason, the safe harbour protection should not avail YouTube. Damages sought were to address the reproduction of copyright-protected content owned by Viacom. The Court rejected this argument holding that the fact that the language of the statute required expeditious removal of infringing material, it meant that the internet service provider (in this case, YouTube) would require prior knowledge of the specific infringing material.[197] The applicable test was, therefore, one of distinction between subjective and objective standard. To have actual knowledge of infringement under the DMCA, an internet service provider (ISP) must subjectively know of specific instances of infringement. To have the

194 Leonard P, 'Safe harbors in choppy waters – Building a sensible approach to liability of internet intermediaries in Australia' [2010] 3 *J Int'l Media & Ent L* 221, 247.

195 Directive 2000/31/EC of the European Parliament and of the Council of 8 June 2000 on certain legal aspects of information society services, in particular electronic commerce, in the Internal Market ('Directive on electronic commerce').

196 *Viacom International, Inc. v YouTube, Inc.* 676 F.3d 19, United States Court of Appeals, Second Circuit, decision of 5 April 2012, para. 22.

197 Ibid. at para. 89.

requisite offending knowledge of infringement, the ISP must be aware of facts that would have made the existence of specific acts of infringement objectively obvious to a reasonable person.[198] According to Judge Stanton of the US District Court for the Southern District of New York in his summary judgment:

> The tenor of the [DMCA] provisions is that the phrases 'actual knowledge that the material or an activity' is infringing, and 'facts or circumstances' indicating infringing activity, describe knowledge of specific and identifiable infringements of particular individual items. Mere knowledge of prevalence of such activity in general is not enough. That is consistent with an area of the law devoted to protection of distinctive individual works, not of libraries. To let knowledge of a generalized practice of infringement in the industry, or of a proclivity of users to post infringing materials, impose responsibility on service providers to discover which of their users' postings infringe a copyright would contravene the structure and operation of the DMCA. As stated in *Perfect 10, Inc. v. CCBill LLC*, 488 F.3d 1102, (9th Cir. 2007): The DMCA notification procedures place the burden of policing copyright infringement-identifying the potentially infringing material and adequately documenting infringement-squarely on the owners of the copyright. We decline to shift a substantial burden from the copyright owner to the provider.[199]

3.117 Notwithstanding this decision, the Court was persuaded by some of the arguments made by Viacom particularly the argument that specific knowledge of infringement was not required to show the existence of right and ability to control on the part of YouTube. For this reason, the Court remanded this issue to the district court for further proceedings.[200] In April 2013, the district court again ruled in favour of YouTube, and Viacom once again appealed. However, the parties concluded an out-of-court settlement in March 2014, shortly before the time scheduled for oral arguments on the second appeal.[201]

3.118 In the case of *PRS v SoundCloud* instituted in the UK, whether or not the E-Commerce Directive's safe harbour provisions would interpret SoundCloud's business model as making it 'aware of specific facts that would make specific acts of infringement obvious', was not tested after all due to the settlement reached between the PRS and SoundCloud.[202] In the originating processes, PRS had claimed that some of SoundCloud's action amounted to secondary copyright infringement as it allegedly authorised and/or induced its users to infringe. It was alleged that SoundCloud had implemented this infringing behaviour after getting users of its platform to upload copyright-protected music content on its

198 Notwithstanding this decision, the Court was persuaded by Viacom's argument that 'item specific' knowledge was required to prove that YouTube's financial benefit from the infringement. See para. 89(4) of the Judgment.

199 718 F. Supp. 2d at 523.

200 See para. 89(4) of the Judgment.

201 For a record of court filings in this case, see Justia Dockets & Filings (2015). *Viacom International, Inc. et al v YouTube, Inc. et al.* Available at https://dockets.justia.com/docket/new-york/nysdce/1:2007cv02103/302164 (accessed 29 January 2017).

202 See Prsformusic.com (2015). *PRS for Music and SoundCloud reach licensing agreement.* Available at www.prsformusic.com/press/2015/prs-for-music-and-soundcloud-reach-a-multi-territory-licensing-agreement-ending-legal-proceedings (accessed 19 March 2017).

SoundCloud.com platform.[203] In its Statement of Defence, SoundCloud *inter alia* sought to rely on the existence of the safe harbour regime, which it felt shielded it from any potential obligation to seek a licence or face liability for infringement. It averred that its terms of use outlined a free, non-exclusive licensing scheme which it required all users to adhere to in uploading their copyright-protected content. It further alleged that the PRS should have notified it of infringing content to enable SoundCloud to take down the content uploaded by users on its platform.[204]

3.119 As is the case with reliance on South African or Nigerian copyright law, as the case may be in instances where the copyright owner neither uploaded nor authorised the upload of its music content on to the platform, the availability of the safe harbour defence depends on the domestic law. For South Africa, the safe harbour defence may be available to platform firms in appropriate circumstances. In 2002, South Africa enacted the Electronic Communications Transactions Act to recognise the need to protect internet intermediaries from copyright infringement liability given the nature of their services and the way in which the internet operates. In this regard, South Africa's Electronic Communications Transactions Act exempts hosting, caching, linking and conduit intermediaries from copyright infringement liability when they act expeditiously to remove infringing content upon notification.[205] Here, platform firms may be protected only where they are members of an organisation approved by the Minister of Communication.[206]

3.120 As stated earlier, Nigeria does not yet operate a safe harbour regime in its Copyright Act but there is a proposed safe harbour regime in its Copyright Amendment Bill 2015.[207] This would mean that the defence is not available to platform firms sued in Nigeria. Therefore, apart from the general defences discussed below, platform firms sued in Nigeria for secondary infringement would have to prove that its activities did not amount to 'causing another to engage in an infringing act'.

The value gap proposal and the safe harbour regime

3.121 With the emergence of new business models and approaches to deploying digital platforms, there have been calls to abolish or considerably reform the safe harbour regime particularly as it applies to hosting services.[208] Specifically, the regime has been identified as underpinning the copyright terms in the context

203 See para. 6 of the Particulars of Claim.

204 Para. 63 of the Statement of Defence.

205 See Chapter XI, ss 70–79.

206 Comninos A, 'Intermediary liability in South Africa' [2012] *Association for Progressive Communications, Intermediary Liability in Africa Research Papers* 3, 12.

207 See s 51 of the Copyright Amendment Bill.

208 Edwards L, 'Role and responsibility of the internet intermediaries in the field of copyright and related right' (*Wipo.int*, 2011), www.wipo.int/export/sites/www/copyright/en/doc/role_and_responsibility_of_the_internet_intermediaries_final.pdf (accessed 31 January 2017).

of multi-sided music platforms.[209] Also, the regime has been held responsible for the paltry payments or revenue from the platform firms and alleged to be unsupportive of copyright law's objective of incentivising creativity. The claim is that the regime enables massive reproduction of music content and thus, that the platform firms exploit the reproduction right to the detriment or to the exclusion of copyright owners.[210] Seen from this perspective, the failure to ascribe liability to platform firms for the actions of users of the platform in streaming the music content on the grounds that such should be regarded as authorised or induced by the platform firms is held to be a fault arising from the safe harbour regime. This argument as conceptualised in the 'value gap' statement, is that such platform firms should not be able to enjoy the safe harbour protection. Instead, the platform firms should enter into licensing agreements with copyright owners because they are involved in the exploitation of the reproduction right through their users.

3.122 Value gap is the most cited example of the challenge for the copyright system arising from multi-sided music platforms and has been described as a form of unfair competition.[211] According to the IFPI, the value gap makes licensed music platforms to compete unfavourably with unlicensed music platforms. In this regard, the extant copyright law is identified as clearly compelling subscription-based services such as Spotify to seek and obtain a licence from relevant copyright owners prior to operating its platform and deploying the use of music content available on their platform. Conversely, in the case of ad-based services which rely on music content uploaded by the users of the platform to operate their core services, the provisions of the extant copyright law which may require such firm to seek licences *a priori*[212] is weakened. The requirement of licence in this case being to avoid being held liable for authorising the user uploads. This is because the safe harbour regime will not attach infringement liability on the platform firms for platform users' reproduction of music content unless it is shown that the platform firm has the requisite knowledge of infringement. In other words, the enabling of user upload of music content is interpreted as obliging the platform firm to seek a licence. Therefore, the safe harbour exemption which is made on the basis that platform firms are not to be held liable for enabling (or authorising) their users' actions in uploading or reproducing music content, is held to be problematic.[213] According to the IFPI:

> The value gap describes the growing mismatch between the value that user upload services, such as YouTube, extract from music and the revenue returned to the music community – those who are creating and investing in music. The value gap is the biggest threat to the future sustainability of the music industry. . . . Inconsistent applications of online liability laws have emboldened certain services to claim that they are not liable for the music they make available to the public. Today, services such as YouTube, which have developed sophisticated on-demand music platforms,

209 See IFPI 2017 supra at 34.
210 Ibid.
211 Ibid. at 25.
212 See Faturoti 2017 supra.
213 IFPI 2017 supra at 24–28.

> use this as a shield to avoid licensing music on fair terms like other digital services, claiming they are not legally responsible for the music they distribute on their site.

3.123 This statement, when applied to the context of multi-sided music platforms, means that a value gap exists when platform firms are able to procure unfair licensing terms[214] from copyright owners for the use of their music content within the platform. The licensing terms under which platform firms either procure a royalty-free, revenue-free licence or unilaterally impose revenue-sharing arrangements on terms favourable only to them are considered to be unfair.[215] Such conduct results in the platform firm being able to enjoy the benefits of the music content with little or no corresponding revenue to the copyright owner.[216] The objective of incentivising creativity is allegedly derailed in so far as copyright owners are unable to recoup their investments or exploit the right to reproduce their works as a consequence of the conduct.[217] The principal concern is that the business model of the music copyright industry, which involves making considerable investments in music production and artist development, and expectation of revenue from reproduction becomes unsustainable.[218] Platform firms are then able to overrun the copyright owners, resulting in lesser revenue for new (but significant) uses of the copyright owners' creative outputs.[219]

3.124 To understand better why the copyright terms established in multi-sided music platforms is asserted as creating a value gap, some considerations deserve attention. A subscription-based service, which involves a platform firm personally uploading music content on to its platform, is interpreted as directly engaging in the act of reproduction or making available of the music content to the public. As explained in this chapter, such platform firm will require the licence of the relevant copyright owners if it is to avoid liability for copyright infringement.[220] Accordingly, such platform firm may literally be 'at the mercy' of copyright owners whose music content is required to attract subscribers to its platform.[221] Licensing arrangements in such cases are somewhat on a more equitable terrain or more accurately, the copyright owner is able to exercise the control that copyright law intends as it may refuse the licence.[222] However, in the case of multi-sided music platforms, licensing arrangements between the platform firm and the copyright owner are not made before the commencement of the platform firm's services. This is because the reproduction and making available of the music content is made primarily by users of the platform and because

---

214 See IFPI 2017 supra at 33.

215 Ibid.

216 Ibid.

217 The existing link between the exclusive rights and competition in the music copyright industry has already been scrutinised in Chapter 2 on the relationship between copyright and competition.

218 See IFPI 2017 supra at 33.

219 Ibid.

220 See para. 3.5.

221 Ritala 2013 supra at 42–43.

222 Of course, they may overstep their bounds. See Ritala 2013 supra at 42–43; Also Teague 2012 supra at 27–28.

upon meeting the specified conditions, the safe harbour regime exempts platform firms from liability for their users' actions, liability for storing or hosting the copyright-protected content, including any rights of the copyright owner to compel a licence, arises after the fact. In explaining the existence of a value gap, a comparison between payments from 'prior licensed' platform firms and payments from 'post-licensed' platform firms shows the revenue from the latter coming up short.[223] For this reason, the IFPI and several copyright owner groups have lauded proposed legislative reforms to copyright law that would require platform firms that rely on user uploads to seek licensing arrangements *a priori*.[224] Such legislative changes are expected to close the value gap and address the competition concerns. Specifically, the IFPI supported the proposed reforms in the EU in terms of the so-called value gap proposal embodied in the proposed art 13(1) of the Proposal for a Directive on Copyright in the Digital Single Market (DSM).[225] The European Council in 2019 voted in favour of the latest version of the Directive on Copyright in the Digital Single Market (DSM Directive)[226] with the provisions of the proposed art 13 revised and renumbered as art 17.

3.125 Article 17 of the DSM Directive provides that:

1 Member States shall provide that an online content-sharing service provider performs an act of communication to the public or an act of making available to the public for the purposes of this Directive when it gives the public access to copyright-protected works or other protected subject matter uploaded by its users.
An online content-sharing service provider shall therefore obtain an authorisation from the rightholders referred to in Article 3(1) and (2) of Directive 2001/29/EC, for instance by concluding a licensing agreement, in order to communicate to the public or make available to the public works or other subject matter.

2 Member States shall provide that, where an online content-sharing service provider obtains an authorisation, for instance by concluding a licensing agreement, that authorisation shall also cover acts carried out by users of the services falling within the scope of Article 3 of Directive 2001/29/EC when they are not acting on a commercial basis or where their activity does not generate significant revenues.

3 When an online content-sharing service provider performs an act of communication to the public or an act of making available to the public under the conditions laid down in this Directive, the limitation of

223 See IFPI 2017 supra at 33.

224 Ibid.

225 See Directive of the European Parliament and of the Council on Copyright in the Digital Single Market – COM (2016)593.

226 European Parliament legislative resolution of 26 March 2019 on the proposal for a directive of the European Parliament and of the Council on copyright in the Digital Single Market COM(2016)0593-C8–0383/2016–2016/0280 (COD).

liability established in Article 14(1) of Directive 2000/31/EC shall not apply to the situations covered by this Article.

The first subparagraph of this paragraph shall not affect the possible application of Article 14(1) of Directive 2000/31/EC to those service providers for purposes falling outside the scope of this Directive.

4 If no authorisation is granted, online content-sharing service providers shall be liable for unauthorised acts of communication to the public, including making available to the public, of copyright-protected works and other subject matter, unless the service providers demonstrate that they have:

(a) made best efforts to obtain an authorisation, and
(b) made, in accordance with high industry standards of professional diligence, best efforts to ensure the unavailability of specific works and other subject matter for which the rightholders have provided the service providers with the relevant and necessary information; and in any event
(c) acted expeditiously, upon receiving a sufficiently substantiated notice from the rightholders, to disable access to, or to remove from, their websites the notified works or other subject matter, and made best efforts to prevent their future uploads in accordance with point (b).

5 In determining whether the service provider has complied with its obligations under paragraph 4, and in light of the principle of proportionality, the following elements, among others, shall be taken into account:

(a) the type, the audience and the size of the service and the type of works or other subject matter uploaded by the users of the service; and
(b) the availability of suitable and effective means and their cost for service providers.

3.126 Indeed, the cases instituted in the EU and in the US against platform firms as discussed in this chapter, have sought to address the reproduction of copyrighted content arising in the business model context, with specific focus on the perceived 'mismatch' between the value from platform firm's use of music content and the corresponding value received by the music industry.[227] The objective in each of these cases was to prevent platform firms from creating a value gap in the music industry by failing to adequately reward copyright owners for the exploitation of the reproduction right which is exclusive to the copyright owner.[228] In this regard, the US and EU courts have often elaborated similar perspectives, refusing to accept that the respective copyright owners had a valid claim to

227 See *Viacom v YouTube* supra; *GEMA v YouTube* supra.
228 Ibid. See also IFPI 2017 supra at 33.

licensing from platform firms because of their (platform firm) users' activities.[229] While it is to be noted that the value gap proposal has experienced criticisms peculiar to its conflict with other EU Directives, such as the prohibition against the imposition of a general monitoring duty,[230] the similarities in the outcomes of these cases help to explain the misconstruction inherent in the conceptualisation of the value gap as a challenge to the copyright system.

3.127 As identified in this chapter, apart from providing a platform for user uploads of music content and storing music content at the direction of users, the platform firm's activities in relation to the music content and in the implementation of the licensing terms involve indexing, categorisation, deletion and filtering of music content as a way of attracting and retaining customers to the platform.[231] Accordingly, it is argued that the perception that the implementation and application of the copyright terms sits in opposition to the exploitation of the reproduction right is misguided. By extension, the perception that the safe harbour regime requires massive reform, which may exclude platform firms from the safe harbour protection or require licensing for user-uploads is largely unwarranted. In reality, the crux of the copyright terms in multi-sided music platforms as evident from this chapter is hinged on access to the consumer, consumer's data and consumer's attention. Remarkably, the payments and accounting from the platform firms are not connected to the traditional exploitation of the reproduction rights but have been developed by advertising calculations, which are hinged on consumer reach or access.

3.128 The copyright terms in particular, serve the purpose of gaining access to the copyright owners' consumers, consumers' data in terms of their likes and dislikes/tastes, and promotion for the artist (copyright owner). While proponents of the value gap proposal see reproduction rights as the main value metric in the copyright terms, the evidence points to access to the consumer and consumer's data as the main value metric. In the circumstances, it is argued that one of the key copyright law implications of multi-sided music platforms is the erosion of the significance of the reproduction right.

3.129 The argument that the value and utility of the reproduction right diminishes in the context of the copyright terms of multi-sided music platforms contributes to the plethora of calls from scholars and policymakers for a shift in focus for copyright regulation. Concerning the view that the reproduction right as presently constituted should no longer be the exclusive preserve of the copyright owner, it is evident that the reproduction right involving user uploads particularly in multi-sided music platforms context does not result in (much) economic

229 In the relevant cases, the courts in both jurisdictions declined to hold the platform firms liable for their users' activities.

230 See Rosati E, 'Neighbouring rights for publishers: are national and (possible) EU initiatives lawful?' [2016] 47(5) *IIC-International Review of Intellectual Property and Competition Law* 569 (Rosati 2016a).

231 For example, para. 3.65.

value.[232] Rather, it is the indexing, storage and optimisation of user uploads and the provision of access to customer for the purposes of advertising, that generates economic value in multi-sided music platforms context.

3.130 A case in point concerns the introduction of an ancillary copyright protection for press publishers in Italy, Spain and Germany.[233] By virtue of this protection, press publishers have the exclusive right of press products' communication to the public for commercial purposes within one year after being published.[234] In Germany, this right required Google to pay press publishers for its (Google's) use of links to news items from press publishers in its Google News service.[235] In effect, the legislature and the participants considered reproduction rights to be the revenue generator – in other words, the platform firm, Google, was exploiting the reproduction right held by the press publishers. The expectation was that the provision for the ancillary copyright would enable press publishers to earn revenue whenever their press content is reproduced and made available through freemium-based services on search engines.[236]

3.131 Despite this provision, the press publishers in those countries failed to receive any revenue and even lost 'traffic' (access to readers/consumers) when they sought to exploit/enforce the reproduction rights.[237] In the case of Germany, the press publishers were 'forced' to provide Google with a *gratis* licence regarding the ancillary copyright. This is because the revenue generator in the multi-sided platforms involving news content was from advertising and data in terms of 'traffic' and the ancillary right or reproduction right proved to be no revenue earner.[238]

3.132 A paradigm shift from reproduction rights exploitation towards access to consumers can be noticed, particularly in the approach of the platform firms in multi-sided music platforms context. Today, more and more platform firms stress the importance of the access to the consumer by creating ticketing and concert opportunities based on music content that platform users and consumers love.[239]

---

232 See Angelopoulos C, 'EU copyright reform: Outside the safe harbours, intermediary liability capsizes into incoherence' (*Kluwer Copyright Blog*, 6 October 2016), http://copyrightblog.kluweriplaw.com/2016/10/06/eu-copyright-reform-outside-safe-harbours-intermediary-liability-capsizes-incoherence/ (accessed 26 December 2017).

233 See Rosati 2016a supra at 572; Vesterdorf B, 'The effect of failure to notify the Spanish and German ancillary copyright laws' [2015] 5 *European Intellectual Property Review*, https://ssrn.com/abstract=2558029 (accessed 5 September 2017).

234 See Jing-jing Y, 'Review of the 8th Amendment of the German Copyright Act: Ancillary copyright for press publishers: A backward legislation step in the era of the Internet?' [2015] 2 *Journal of Science, Technology and Law* 5.

235 Ibid.

236 See Rosati 2016a supra at 471–473.

237 Ibid. See also Stadler 2007 supra at 903 where Stadler makes a convincing argument against the utility of the reproduction rights for copyright owners.

238 See Ramalho A, 'EU competence to create a neighbouring right for publishers? The small pieces make up the big picture' (*Kluwer Copyright Blog*, 5 September 2016) http://copyrightblog.kluweriplaw.com/2016/09/05/eu-competence-create-neighbouring-right-publishers-small-pieces-make-big-picture/ (accessed 26 December 2017); Höppner T, *EU copyright reform: the case for a related right for press publishers*. CREATe Working Paper 2017/08 (April 2017).

239 See Hu 2017 supra.

Therefore, it is argued that it behoves copyright owners to monetise access to the consumers of their music content. Further, the copyright terms should not be viewed as an exploitation or exercise of reproduction rights or based on the safe harbour regime, but rather as a method deployed by the platform firms to gain access to the consumers and consumers' data.

3.133 In this context, the deployment of multi-sided music platforms necessarily entailed a new approach to the analysis of the scope of copyright protection, particularly the parameters of the reproduction right as value metric. The fact that the source of revenue within the business model flows from advertising may be interpreted to mean that the copyright system based on and the economic right of reproduction of music content (or any copyrighted content) have been jettisoned as the value metric in the copyright ecosystem. The new value metrics operate outside the reproduction of content to generate revenue from the interaction with the content. In these cases, the exploitation of the reproduction rights is discarded, and its 'monetisation' superseded by other income streams. Multi-sided music platforms introduce revenue streams that are more external to the remuneration system based on the reproduction of music content. As such, a copyright law system focused on the expectation of revenue from every reproduction of copyright-protected content blurs the consideration of other viable revenue opportunities that free and/or uninhibited reproduction may have offered. It is argued that such restriction is disadvantageous because digitisation involves such rampant reproduction to the extent that making reproduction exclusive to the copyright owner is near futile. The focus is no longer on leveraging on the reproduction rights *per se*; the focus is on the consumer. The very implication of the copyright terms within multi-sided music platforms is to remove the focus on copyright protection system based on reproduction and place it squarely on the consumers of the 'business opportunity' created by the music content. It follows that the platform firm's activity cannot be properly assessed through the lens of reproduction. The focus here is on the activities of the platform firm itself, which clearly does not amount to reproduction of the music content.

Limitations regarding the subject matter of protection

3.134 As indicated earlier, a defendant in an action for copyright infringement may escape liability if such defendant's actions fall within activities limited and/or exempt from copyright protection. Limitations and exceptions such as limit on copyright subject matter, originality and fixation requirements, the exclusion of ideas, and the duration of rights, are of more general application and may not be specifically relevant to the online context of multi-sided music platforms.[240]

240 See Challis B, '*The 1709 Blog: What's wrong with the 'Blurred Lines' copyright ruling?*' (The1709blog.blogspot.com, March 2015), http://the1709blog.blogspot.com/2015/03/whats-wrong-with-blurred-lines.html (accessed 7 April 2015); Corbett 2011 supra at 515; Heald 2014b supra; Elkin-Koren 2016 supra at 4, 12–14.

Nevertheless, they are discussed in the ensuing paragraph as they may still avail a defendant sued for copyright infringement.

3.135 Copyright protects only original expressions and does not protect ideas, procedures and the like. According to the TRIPS Agreement to which both South Africa and Nigeria are signatories, 'copyright protection shall extend to expressions and not to ideas, procedures, methods of operation or mathematical concepts as such'.[241] Even when copyright subsists in a work, copyright applies only to copying the expression or substantial part thereof, but it is not an infringement to copy any facts contained therein or any idea, process, system and so on that the work describes.[242] As a result, a defendant may be able to show that he is not liable for copyright infringement because copyright does not subsist in the work allegedly infringed.

3.136 On a related matter, copyright law requires that for a work to be eligible for copyright under the Copyright Act, sufficient effort must have been expended on the work to give it an original character and it must have been fixed in a definite medium directly perceivable or perceivable with the aid of any device or machine.[243] In essence, the originality requirement demands that the work is an independent creation of the creator and that some exertion is expected from the author. In South Africa a work is considered original if, in addition to independent creation, 'sufficient skill and effort' have been expended in creating it.[244]The originality requirement is interpreted in substantially the same way in Nigeria.[245]

3.137 By protecting only original expressions, copyright protection will by implication be unavailable to works that do not measure up to such standards. Therefore, a defendant in an action for copyright infringement may aver in its defence that the work alleged to have been infringed is not original.

3.138 In *Moneyweb (Pty) Limited v Media 24 Limited and Another*, the High Court of South Africa held that four of the contested news articles did not enjoy copyright protection because those articles failed the originality test. In applying the originality test, the court considered whether the articles were verbatim report of the interview transcripts on which they were based and concluded that it was not evident how much of the article was the writer's own work or a repetition of what the writer heard.[246]

---

241 Article 9(2) TRIPS Agreement.

242 Indeed, the fact that the making of a work involved some form of copyright infringement would not alone constitute grounds for ineligibility. See s 1(4) of the Nigerian Copyright Act. See also Ola 2014 supra at 12.

243 See section 1(2)(a) and (b) of the Nigerian Copyright Act. Also, see the South African case of *Waylite Diary CC v First National Bank Ltd* 1995 (1) SA 645.

244 See Harms 2012 supra at 201–209. Also Dean OH, *Handbook of South African Copyright Law*, loose-leaf updates (Juta 2006), paras 1.15–1.17.

245 Nwogu M, 'Copyright law and the menace of piracy in Nigeria' [2015] 34 *JL Pol'y & Globalization* 113, 114–115.

246 Paras 25, 28, 34 and 39.

Limited term of protection

3.139 Copyright protection does not exist in perpetuity. Rather, the protection lasts for a stated period. In the case of Nigeria, the term of copyright protection in a musical work is life of the author plus 70 years.[247] Upon the expiration of the term of protection, the protected work is said to enter the public domain.[248] A work created in 1920, whose author died in 1950, will enter the public domain in 2020. Once a given work enters the public domain, there is no risk of infringement and no need for permission or licence to use the work. As a defence to copyright infringement, a defendant may aver that copyright term in the allegedly infringed work has expired.[249]

Actions outside the exclusive rights framework

3.140 The exclusive rights available to the copyright owner are specifically delineated under the copyright statute. The rights that are of particular application in the context of multi-sided music platforms have been discussed in this chapter. It therefore goes without saying that activities which do not fall within the scope of the exclusive rights framework would not form the subject matter of an action for copyright infringement.[250] Accordingly, in defending an action for copyright infringement in the context of multi-sided music platforms, the defendant may in appropriate circumstances show that the alleged infringing activities are outside the scope of the exclusive economic rights available to the copyright owners under the copyright framework.

Copyright terms and the scope of the limitations and exceptions framework

3.141 The parameters of what users of protected work can do in relation to any protected work depends, not only on the scope of copyright protection, but also on the limitations and exceptions to copyright protection.[251] Put differently, the scope of limitations and exceptions to copyright protection may determine whether or not a copyright user's activities require a licence. In the context of the multi-sided music platforms and the copyright framework, a defendant may in appropriate circumstances show that its activities in relation to the music content fall within the relevant limitations and exceptions to copyright protection.

---

247 See s 2(2) and the First Schedule to the Nigerian Copyright Act. The duration of protection in the case of South Africa is 50 years. See s 3(2) of the South African Copyright Act.

248 Corbett 2011 supra at 518.

249 Erickson and Kretschmer 2014 supra at 6; Deazley R, *Rethinking copyright: history, theory, language* (Edward Elgar 2006), 118. Also Greenleaf G and Bond C, 'Public rights in copyright: What makes up Australia's public domain' [2013] 23 *Australian Intellectual Property Journal* 111, 132.

250 This is one of the maxim of statutory interpretation: *expressio unius personae vel rei, est exclusio alterius or inclusio unius est exceusio alterius* – meaning 'the express mention of one person or thing is the exclusion of another or the inclusion of one is the exclusion of another; respectively'. See *Attorney-General of the Federation & 2 Ors v Alhaji Atiku Abubakar & 3 Ors* (S.C. 31/2007) [2007] NGSC 118 (20 April 2007).

251 See Chapter 2.

The scope of the limitations and exceptions under international copyright framework

3.142 Article 9(2) of the Berne Convention, to which both South Africa and Nigeria are signatories, provides the parameters for Member States to formulate limitations and exceptions to copyright protection. These parameters provide a test widely referred to as the 'three-step test'. The first step of this test requires the identification of the particular purpose the limitations and exceptions would serve (that is, the limitations and exceptions should be dedicated to 'certain special cases'). The second step requires the limitations and exceptions not to conflict with a normal exploitation of the work. The third step considers whether the limitations and exceptions would otherwise unreasonably prejudice legitimate interests of the author or copyright owner.[252] In the case of the Berne Convention, this test is limited to the reproduction right. Article 9(2) of the Berne Convention provides that

> It shall be a matter for legislation in the countries of the Union to permit the reproduction of such works in certain special cases, provided that such reproduction does not conflict with a normal exploitation of the work and does not unreasonably prejudice the legitimate interests of the author.

3.143 Article 13 of the TRIPS Agreement expands the scope of the three-step test to apply to all the exclusive rights granted to authors and copyright owners. It provides: 'Members shall confine limitations or exceptions to exclusive rights to certain special cases which do not conflict with a normal exploitation of the work and do not unreasonably prejudice the legitimate interests of the right holder'. Further, by requiring Member States to 'confine limitations or exceptions to exclusive rights' in terms of the three-step test, the TRIPS Agreement somewhat reconfigured the test into a check for the appropriateness of the limitations and exceptions adopted by Member States. It also provided a process by which Member States can challenge another Member State's adoption of limitations and exceptions that fail the three-step test.[253] The WCT specifically permits Contracting Parties to 'devise new exceptions and limitations that are appropriate in the digital network environment'.[254]

3.144 Member States of these treaties have in their copyright laws adopted many limitations and exceptions to the exclusive rights, which they consider to be compliant with the three-step test.[255] For instance, specific exceptions such as the fair dealing exceptions available in many jurisdictions including South

252 See Senftleben M, *Copyright, limitations, and the three-step test: an analysis of the three-step test in international and EC copyright law* (Vol. 13 Kluwer Law International 2004), 47–51 (Senftleben 2004); Samuelson P, 'Justifications for copyright limitations and exceptions', in Okediji R (ed), *Copyright Law in an Age of Limitations and Exceptions* (New York: Cambridge University Press 2017), 35.

253 See Article 64 of the TRIPS Agreement.

254 See Agreed Statement concerning art 10. Article 10 refers to the three-step test and the limitation and exceptions to copyright protection, generally.

255 See Samuelson 2017 supra at 24–25.

Africa and Nigeria as indicated in Chapter 2 are considered compliant with the three-step test.[256] Few cases have analysed the meaning of each of the steps of the three-step test.

3.145 In resolving the dispute between the EU and the US over an exception to the rights holders' copyright in US copyright law,[257] the WTO panel's decision extensively analysed each of the steps. On the first step, the WTO panel held that the scope of any limitation to copyright protection must be known and particularised.[258] On the second step, the WTO panel took the view that the term 'normal' consists of a dynamic element capable of taking into account technological and market developments.[259] Essentially the panel established that not only actual but also potential effects are to be considered when assessing the permissibility of copyright exceptions and limitations.[260]

3.146 With respect to the third step test, the WTO panel stated that the analysis would require the following stages: a definition of the 'interests' of right holders at stake and which attributes make them 'legitimate', then, an understanding of the term 'prejudice' and the level of prejudice that may be considered 'unreasonable'.[261]

3.147 Regarding the meaning of 'interests', the WTO panel observed that 'interests' are not necessarily confined to actual or potential economic issues.[262] It further noted that the term 'legitimate' refers to both lawfulness and legitimacy 'in the context of calling for the protection of interests that are justifiable in the light of the objectives that underlie the protection of exclusive rights'.[263] On the question of what degree of 'prejudice' would be necessary to qualify as 'unreasonable', the panel concluded that the 'prejudice to the legitimate interests of right holders reaches an unreasonable level if an exception or limitation causes or has the potential to cause an unreasonable loss of income to the copyright owner'.[264] However, the WTO panel adopted the view expressed in the Guide to the Berne Convention[265] that the prejudice contained in the third step of the three-step test may not be unreasonable if the rights holder is equitably compensated, for example through a system of non-voluntary licensing with equitable remuneration.[266]

3.148 While the WTO decision has been criticised for focusing exclusively on economic interests, there is no doubt that it has shed some light on how the test is

256 Schönwetter 2009 supra at 89–91.

257 United States – Section 110(5) of the U.S. Copyright Act, document WT/DS160/R. For a detailed examination of the panel decision and a brief outline of the WTO dispute settlement procedure, see Oliver J, 'Copyright in the WTO: The Panel Decision on the Three-Step Test' [2001] 25 *Colum JL & Arts* 119.

258 See para. 6.108 of the decision.

259 Ibid. at para. 6.166.

260 Ibid. at para. 6.180.

261 Ibid. at para. 6.222.

262 Ibid. at para. 6.223.

263 Ibid. at para. 6.224.

264 Ibid. at para. 6.229.

265 See WIPO Guide to the Berne Convention (1978) 55–56.

266 See para. 6.229 of the decision.

to be understood. In general terms, most courts have, in line with the WTO Panel decision adopted a rather restrictive and rights holders-focused approach.[267]

3.149 In the *Mulholland Drive* case,[268] for instance, the claimant argued that some technological protection measures (TPMs) unlawfully prevented him from exercising his rights under the private copy exceptions. The French Supreme Court held *inter alia* that the private copying exception was, at least in relation to movies and audio-visual works, usually in conflict with the normal exploitation of the work and therefore in breach of the second step of the three-step test. In this context, the French Supreme Court expressly stressed the importance of the DVD market for the movie industry for recovering the costs of producing a movie.

3.150 It appears from the foregoing cases that the test favours a specific provisions approach, as a general clause exception or limitation may be more likely to violate the requirements contained in the first step of the three-step test.[269] It also appears that the 'prejudice' contained in the third step of the three-step test may not be unreasonable if the rights holder is, for instance, equitably remunerated through a system of non-voluntary licensing.[270]

3.151 These considerations may have informed the approach of many jurisdictions, which have made provisions for compulsory or statutory licences as a limitation to exclusive rights in that they permit certain uses of protected works subject to an obligation to pay for such use under a compulsory or statutory licence.[271]

3.152 In the case of usage and access terms implemented in multi-sided music platforms, these indicate *inter alia*, the uses to which platform firms may put the music content. Such uses have been described in this chapter and include storing and indexing of the music content in a manner that will optimise search engine uses of the music content.[272] Further, such uses enable platform users to engage with and interact with the work in the course of social consumption and production.[273] The pertinent question is whether such use may be regulated by the scope of limitations and exceptions to copyright protection. As Samuelson rightly points out, 'users' interests are often examined through the prism of Limitations and Exceptions (L&E) to copyright'.[274] Accordingly, the potential for applying copyright law to regulate the activities of multi-sided music platforms is evident where the consideration is whether the restrictions imposed by the

267 Geiger C, 'Rethinking copyright limitations in the information society: The Swiss Supreme Court leads the way' [2008] 39(8) *IIC* 943.

268 French Cour de Cassation, 1st Civil Division, decision of 28 February 2006.

269 Schönwetter 2009 supra at 106.

270 See para. 6.229 of the WTO decision.

271 Samuelson 2017 supra at 12.

272 See Rosati E, 'Linking for profit, technical means and burden of proof – German BGH applies CJEU case law to Google's Image Search' (*The IPKat*, 18 December 2017), http://ipkitten.blogspot.com.ng/2017/12/linking-for-profit-technical-means-and.html (accessed 23 December 2017).

273 Elkin-Koren 2011 supra.

274 See Samuelson 2017 supra at 12. See also Elkin-Koren 2016 supra at 4, 12–14.

copyright terms are over and above those covered by the scope of copyright protection and/or limitations thereto.

3.153 In the case of *Society of Composers, Authors and Music Publishers of Canada v Bell Canada ('Bell')*,[275] decided by the Canadian Supreme Court, the plaintiff challenged as infringing, the activities of the defendant in permitting its customers to listen to 30-second preview of songs to enable them make a decision regarding downloading the full song for a fee. The defendant denied that such conduct amounted to infringement and instead argued that its permission of 30-second song preview was in fact, within the research category of the fair dealing exception. The Canadian Supreme Court agreed with the defendant's argument that 30-second song previews could be treated as consumer research and would therefore qualify as fair dealing. The Court concluded that 'limiting research to creative purposes would also run counter to the ordinary meaning of 'research', which can include many activities that do not demand the establishment of new facts or conclusions. It can be piecemeal, informal, exploratory, or confirmatory. It can in fact be undertaken for no purpose except personal interest'.[276]

3.154 Similarly, the Canadian Supreme Court in *Alberta (Education) v Canadian Copyright Licensing Agency ('Alberta Education')*[277] interpreted 'private study' (a fair dealing category) widely in holding that it may include teacher instruction. The Court therefore held that private study 'should not be understood as requiring users to view copyrighted works in splendid isolation'.[278]

3.155 These decisions indicate the possibility that the fair dealing exception and indeed, other limitations and exceptions to copyright may be interpreted broadly and applied to a wide range of innovative uses that do not require the consent of copyright owners.[279] However, whether the fair dealing exception may be interpreted as extending to the copyright terms in the context of multi-sided music platforms depends on two factors. These involve the consideration of whether the activities may be construed as research, private study or other specific activities listed under the fair dealing category and whether such use is fair.[280]

3.156 Furthermore, there is also the possibility, as suggested in Chapter 6 of this book, of treating the platform firm's activities as regulated use and apply a compulsory and statutory licence as a limitation to the copyright protection covering the music content. The interpretation of digitisation and indexing of

---

275 2012 SCC 36, [2012] 2 SCR 326 (*Bell*).

276 *Bell* supra at para. 22.

277 2012 SCC 37, [2012] 2 SCR 345 (*Alberta Education*).

278 *Alberta (Education)* supra at para. 27.

279 Katz A, 'Fair use 2.0: the rebirth of fair dealing in Canada', in Geist M (ed), *The Copyright Pentalogy: How the Supreme Court of Canada Shook the Foundations of Canadian Copyright Law* (University of Ottawa Press 2013), 93.

280 See Geist M (ed), 'Fairness found: How Canada quietly shifted from fair dealing to fair use', in *The Copyright Pentalogy: How the Supreme Court of Canada Shook the Foundations of Canadian Copyright Law* (University of Ottawa Press 2013), 176–177.

protected works for library collections as fair use is instructive. In the US, the courts have accepted as fair use, the making of copies of texts and images for the purpose of indexing their contents and showing parts of same in search results.[281] Similar consideration has been extended to non-profit organisations indexing books to develop a searchable database that will assist researchers in the case of *Authors Guild, Inc. v HathiTrust*.[282]

3.157 In these circumstances, it appears that the activities of platform firms as embodied in the copyright terms may be interpreted as fair use or fair dealing using an expansive interpretation of the latter. However, the fact that the indexing and optimisation in the case of the platform firms is undertaken for profit may change the tenor of such interpretation. Indeed, such indexing differs from that undertaken in the context of (non-profit) libraries, which is usually for the purpose of lending the books to the public. Accordingly, while the said activities may be permissible, the platform firm may be obligated to pay a fee under a compulsory licence. The commercial context of such activities may provide the rationale for the creation of a compulsory licence for the implementation of the copyright terms in the context of multi-sided music platforms.[283]

The scope of the limitations and exceptions framework (South Africa)

3.158 The most relevant limitation and exception to copyright protection in the context of multi-sided music platforms, would be the fair dealing exception[284] and the limitation to copyright protection imposed by statutory and/or compulsory licences.[285]

3.159 In South Africa, the fair dealing exceptions in the Copyright Act apply to literary (which includes dramatic) and musical works, artistic works, cinematographic films, sound recordings, broadcasts, programme-carrying signals, published editions and computer programs.[286] The fair dealing provisions in the current Act permits dealing with the work for research and private study, personal or private use, criticism and review, and reporting current events. The Act does not define the notion of fairness and as such the court has a wider discretion to consider everything relevant to the copyright owner's rights and the public interest, in the specific context of the facts of each case, before reaching a decision as to whether an infringement occurred.

3.160 The fair dealing exceptions contemplated by section 12(1) of the Copyright Act have not been subject of judicial interpretation until the case of *Moneyweb (Pty) Limited v Media 24 Limited and Another*. However, the fair dealing

281 See *Kelly v Arriba Soft Corp.*, 336 F.3d 811 (9th Cir. 2003); *White v West Pub. Corp.*, – F. Supp. 2d – (S.D.N.Y. 2014).

282 755 F.3d 87 (2d Cir. 2014). See also *A.V. v iParadigms, LLC*. 562 F.3d 630 (4th Cir. 2009); Samuelson 2017 supra at 18–19.

283 Samuelson 2017 supra at 27.

284 See Samuelson 2017 supra at 36–42.

285 Ibid. at 13.

286 For the full bouquet of the fair dealing exception, see ss 12–19B of the South African Copyright Act.

exception examined in that case pertained to 'reporting current event in a newspaper, magazine or some other periodical' as contained in section 12(1)(c)(ii) of the Act.[287] Currently, it is uncertain whether the activities of the platform firm in the context of multi-sided music platforms would fall within any of the fair dealing categories. At this point, however, it becomes important to acknowledge two things. First, it is possible to stretch the meaning of the specific fair dealing exceptions to accommodate the activities undertaken by the platform firm in the context of multi-sided music platforms. In the *Bell* case discussed earlier, the court interpreted the 'research' fair dealing exception to include consumer research. Second, the copyright law reform process currently ongoing in South Africa and Nigeria present an opportunity for the fair dealing exception to be specifically accommodating of the activities of the platform firms. However, this approach has the potential to engender conflicting interpretations. In the circumstances, it appears the best viable solution is to ensure that fair dealing exceptions need to offer a measure of legal certainty. In the absence of such certainty, users of copyright-protected content may err on the side of caution by avoiding uses of such content in any manner that is not explicitly permissible. As a result, creativity may be stifled.

3.161 It has been suggested that the bouquet of exceptions in the Copyright Amendment Bill be expanded to include such copying for indexing and storage purposes on the grounds that while such use involves copying, the copying does not affect the copyright owners' market.[288] Conversely, expanding the scope of exclusive rights to cover such uses may engender similar results as occurred in the *German Press Publishers* case discussed earlier. Again, the inclusion of a *gratis* licence scheme within the copyright terms discussed earlier in this chapter, lends credence to this argument.

The scope of the limitations and exceptions framework (South Africa)

3.162 The Nigerian situation is quite similar to the scenario in South Africa. The Nigerian fair dealing exception like its South African counterpart permits research and private study, personal or private use.[289] The second schedule to the Nigerian Copyright Act deals generally with exceptions to copyright infringement, particularly, paragraph (a) provides for fair dealing as follows:

> The doing of any of the acts mentioned in the said section 6 by way of fair dealing for purposes of research, private use, criticism or review or the reporting of current events, subject to the condition that, if the use is public, it shall be accompanied by an acknowledgement of the title of the work and its authorship except where the work is incidentally included in a broadcast.

287 *Moneyweb (Pty) Limited v Media 24 Limited* supra at paras 101–105.

288 See Sag 2009 supra at 1607–1682; Sag M, 'Orphan works as grist for the data mill' [2012] *Berkeley Technology Law Journal* 1503; Jockers M, Sag M and Schultz J, 'Digital archives: Don't let copyright block data mining' [2012] 490(7418) *Nature* 29; Riby-Smith 2017 supra.

289 Ekpa F and Kure B, 'Fair dealing as an exception to the infringement of copyright: an obstacle to the effective enforcement of copyright claims in Nigeria' [2015] 2 *Idah Bar Journal of Contemporary Legal Issues* 245, 247–250.

3.163 Similar to South Africa, there is no clear definition of what the concept of fairness means in relation to the term 'fair dealing' under the Nigerian Copyright Act. Again, for the meaning and criteria to be applied in determining fairness in dealing with a given work falls within the discretion of the courts. However, courts may look at whether an objective viewer would consider that, the person is genuinely using the material for one of the purposes set out in the Act; and their use of it is fair in that context.[290] Factors that may be considered in working out whether a use is 'fair' include whether the person using the material is doing so for commercial purposes, and whether the copyright owner is financially prejudiced because of the use. The mere fact that the person using the material is not making a profit does not make it fair.

3.164 Typically, the fair use model applicable in the US, Israel and the Philippines is widely considered as more expansive and flexible because of its open-ended nature, while the fair dealing model is considered narrow because of its closed, specific nature. This is not an attempt to discuss the advantages and/or disadvantages of the approach to the definition of the fair dealing exception. It is only pertinent to note that in appropriate circumstances, a defendant may show that his activities in relation to protected content amounts to fair dealing with the work.

290 Ibid. at 258.

CHAPTER 4

Multi-sided music platforms and privacy law

Introduction

4.1 Data (used interchangeably with information) has been defined as 'facts or information, especially when examined and used to find out things or to make decisions'.[1] From this definition, it is evident that data covers a range of items ranging from basic information, such as names, addresses and email addresses to more complex information involving bank records, health records, trade secrets of companies etc. Data is subject of diverse uses and has been described as the oil of the digital era.[2] Indeed, it has been reported that five of the most valuable listed companies in the world (Microsoft, Facebook, Apple, Amazon and Alphabet Inc. (the parent company of Google)) deal with data.[3]

4.2 As noted in the introductory chapter, the design and implementation of multi-sided music platforms have led to an exponential increase in the volume of data provided and collated by platform firms. Platform firms require users such as copyright owners (when they upload music content) and other uploaders to complete some form of registration before they can upload content to the platform. Such registration systems will inevitably lead to the provision of personal data such as email addresses, names, gender, age and in some cases, residential or business addresses. In terms of multi-sided music platforms, data is deployed alongside copyright-protected music content in digital advertising. This raises the question of how personal data are being processed and whether privacy rights are being respected on multi-sided music platforms.

4.3 This chapter looks at the use of personal data (i.e. data processing)[4] in multi-sided music platforms and the privacy protection legal framework that regulate such uses in South Africa and Nigeria. It analyses the pertinent rights

1 'Data Noun – Definition, Pictures, Pronunciation and Usage Notes | Oxford Advanced American Dictionary at Oxfordlearnersdictionaries.Com' (*Oxfordlearnersdictionaries.com*, 2019), www.oxfordlearnersdictionaries.com/definition/american_english/data (accessed 6 July 2019).

2 'The World's Most Valuable Resource Is No Longer Oil, But Data' (*The Economist*, 6 May 2017), www.economist.com/leaders/2017/05/06/the-worlds-most-valuable-resource-is-no-longer-oil-but-data (accessed 6 July 2019).

3 Kim E, 'More than half of online sales growth in the US came from Amazon last year' (*Business Insider*, 2 February 2017), www.businessinsider.com/amazon-drives-more-than-half-us-ecommerce-growth-2016-2017-2?IR=T (accessed 6 July 2019).

4 'Processing' refers to 'any operation or activity or set of operations, whether or not by automatic means, concerning personal information'. See section 1.1(r) of Nigeria Data Protection Regulation 2019.

granted to data subjects (including copyright owners) vis-à-vis the terms of use and privacy policy indicated by platform firms.

4.4 Most of the data that has been collected and processed by platform firms are data of/about identifiable persons (personal data) or data relating to such persons, both natural and legal persons. The unbridled use of such data in the hands of private firms and public institutions have led to and have the potential to lead to abuse or misuse of such information.[5] In response to the exponential increase in data collation and innovation in uses of data,[6] many countries have recognised the need to provide statutory and regulatory safeguards for persons in order to prevent an invasion of their privacy and individual liberties. Such laws are referred to differently in different countries – while some countries use the expression 'data law' or 'data protection laws', others refer to such laws as 'privacy protection laws'. However, there is no dispute that these laws (by whatever name called) are geared towards the protection of privacy and individual liberties.

4.5 Between 2017 and 2018, the number of countries that have enacted privacy protection laws rose by 10%, from 120 to 132.[7] As at January 2019, the Global Table of Data Privacy Laws show that 28 countries have official bills for privacy protection in various legislative stages.[8] These privacy protection laws and official bills have been confirmed to fulfil international minimum standards for privacy protection.[9] In this regard, South Africa's Protection of Personal Information Act No. 4 of 2013 falls within this category. Nigeria's National Information and Technology Development Agency recently issued the Nigeria Data Protection Regulation 2019 (the 'Regulation'), stipulating data protection rules that meet the international minimum standards for privacy protection.[10]

4.6 Two of the most pertinent issues relating to multi-sided music platforms and their data processing activities are how such data is being processed and whether privacy rights are being respected.[11] These concerns raise issues in relation to many aspects of the business activities of copyright owners as possible data subjects, with examples including:

5 Ludington S, 'Reining in the data traders: A tort for the misuse of personal information' (2006) 66 *Md L Rev* 140.

6 Ohm P, 'Broken promises of privacy: Responding to the surprising failure of anonymization' (2009) 57 *UCLA L Rev* 1701.

7 Greenleaf G, 'Global data privacy laws 2019: 132 national laws & many bills' [2019] 157 *Privacy Laws & Business International Report*, 14–18.

8 Ibid. Nigeria's Digital Rights and Freedom Bill 2016 is listed as the official privacy protection bill awaiting presidential assent. It is to be noted that in March 2019, Nigeria's president declined assent to the bill.

9 Ibid.

10 Data Protection Regulation 2019, https://nitda.gov.ng/wp-content/uploads/2019/01/Nigeria%20Data%20Protection%20Regulation.pdf (accessed 1 July 2019).

11 Koornhof P and Pistorius T, 'Convergence between competition and data protection law: A South African perspective' [2018] 8(3) *International Data Privacy Law* 277–283.

- Who may qualify as data subject with rights within the applicable privacy laws;
- Copyright owners requiring access to processed personal data to gauge public perception and reception to their uploaded content;
- Copyright owners requiring access to processed personal data to inform the creation of new content.

4.7 The question is whether the rights afforded to persons under the relevant privacy laws admit of these interests and potential requests of copyright owners and uploaders in South Africa and Nigeria.

Legal framework for data protection

4.8 Privacy protection is considered an extension of the fundamental right of citizens to privacy and as earlier stated, the number of privacy protection laws have continued to rise over the years. These laws aim at preventing what are considered as infringement of fundamental human rights such as unauthorised disclosure of personal data, unlawful storage of personal data and other forms of abuse or misuse of personal data.

4.9 In many countries, there are laws requiring various parts of the private sector such as e-commerce, consumer transactions, medical records etc. to comply with a particular data protection principle such as data security, data quality or individual participation. Examples include e-commerce laws in Indonesia and Turkey, both limited to e-commerce; data privacy principles in Brazil's 2014 Marco Civil law, limited to the internet; several sectoral privacy laws in the US which deal with parts of the US private sector, etc.[12] Nigeria and South Africa have laws that impose obligations for privacy and data protection, respectively.

4.10 In the case of South Africa, section 14 of the 1996 Constitution provides for the right to privacy. Section 10 of the Constitution also contains a right to human dignity. The Constitution further enjoins the courts to consider international law when interpreting legislation.[13]

4.11 Apart from its Constitution, other statutes in South Africa require specified public and private parties to protect personal data and privacy in various ways. These statutes include the National Health Act 61 of 2003; the National Credit Act 34 of 2005; the Consumer Protection Act 68 of 2008; the Electronic Communication and Transactions Act 25 of 2002; and the Promotion of Access to Information Act 2 of 2000. However, the Protection of Personal Information, Act 4 of 2013 (POPI) is the primary legislation regulating data protection in South Africa.[14]

---

12 Greenleaf G, 'Sheherezade and the 101 data privacy laws: Origins, significance and global trajectories' [2014] 23 *JL Inf & Sci* 4.

13 See ss 39(1)(b)), 233.

14 See Koornhof and Pistorius 2018 at 279–280.

4.12 Apart from section 37 of Nigeria's 1999 Constitution (as amended) that protects the rights of citizens to their privacy and the privacy of their homes, correspondence, telephone conversations and telegraphic communication, certain provisions of the Freedom of Information Act No. 4 of 211, the Cybercrimes (Prohibition, Prevention etc) Act 2015, Consumer Code of Practice Regulations 2007 issued by the Nigerian Communications Commission for the telecommunication sector,[15] the Consumer Protection Framework issued by the Central Bank of Nigeria in 2016 impose various data protection obligations. For instance, section 1 of the Freedom of Information Act No. 4 of 2011 gives citizens the right of access to public records and information, while section 14 prevents a public institution from disclosing personal information to the public unless the individual involved consents to the disclosure.

4.13 The Digital Freedom Rights Bill 2016, which provides for 'the protection of the human rights online, to protect internet users in Nigeria from infringement of their fundamental freedoms and to guarantee the application of human rights for users of digital platforms and/or digital media and for related matters'[16] has been touted as a comprehensive and internationally compliant privacy protection statute.[17] However, even though the two national legislative houses have passed the Bill and sent same to the president for his assent, the president has declined assent to the Bill.[18] Nevertheless, in January 2019, the National Information Technology Development Agency ('NITDA/the Agency') issued the Nigerian Data Protection Regulation 2019, pursuant to its powers under section 6(c) of the National Information Technology Development Agency Act 2007 (NITDA Act). This Regulation, which is the focus of this chapter in relation to Nigeria, is the first comprehensive legislation on data protection and privacy legislation in Nigeria.

4.14 While these laws are a welcome development, the Committee of Ministers of the Council of Europe, the Organisation for Economic Co-operation and Development (OECD) and indeed, many other international organisations have respectively noted that disparities in national legislations for privacy protection pose a danger to the cross-border free flow of personal data. It was suggested that given the number of sectors (health, banking, security etc.) that rely on such cross-border free flow of personal data to effectively operate, disparities in national legislation might cripple such sectors. Also, it was noted that some of these laws lacked provisions for protecting and safeguarding the crucial privacy rights of individual access and correction.[19]

---

15 For example, s 9.

16 See the preamble to the bill (*Eie.ng*, 2019), http://eie.ng/wp-content/uploads/2016/06/Digital-Rights-and-Freedom-Bill-2016.pdf (accessed 8 July 2019).

17 See Greenleaf 2019 supra.

18 Ekwealor V, 'Nigeria's president refused to sign its Digital Rights Bill, what happens now?' (*Techpoint.Africa*, 27 March 2019), https://techpoint.africa/2019/03/27/nigerian-president-declines-digital-rights-bill-assent/ (accessed 8 July 2019).

19 See Greenleaf G, 'China – From warring States to Convergence?' in *Asian Data Privacy Laws: Trade and Human Rights Perspectives* (OUP, 2014); Organisation for Economic Co-operation

4.15 For this reason, international organisations such as the OECD and the Council of Europe have come up with guidelines that would help to harmonise national privacy protection legislations while ensuring balanced protection of human rights and free flow of data. The OECD/Council of Europe data protection principles are much more widely accepted as there is a large number of data privacy laws embodying their proposed minimum set of data protection principles.[20] In summary, the OECD/Council of Europe standards require that a law must satisfy the following principles as minimum standards:[21]

- Collection limitation;
- Data quality;
- Purpose specification;
- Use limitation;
- Security safeguards;
- Openness;
- Individual participation (i.e. right to access and challenge person data; generally regarded as the most important privacy safeguard).[22]

4.16 Various international bodies accept the use of these standards as criteria for whether a country has a 'data privacy law'.[23] In particular, the Global Table of Privacy Laws[24] prepared by Graham Greenleaf, Professor of Law and Information Systems at the University of New South Wales, using these standards, is regarded as one of the most authoritative assessment of the global tally of countries with data privacy laws.[25]

4.17 While the acceptance of national privacy legislations based on these standards does not provide or indicate the effectiveness of such legislations; they at least indicate the existence of internationally accepted national framework for privacy protection in a given country.[26] South Africa's Protection of Personal

and Development, '*OECD Guidelines on the Protection of Privacy and Transborder Flows of Personal Data – OECD*' (oecd.org, 2013), www.oecd.org/internet/ieconomy/oecdguidelinesontheprotectionofprivacyandtransborderflowsofpersonaldata.htm (accessed 8 July 2019).

20 See Greenleaf G, 'The influence of European data privacy standards outside Europe: Implications for globalisation of Convention 108' (2012) 2(2) *International Data Privacy Law* 68–92.

21 See Organisation for Economic Co-operation and Development, '*OECD Guidelines on the Protection of Privacy and Transborder Flows of Personal Data – OECD*' (oecd.org, 2013), www.oecd.org/internet/ieconomy/oecdguidelinesontheprotectionofprivacyandtransborderflowsofpersonaldata.htm (accessed 8 July 2019).

22 For a detailed explanation of these principles, see ibid.

23 For example, the European Commission *Exchanging and Protecting Personal Data in a Globalised World* (Communication from the Commission to the European Parliament and the Council), 10 January 2017, COM(2017) 7 final, footnote 32; 'UNCTAD | Summary Of Adoption Of E-Commerce Legislation Worldwide' (*Unctad.org*, 2019), https://unctad.org/en/Pages/DTL/STI_and_ICTs/ICT4D-Legislation/eCom-Global-Legislation.aspx (accessed 9 July 2019).

24 Greenleaf G, 'Global Tables of Data Privacy Laws and Bills (5th Ed 2017)' [2017] 145 *Privacy Laws & Business International Report* 14–26; Greenleaf 2019 supra.

25 See Greenleaf G, 'Global data privacy laws 2015: 109 countries, with European laws now a minority' [2015] 133 *Privacy Laws & Business International Report*.

26 Ibid.

Information Act and Nigeria's Data Protection Regulation 2019 respectively meet these criteria. Accordingly, this chapter looks at the main compliance issues and the prospects and challenges as it relates to multi-sided music platforms.

Protection of Personal Information Act

4.18 As stated in the preamble to the Protection of Personal Information Act, the purpose of the Act is to regulate 'the processing of personal information by public and private bodies in a manner that gives effect to the right to privacy subject to justifiable limitations that are aimed at protecting other rights and important interests'.[27] This objective corresponds to the values of international standards such as the OECD Data Protection Guidelines and the guidelines proposed by the Council of Europe.[28] However, the bulk of the Act is not yet in force, given that it requires a proclamation by the president of South Africa.[29]

4.19 However, the president has made a proclamation regarding certain sections of the Act such as the definitions section (section 1); the provisions relating to the Information Regulation (Part A of Chapter 5); regulations that may be made by the relevant minister and the information regulator and the procedure for making such regulations (sections 112 and 113).[30]

4.20 While the definitions in section 1 of the Act are in force already; they do not impose obligations on the persons regulated or protected by the Act. However, they offer an indication of how the law characterises the various subjects of legislation. Section 1 of the Act defines the following key terms: data subject, responsible party, operator, personal information and also regulator. A 'data subject' is the person to whom the personal information relates. A 'responsible party' is the public or private body or person which, alone or in conjunction with others, determines the purpose of and means for processing personal information. An 'operator' is the person who processes personal information for a responsible party in terms of a contract or mandate, without coming under the direct authority of that party. The 'regulator' is the information regulator established in terms of section 39 of the Act. By virtue of section 39 of the Act, the regulator is a juristic person whose functions include monitoring and enforcing compliance by public and private bodies with the provisions of the Act. The term 'personal information' is defined as information relating to an identifiable, living, natural person, and juristic persons. The category of information recognised as personal information is inexhaustive as the Act uses the expression 'including but not limited to' in providing a list. The use of the expression 'includes' suggests that in appropriate circumstances, other information may qualify as personal information.

27 See the preamble to the Act.

28 Greenleaf 2019 supra.

29 See s 115 of the Act.

30 'Proclamation by the President of the Republic of South Africa, No. R. 25, 2014' (*Saica.co.za*, 2014), www.saica.co.za/Portals/0/Technical/LegalAndGovernance/37544_pro25.pdf (accessed 8 July 2019).

4.21 The Act provides eight conditions for the lawful processing of personal information. These principles include:

- Accountability (section 8);
- Processing limitations such as lawfulness, consent etc. (sections 9 to 12);
- Purpose specification and limited retention (sections 13 and 14);
- Compatibility with purpose of collection (section 15);
- Information quality (section 16);
- Openness (sections 17 and 18);
- Security safeguards (sections 19 to 22);
- Data subject participation (sections 23 to 25).

4.22 In terms of data subject participation, which is considered the most important privacy protection safeguard, a data subject under the Act has the right to request a responsible party to confirm whether or not the responsible party holds personal information about the data subject, and to request the record itself.[31] A data subject also has the right to request a responsible party to correct or delete personal information about the data subject that is inaccurate, irrelevant, excessive, out of date, incomplete, misleading or obtained unlawfully.[32]

4.23 By virtue of section 5 of the Act, data subjects have the following rights:

- Right to lawful processing of their personal information (section 3);
- Right to notification regarding the collection or acquisition of their personal information (section 5(a));
- Right to establish the existence of personal information and request access to such information (section 5(b));
- Right to request the correction, destruction or deletion of their personal information (section 5(c));
- Right to object to processing that is contrary to their interests or the performance of a public duty (section 5(d));
- Right to object to the processing of their personal information for purposes of direct marketing (section 5(e) and (f));
- Right to object to automated processing (section 5(g));
- Right to complain to the regulator (section 5(h));
- Right to institute civil proceedings in court (section 5(i)).

4.24 The Act shares several similarities with the EU General Data Protection Regulations (GDPR). For instance, both legislations include the provisions guiding the different categories of data and identify a special category of personal data which the Act refers to as 'special personal information'.[33] This special category of data includes personal information concerning religious or philosophical

31 Section 23 of the Act.
32 Section 24 of the Act.
33 See s 26 of the Act. These are referred to as 'sensitive personal data' under the GDPR 2016.

beliefs, trade union membership, race or ethnic origin, health or sex life, political persuasion or biometric information of a data subject. Similar to the GDPR, such special category of data may be legally processed where it has been made publicly available by the data subject.[34]

The Nigeria Data Protection Regulation 2019

4.25 In January 2019, Nigeria's National Information and Technology Development Agency (NITDA) issued the Nigeria Data Protection Regulation 2019 (the 'Regulation'). According to its preamble, the Regulation was issued pursuant to NITDA's mandate under the NITDA Act[35] to, *inter alia*:

> Develop regulations for electronic governance and monitor the use of electronic data interchange and other forms of electronic communication transactions as an alternative to paper-based methods in government, commerce, education, the private and public sectors, labour, and other fields, where the use of electronic communication may improve the exchange of data and information.

4.26 The Regulation has the status of law, as it is a subsidiary legislation made by a public agency acting within its powers under a primary law.[36] Unlike its South African counterpart, the Regulation became effective from the date of its issuance, having been approved by the NITDA Board. However, like its South African counterpart, the Regulation shares several similarities with the GDPR. For instance, both legislations include the provisions guiding the different categories of data and identify a special category of personal data which the Regulation refers to as 'sensitive personal data'.[37] This special category of data include personal information concerning religious or other beliefs, trade union membership, race, ethnicity, criminal records etc.[38]

4.27 The Regulation regulates the activities of 'Data Controllers' and 'Data Administrators' in their use of the personal data of all natural persons who are Nigerian citizens or who live in Nigeria.[39] Data Controller is defined under the Regulation as a person who determines the purposes for and the manner in which personal data is or is to be processed.[40] A Data Administrator under the Regulation is a person who processes personal data.[41]

4.28 Under the Regulation, 'personal data' is defined to include a name, address, photo, email address, bank details, medical information, posts on social

34 See s 27 of the Act.

35 National Information and Technology Development Agency Act No. 28 of 2007.

36 Okoeguale H, 'Strengthening legislative controls over delegated legislation in Nigeria' (2019) 10(2) *Nnamdi Azikiwe University Journal of International Law and Jurisprudence* 35–41.

37 See s 1.3(v).

38 Ibid. Unlike the GDPR though, the availability of such sensitive data publicly, does not provide legal basis for their processing.

39 Section 1.2 of the Regulation.

40 Section 1.3(g) of the Regulation.

41 Section 1.3(f) of the Regulation.

networking sites, computer internet protocol (IP) address and any other information relating to an identified or identifiable natural person referred to as 'data subject'.[42]

4.29 Also, in defining 'an identifiable natural person', the Regulation stipulates that it must be a person who can be identified, directly or indirectly in particular reference to an identifier such as the various examples of 'personal data' already provided.[43] This would include information that may be used on its own or used with other information to identify, contact or locate a natural person, whether directly or within a context.[44]

4.30 As persons who determine how personal data is processed or will be processed, Data Controllers are mandated by the Regulation to process personal information in accordance with the legal basis provided by the Regulation.[45]

4.31 The legal basis for processing include any of the following: the processing has been consented to by the data subject; the processing is for the performance of a contract; the processing is required for compliance with a legal obligation; etc.[46] Following the literal rule of statutory interpretation, the use of the expression 'any' would mean that either of the previously stated bases would suffice as legal basis under the Regulation.[47]

4.32 In terms of consent, the Regulation requires express consent and the Data Controller must be able to show that the data subject has validly given her consent. For multi-sided music platforms, which regard use of the platform as indication of consent to processing of personal data, it is doubtful that such would qualify as valid consent under the Regulation. However, it seems the use of personal information is with the knowledge of the users of the platform, given the detailed explanation on some platforms regarding their activities with respect to personal data they collect.

4.33 Prior to obtaining or processing personal data, the Data Controller is required to provide the data subject with certain information such as the identity and contact details of the Data Controller; the purpose for which the data will be processed as well as the legal basis; recipient(s) of the data; the period for storing personal information; rights of the data subject; possible transfer of the information to third parties, foreign countries or international organisation.[48]

4.34 Under section 2.13, data subjects have the following rights: right to request access to personal data; right to rectify the information and to have it in a portable format; the right to erasure or deletion of the information; restriction in processing the information and the right to transfer the information to a third party; the right to know their rights. These are substantially similar to the rights

42 Section 1.3(q) of the Regulation.
43 Section 1.3 of the Regulation.
44 This aligns with minimum standards of the OECD Guidelines 2013.
45 See s 2.2 of the Regulation.
46 Ibid.
47 See *Ifezue v Mbadugha* (1984) 5 SC 79.
48 See s 2.13.6 of the Regulation.

available to data subjects under South Africa's Protection of Personal Information Act.

Applicability of the data protection legal frameworks in South Africa and Nigeria

4.35 Before focusing exclusively on the copyright and privacy terms, as they currently exist in multi-sided music platforms, it is important to first consider the applicability of the data protection legal frameworks in South Africa and/or Nigeria. As indicated in the introductory chapter, platform firms are internet companies but may be established as legal persons in specific jurisdictions outside Nigeria and/or South Africa. This raises the question of whether South African and/or Nigerian law may apply to their services.

4.36 Section 3(1) of the Protection of Personal Information Act provides that:

> This Act applies to the processing of personal information
>
> (a) entered in a record by or for a responsible party by making use of automated or non-automated means: Provided that when the recorded personal information is processed by non-automated means, it forms part of a filing system or is intended to form part thereof; and
> (b) where the responsible party is – (i) domiciled in the Republic; or (ii) not domiciled in the Republic but makes use of automated or non-automated means in the Republic, unless those means are used only to forward personal information through the Republic.

4.37 The Act uses the expression 'and' meaning that both conditions in section 3(1)(a) and (b) would apply. Accordingly, the application of the Act is limited to processing of a 'record'[49] containing personal information where made by a responsible person domiciled in South Africa or a responsible person who makes use of automated or non-automated means in South Africa. These criteria would be used to assess the applicability of the Act with respect to data processing activities relating to South African data subjects.

4.38 It appears the Act would apply to most platform firms in so far as they process records containing personal information given that most platform firms are either domiciled in South Africa or use automated or non-automated means in South Africa. In any event, section 3(2)(b) permits the application of other legislations where such legislations 'provides for conditions for the lawful processing of personal information that are more extensive than those set out in Chapter 3'. Given that the Constitution mandates courts to 'prefer any reasonable interpretation of the legislation that is consistent with international law over any alternative interpretation that is inconsistent with international law' when interpreting legislation,[50] it may be that other international laws on privacy such as the GDPR may

49 As defined in s 1 of the Act.
50 Section 233 of the Constitution of the Republic of South Africa.

be interpreted to bring erring companies in line even when they would ordinarily escape liability under the Act.

4.39 By virtue of section 1.2(a) and (b) of the Nigerian Data Protection Regulation 2019, the Regulation applies to all transactions intended for the processing of personal data and to actual processing of personal data in respect of natural persons in Nigeria; and to 'natural persons residing in Nigeria or residing outside Nigeria but of Nigerian descent'.

4.40 Corollary to the foregoing, companies are directly responsible for data protection compliance as long as they are processing the personal data of Nigerian citizens, notwithstanding the location of the company.

4.41 Having shown the possible applicability of the legal frameworks for data protection in Nigeria and South Africa, the next paragraphs look at the terms of use and privacy policy of platform firms through the lens of the Protection of Personal Information Act and the Nigerian Data Protection Regulation, respectively. The focus will be on those aspects of the two statutes that influence how platform firms deal with individuals (and firms) that supply the platforms with copyright-protected music content; some aspects of these legislations are not touched on at all. Specifically, the focus does not consider aspects of the Regulation that do not concern multi-sided music platforms as the term is used in this book.

Privacy terms, data processing and multi-sided music platforms

4.42 When copyright owners and platform users upload music content and access the platform, they provide personal information to the platform firms.[51] In most multi-sided music platforms, platform users (including copyright owners) are required to register on the platform in order to upload protected content. Such registration would involve the provision of names, phone numbers, email addresses and other personal information. Platform firms also collect the content created, uploaded, or received from others when using their services. This includes things like written and received emails, saved videos and photos and even comments made by users on uploaded content.[52] Essentially, within the context of multi-sided music platforms, data of copyright owners and uploaders; data relating to copyright owners and data regarding the content uploaded by copyright owners are collected and processed.

4.43 These data are processed and used by the platform firms to decipher a user's language, ads they will find useful, people that matter most to the users online and videos or content the user may like. As stated in Chapter 3, watching music content from a specific artist will prompt the platform to show the user other content from such artist as well as content from the same genre of music as

51 See *Policies.google.com* (22 January 2019), https://policies.google.com/privacy?hl=en (accessed 5 July 2019).

52 Ibid. See also Kumaraguru P, Cranor L, Lobo J and Calo S, 'A survey of privacy policy languages'. In *Workshop on Usable IT Security Management (USM 07): Proceedings of the 3rd Symposium on Usable Privacy and Security, ACM.* 2007.

the one being watched.[53] The key takeaway from the foregoing is that in uploading and/or assessing music content, users provide platform firms with a significant amount of personal information.

4.44 When considering how complaint a platform firm (or any responsible party/data controller) is, the privacy policy (whether provided in a single document or as part of the platform's terms of use or terms of service) is usually the first port of call. For some platform firms such as YouTube, Facebook, and SoundCloud, the terms of use come with a privacy policy which explains the kind of information the platform collects, the uses to which such content are put and also, the rights or options open to platform users including copyright owners and uploaders. The platform firms also collect information in or about the protected content that uploaders provide. For example, date a file was created. According to Google's Privacy Policy, when users use their services:

> We collect information about the apps, browsers, and devices you use to access Google services, which helps us provide features like automatic product updates and dimming your screen if your battery runs low. The information we collect includes unique identifiers, browser type and settings, device type and settings, operating system, mobile network information including carrier name and phone number, and application version number. We also collect information about the interaction of your apps, browsers, and devices with our services, including IP address, crash reports, system activity, and the date, time, and referrer URL of your request.[54]

4.45 In general terms, platform firms use the information they collect to provide their services and improve on their product and service offerings. They may also use collected information to develop new services and of course serve personalised ads. The collated information may also be shared with third parties usually referred to in most privacy policies as 'partners'.[55] Such partners include developers, publishers, advertisers, copyright owners and other persons or firms, who have a contractual agreement with the platform firms. The information shared is usually anonymised and non-identifiable personal information such as information that show trends about the general use of their services. Notably, information about consumer patterns are anonymised[56] and/or pseudonymised[57] and shared with copyright owners by way of 'views' and analytics. Specifically, the revenue-sharing agreement discussed in Chapter 3 of this book,[58] may

53 See Chapter 3, para. 3.26.

54 *Policies.google.com* (22 January 2019), https://policies.google.com/privacy?hl=en (accessed 5 July 2019).

55 Ibid.

56 Basically, anonymisation involves the removal of both direct and indirect identifiers that may lead to the identification of a particular person. See Mahrt M and Scharkow M, 'The value of big data in digital media research' [2013] 57(1) *Journal of Broadcasting & Electronic Media* 20–33.

57 Under art 3 of the GDPR for instance, 'pseudonymisation' is defined 'the processing of personal data in such a way that the data can no longer be attributed to a specific data subject without the use of additional information, as long as such additional information is kept separately and subject to technical and organizational measures to ensure non-attribution to an identified or identifiable individual'.

58 See Chapter 3, paras 3.11–3.14.

indicate what obligations platform firms have regarding the disclosure of personal information that may help copyright owners make business decision. However, it is doubtful that such information would include the nature of user engagement with protected content beyond view counts and analysis that copyright owners may independently make from comments section. For instance, Facebook indicates in its privacy policy that

> We provide aggregated statistics and insights that help people and businesses understand how people are engaging with their posts, listings, Pages, videos and other content on and off the Facebook Products. For example, Page admins and Instagram business profiles receive information about the number of people or accounts who viewed, reacted to or commented on their posts, as well as aggregate demographic and other information that helps them understand interactions with their Page or account.[59]

4.46 For copyright owners, processed data (e.g. in the form of analytics and measurement) can help them understand how their content is used and/or more importantly, received/perceived by the public.[60] For example, Facebook's data policy indicates that it used the information that it has of users to help advertisers and other partners measure the effectiveness and distribution of their ads and services, and understand the types of people who use their services and how people interact with their websites, apps and services.[61]

4.47 To underscore the importance of data to copyright owners, a popular US video streaming platform provides a good example. In 2018, Netflix disclosed that over 45 million accounts watched one of its recent movies at the time, *Birdbox*, in the first week of the movie's opening on the platform.[62] While such disclosure was welcome (and rare for Netflix), many movie and film producers complained that more information was needed regarding the reception of the movie and other Netflix movies as well.[63] It was widely asserted that information such as the number of people who watched the entire film, demographics of viewers, what constituted 'view count' etc. would enable producers gauge and interpret public reaction to their movies. It was alleged that Netflix's withholding of such crucial viewership information was to the detriment of the business and

59 'Data Policy' (*Facebook*, 19 April 2019), www.facebook.com/policy.php (accessed 5 July 2019).

60 See Doyle G, 'Television production: Configuring for sustainability in the digital era' [2017] 40 *Media, Culture & Society* 285–295. Also Akan J, 'Private equity investors are making a big bet on afrobeats' rapid rise up the global charts' (*Quartz Africa*, 31 January 2019), https://qz.com/africa/1539118/don-jazzys-mavin-gets-multimillion-dollar-investment/ (accessed 9 July 2019).

61 'Data Policy' (*Facebook*, 19 April 2019), www.facebook.com/policy.php (accessed 5 July 2019).

62 Clark T, 'Netflix says a record-breaking 45 Million accounts watched 'Bird Box' in its first week, but we don't know how many finished the movie' (*Business Insider*, 28 December 2018), www.businessinsider.com/netflix-says-45-million-accounts-watched-bird-box-in-first-week-2018-12?IR=T (accessed 8 July 2019).

63 Guerrasio J, 'Netflix's record-breaking viewership for 'Bird Box' has sparked debate In Hollywood, and some believe the company's lack of transparency hurts filmmakers' (*Business Insider*, 31 December 2018), www.businessinsider.com/netflix-bird-box-sparks-debate-over-data-in-hollywood-2018-12?IR=T (accessed 8 July 2019).

creative/productive patterns of film producers.[64] There were also concerns that the data from Netflix was not verified by a third party measurement company in the way TV ratings and box-office results generally are.

4.48 Notably, disclosure of processed personal information or data is usually based on contractual arrangements between the platform firms and the relevant 'partner'. In such case, platform firms may be under no obligation to share such information with partners. Platform firms also decide what information they share with partners and how such information is shared. For instance, Facebook has indicated that it is

> In the process of restricting developers' data access even further to help prevent abuse. For example, we will remove developers' access to your Facebook and Instagram data if you haven't used their app in three months, and we are changing login, so that in the next version, we will reduce the data that an app can request without app review to include only name, Instagram username and bio, profile photo and email address. Requesting any other data will require our approval.[65]

4.49 Despite the benefits of sharing such information and the fact that anonymisation may comply with the regulatory requirements of privacy laws,[66] there is the possibility that copyright owners may require more information than the platform firms are willing to share.[67] Also, the possession and control of data imbue the platforms with significant powers which, if unchecked, may be abused or misused against copyright owners and other firms.[68]

4.50 In *Six4Three v Facebook*, Six4Three claimed that access to Facebook's user data was crucial to its existence as a company and that in restricting and/or denying access to the said data; Facebook crippled its (Six4Three's) business.[69] Also, in *Styleform IT v Facebook*, the plaintiff alleged that access to user data was crucial to its business operations and (the manner of) restriction to such access was anti-competitive and an intentional interference with contract.[70] Both cases are currently ongoing in the respective courts.

4.51 In terms of rights available to platform users regarding the collection and processing of their personal information, it is noted that users may choose how much information to provide and may enjoy a degree of control (through the platform firm's privacy settings) in terms of how their personal data is used. However, given the wide avenues for data collection, a user may not completely escape providing their personal data so long as they use the platform.

---

64 Ibid.

65 'Data Policy' (*Facebook*, 19 April 2019), www.facebook.com/policy.php (accessed 5 July 2019).

66 Because data within the scope of the regulations are such as may be identified or identifiable.

67 Doyle G, 'Television and the development of the data economy: Data analysis, power and the public interest' [2018] 9 *International Journal of Digital Television* 56–58.

68 Ibid.

69 Case Number CIV 533328. See www.documentcloud.org/documents/5775209-CIV533328-12.html#document/p106/a493727.

70 Case Number CGC-18–571075. See www.documentcloud.org/documents/5433610-Styleform-IT-v-Facebook.html.

4.52 Substantively, users may export their uploaded content and may also request removal of content and/or their personal information. It is to be noted that this is merely a request, which may or may not yield the desired result. In most cases, the platform firm would only remove content if the requesting user were uniquely identifiable within the content she seeks to have removed. The platform firms consider factors such as image or voice, full name, financial information, contact information and other personally identifiable information in determining whether a requesting user is uniquely identifiable.[71]

4.53 It is important to note that there are platform firms within the context of this book that do not provide a privacy policy on their platform. However, this does not mean that such firms do not collect and/or process personal information. For this reason, the discussions in this chapter are applicable to them also and as a matter of compliance, such firms need to formulate and provide a privacy statement or policy to the public. Both the Protection of Personal Information Act and the Regulation require the provision of such a document.[72]

Privacy protection in South Africa and Nigeria and multi-sided music platforms

4.54 As earlier stated, South Africa's Protection of Personal Information Act is yet to come into force as the bulk of its provision is awaiting presidential proclamation. For Nigeria, while the Data Regulation is already in force, the interpretation, adequacy and/or efficacy of its provisions in protecting personal information and rights of data subjects are yet to be tested given its recent provenance. However, both legislations contain similar provisions with respect *inter alia* to the right of access for data subjects. For this reason, both legislations are considered together in this section with relevant differences highlighted where applicable.

4.55 Corollary to the foregoing, a crucial part of the analysis of the copyright terms implemented in multi-sided music platforms hinges on their relationship to the scope of the rights of data subjects. As the privacy terms involve uses to which user data may be put,[73] the question of their alignment with the privacy law framework must be answered from the perspective of the relationship between the privacy terms and the rights available within the privacy framework. In particular, it may be argued that despite the benefits of granting copyright owners access to data relating to them, the privacy terms may not be amenable to be applied towards promoting competition in the music copyright industry.

4.56 Accordingly, the pertinent question relates to whether the activities of the platform firms are within or outside the scope of the rights available to

---

71 In deciding to remove, Google states that it considers public interest, newsworthiness, and consent. See *Policies.google.com* (22 January 2019), https://policies.google.com/privacy?hl=en (accessed 5 July 2019).

72 See s 18 of the Act and s 2.5 of the Regulation, respectively.

73 See Chapter 3, paras 3.24–3.28.

the copyright owners as data subjects under the privacy law framework. In this regard, the most relevant rights for copyright owners as data subjects in the context in which multi-sided music platforms operates, would be the right of access and the right of complaint or the right to seek redress.[74] It is argued that the other data subject rights recognised by the Protection of Personal Information Act in the case of South Africa and the Data Protection Regulation in the case of Nigeria, leaves the data in the hands of the platform firms. Indeed, with the exception of the right to request access to personal data, which means the data may be given or provided to the data subject, most of the other rights of data subjects relate to actions which the platform firm may take without handing over the data to the data subject.

4.57 The next paragraphs examine the privacy terms with reference to the right of access and the right to seek redress and identifies whether there is a fit between such rights and the implementation of the terms in multi-sided music platforms.

Multi-sided music platforms and right of access to personal information in South Africa and Nigeria

4.58 To reiterate, the privacy terms applicable within most multi-sided music platforms require some sort of personal information from copyright owners and uploaders in the form of names, email address and uploaded content. Such information falls within the definition of 'personal information' under the Protection of Personal Information Act and 'personal data' in the case of Nigeria.

4.59 The previous paragraphs have dealt with the definition of data controller in the two legislations.[75] Going from the privacy terms in multi-sided music platforms as discussed earlier, it is evident that platform firms qualify as data controllers within the meaning of the two legislations. By the same token, copyright owners and uploaders clearly qualify as data subjects, with a caveat. South Africa's Protection of Personal Information Act defines 'data subject' and 'personal information' with reference to information relating to natural persons and existing juristic persons.[76] In contrast, Nigeria's Data Regulation, in defining 'data subject', 'personal data' or 'personal identifiable information' stipulates that it would involve information relating to an identified or identifiable *natural person*.[77] In other words, while corporate information being information about artificial persons are excluded from the ambit of the Regulation in the case of Nigeria,[78] such information would be covered and personal data of a data subject under section 1 of South Africa's Protection of Personal Information Act.

74 Doyle 2018 supra at 57.
75 See paras 5.20 and 5.27.
76 See s 1 of the Act.
77 Section 1.3 of the NITDA Data Protection Regulation.
78 Unless such corporate information relates to natural persons.

4.60 Corollary to the foregoing, individual copyright owners and uploaders may qualify as data subjects with the attendant rights under both legislations. But in the case of Nigeria, copyright owners and uploaders who operate registered accounts as firms or in the name of their firms may not qualify as data subjects under the Regulation unless the relevant information relates to natural persons. This leaves the status of record companies and similar firms that operate corporate platform accounts dangling.

4.61 As data subjects, copyright owners may request access to their personal data. This would include data relating to them. Can copyright owners and uploaders as data subjects request more information from the platform firms? And could the platform firms validly refuse such access? Notably, copyright owners and uploaders are typically desirous of a specific kind of data – data that provide them with information needed to run their businesses as copyright owners. As stated in Chapter 3 of this book, access to consumers and consumer data are the new value metric for the music copyright industry.[79]

4.62 There are two aspects to the significance of the right of access: one is the information or data that the platform firm does provide, and the second aspect is the possibility of the copyright owners require broader access or more information. Regarding the first aspect, the platform firms as earlier stated provide this data based on contractual relationship with copyright owners and other third parties as 'partners'. This leads to the question of what such 'partners' go on to do with such data. It is possible, based on the nature of certain uses, for the 'partners' to become data controllers or responsible parties within the meaning of the Regulation and the Act, respectively. This may be particularly so if the 'partners' decide how personal data is dealt with, bearing in mind that these data, while relating to the relevant 'partner' may also contain data about other users. In such cases, platform firms may need to put in place measures to ensure that 'partners' adhere to the eight principles of the Act or the Regulation, as the case may be.

4.63 Still on the first aspect, the provision of data based on contractual obligations may mean that the volume and nature of data provided is at the discretion of the platform firms. Access may be 'turned on and off' like the proverbial tap. Platform firms may claim compliance with privacy regulations and refuse access. This may be problematic for copyright owners who rely on such access to make crucial business decisions. Indeed, this was the subject of the suit in *Six4Three v Facebook* mentioned earlier.[80] It is submitted that this brings to question the appropriate balance between data access requests and the interests of other data subjects.[81]

4.64 On the second aspect, the copyright owners and uploader may be requesting access as data subjects simpliciter. As data controllers, platform firms will

79 See Chapter 3, paras 3.20 and 3.128.

80 *Six4Three v Facebook* supra.

81 Simbro EM, 'Disclosing stored communication data to fight crime: The US and EU approaches to balancing competing privacy and security interests' (2010) 43 *Cornell Int'l LJ* 585.

have a legal responsibility to respond to such request for access to personal data of data subjects which they hold ('subject access request'). The questions here relate to procedures for exercising the right or making the request; the nature of data or personal information covered and whether the platform firm as responsible party (in terms of the Act) or data controller (in terms of the Regulation) has a discretion regarding providing access. The next paragraphs deal with these issues seriatim.

4.65 Regarding the procedure for making request for access, section 25 of the Act stipulates that sections 18 and 53 of the Promotion of Access to Information Act apply to subject access request. Under the Promotion of Access to Information Act, sections 18 and 53 indicate substantially similar procedure for subject access requests. However, while section 18 deals with access requests made to a public body, section 53 deals with requests to a private body. Given that platform firms are private bodies, reference is made to section 53.

4.66 Section 53 indicates that subject access requests must be made in the prescribed form to the relevant private body. It is submitted that the prescribed form requires stringent information for a request to be valid. Under the prescribed form, requesters are required *inter alia* to not only identify the right they seek to exercise or protect but to also provide an explanation of why the requested record is required for the protection of the identified right. According to section 53 of the Promotion of Access to Information Act:

> (1) A request for access to a record of a private body must be made in the prescribed form to the private body concerned at its address, fax number or electronic mail address.
>
> (2) The form for a request for access prescribed for the purposes of subsection (1) must at least require the requester concerned –
>
> (a) to provide sufficient particulars to enable the head of the private body concerned to identify –
>
> (i) the record or records requested; and
> (ii) the requester;
>
> (b) to indicate which form of access is required;
> (c) to specify a postal address or fax number of the requester in the Republic;
> (d) to identify the right the requester is seeking to exercise or protect and provide an explanation of why the requested record is required for the exercise or protection of that right;
> (e) if, in addition to a written reply, the requester wishes to be informed of the decision on the request in any other manner, to state that manner and the necessary particulars to be so informed; and
> (f) if the request is made on behalf of a person, to submit proof of the capacity in which the requester is making the request, to the reasonable satisfaction of the head.

4.67 In the case of Nigeria, the Regulation merely require subject access requests to be made under a 'formal process'[82] but does not indicate what constitutes such.

4.68 Regarding the question of the nature of data that may be requested, the Act stipulates that where a responsible party is processing the personal information of a data subject, such data subject has the right to the record or description of the personal information about the data subject held by the responsible party.[83] It seems from the wording of the Act that a description of the information held may suffice.

4.69 Evidently, although both legislations make provisions for right of access and procedures for dealing with subject access requests, as noted earlier, some information may not be provided even though they may qualify as personal data or personal information. There is little clarity as to what sort of information the data subject must be given. For instance, would the raw data suffice or can processed data be subject of access requests? The Regulation defines 'Data Subject Access Request' as the mechanism for an individual to request a copy of their data under a formal process and payment of a fee.[84] It seems from this definition that only the raw data may suffice. Where the platform firm holds data that is logged against non-obvious identifiers such as an IP address or cookie rather than against information that is more clearly related to a specific data subject, it may be easy or reasonable for the platform firms to refuse access to such data. This may be on the grounds that it may be difficult to ascertain with certainty that providing such information will not also mean providing information relating to other persons that may be associated with that identifier. Also, even though such information may be anonymised, it may nonetheless be capable of being associated with other information that may make the information identifiable of another person. For instance, in the case of YouTube multi-channel network mentioned in Chapter 3 of this book,[85] the aggregators manage multiple channels belonging to various copyright owners and YouTube provides reports and analytics for all the channels in a single document. In preparing reports to each copyright owner under the 'network', the operator of the multi-channel network (i.e. the aggregator) cannot simply forward the YouTube report to each copyright owner. Instead, the operator must separate each copyright owner's data and prepare a separate report.[86]

4.70 More significantly, it seems that apart from information relating to certain records of South African Revenue Service, disclosure that could reasonably be expected to endanger the life or physical safety of an individual, trade secrets of a third party and other information exempted by the applicable sections of Chapter 4 of Part 2 and Chapter 4 of Part 3 of the Promotion of Access to

82 See s 1.1(l) of the Regulation.
83 See ss 5(b) and 23(1) of the Act.
84 See s 1.3(l) of the Regulation.
85 See Chapter 3, para. 3.12.
86 It is submitted that this brings questions of accountability and transparency.

Information Act,[87] the responsible party has no discretion regarding disclosure.[88] Instead, the responsible party must disclose the information sought.

4.71 In terms of the Regulation, the data controller may or may not provide the requested access. Where it elects to provide access, the Regulation requires that it is done in a 'concise, transparent, intelligible and easily accessible form'.[89] Where it elects not to grant access, it is required to provide reasons and indicate that the data subject may lodge a complaint with a supervisory body.[90]

4.72 Furthermore, for the copyright owners and uploaders, the nature of their need for access may necessitate more frequent requests than the platform firms may reasonably be expected to respond to. The key issue for subject access requests in this context thus moves from being a question of rectification or erasure to being a question of business or enterprise interest (i.e. needing access to assist with business decisions). In addressing access requests that are 'manifestly unfounded or excessive' because of their 'repetitive character', the Regulation permits the data controller to charge a reasonable fee taking into account the cost of providing the information or to refuse to act on the request and write a letter to that effect with NITDA in copy.[91] Given the almost non-existent cost of providing access via electronic means, charging fees for access may not be enough to deter repeated requests. Given this, platform firms may be likely to elect to refuse access. However, they have the burden of demonstrating that requests are manifestly unfounded or excessive.[92]

4.73 In the case of South Africa, the Act does not make provisions limiting or regulating the number of subject access requests that may be made. However, it does allow some discretion in terms of timing of response to such requests. In this regard, the Act requires the responsible party to provide access to the information 'within a reasonable time'.[93]

4.74 In reality, platform firms may be able to refuse copyright owners data access in the name of preventing abuse of such data access.

Multi-sided music platforms and enforcement of privacy rights in South Africa and Nigeria

4.75 The Act stipulates that the Regulator may issue a code of conduct, which may *inter alia* indicate how complaints regarding breaches of the provisions of the Act may be made.[94] However, such codes of conduct cannot interfere with the provisions of Chapter 10 on enforcement.

87 Promotion of Access to Information Act No. 2 of 2000.

88 See s 23(5) of the Act which provides that 'if a request for access to personal information is made to a responsible party and part of that information may or must be refused in terms of subsection 4(a), every other part must be disclosed'.

89 See s 2.13.1 of the Regulation.

90 See s 2.13.2 of the Regulation.

91 See s 2.13.3(a) of the Regulation.

92 See s 2.13.3 of the Regulation.

93 See s 23(1)(b)(i) of the Act.

94 See s 60 of the Act.

4.76 In terms of enforcement of rights under the Act, data subjects may submit a complaint to the Regulator, in writing, alleging interference with the protection of the personal information of a data subject.[95] Upon receipt of a complaint, the Information Regulator may conduct an investigation, act as conciliator in relation to the interference with the protection of the personal information or take other actions as stipulated in section 76 of the Act. The Regulator may also refer a complaint to another regulatory body that may be more suited to address the nature of the complaint.[96]

4.77 Where the Regulator decides to investigate, it will consider *inter alia* the subject matter of the complaint and any response provided by the responsible party. The Regulator may procure a settlement between the parties and may also secure an assurance from the responsible party that the offensive action will not be repeated.[97]

4.78 From the foregoing and the general wording of the Act, it seems that the Act is more inclined to encourage rather than force compliance with the rights of data subjects. The payment of fines (up to R10 million) is limited to the commission of an offence.[98] Offences include failure to notify the Regulator of processing undertaken without prior authorisation,[99] obstructing the Regulator,[100] breach of confidentiality,[101] failure to comply with enforcement or information notices[102] etc.

4.79 Data subjects may also institute a civil action for damages against a responsible party for breach of the conditions for lawful processing of personal information.[103]

4.80 In the case of Nigeria, where a data subject believes that her rights have been infringed and consequently, there has been a breach of the Regulation, such data subject may seek redress in court.[104] Also, NITDA may set up an Administrative Redress Panel to, *inter alia*, investigate any allegation of breach of the Regulation and determine appropriate redress within 28 working days. Given its terms of reference under section 3.2.1, it appears the Administrative Redress Panel can only act on the basis of a complaint or allegation and cannot act *suo motu*.

4.81 Unlike its South African counterpart, the Regulation stipulates penalties for breach of the data privacy rights of data subject. The penalty is a fine of 2% of annual gross revenue or 10 million naira, whichever is greater, in the case of more than 10,000 data subjects and 1% of the annual gross revenue or 2 million naira, whichever is greater, in the case of fewer than 10,000 data subjects.[105]

---

95 Section 74(1) of the Act.
96 Section 78 of the Act.
97 Section 80 of the Act.
98 See s 109 of the Act.
99 See s 59 of the Act.
100 Section 100 of the Act.
101 Section 101 of the Act.
102 See s 103 of the Act.
103 Section 99(1) of the Act.
104 Section 3.2.1 of the Regulation.
105 Section 2.10 of the Regulation.

4.82 While this is laudable in that the hefty fine may compel compliance, it poses a conundrum as to how the number of data subjects may be assessed. For instance, would 10,000 data subjects mean that for breach of the data privacy rights of a single data subject, a penalty may be awarded on the basis of the number of data subjects that a data controller deals with? Or would 10,000 data subjects need to bring an action for the penalty to apply?

4.83 On a related matter, both legislations place the right to seek redress solely on a data subject. This is unlike the GDPR that give data subjects the right to mandate a consumer protection body to exercise their rights and bring claims on their behalf.[106] With the expertise and funds that consumer protection bodies may have at their disposal, it is submitted that it would have been helpful if such mechanism were available to data subjects in the case of South Africa and Nigeria.

Conclusion

4.84 Essentially, within the context of multi-sided music platforms, the privacy protection laws may not offer much protection for copyright owners as 'firms' who are data subjects. For one, the legislations in South Africa and Nigeria are not categorical about the nature of information that may be covered by the right of access. Further, in the case of South Africa, the data subjects have to comply with the provision of stringent information before they may validly request access to personal information. For Nigeria, the Regulation more or less leaves compliance with access requests at the discretion of the data controllers as it may be easier to refuse access than to grant access in certain instances. Specifically, when it comes to access to information relating to economic interests, data controllers such as platform firms may pick and choose the information they disclose.

4.85 That said, the Protection of Personal Information Act is not yet in force in South Africa and the Data Regulation in Nigeria is still at its infancy. Given that the efficacy of any legislation is in its enforcement, one must needs watch developments when the Act comes into force in South Africa and as time goes in the case of Nigeria. In the meantime, copyright owners in the context of multi-sided music platforms may have to resort to other regimes or other legislations that impose similar privacy protection obligations in order to secure the necessary access to information.[107]

106 Article 80 GDPR.
107 This is discussed in Chapter 6.

CHAPTER 5

Competition law infractions

Introduction

5.1 As explained in Chapter 2, competition law complements both copyright law and privacy protection laws in the achievement of their respective objectives. In the case of copyright, competition law may apply to restrict the exercise of copyright to protect the public interests as copyright and other intellectual property rights (IPRs) do not stand in the way of competition law application. Regarding privacy protection, competition law may apply to restrict anti-competitive uses and abuses of data or personal information. Competition law may also apply to ensure that dominant and economically powerful firms, be they distributors or even copyright owners themselves, companies or persons that process data do not derail the legitimate distribution of copyright products or the privacy rights of persons and companies. Accordingly, copyright owners, users of copyright-protected content including platform firms, companies and persons that process data are in the focus of competition law so long as they are involved in economic activities.[1]

5.2 This chapter looks, *inter alia*, at application of competition law to the manner in which copyright protected music content and user data are deployed on multi-sided music platforms generally, and to the relationship between platform firms and other firms using their services or rendering similar services.[2] In South Africa, while platform firms within the context of copyright and privacy protection laws as discussed in this book, have not been the subject of competition law scrutiny, the activities of firms which like platform firms, own and operate distribution systems for copyright-protected content have been subject of

---

1 Competition law only applies to economic or commercial activities. See s 3(1) of the South African Competition Act; s 2(2)(c) of the Nigerian Federal Competition and Consumer Protection Act. The Competition Act (in the case of South Africa) and the Competition and Consumer Protection Bill (in the case of Nigeria) do not explicitly define 'economic activity'. However, the term has been defined in several decided cases. For example, *Competition Commission v American Natural Soda Ash Corporation II 49/CR/Apr00 and 87/CR/Sep00; American Natural Soda Ash Corporation and Another v Competition Commission of South Africa and Others (12CAC/DEC01)* [2002] ZACAC 5.

2 See *inter alia*, Polverino 2012 supra at 3–4; Gal and Rubinfeld 2015 supra at 3–5; Wagner-von Papp F, Unilateral conduct by non-dominant firms: A comparative reappraisal [2015] *ASCOLA Series* 13–5 (Wagner 2015).

judicial and quasi-judicial proceedings.[3] Nigeria, as earlier stated, only recently (2019) enacted a substantive competition statute.

5.3 These circumstances, notwithstanding, the activities of multi-sided platforms have been the subject of much debate in both the EU and in the US. Particularly in the EU, the EU competition authority (the European Commission) has beamed the competition law searchlight on the potential anticompetitive conduct implemented by undertakings that facilitate access to copyright products in the open business model context similar to those of multi-sided music platforms.[4] In particular, the European Commission, although recognising that the open business model in itself 'does not raise competition concerns',[5] also noted that it could raise competition concerns in relation to business practices, policies or contractual rules surrounding its implementation.[6]

5.4 Accordingly, this chapter builds on these experiences to discuss the following:

- The general nature and types of conduct regulated and prohibited by competition law;
- Copyright terms and privacy terms applied in multi-sided music platforms from a competition law perspective;[7]
- How competition law infractions may occur in multi-sided music platforms vis-à-vis the use of copyright-protected music content and personal data;
- Identifying possible defences.

Nature and types of conduct regulated by competition law

5.5 In each market, there are several market participants, which include firms engaged in different economic activities, their suppliers, customers and/or consumers. A key feature of markets is the existence of firms, which are not equal in size, market reach and/or consumer size. In practical terms, firms in both vertical relationships[8] and horizontal relationships[9] differ in size and economic strength. It is possible for inequality of economic power in vertical relationships to affect

3 See *DW Integrators* supra; *Mandla Matla Publishing* supra. In these cases, the competition enforcer did not find any offensive conduct under the Competition Act.

4 See, e.g., European Commission [2016] *Antitrust: Commission sends Statement of Objections to Google on Android operating system and applications*. Available at http://europa.eu/rapid/press-release_IP-16-1492_en.htm (accessed 6 January 2017) (Google Android Statement).

5 Ibid.

6 Ibid. In particular, the Commission stated that its concerns 'relate to the conditions for use of Google's proprietary apps and services on Android devices, which are not open source'.

7 Economic or commercial activities.

8 'Vertical relationship' means the relationship between a firm and its suppliers, its customers, or both. See s 1(xxxiii)(ii) of the South African Competition Act.

9 'Horizontal relationship' means a relationship between competitors; See s 1(xiii) of the South African Competition Act.

the ability of horizontally related firms to compete.[10] Put differently, economic inequality between vertically integrated firms may affect competition in markets in which firms are horizontally integrated. From the perspective of the dominant or economically stronger firm, such economic imbalance may reinforce its market power in the relevant market apropos its competitors. From the perspective of the weaker firm, it may affect its ability to effectively compete on the downstream market for the production of goods.[11]

5.6 As a market regulatory legal tool which is concerned only with the effects which the conduct of market participants have on a given market,[12] competition law will interfere with the freedom of market participants to enter into business dealings as long as the business transactions affects the relevant market.

5.7 There is a close connection between competition and market participation, which, from a legal perspective, occurs through economic relationships and contractual terms, set by (or between) market participants.[13] From a competition law perspective, specifically, economic relationships and contractual terms are regulated for the purpose of eliminating and penalising anticompetitive conduct and/or conduct that restrict competition. Such conduct may be cartels, abuse of dominance or specified restrictive agreements. In the case of mergers, competition law regulates contractual provisions and relationships by monitoring (and approving or refusing to approve) prospective contractual relationships that have the likelihood of affecting the openness and competitiveness of a market.[14] The purpose of these regulatory activities is to protect and/or promote competition.

5.8 There are two dimensions to the promotion and/or protection of competition. First, it is to be understood that the broad principle behind the protection of competition through competition law is the definition and calibration of a 'relevant market'. Whether any unilateral or concerted conduct (whether by or between horizontally or vertically related firms) restricts competition is assessed from the standpoint of a relevant market. In this context, the definition of 'market' usually relies on monetary exchanges so that in the case of multi-sided music platforms where music content is distributed free of charge or data is provided for free; it may be difficult to define the relevant market.[15] Similarly, assessing

10 See Boy L, 'Abuse of market power: controlling dominance or protecting competition?' in Ullrich H (ed), *The Evolution of European Competition Law: Whose Regulation, Which Competition?* (Edward Elgar 2006), p. 216.

11 In terms of copyright, the downstream would be the market for the creation and production of music content

12 Bakhoum 2017 supra at 4.

13 Market participants include firms and their suppliers or firms and their customers and/or consumers.

14 Competition law also permits the conduct of market inquiries. See Koornhof P and Pistorius T, 'Convergence between competition and data protection law: A South African perspective' [2018] 8(3) *International Data Privacy Law* 278–279.

15 See Gal and Rubinfeld 2015 supra at 3–5; See also Bakhoum M, 'Abuse without dominance in competition law: abuse of economic dependence and its interface with abuse of dominance', in Nihoul P (ed) (2017), *Abuse Regulation in Competition Law: Past, Present and Future, ASCOLA series*, 15. Available at https://ssrn.com/abstract=2703809 (accessed 10 March 2017).

whether the conduct of any firm is anticompetitive (abuse of dominance) requires that such firm enjoys a dominant position in a relevant market and abuses such dominant position.[16] To define and assess dominance, competition law examines the economic status or influence[17] of market participants – the 'market' having been defined prior. As such, the conceptual approach to assessing economic influence, under competition law, relies on market power[18] and/or market share[19] of the participants in a relevant market. Accordingly, whether the copyright and privacy terms and resultant economic relationships are directed to exclude competitors or to exploit suppliers and/or consumers, the primary requirement is that such rules or relationships must affect competition in the relevant market. Otherwise, such rules or relationships may not be painted with the anticompetitive brush.

5.9 But certain approaches to business practices in business relations may in fact extend the reach of competition law to vertical contractual relationships between firms, which are not competing in the same market or in any defined market and which do not hold a dominant position as per a specific market. In protecting the ability of market participants to compete, competition law can also go beyond encouraging formal economic equality between market participants[20] and keeping the market open and competitive.[21] Competition law aims to rectify the adverse effects of inequalities in contractual relationships, which erodes competition.[22] This is particularly the case in jurisdictions, which have concentrated markets and where copyright markets are not functioning due, *inter alia*, to concentration of economic power.[23]

5.10 Second, competition law may protect and promote competition by scrutinising the conduct of one party in a contractual or business relationship, even where such party does not hold a dominant position in relation to any relevant market.[24] In such instance, it may hold that competition may also be restricted or adversely affected when a market participant enjoys a stronger economic position vis-à-vis its supplier or trading partner and relies on its position of economic strength to decimate the weaker trading partner's ability to compete or remain

16 This is the approach to the concept of abuse of dominance in South Africa. See *Sasol Oil (Pty) Ltd v Nationwide Poles CC* (49/CAC/Apr05). This approach is largely based on the influence of competition law in the EU. See also Bakhoum 2017 supra at 1.

17 Ibid.

18 See Drexl J, 'The relationship between the legal exclusivity and economic market power. links and limits', in Govaere I and Ullrich H (eds), *Intellectual Property, Market Power and the Public Interest* (Lang 2008), 16–18.

19 South African Competition Act 1998 assesses dominance from a combined market share and market power approach. See s 7 of the Act.

20 Bakhoum 2017 supra at 4–5.

21 See Drexl 2008 supra at 16–18.

22 See Hughes 2009 supra at 392; Wagner 2015 supra at 10–15.

23 See Bakhoum M, 'A dual language in modern competition law? Efficiency approach versus development approach and implications for developing countries'. [2011] *World Competition* 495; Gal MS and Fox EM, 'Drafting competition law for developing jurisdictions: learning from experience', in Gal M, Bakhoum M, Drexl J, Fox E and Gerber D (eds), *The Economic Characteristics of Developing Jurisdictions: Their Implications for Competition Law* (Edward Elgar 2015), 296–356.

24 See Drexl 2013 supra at 42. See also Bakhoum 2017 supra at 26.

in its business.[25] Competition is affected in such instance even in the absence of a dominant position in the regular competition law sense[26] because the choices available to a market participant to conduct its business are undermined.[27] The imbalances in the relationship of the market participants coupled with the certain contractual terms have the potential to erode competition especially when they undermine market participants from having an equitable opportunity to participate in the copyright market.[28] Indeed, competition law has been applied to cases where an undertaking, which is a distributor of copyright-protected content, exercises its proprietary rights in the distribution system to the detriment of the copyright market.[29]

Restrictive agreements

5.11 Restrictive agreements may be between firms in either a horizontal relationship or a vertical relationship. Specifically prohibited restrictive agreements include formation of price cartels – agreements in which firms (including copyright owners) use copyright or data for sharing markets or in entering into market-foreclosure agreements; exclusivity agreements regarding the distribution of works, resale-price maintenance, and the like. Sections 4 and 5 of the Competition Act (in the case of South Africa) and section 59 of the Federal Competition and Consumer Protection Act (in the case of Nigeria) cover such prohibited restrictive agreements. Where copyright owners or copyright users (including platform firms) enter into agreement or contractual arrangements that have the effect of restricting competition by foreclosing the distribution of copyright products, such may be addressed by the relevant competition statute. Such application of competition law complements the goal of copyright law in ensuring wider distribution of copyright-protected products. Also, personal data may be processed and shared between competing firms and used to fix prices resulting in anti-competitive effects.

Unilateral conduct: abuse of dominance

5.12 Competition law may also apply to unilateral conduct by firms (whether copyright owners, copyright users, distributors or data processors), which enjoy a dominant position in the market for distribution of creative works or the market for data and/or data analytics, to prohibit them from abusing their dominant

25 See Hughes 2009 supra at 389–392.

26 Competition statutes usually stipulate legal and economic criteria for assessing dominance.

27 Bakhoum 2017 supra 5 at 2 and 21; Këllezi P, 'Abuse below the threshold of dominance? Market power, market dominance, and abuse of economic dependence', in *Abuse of Dominant Position: New Interpretation, New Enforcement Mechanisms?* (Springer 2008), 62.

28 Section 2(e) South African Competition Act; Section 1(a) Federal Competition and Consumer Protection Act.

29 See Drexl 2013 supra at 167.

market positions to the detriment of the market.[30] In the case of conduct by the relevant copyright owner, competition law may apply to restrict the exercise of copyright protection.[31] Indeed, the so-called interface between copyright and competition law has been the attempts to apply competition law to address what is perceived as the undue exercise of copyright or other intellectual property rights. The exclusive nature of the copyright owner's rights is interpreted as conferring the copyright owner with market power in the competition law sense.

5.13 Specifically, based on the right to exclusivity conferred on the copyright owner under the Copyright Act, such copyright owner may, where he has the requisite dominant position, contravene section 8 of the South African Competition Act that deals with the 'abuse of a dominant position'. Section 8 provides:

> It is prohibited for a dominant firm to:
>
> (a) charge an excessive price to the detriment of consumers;
> (b) refuse to give a competitor access to an essential facility when it is economically feasible to do so;
> (c) engage in an exclusionary act, other than an act listed in paragraph (d), if the anti-competitive effect of that act outweighs its technological, efficiency or other pro-competitive, gain; or
> (d) engage in any of the following exclusionary acts, unless the firm concerned can show technological, efficiency or other pro-competitive, gains which outweigh the anti-competitive effect of its act:
>
> (i) requiring or inducing a supplier or customer to not deal with a competitor;
> (ii) refusing to supply scarce goods to a competitor when supplying those goods is economically feasible;
> (iii) selling goods or services on condition that the buyer purchases separate goods or services unrelated to the object of a contract, or forcing a buyer to accept a condition unrelated to the object of a contract;
> (iv) selling goods or services below their marginal or average variable cost; or
> (v) buying-up a scarce supply of intermediate goods or resources required by a competitor.

5.14 Any such conduct will constitute a contravention of the Competition Act. Similarly, other firms outside the copyright owner may be subject of competition law enforcement under this provision, in the interest of the distribution of copyright products. However, the copyright owner or some other relevant firm may be able to escape the brunt of this section if he/she/it qualifies for an exemption in terms of section 10(4) of the Act.[32] Section 10(4) of South Africa's Competition Act provides that firms can apply to the Competition Commission to exempt 'an

30 See s 8(a) and (b) of the South African Competition Act.

31 See Drexl 2013 supra at 40.

32 Section 10(4) of the Competition Act 89 of 1998 (South African Competition Act); Hartzenberg T, 'Competition policy and practice in South Africa: promoting competition for development symposium on competition law and policy in developing countries' [2005] *Nw J Int'l L & Bus* 26, 667.

agreement or practice, or category of agreements or practices, that relates to the exercise of intellectual property rights, including a right acquired or protected in terms of the . . . Copyright Act, 1978 (Act No. 98 of 1978)'.[33] An exemption granted by the Competition Commission ensures that even when an agreement or practice falls within the prohibited or restricted acts in Chapter 2 of the Act, such agreement or practices will be deemed not to have offended the provisions of the Competition Act, particularly Chapter 2.[34] However, in the absence of the grant of an exemption either because an application was refused[35] or the specified term of exemption has lapsed[36] or an exemption granted was revoked,[37] the agreement or practices that fall within the prohibited or restricted acts will bear the brunt of the Competition Act. It is important to know that the exemption is not automatic and instead, the exemption has to be sought via an application.

5.15 In Nigeria, there is also a similar list of conduct prohibited as abuse of dominance.[38] A copyright owner who 'enjoys a position of economic strength enabling it to prevent effective competition being maintained on the relevant market and having the power to behave to an appreciable extent independently of its competitors, customers and ultimately of the consumers' will be considered to occupy a dominant position in a relevant market.[39] Where such copyright owner abuses its dominant position, it may be liable to comply with the directives of the Federal Competition and Consumer Protection Commission[40] and where the abuse persists, to criminal conviction and 'a fine not exceeding 10% of its turnover in the preceding business year or such higher percentage as the court may determine under the circumstances of the particular case'.[41]

5.16 In essence, competition law can apply to the conduct of copyright owners when they exercise their exclusive rights. It may also apply to the conduct of platform firms in their use of copyright-protected works.

Abuse of dominance: copyright owners

5.17 Copyright owners may be alleged to have abused their dominant market position either by exercising their exclusive rights or by acting outside the scope

33 However, some competition statutes exempt intellectual property rights (IPRs) including copyright from the application of competition law. Examples include Poland, Mexico and Peru. It is to be noted that even in these countries, there may be room to interpret the exemption provisions to permit competition law scrutiny on matters regarding the exercise of intellectual property rights. See Drexl 2013 supra at 45–47.

34 Chapter 2 of the South African Competition Act deals with situations where an agreement restricts competition to the extent prohibited by the Act as well as situations where a firm abuses its dominant position in a defined market.

35 See s 6 of the South African Competition Act.

36 Section 10(4A) of the South African Competition Act.

37 Section 10(5) of the South African Competition Act.

38 Section 72(2) of the Federal Competition and Consumer Protection Act 2019 (Nigerian Competition Act).

39 Section 70(2) of the Nigerian Competition Act.

40 Such directive may include a 'cease-and-desist' order. See s 73(1) of the Nigerian Federal Competition and Consumer Protection Act.

41 See s 74(1).

of copyright protection.[42] In the context of licensing practices for online music, Harrison explains:[43]

> Licensing practices seem to fall into three ranges. In the first range, the copyright holder uses its power simply to preclude free riding. Efforts of this sort find a safe haven within copyright laws. At the next level, the effort is to expand the effect of exclusivity beyond that granted by copyright but not to the point of having an impact on an economically significant market. Finally, the use of the exclusivity may have a sufficient impact on an economically significant market to raise an antitrust issue.

5.18 However, as stated earlier, such application and indeed, other external doctrines are largely applied when copyright protection is regarded as a monopoly right, which may be abused to the detriment of competition. In such instances, competition law may be applied to restrict the exercise of copyright and direct the issuance of a compulsory licence in the interest of competition.

5.19 In *Magill*,[44] the European Commission's decision, which was upheld by the Court of First Instance and Court of Justice, required the broadcasters for television programme listings to grant a licence to third parties willing to publish a comprehensive weekly guide. The courts found that the firms under investigation enjoyed a de facto monopoly over the information used to compile listings. It was also found that their refusal to license was an abuse of their dominant position, as the refusal prevented the appearance of a new product for which there was a potential consumer demand ('new product test'). The 'new product test' primarily focuses on the development of new products for consumers in the downstream market.[45] This interpretation was also supported by the fact that there was no actual or potential substitute to the product, and that there was no objective justification for a refusal. Rather, the IPRs owners were reserving for themselves the secondary market of weekly guides by refusing to license IPRs that were indispensable for operating in the secondary market. All these factors represented 'exceptional circumstances', which ultimately led the Commission to apply competition law and impose a compulsory licence.

5.20 While Magill was unclear as to whether the 'exceptional circumstances test' was cumulative or separate,[46] the test itself strongly influenced further decisions of

42 For instance, the copyright misuse doctrine in the US is invoked when a defendant in an infringement suit argues that the copyright owner's action is tantamount to an attempt to extend protection beyond the scope of copyright law. See the case of *Lasercomb Am. Inc. v Reynolds*, 911 F.2d 970 (4th Cir. 1990); Harrison, JL, 'Online music: antitrust and copyright perspectives' [2002] *Antitrust Bull* 47, 483–484.

43 Harrison 2002 supra at 486.

44 Joined Cases C 241–242/91 P, *Radio Telefis Eireann & Independent Television Publications v European Commission* [1995] 4 C.M.L.R. 718 (*Magill*).

45 Colston C and Galloway J, *Modern Intellectual Property Law* (Taylor & Francis 2010), 432.

46 Other criticisms of the decision related to the absence of guidance on the defences IPRs holders may oppose, in terms for instance of objective justifications and the potential negative effects of the decision on innovators' incentives to invest time and money on research. See Aitman D and Jones A, 'Competition law and copyright: has the copyright owner lost the ability to control his copyright?' [2004] *European Intellectual Property Review*, *26*(3), 137–147.

the EU courts especially in the cases of *IMS Health*[47] and *Microsoft*.[48] These later cases contributed to expand the scope of *Magill*.

5.21 In *IMS Health*, the CJEU substantially followed *Magill* and also stated that the tests proposed in the *Magill* case was to be applied cumulatively and that both tests must be satisfied for the finding of a competition violation. Specifically, the court took the view that a compulsory licence should not be issued where the competitors only propose 'clones' of the main product. Only the advancement of innovative processes, through development of new products, may justify a limitation of IPRs through the grant of a compulsory licence ('innovation balance test').[49]

5.22 In *Microsoft*, the court further expanded on the tests proposed in the *Magill* and *IMS Health* cases. The court broadened the 'new product test' by interpreting it as a 'limitation to technical development to the prejudice of consumers under Article 102(b)'.[50] In the court's view, a compulsory licence was justified where the complainant has shown that the refusal to licence is likely to harm consumers.[51] Here, consumer harm for this purpose is primarily interpreted in terms of consumer choice, or lack of it.[52] This interpretation has been criticised as capable of discouraging investments into innovative but costly research.[53]

5.23 In all, these EU cases show the role of competition law in the exercise of copyright. The application of competition law to restrict the exercise of IPRs can only be made in 'exceptional circumstances' and mere existence of IPR will not confer dominance. The decision in these cases especially as to the test to be applied in determining what would constitute 'exceptional circumstances' in which a competition authority would interfere with the exercise of copyright and issue a compulsory licence; is noteworthy for the direction it provides on the relationship between IP generally and competition law.[54] It is also significant for the direction it offers on when competition law will impose compulsory licence.

5.24 Notably, the application of competition law to restrict the exercise of copyright per se has rarely yielded the expected result of interfering with copyright protection.[55] Two South African, two cases are instructive.

---

47 Case C-481/01 *IMS Health GmbH v NDC Health GmbH* [2004] 4 C.M.L.R. 28 (*IMS Health*).

48 Case C-3/37.792 *Microsoft* [2007] O.J. L32; and Case T-201/04 *Microsoft v European Commission* [2007] E.C.R. II-03601 (*Microsoft*).

49 See Anderman S, 'Does the Microsoft case offer a new paradigm for the "exceptional circumstances" test and compulsory copyright licenses under EC Competition Law?' [2004] *Competition Law Review*, *1*(2), 13. Also Park 2010 supra at 72; McMahon K, 'Interoperability: indispensability and "special responsibility" in high technology markets' [2007] *Tul J Tech & Intell Prop*, 9, 123.

50 *Microsoft* supra at para. 647.

51 *Microsoft* supra at para. 650. See Anderman S, '*Microsoft v Commission* and the interoperability issue' [2008] *European Intellectual Property Review*, 30(10), 399.

52 Colston C and Galloway J, *Modern Intellectual Property Law* (Taylor & Francis 2010), 432.

53 See Gürel B, 'An external method for establishing the balance in intellectual property rights' scope: Article 102 of the TFEU' [2009] *Global Antitrust Review*, 10, 66; Park JH, *Patents and Industry Standards* (Edward Elgar 2010), 75. Other criticisms related to the objective justification, which the rights holder may put forward to defend a competition law infringement.

54 For more discussion on this relationship, see Drexl J (ed.), *Research Handbook on Intellectual Property and Competition Law* (Edward Elgar 2010).

55 See Drexl 2013 supra at p. 42.

5.25 In *DW Integrators CC and SAS Institute (Pty) Ltd*[56] decided by the South African Competition Tribunal, the defendant, a large software firm, which holds IPRs on software program was alleged to have abused its dominant position. SAS Institute (Pty) Ltd ('SAS') had an arrangement with DW Integrators CC ('DWI') and had licensed DWI to use the IPRs in its business of supporting other firms using the SAS software programs. SAS, however, refused to continue this agreement and DWI sought an 'interim relief'[57] on the grounds that the refusal of SAS was anti-competitive. DWI argued, *inter alia*, that SAS's software constituted an essential facility and, therefore, SAS was under a duty to license to DWI. While the Tribunal did not consider whether the software indeed constituted an essential facility since DWI had failed to establish the relevant market,[58] the Tribunal suggested that there were other suppliers of similar software.[59] Furthermore, the Tribunal refused to accept the market definition proposed by DWI because DWI had narrowly defined the market to make SAS a dominant market operator. Specifically, the Tribunal did not accept DWI's argument that SAS's IPRs constituted a proper market and that SAS's refusal to license was an attempt to leverage market dominance to the service market.[60] Rather, the Competition Tribunal advised that 'caution is particularly well-advised when dealing with the interface between antitrust and intellectual property'.[61] In this regard, the Tribunal relied on the decision of the US Federal Circuit Court in the case of *Atari Games Corp. v Nintendo of America, Inc.*,[62] where the court warned that

> the danger of disturbing the complementary balance struck by Congress is great when a court is asked to preliminarily enjoin conduct affecting patent and antitrust rights. A preliminary injunction entered into without a sufficient factual basis and findings, though intended to maintain the status quo, can offend the public policies embodied in both the patent and the anti-trust laws.

5.26 In *Mandla-Matla Publishing (Pty) Ltd v Independent Newspapers (Pty) Ltd*,[63] the complainant argued that the respondent's action in holding back information on the distribution of the IsiZulu newspaper and in insisting on providing the information only if the complainant and its business partner entered into distribution agreements for certain districts, was anti-competitive.

5.27 The Tribunal affirmed the decision of the Competition Commission against the complainant. The Tribunal found that instead of restricting distribution, the respondent's conduct actually resulted in broader circulation and more sales. Accordingly, the Tribunal held that such situation was pro-competitive

56 14/IR/Nov99) [2000] ZACT 16 (1 May 2000) (*DW Integrators*). See also Brand J, Intellectual property and the abuse of dominant position in South African competition law [2005] *S. African LJ*, 122, 907; Drexl 2013 supra; Van Aswegen 2003 supra at 118–119.

57 See s 59 of the South African Competition Act.

58 *DW Integrators*, paras 23 and 31.

59 Ibid. at para. 25.

60 Ibid. at para. 24.

61 Ibid. at para. 18.

62 897 F.2d 1572, 1577 (Fed. Cir. 1990).

63 *Mandla-Matla Publishing* supra.

as the complainant was compelled to build up its own distribution network in response to the respondent's competitive advantage. The Tribunal took the view that the claim could only be justified under essential-facilities doctrine.[64] Therefore, the Tribunal considered the claim to grant access to respondent's distribution system as 'anti-competitive' as the refusal had even promoted competition.[65] Further, although the Tribunal found that the respondent had exercised market dominance in convincing distributors not to sell the complainant's newspaper,[66] such conduct had no anti-competitive effect as required for a competition law infraction.[67] For this reason, the complaint was dismissed.[68]

5.28 In summary, the application of competition law in cases outside the 'internal safeguards' provided by copyright law has traditionally been undertaken to curtail the copyright owner's undue exercise of his exclusive rights. The possible anti-competitive effects of conduct relating to the exercise of copyright may result in the application of competition law to restrict the exercise of the exclusive rights. With its rules on monopoly and abuse of market dominance, competition law can be applied to cases where a copyright owner refuses to issue a licence and may be applied to restrict the exclusivity of rights where the exercise of such right appears excessive and detrimental to consumer welfare.[69] However, such restrictive application of competition law to the exercise of copyright by the copyright owner is typically unsuccessful due to the availability of substitutable copyright products that whittle down the required market power of the copyright owner.

Abuse of dominance: platform firms

5.29 The prohibitions stipulated within competition law may apply to the conduct of any firm so long as such conduct restricts competition and/or the relevant firm is in a market dominant position in terms of the competition statute. This argument may be particularly apposite for the platform firms in the context of multi-sided music platforms where the focus is on the import of the actions and activities of the platform firms as distributors and users of copyright-protected music content and as data processors.[70] In the case of copyright-protected music content, its point of divergence from the traditional copyright and competition law interface relates to its application to the conduct of other persons or firms (outside the copyright owner exercising its exclusive rights), which deal with content or product protected by copyright law.

5.30 For platform firms, competition law applies as a distinct body of law and there is no conflict in the traditional sense between the two fields of copyright

64 *Mandla-Matla Publishing* supra at para. 53.
65 Ibid. at para. 54.
66 Ibid. at para. 63.
67 Given that respondent's conduct had indeed enhanced competition. Ibid. at para. 99.
68 Ibid. at para. 100.
69 Consumer Focus 2011 supra at 6–8. See also Drexl 2013 supra at 40–41.
70 As shown from Chapters 3 and 4.

and competition law.[71] The focus would be on the conduct of the platform firm rather than the conduct of the copyright owners as explored in the cases discussed earlier.

5.31 When competition law is applied to the conduct of platform firms in using copyright-protected content, competition law complements the role of copyright law in incentivising creativity and encouraging the wider dissemination of copyright works.[72] In this regard, competition law is not applied to restrict the exercise of copyright but rather, competition law uses its legal tools in a complementary manner to serve the same goals of incentivising creativity and enhancing consumer welfare.[73]

5.32 The copyright terms established unilaterally by the platform firms are contractual provisions. Being contractual provisions, they are legal instruments used to formalise business and/or economic dealings between the various market participants, namely, the copyright owner, the platform firm, the consumers and the advertising companies.[74]

5.33 As discussed in Chapter 3 of this book, the copyright terms constitute a unilateral contract and therefore, are not the product of concerted behaviour between platform firms and users of the platform (including copyright owners). More importantly, the copyright terms indicate what the relevant platform firm may do with the copyright-protected music content and how the relevant platform firm may deal with others who use the platform in relation to such protected content. This interface between the copyright terms applicable in the context of multi-sided music platforms and competition law in South Africa and Nigeria are explored in the next section. These copyright terms constitute unilateral conduct on the part of platform firms.[75] Accordingly, in the next sections, reference is only made to abuse of dominance or to unilateral conduct.

Copyright terms from a competition law perspective

5.34 The copyright terms have been extensively discussed in Chapter 3 of this book. Several aspects of the copyright terms raise specific competition law questions and the consideration of the effect of the copyright terms on competition

71 See for instance Drexl's work, which goes beyond the copyright and competition interface (that is, where the exercise of copyright produces anticompetitive effects, inviting the application of competition law) to deal with the complementary role of competition law in relation to the objectives of copyright law. Drexl 2013 supra at p. 16.

72 See Santos A, 'Nurturing creative industries in the developing world: The case of alternative systems of music production and distribution' [2013] *Mich St U Coll L Int'l L Rev*, 21, 623.

73 Consumer Focus 2011 supra at 2, 18. Also Russi 2011 supra at 170; Polverino 2012 supra at p. 1, Newman 2013 supra at 1443; Santos 2013 supra at 624; Gal M and Rubinfeld D, 'The hidden costs of free goods: Implications for antitrust enforcement' [2015] *UC Berkeley Public Law Research Paper No. 2529425*, 40. Available at http://ssrn.com/abstract=2529425.

74 See First H and Waller S, 'Antitrust's democracy deficit' [2013] *Fordham Law Review*, 81, 2571.

75 See Google Android Statement supra. In commencing investigation against Google, the European Commission was vociferous in condemning the contractual rules and relationships set and reinforced by Google in relation to the dissemination of the Android software.

may be undertaken from various respects. It may relate to a distribution system as represented by the platform; a long-standing business relationship between two firms; and/or the services that are required for the copyright market[76] to function properly.[77] Competition may be affected where a firm (such as a platform firm) depends on another firm (a supplier)[78] to distribute copyright products or where a firm (such as the copyright owner) depends on another firm (a distributor)[79] to distribute its copyright-protected content. In the case of multi-sided music platforms, the relative dominance of platform firms may affect the individual freedom of copyright owners where, the copyright owner as a supplier or a distributor depends 'exclusively' on the facilitating platform as a distributor or a supplier and does not have equivalent alternatives. Exclusivity in this case may arise as a result of the unique offerings of each platform firm. Apart from distribution systems, other issues relate to the significance of the platform firm's ability to obtain a *gratis* licence in respect of the music content, the exclusion of copyright owners based on firm size and repertoire size as evident from the revenue-based licensing terms, amongst others.[80]

5.35 As noted in Chapter 3, the *gratis* licensing term indicated in multi-sided music platforms relates to the grant of a royalty-free or *gratis* licence by each person uploading music content to the relevant platform.[81] This particular provision is aimed at ensuring that the platform firm may deploy the music content in providing its advertising services, without incurring liability for copyright infringement. The implications of such *gratis* licence in relation to the platform firm's use of the music content particularly in cases where the uploader is not the copyright owner has been discussed in Chapter 3 from the perspective of copyright law.[82]

5.36 As a business entity investing creative efforts and funds towards the production of music content, the grant of a *gratis* licence to platform firms particularly for the use of the music content in a commercial context may create concerns for copyright owners. Indeed, as was shown in Chapter 3, copyright owners are increasingly concerned about the viability of the music copyright sector in the face of multi-sided music platforms and their provision of music content free of charge.[83] An additional issue is that of challenges in terms of resources required by copyright owners to monitor and challenge the removal of their music content from platforms that have them without the copyright owners' consent.

76 See Ritala 2013 supra at 25; Drexl 2013 supra at 42.

77 See Ritala 2013 supra at 25; Drexl 2013 supra at 42.

78 Based on this perspective, Ritala suggests that the US removes the dichotomy between interactive and non-interactive service in order to have compulsory licensing apply for all firms operating as a digital music service. See Ritala 2013 supra at 25.

79 See the subject of the dispute in the case of *Attrakt v Google* supra discussed below.

80 See Alexiadis P, 'Forging a European competition policy response to online platforms' [2017] *Business Law International*, *18*(2), 93–97; Verhaert J, 'The challenges involved with the application of art 102 TFEU to the new economy: a case study of Google' [2014] *ECLR*, 35(6), 265–267.

81 See Chapter 3, para. 3.6.

82 See particularly, paras 3.85–3.91.

83 Hence, the value gap proposal.

5.37 Apart from the *gratis* licence, the licensing terms also provide for a revenue-based licensing regime. In this regard, selected copyright owners can share advertising revenue received by the platform firms for the use of the music content to render advertising services. Music content identified by participating partners is excluded from the platform and those uploaded by the said participating partners are monetised through advertising. The conditions for acceptance into the revenue-based licensing scheme vary across platforms. In most cases, selected copyright owners are obliged to own exclusive rights to a substantial body of original material that is frequently uploaded by the platform users. By implication, smaller copyright owners are excluded from the revenue-based licensing scheme.[84] Furthermore, by implementing contractual provisions regarding the payment and termination of payment, the revenue-based licensing terms may have a significant effect on competition in the copyright market. Similar to the case of the terms relating to *gratis* licence, the question is whether there is adherence to competition law requirements in view of the parameters for exclusion or inclusion of copyright owners from the revenue-based licensing scheme. Additionally, there is also the question of how the conduct of platform firm in relation to the copyright terms affects competition in terms of market participation by copyright owners and/or other platform firms. Possible issues relate to the feasibility for smaller platform firms to put such a system in place and whether the licensing terms in particular, impede market entry for other platform firms by unduly raising their costs.

5.38 Another concern with respect to the revenue-based licensing terms relate to the provision indicating that the copyright owners' access to the platform or revenue share may be withdrawn or restricted at any time on any stated or unstated grounds.

5.39 Contracts remain a crucial factor in the sustenance of the business model deployed by platform firms and in the exploitation of copyright-protected music content. But, within the copyright terms established in the context of multi-sided music platforms, the copyright owner (and every platform user) is compelled to relinquish its control of these contracts to the platform firm. Also, the popularity of the music content is the catalyst for the realisation of the economic interests of the copyright owner. As such, the copyright owner is reliant on the platform firm to indicate the popularity levels through number of views, number of clicks on ads displayed during music consumption; number of subscriptions and/or the number of downloads. The popularity levels trigger market forces as they determine the advertising revenue, if any that accrues from interaction with the music content embodying the copyright work. The popularity levels established on one platform may also determine revenue from other avenues such as live performance events, social media and brand relationships.[85] Indeed, number of social media followers, number of concerts in a given period, social media post views

84 See Chapter 3, para. 3.12.

85 Cooke C, 'Dissecting the digital dollar, part one: how streaming services are licensed and the challenges artists now face' [2015] *Music Managers Forum report*.

are all metrics that corporate brands look at to select brand ambassadors.[86] The operation of market forces in this context result in heightened reliance on platform firms, which dictate contractual rules that could undermine the economic freedom of the copyright owner.

5.40 The concentration of economic powers in the hand of the platform firm affects not only the structure of the market, but also the individual freedoms of copyright owners as market participants. As suggested by Bakhoum, the difference between economic freedom represented in voluntary contractual agreements and that represented in market participants' respective opportunity to compete is the determinant of competitiveness.[87] In the case of the multi-sided music platforms, parties have clearly exercised 'formal' economic freedom as copyright owners place their music content on platform that enable consumers to access the content at zero prices. However, there is the likelihood that the economic freedom of the copyright owners to compete in the market created by the platform firm's copyright terms may be limited.[88] This is particularly so because of possible lock-in effects.

5.41 In a revenue-based licensing arrangement, which has the effect of locking in copyright owners, the freedom of competition of the copyright owners as the weaker party to shift to another distributor may be considerably restricted. This is because the option of switching to another platform firm or to other platforms is not a real option as users and copyright owners lose the mileage that has accrued on any specific platform if they switch. For instance, leaving YouTube and deleting uploaded content would take out the number of views and channel subscribers gained. Also, due to the fact that popularity levels generated on a specific platform is crucial for revenue generation, there is the fear that a decision by the platform firm to shut out the copyright owner from the platform may result in economic losses for the copyright owner.

5.42 Protecting economic freedom and freedom to compete may therefore justify competition law intervention to protect the copyright market against 'structural restrictions' and the copyright owners against 'coercion'.[89]

5.43 In essence, the nature of the contractual relationship involved in the creation and use of a platform highlights how the copyright terms in the case of multi-sided music platforms in particular, can be used to restructure the market by stabilising or enhancing the market share of the platform firms as an economically stronger party and by limiting the freedom to compete of the weaker party.[90] The implementation of the contractual terms may also result in the abuse of a dominant position, which is an anticompetitive conduct.[91] Although it did not involve the use of copyright-protected content, the case of *Attrakt v Google*

86 See Booth and Matic 2011 supra at 187.
87 Bakhoum 2017 supra at 17.
88 Heald 2014 supra at 313.
89 Bakhoum 2017 supra at 21.
90 See *Attrakt v Google* para 8; Boy 2006 supra.
91 See *Attrakt v Google* supra at para 9.

offers a good example of how contractual terms may be implemented in an anti-competitive manner. It is particularly apposite to the copyright terms in multi-sided music platforms because the contractual terms pertinent to the case are on all fours with *AdSense*, which is one of the copyright terms of YouTube in Nigeria and South Africa.[92]

Attrakt v Google

5.44 In Italy, the Court of Milan dealt with a case that illustrates, in the advertisement sector, how contractual provisions may affect the economic freedom of a market participant and thus, competition in a given market. The contractual terms may strengthen the economic power and position of a market participant vis-à-vis its competitors. The rules may also limit the freedom and ability of other market participants to participate in other markets. In the case of *Attrakt S.R.L. v Google Ireland Limited* ('*Attrakt v Google*'),[93] Google, which is active in the search engine and advertising business, created two separate contractual relationships with its search engine and advertising partner, Attrakt S.L.R., an Italy-based search engine company. These two contracts were linked to each other and used by Google to control the contractual relationship and create a situation where its conduct undermined the continued participation of Attrakt in the market.

5.45 With Attrakt as a trading partner, Google agreed on a publishing and revenue share service that enabled Google to display advertisements on Attrakt's website and share accruing revenue from the advertisements with Attrakt.[94] Parallel to that, there was another contract for Google to provide advertising services to Attrakt which enabled Attrakt to display its website links on Google's site and advertising network (referred to as 'AdWords') upon payment to Google.[95] These contracts are interrelated such that Attrakt paid Google to attract users to its (Attrakt's) site based on the AdWords agreement and relied on Google to make returns form these payments, based on the AdSense agreement. The AdSense agreement obliged Google to pay Attrakt when users clicked on the ads appearing on Attrakt's website. With Attrakt and indeed each AdSense partner,[96] Google was exclusively in charge of selecting ads to be included as part of the search results depending on the particular website user. Google's selection could not be modified and only Google knew and could account for remuneration earned from clicks.[97] Provisions were inserted in the AdSense contract directing Attrakt to follow Google's directives and to permit Google to control announcements and position of announcements on Attrakt's site, links and search results.[98] In addition to these provisions that obliged Attrakt to largely conduct its business based on Google's

92 Chapter 3, para. 3.14.
93 See *Attrakt v Google* supra.
94 *Attrakt v Google* para. 5.
95 Ibid.
96 Attrakt v Google supra at para. 6.1.
97 *Attrakt v Google* para. 6.
98 *Attrakt v Google* para. 6.1.

directives, additional provisions related to Google's exclusive control of revenue accounting and payments were included.[99] A limitation of liability clause states that Google's liability in the event of any breach is limited to a stated sum. This provision prevents the AdSense partner from collecting actual monies owed by Google in the event of a suit or from collecting potential damages as may be assessed by a court. This may result in huge losses especially for a small firm. In the light of all these provisions, the Court accepted the existence of a dependency between Google and its trading partner, Attrakt. The Court concluded that a situation of economic dependence existed between the parties.[100] Further, the court took the view that Google's conduct amounted to an abuse of dominance as well.[101]

5.46 Analysed individually, Google's position and actions under the AdSense contract was a legitimate exercise of its right to run its business as it sees fit and to accept or refuse to deal with any business entity or individual.[102] Indeed, the Court acknowledged that 'it is certainly true that in fixed term contracts, withdrawal is permitted, in order to reflect the need to avoid an obligatory binding agreement from persisting perpetually'.[103]

5.47 However, analysed together, with regard to their actual effects on the market, the two contracts allow Google to 'create' a firm (Attrakt) that is economically dependent on it. The Court found:

> An examination of the contracts and correspondence exchanged by the parties to the action reveals a decidedly unbalanced picture in favour of the defendant Google, which, from the setting-up of the contractual relationship until its conclusion, dictated the conditions, time schedule and modifications to be implemented on the site owned by Attrakt. It continually made demands of Attrakt of all kinds, aimed basically at monitoring developments in the contractual relations and the possibility of growth on the part of Attrakt. The continual requests for information, the directives and controls constitute clear evidence of the fact that, apart from a business form, unbalanced in favour of the defendant, who decided the fees to be paid and the shares, on the other hand, to which it was entitled for intermediation activities, the Google company was aware of the operations carried out by Attrakt, and hence no increase or anomalous development in the advertising displayed could escape it, unless it was permitted by the company or, even encouraged. The increase in turnover stemming from the contracts was always observed with interest by Google, which, on its part, encouraged the AdWords campaign and received punctual, immediate replies from Attrakt – as it acknowledged itself in the correspondence – on the operating methods used to earn profits, with regard to the interdependent relationship between the two AdWords and AdSense contracts, as well as the technical aspects with which users were redirected to the Attrakt landing-page.[104]

99 Ibid.

100 *Attrakt v Google* para. 6.2.

101 See *Attrakt v Google* para. 9.

102 Both parties had similar termination rights. See para. 7.1 of the judgment citing relevant portions of art 7 of the AdSense contract. Indeed, in its correspondence with Attrakt, Google indicated that '[it] understood that [Attrakt] may want more information about [its] account activity. However, because we have a need to protect our proprietary detection system, we are unable to provide our publishers with any details about their account activity'. See *Attrakt v Google*, para. 5.

103 *Attrakt v Google* para. 7.1.

104 *Attrakt v Google* para. 6.2.

5.48 The two contracts enabled Google to plan and coordinate its advertising distribution services. The costs to leave the Google platform or to shift to another platform were high enough to deter Attrakt from leaving the platform. In this regard, Attrakt's profits were exclusively reliant on the difference between the income received through the AdSense contract, and the spending it made on the AdWords contract.[105]

5.49 It is evident from the foregoing that the economic powers of the parties were clearly unequal, with Google being the economically dominant party. Further, in both contracts executed by the parties, Google clearly had the upper hand and significantly, could terminate the contract at any time.[106] The foundation of Attrakt's business was based on Google's direction and will.[107] It was therefore important that termination of the contract by Google must be made for good reason and preferably, followed with payments of any monies due Attrakt.[108] In the absence of these steps necessitated by the very nature of the contractual relationship and economic position of the parties, Google exercise of its termination powers and failure to pay outstanding monies to Attrakt resulted in the pronouncement of a 'death sentence' on Attrakt's business.

5.50 From the foregoing, it can be seen that the conduct of economically strong or dominant firms and the effect of such conduct on competition can be addressed by the competition law concept of abuse of dominance.

Privacy terms from a competition perspective

5.51 Similar to the copyright terms, the relevant privacy protection rights in the context of multi-sided music platforms have been discussed in Chapter 4 of this book. To reiterate, the right to request access to personal data and the right to seek redress in the event of a breach of data subject rights were considered as most relevant to the context of multi-sided music platforms. It was also established that in terms of economic strength, platform firms who are data processors are significantly stronger than copyright owners, uploaders and other data subjects especially in the context of South Africa and Nigeria. Given these circumstances, it could be a concern where the relevant privacy protection laws

105 *Attrakt v Google* para. 6.2.

106 By virtue of Clause 7 of the AdSense contract, Google 'may, at any time, terminate all or part of the programme, terminate this Contract and suspend or terminate the participation of any Property in the Programme, either in whole or in part'. See *Attrakt v Google* para. 7.1.

107 For instance, Clause 6.2 of the AdSense contract provided that Google's share of profits on advertising announcements of third party advertisers would be established by Google 'at its discretion' and that payment would be calculated 'exclusively on the basis of registers kept by Google'. See also Clause 11.3 of the AdSense contract by virtue of which Google's liability cannot 'exceed 125% of the net amount paid by Google to Attrakt over the last 12 months immediately prior to the moment at which liability first arose'. See *Attrakt v Google* para. 7.1.

108 According to the court, 'In the event, therefore, of proven disparity between the strengths of the contracting parties, an assessment by the court as to whether or not the withdrawal was abusive must be wider and more rigorous, and may be made regardless of whether negligence or specific intent to harm are involved'. See *Attrakt v Google* para. 7.

struggle to guarantee the effectiveness of data protection rights vis-à-vis the economically stronger and dominate firms that process personal data particularly on the internet.

5.52 Given that competition law has the legal tools to interfere with the exercise of economic or market power in appropriate circumstances, it is inevitable that it would be drawn into an analysis of privacy regimes, especially as a way to secure or strengthen the protection of privacy protection rights. Also, in the wave of wider provisions for privacy protection across many countries, there is recognition that firms may use the quality of privacy protection of its products and/or services as a tool to gain competitive advantage. By extension, privacy terms may constitute a parameter with which to gauge the presence or absence of competition in a given market.[109]

5.53 In *Six4Three v Facebook*, Six4Three sought several reliefs from the court and in particular asked the court to direct Facebook to restore its access to the user's data.[110] In terms of the statement of claim in that case, Facebook was alleged to have unlawfully controlled its competitors by first offering and subsequently restricting the competitors' access to user data needed to operate their business.[111] On its part, Facebook has been alleged to cite compliance with privacy regulations as to what informed its actions in restricting third party access to its users' data.[112]

5.54 At the heart of lawsuits of this nature is the question of the role of privacy laws in the quest for balance between competition in the marketplace and the need for access to personal information. The facts of the case instituted by Six4Three are framed in competition law terms. According to Six4Three, Facebook engaged in a 'series of fraudulent and anti-competitive schemes' as allegedly evident from the following facts:

- From 2010 until April 30, 2015, Facebook granted Six4Three (and other developers) access to users' data including data relating to users through a system – 'Graph API'.[113]
- Based on such access and the continued promise of access, Six4Three created its business model.
- Subsequently, Facebook indicated that it would be removing apps' (including Six4Three) access to user data. Facebook eventually removed access.

109 Lynskey O, 'At the crossroads of data protection and competition law: time to take stock' [2018] 8(3) *International Data Privacy Law* 179–180.

110 Case Number CIV 533328. See www.documentcloud.org/documents/5775209-CIV533328-12.html#document/p106/a493727.

111 See Solon O and Farivar C, 'Inside Bikini-Photo Startup Six4three's Scrappy Battle to Put Facebook on Trial' (NBC News, 16 April 2019), www.nbcnews.com/tech/social-media/inside-bikini-photo-startup-six4three-s-scrappy-battle-put-facebook-n995016 (accessed 9 July 2019).

112 Ibid.

113 'Facebook Unveils Platform for Developers of Social Applications | Facebook Newsroom' (Newsroom.fb.com, 24 May 2007), https://newsroom.fb.com/news/2007/05/facebook-unveils-platform-for-developers-of-social-applications/ (accessed 7 July 2019).

- If Facebook had been transparent about subsequent restriction of access to user data, Six4Three would not have commenced operations in the first place.

5.55 Seen from this perspective, the analysis of the privacy terms may also be undertaken from the concept of abuse of market dominance or unilateral conduct, as is the case with the copyright terms.[114]

Copyright and privacy terms and the respective competition law regimes in South Africa and Nigeria

5.56 Corollary to the foregoing, the next paragraphs consider how competition law rules in South Africa and Nigeria respectively may apply to the copyright terms and the privacy terms as implemented in the context of multi-sided music platforms. In particular, the focus is on the statutory provisions relating to abuse of dominance or dominant market position.

Copyright terms

South Africa

5.57 After the abolition of apartheid and the subsequent removal of trade sanctions, the South African government commenced a process to comprehensively reform competition law through the Department of Trade and Industry (DTI) in 1997. The aim was to devise a framework that ensures that the days of monopolies and highly concentrated markets were over and that real opportunities existed for all South Africans to participate in world markets.[115] Consequently, South Africa enacted the Competition Act 1998, which became fully operative in September 1999. The Competition Act 1998 repealed the Maintenance and Promotion of Competition Amendment Act, 1990 and previous related laws thereto.

5.58 The South African competition enforcers (Competition Commission, Competition Tribunal and Competition Appeal Court) are yet to deliberate on the import of the use of copyright-protected music content in the context of multi-sided music platforms. Yet, the debate about the application of competition law to the activities of platform firms as distributors of copyright-protected content continues unabated. As stated earlier, the activities of platform firms have been the subject of much debate in the EU and in the US, particularly with respect to the appropriateness or otherwise of applying competition law rules to regulate them.[116] The prohibition against unilateral conduct amounting to abuse of

114 Kornoff 278.

115 Chabane N, 'An evaluation of the influence of BEE on the application of competition policy in South Africa', in *Trade and Industrial Policy Strategies Annual Forum, Johannesburg* (2003); Dale S (2016). *Case Study: South Africa – Equal opportunity to compete*. IDRC – International Development Research Centre. Available at www.idrc.ca/en/article/case-study-south-africa-equal-opportunity-compete (accessed 25 November 2016); Hartzenberg 2005 supra at p. 667.

116 See *inter alia*, Polverino 2012 supra at 3–4; Gal and Rubinfeld 2015 supra at 3.

dominance is dealt with under section 8 of the Competition Act. This provision may be applied to assess the implementation of the copyright terms implemented in the context of multi-sided music platforms. The conduct listed under section 8 of the Competition Act include charging of excessive prices, refusal of access to an essential facility, requiring or inducing a supplier or customer to not deal with a competitor, refusing to supply scarce goods to a competitor when supplying those goods is economically feasible, selling goods or services on condition that the buyer purchases separate goods or services unrelated to the object of a contract, forcing a buyer to accept a condition unrelated to the object of a contract, selling goods or services below their marginal or average variable cost, or buying-up a scarce supply of intermediate goods or resources required by a competitor.[117] Each of these conduct, apart from excessive pricing and refusal of access, is presumed anti-competitive unless the firm concerned can show technological, efficiency or other pro-competitive gains that outweigh the anti-competitive effect of the Act.

5.59 There are significant similarities between South Africa's approach to applying abuse of dominance provisions and that of the EU. For instance, the abuse of dominance provisions in section 8 of the Competition Act is similar to that found in Article 102 of the EU's TFEU. It is therefore reasonable to anticipate that in cases of alleged abuse of dominance, South Africa's competition enforcers will apply competition law in a similar manner as its EU counterpart. Similar to the position within the EU competition law framework, South African competition law is applied to economic activities on the basis of whether such activity affects the competitive process or efficiency in the marketplace. In relation to conduct, which amounts to abuse of dominant market position, competition law intervention requires that the alleged offending firm be in a dominant position;[118] and the conduct complained of must affect competition in a relevant market.[119] Each criterion, in turn, requires a specific approach.

5.60 Dominance is assessed based on the existence of market power which is analysed vis-à-vis other competitors' market shares in the relevant market.[120] According to section 7 of the Competition Act, a dominant firm is one that holds at least 45% of a given market; or at least 35% of the market in the absence of proof that it has market power or less than 35% of the market and market power. 'Market power' under the Competition Act, means the 'power of a firm to control prices, or to exclude competition or to behave to an appreciable extent independently of its competitors, customers or suppliers'.[121] In defining market

117 See s 8 of the Competition Act.

118 International Competition Network (ICN) (2008). *Report on Abuse of Superior Bargaining Position*. Japan, 10. Available at www.internationalcompetitionnetwork.org/uploads/library/doc386.pdf (accessed 9 March 2017); Bakhoum 2017 supra 5 at 16. Under EU law, abusive behavior can only constitute an infringement if performed by a dominant firm.

119 ICN Report 2008 supra at 10. Also see Bakhoum 2017 supra at 16.

120 See ICN Report 2008 supra at 19; Bakhoum 2017 supra at 17; s 7 of the South African Competition Act.

121 See s 1(xiv) of the Competition Act.

power, the South African Competition Act adopts the EU approach in the decision of the court in the case of *United Brands Company and United Brands Continentaal BV v Commission of the European Communities*[122] where market power was defined as the power of a firm to behave independently towards its competitors, customers and consumers.[123] In that case, the court accepted the behaviour of United Brands as evident of its dominant position because it found that United Brands was able to enjoy a position of 'economic strength' which enabled it to 'prevent effective competition being maintained on the relevant market by giving it the power to behave to an appreciable extent independently of its competitors, customers and ultimately of its consumers'.[124] The court held that such behaviour by an undertaking in a dominant position where it succeeds in eliminating a competitor established in the market, would have repercussions on the 'patterns of competition'.[125]

5.61 In the context of multi-sided music platforms and the copyright terms as described in this book, the question, as earlier stated is whether the copyright market is a 'valid' market in which the *gratis* licencing terms and the other copyright terms enabling its establishment and implementation may attract competition law scrutiny under section 8 of the Competition Act. The dominance in question largely relates to the relationship between the platform firms and the copyright owner so that the considerations highlighted in the general discussion of abuse of dominance earlier in this chapter,[126] regarding the issuance of a compulsory licence under competition law, may be more apposite for a copyright law-based statutory licence.[127] The relationship between the platform firms and the copyright owner amounts to a vertical relationship, as copyright owners may be suppliers to or, customers of the platform firm.[128] Furthermore, by providing a free platform that enables massive reproduction of music content, platform firms occupy a unique and powerful position in relation to the distribution of music content. Accordingly, while the platform firm may not have the requisite 35% and/or above 35% of the market for the production and distribution of music content, it does have the power to behave independent of the copyright owners and other users of its platform (market power).[129]

---

122 [1978] ECR I-00207, para. 65 (United Brands); C-85/76, *Hoffmann-La Roche/Commission* [1979] ECR I-00461, para. 38.

123 See *United Brands* supra at para. 38. See also ICN Report 2008 supra at 22.

124 FitzPatrick MH, '*United Brands Company v. Commission of the European Communities*: window to price discrimination law in the European Economic Community' [1979] *Nw J Int'l L & Bus*, 1, 338; Maliszewska-Nienartowicz J. 'The abuse of the dominant position within the internal market of the European Community: From theoretical assumptions to practice' [2007] *Interdisciplinary Management Research*, 3, 429–448.

125 See *United Brands* supra at para. 112.

126 See paras 4.14 to 4.28.

127 See Chapter 6.

128 See s 1(xxxiii)(ii) of the South African Competition Act.

129 See, for example, the Swiss Cartel Act, which modifies the definition of 'dominance' and provides that, 'The term "enterprises having a dominant position in the market" means one or more enterprises being able, as regards supply or demand, to behave in a substantially independent manner with regard to the other participants (competitors, suppliers or customers) in the market'. See art 4

5.62 However, the behaviour of a dominant firm would only be abusive if such behaviour falls under the conduct prohibited as such under the Act.[130] In the case of South Africa, section 8 of the Competition Act contains a closed list of conduct prohibited for dominant firms. Therefore, unlike art 102 TFEU which prohibits 'any abuse' by a dominant firm and contains a non-exhaustive list of conduct considered abusive, South African Competition Act appears to consider only the listed conduct in section 8 as abusive.[131] Accordingly, while art 102(2) TFEU does not exclude the possibility of recognising abuses not mentioned in art 102(2) TFEU,[132] section 8 of the Competition Act may not recognise conduct outside the list provided in the Act.[133]

5.63 Some specific aspects of the copyright terms that raise competition law questions include: the potential of the *gratis* licensing scheme to exclude copyright owners from the copyright market based on loss of revenue; the aspect of the revenue-based licensing rule that excludes copyright owners with smaller number of music content. These issues may be considered in relation to section 8(c) of the Competition Act given that other paragraphs of section 8, as listed in paragraph 4.10 of this chapter, deal with specific matters such as excessive pricing,[134] refusal of essential facilities to a competitor,[135] tying[136] and the like.[137] While excessive pricing covered by section 8(a) relates to instances where a dominant undertaking, which holds dominant market power, charges prices that are above the competitive pricing level, refusal of essential facilities prohibited under section 8(b) relates to cases where the dominant firm has a product or facility which is considered crucial for competitors to compete.[138]

II Swiss Cartel Act (Federal Act on Cartels and Other Restraints of Competition of 6 October 1995, Systematic Compilation of Federal Law (SR) 251), amended pursuant to Paragraph I of the Federal Act of 20 June 2003, in force from 1 April 2004 (AS 2004 1385, 1390; BBl 2002 2022). See also Këllezi 2008 supra at p. 66.

130 See Drexl 2013 supra at p. 111.

131 Section 8 uses the expression 'it is prohibited for a dominant firm to'. Cf. art 102(1) TFEU which uses the expression 'any abuse'.

132 See Case C-95/04 P *British Airways v Commission* [2007] ECR I-2331, paras 57–59, where it was held that competition law enforcers are not prevented from recognising abusive conduct relating to rebates beyond the requirements of art 102(2)(b) TFEU.

133 This is one of the maxim of statutory interpretation: *expressio unius personae vel rei, est exclusio alterius or inclusio unius est exceusio alterius* – meaning 'the express mention of one person or thing is the exclusion of another or the inclusion of one is the exclusion of another; respectively'. See *Attorney-General of the Federation & 2 Ors v Alhaji Atiku Abubakar & 3 Ors* (S.C. 31/2007) [2007] NGSC 118 (20 April 2007)

134 See s 8(a) of the Act.

135 See s 8(b) of the Act.

136 See s 8(d)(iii) of the Act. 'Tying' is defined as a dominant firm (or firm with substantial market power) selling one product (the tying product) only on the condition that the buyer also purchases a different (or tied) product, or agrees that it will not purchase the tied product from another supplier.

137 See Parr G (2011), Squeezing the margin squeeze abuse into the South African Competition Act. In *University of Johannesburg: conference on competition law and economics, 3–4 October 2011*. Available at www.compcom.co.za/wp-content/uploads/2014/09/UJ-Margin-Squeeze-Geoff-Parr-26-Sept-2011.pdf (accessed 23 May 2018).

138 See the cases of *DW Integrators* and *Mandla-Matla Publishing*, respectively discussed in this chapter.

5.64 Section 8(c) of the South African Competition Act contains a catch-all provision on exclusionary acts. It prohibits dominant firms from engaging in any action that prevents or impedes another firm entering into, or expanding within a market (exclusionary act).[139] Such conduct is only prohibited if it is shown that the anti-competitive effect of the exclusion outweighs its technological, efficiency or other pro-competitive gain. Accordingly, in the case of the *gratis* licensing term where the copyright owner may be inhibited from investing in creative and distributive efforts due to the absence of revenue, the question is whether the anti-competitive effect of such exclusion outweighs any pro-competitive gains. In the case of the revenue-based licensing term smaller copyright owners are excluded based on the size of their copyright portfolio. Similarly, the question from a competition law perspective is whether the anti-competitive effect arising from treating copyright owners differently based on the quantity of content in which rights are held outweighs the pro-competitive or other gains from such exclusion.

5.65 It seems from the wording of section 8(c) that the onus lies on the copyright owner to show that the anti-competitive effect of such exclusion outweighs its technological, efficiency or other pro-competitive gain. By extension, there appears to be a presumption that 'exclusionary acts' by dominant firms are pro-competitive ab initio or at least are not sufficiently anti-competitive.[140] The exercise of dominance resulting in excluding a market participant is, in most cases, perceived as evidence of competition and controlling such dominance and concentration of economic power is likely to restrict competition.

5.66 In *VG Media Gesellschaft zur Verwertung der Urheber- und Leistungsschutzrechte von Medienunternehmen mbH v Google Inc. ('German Press Publishers')*, the German competition regulator, *Bundeskartellamt*, declined to initiate formal proceedings against Google on grounds, *inter alia*, that it accepted that there was objective justification (i.e. avoidance of damages for copyright infringement) for Google's actions and as such it cannot be compelled to pay royalties for the use of news content.[141]

5.67 In the case of South Africa, it has been posited that because a small business will typically hold a market share of 10% or less in any defined market, it would be unlikely that the exit of the small business will provide proof of sufficient anti-competitive effect as to trump other pro-competitive gains in the

---

139 'Exclusionary act' means an act that impedes or prevents a firm entering into, or expanding within, a market. See s 1(x) of the Act.

140 See Gal and Fox 2015 supra at 332. See also Fox E, 'Comment: abuse of a dominant position: the Americanization of European competition law? The critical role of perspective', in Ullrich H (ed.), *The Evolution of European Competition Law: Whose Regulation, Which Competition?* (Edward Elgar 2006), 235.

141 *Bundeskartellamt*, decision of 9 September 2015, case B6–126/14, *VG Media Gesellschaft zur Verwertung der Urheber- und Leistungsschutzrechte von Medienunternehmen mbH v Google Inc*,. An English translation of the decision is available at www.bundeskartellamt.de/SharedDocs/Entscheidung/EN/Fallberichte/Kartellverbot/2016/B6-126-14.pdf?__blob=publicationFile&v=2.

market.[142] Viewed from this perspective, it may be an uphill task to challenge the business practices that led to the exclusion or exit of the copyright owner (as a small business) as sufficiently anticompetitive. The following statement made by the South African Competition Commission confirms this reasoning:

> The hurdle for proving abuse-of-dominance cases are significant, they require extensive legal and economic analysis. This is evident in the small number of cases where abuse of dominance has been found and the extensive evidence that has been required for these findings. ...[143]
>
> . . . [it] should be noted that cases that deal with abuse of market power are often difficult to prove in practice. Specifically, complaints relying on those sections of the Competition Act wherein a small business must prove a substantial prevention or lessening of competition in a particular relevant market are often unsuccessful.[144]

5.68 Prohibited practices are prosecuted under the Competition Act either as restrictive agreements, which have the effect of substantially preventing or lessening competition in a market (sections 4 and 5), or as an abuse of a dominant position (sections 8 and 9). The abuse of dominance provisions of the Competition Act in particular, outlaw a range of exclusionary acts that are most likely to affect small businesses as existing firms or new entrants seeking access to markets. While the prohibited practices in Chapter 2 of the Competition Act may engender a consideration of the interests of small businesses or firms,[145] the likelihood of finding antitrust liability in most of these cases when the offending effect is the exit of a small firm, is low.

5.69 It is possible to argue that where the copyright owner as a market participant loses the opportunity and freedom to compete within the economy and to access alternatives both as supplier and 'buyer', the *gratis* licensing term has the effect of substantially reducing competition.[146] Here, it is to be noted that as indicated in previous chapters, the protection of the economic freedom of the copyright owner contributes to keeping the copyright market open and competitive. The existing link between competition and SMEs participation in the market has already been drawn in Chapters 2 and 3 of this book. Sometimes the exclusion of protected works from the market does not have significant effect. The crucial competition issue here is the exclusion of the copyright owner, a small business/SME from the economy and economic participation. It is argued that in the context of multi-sided music platforms, the *gratis* licensing terms as embodied in the terms of use or service, create a situation where the economic

142 See Kampel K (2004), *Competition law and SMEs: Exploring the competitor/competition debate in a developing democracy* (No. 30655). University of Manchester, Institute for Development Policy and Management (IDPM). See also Du Plessis L (2015). *How does competition law enforcement benefit small business*. Competition News, Edition 53. Available at www.compcom.co.za/wp-content/uploads/2015/03/Competition-Commision-September-Newsletter.pdf, p. 8 (accessed 5 March 2017).

143 See Compcom.co.za (2017). *Abuse of dominance | The Competition Commission of South Africa*. Available at www.compcom.co.za/abuse-of-dominance/ (accessed 6 February 2017).

144 See Du Plessis 2015 supra at 8.

145 Ibid. at 7.

146 Bakhoum 2017 supra at 15.

freedom of the copyright owner depends largely on the platform firm. Indeed, in some instances, leveraging on such economic dependence presents dire consequences for competition in the copyright market. The fact that the platform firms deliberately refrain from taking proportionate measures to prevent the availability of infringing content, taking advantage of the delays and inefficiencies that come with notice and takedown procedures (i.e. the copyright owner first has to identify the content, notify the platform and await takedown), may lend credence to the anticompetitive assessment. Also, the question of whether it is feasible for copyright owners and/or smaller platforms to put such a system in place and whether such will raise their costs (thereby impeding their market entry) may be proof of anti-competitive effect.

5.70 The European Commission in its investigations and complaints against Alphabet Inc. took a similar approach where the Commission indicted Google (which has Alphabet as its parent company) for the contractual terms which Google stipulated for the use of its Android[147] software in mobile phone operating systems.[148] The result of the Commission's investigation considered Google as dominant in the markets for 'general internet search services, licensable smart mobile operating systems and app stores for the Android mobile operating system'. Google was found to hold market shares of more than 90% in each of the identified markets in the European Economic Area (EEA).[149] Having established Google's market dominant position, the Commission went on to identify the potentially infringing conduct inherent in the business practices and contractual stipulations for using the Android open business model. While the Commission expressed the view that by itself, Android was pro-competitive, Google, in offering a platform that facilitated the deployment of an open business model (Android), stipulated contractual terms that raised antitrust concerns. According to the Commission, the following business practices were anticompetitive:

1 Requiring manufacturers to pre-install Google Search and Google's Chrome browser and requiring them to set Google Search as default search service on their devices, as a condition to license certain Google proprietary apps.
2 Preventing manufacturers from selling smart mobile devices running on competing operating systems based on the Android open source code.

147 Android, owned by Google Inc., is an open-source operating system, meaning that it can be freely used and developed by anyone to create a modified mobile operating system. See Clark T '*Google v. Commissioner*: a comparison of European Union and United States antitrust law' [2006] *Seton Hall L Rev*, 47, 1021.

148 See Cardoso R and Ren R (2016). *European Commission – Press Releases – Press release – Antitrust: Commission sends Statement of Objections to Google on Android operating system and applications*. Europa.eu. Available at http://europa.eu/rapid/press-release_IP-16-1492_en.htm (accessed 14 March 2017).

149 Ibid.

3 Giving financial incentives to manufacturers and mobile network operators on condition that they exclusively pre-install Google Search on their devices.

5.71 In considering the effects of the identified business practices and contractual rules, on the relevant markets, the Commission found that the conduct would have the following effects: (1) strengthen Google's dominant position in general internet search services; (2) impede the ability of Google's competitors in the mobile browsers market to compete with Google; (3) obstruct the development of operating systems based on the Android open source code; and (4) hinder the opportunities that the Android open source code would offer for the development of new apps and services.[150]

5.72 Some scholars have condemned this approach as an inappropriate challenge to Google's very business model.[151] In particular, Colomo compared the facts of the investigation with the facts in *Pronuptia de Paris GmbH v Pronuptia de Paris Irmgard Schiligallis* (*Pronuptia*),[152] arguing that the Commission needs to show that it assessed the conditions of competition with and without Google's business practices before expressing competition concerns.[153] However, it is argued that analysis such as Colomo's sets a single agenda for competition law enforcement.[154] Such agenda relates to the application of competition law only when the competition process manifested in the absence of efficiency is affected. But, as Evenett rightly noted:

> competition law is a multifaceted tool and can be adapted to different circumstances. For example, the presence in many developing countries of a large informal sector in certain markets may alter assessments of the number of substitutes available to buyers and therefore the assessment of the market power of incumbent firms. This consideration may not be that important in implementing competition law in the highest income countries.[155]

5.73 Conversely, despite the possibility that the incentive for continued investment in creative efforts may be reduced by the *gratis* licencing and circumstances regarding its grant and use, there is no compulsion under competition law for platform firms to procure a paid licence in every case. This is especially so in view of the requirement to show that the anticompetitive effect of such contractual term outweighs the 'technological, efficiency or other pro-competitive,

150 Ibid.

151 See Van Loon 2012 supra at 34. See also Colomo P (2016). *Android meets Pronuptia, or why software licensing is like a franchising agreement.* Chillin' Competition. Available at https://chillingcompetition.com/2016/04/25/android-meets-pronuptia-or-why-software-licensing-is-like-a-franchising-agreement/ (accessed 9 March 2017).

152 Case 161/84.

153 Ibáñez Colomo P and Lamadrid de Pablo A, 'On the notion of restriction of competition: what we know and what we don't know we know', in Gerard D, Merola M and Meyring B (eds), *The Notion of Restriction of Competition: Revisiting the Foundations of Antitrust Enforcement in Europe*. Available at https://ssrn.com/abstract=2849831 (accessed 9 March 2017).

154 Evenett 2015 supra at 16–18.

155 Ibid. at 18. See also Bakhoum 2017 supra at 19.

gain' resulting from such rule.[156] Such proof may be hard to find when the efficiency in the distribution of music content arising from the implementation of the copyright terms is considered.[157] The likelihood of wider distribution of copyright-protected content and the existence of incentive for continued creativity are key parameters for assessing competition consequences. This criterion was applied by the Japanese competition authority to promote competition in the distribution of sound recordings through ring tones. In the relevant cases, the complaint was that the actions of the distributor firm that owns the distribution system amounts to abuse of dominance.[158] For one, both parties benefit from the *gratis* licence: the platform firm is able to use the music content for advertising, the copyright owners benefit from the visibility and free distribution provided by the existence of the platform.[159] Within the music industry, 'plugging' has been a significant part of the business model and a key mechanism for promoting new music content. According to Towse, plugging could be an 'expensive affair' with copyright owners spending thousands of pounds to promote new music content in seaside resorts and on the radio.[160] In the context of multi-sided music platforms, the opportunities presented by the free access to the platform are significant. At no cost to the copyright owner, its music content can be presented and promoted to the millions of platform users and advertisers. As a practical example, *NotJustOk.com*, available in South Africa and Nigeria, has come to represent a powerful tool for plugging of new music content. In this regard, the platform provides the much-needed traction that copyright owners seek with providing music content free of charge and overcomes the constraints of geographical location (limited reach) and the inconvenience of online infringement. Secondly, showing the absence of the usual hitches in the music content distribution process can offer proof of efficiency (or other pro-competitive gain) and by extension, provide a competition law defence for the platform firms. For example, collecting societies have relied on their administrative systems and databases to show their efficiency and necessity for the music copyright industry.[161] Indeed, YouTube and its Content ID tool may be prime example of technological and/or efficiency gain. From the database that offers a centralised location for a large volume of copyrighted content to the ability to monetise what may be infringing use, the Content ID tool may be evidence of technological and efficiency gains. Furthermore, there is nothing stopping the copyright owners from designing their own distribution system. However, network effect is to be considered and also the fact that the

---

156 See s 8(c) of the Competition Act.

157 See Heald 2014 supra at 317–319; Okorie, C, *Use of music aggregation in the UK and Nigeria* (Masters, University of Strathclyde 2014), 24–27.

158 See Japanese Fair Trade Commission (JFTC) decision of 26 April 2005, Case No. 3 (Kan) of 2005, Toshiba EMI Ltd; Drexl 2013 supra at 156.

159 See Chapter 3, para. 3.18.

160 Towse 2017 supra at 415.

161 See Hviid M, Schroff S and Street J, 'Regulating collective management organizations by competition: An incomplete answer to the licensing problem' [2016] *J Intell Prop Info Tech & Elec Com L*, 7, 256.

systems are designed in such manner that illegal uploads will continue regardless of whether the copyright owner participates or not. So, then, it comes down to weighing the degree of pro- and anti-competitive effects.

5.74 Furthermore, given the fact that the copyright terms result in consumers enjoying (legal) access to the music content at no cost, it may be problematic to show that the anti-competitive effect of excluding some copyright owners based on a *gratis* licence granted to platform firms on their own volition outweigh such pro-competitive gain.[162] As the US explained in response to the question posed by the International Competition Network (ICN):[163]

> in the absence of harm to competition, governments generally should make every effort not to interfere in privately-negotiated contracts. The package of terms that make up a contract between parties in a vertical relationship reflects the parties' agreement as to how to allocate rights and risks between them in an efficient manner.

5.75 Such position may exist in the context of the copyright terms as used in multi-sided music platforms.[164] Without substantial anti-competitive effect shown, it appears that the Competition Act may not be applicable to scrutinising the specific issues of exclusion arising from the copyright terms as implemented in multi-sided music platforms. However, it is argued that the showing of significant anticompetitive effect requires a balancing between safeguarding competition in the market, respecting freedom of contract and protecting the freedom of competition of weaker parties against powerful business partners.[165] In this regard, the presence or existence of countervailing power on the part of the copyright owner is a factor in assessing the effect of the copyright terms on competition.[166] The protection and promotion of competition in economic activities is not limited solely to the achievement of efficiency[167] and/or consumer welfare goals.[168] The protection and promotion of competition is also curtailed when the economic freedom of copyright owners as market participants is denied.[169] At the foundation of competition law in South Africa, is the intent to control concentration of economic power in the public interests.[170] The copyright terms used

162 See Van Loon 2012 supra at 35.

163 The International Competition Network (ICN) had enquired as to why the United States' antitrust rules will not regulate or intervene in contractual relationships or positions. See ICN Report 2008 supra at 17. See also Katz and Veel supra at 144–145; *Verizon Communications Inc. v. Law Offices of Curtis V. Trinko*, 540 U.S. 398 (2004).

164 Drexl 2013 supra at 177.

165 Bakhoum 2017 supra at 17–18; Boy 2006 supra at 218.

166 ICN Report 2008 supra at 26.

167 Behrens P and Fox E, 'Abuse of market power: controlling dominance or protecting competition?' in Ullrich H (ed), *The Evolution of European Competition Law: Whose Regulation, Which Competition?* (Edward Elgar 2006), 228.

168 Bakhoum 2017 supra at 18.

169 Ibid.

170 See Hodge J, Goga S and Moahloli T, 'Public interest provisions in the South African Competition Act: A critical review' [2012] *The Development of Competition Law & Economics in South Africa* 10. See Fox EM, 'Equality, discrimination, and competition law: lessons from and for South Africa and Indonesia' [2000] *Harv Int'l LJ*, 41, 579 (Fox 2000). The intent to control concentration of economic power is a common foundational feature of competition law in many countries including

in multi-sided music platforms create new forms of concentration of economic power due to their very approach to openness and free (universal) access to music content. Such approach, as reflected in the copyright terms, gives platform firms (non-copyright firms), the latitude to concentrate economic power that dictates the pace of the music copyright industry. This concentration of economic power through openness and resulting contractual terms gives platform firms as stronger economic entities, leveraging powers vis-à-vis the copyright owners as small businesses and therefore, weaker trading partners. Where it reaches a critical level, such concentration of economic power is likely to affect the structure of the market and the freedom of competition of markets participants in economically weaker positions.[171]

5.76 This situation can be illustrated in situations where the platform firm can terminate the contract for any and no reason. The timing and circumstances of such termination may be such that the copyright owner not only loses significant revenue but may also be limited in its ability to shift to another facilitating platform as a trading partner. These kinds of policies and their implementation may limit not only the economic freedom of the copyright owner as the weaker party (vertical approach), but may also strengthen the market power of the relatively dominant firm (horizontal approach). Consequently, the market may be affected.

5.77 To understand better how copyright terms in multi-sided music platforms create a situation of economic dependence between owners of platform firms or distributing systems and owners of copyright in music content, some considerations deserve attention. A technological or distribution platform which is essential to distribute music content at zero price has a much higher value *ex post* than *ex ante*,[172] because at the start of the process, several alternative platforms are potentially available. Once one platform has been involved and network effects set in, competition ends between platforms that may be foregone without significant financial consequences. As a concept, network effects occur where a product or service gains additional value as more people use it.[173] For instance, in the case of multi-sided music platforms, a platform may become more valuable to a copyright owner because of the number of views the copyright owner's music content may have generated on the platform. It is clear, then, how the copyright terms as contractual provisions may well create a situation of economic dependence. To exercise and maintain its dominance in the distribution system, the platform firm may threaten to block the distribution of the music content by removing

the US, Germany and Japan. See Fox 2006 supra at p. 235. Also Gerber D, *Law and Competition in Twentieth Century Europe* (Clarendon Press 2003), 232; Hiyashi S, "The goals of Japanese competition law', in Drexl J, Idot L and Monéger J (eds), *Economic Theory and Competition Law* (Edward Elgar 2009), 56–57.

171 Bakhoum 2017 supra at 20.

172 Ibid. at 13; Wagner 2015 supra at 13.

173 See Katz A, 'A network effects perspective on software piracy' [2005] *University of Toronto Law Journal*, 55(2), 164. On the regulatory implications of network effects, see Lemley MA and McGowan D, 'Legal implications of network economic effects' [1998] *Cal L Rev*, 86, 479; Gal and Rubinfeld 2015 supra.

access to the platform.[174] That is why Ginsburg suggested that the recognition and enforcement of the entirety of the author and copyright holder's monetary and moral interests is the most viable way of securing the position of the author within copyright law.[175]

5.78 However, the competitive effects of the copyright terms used in multi-sided music platforms have yet to attract the scrutiny of the South African competition regime. Such inattentiveness, it is argued, appears to be out of touch with the development needs of emerging economies such as South Africa where contractual processes and provisions between two economically unequal firms (one being dominant in relation to the other) are rife and may adversely affect competition in downstream markets.[176]

5.79 However, in addition to promoting efficiency, the Competition Act also includes provisions that hint at the possibility of considering the economic and contractual position of firms in promoting competition in the South African economy.[177] In this regard, section 2(e) of the Act provides that one of the objectives of the Act is to 'to ensure that small and medium-sized enterprises have an equitable opportunity to participate in the economy'. As Fox points out, South Africa's Competition Act explicitly enables the promotion of competition in order to advance market access of SMEs, highlighting the important link between competition and inclusiveness and equity of market participants and market participation.[178] However, while the provisions of section 2(e) of the Act seems to validate the call for the recognition of the effect of business conduct on small businesses and on loosely defined markets, the Competition Appeal Court in *Sasol Oil (Pty) Ltd v Nationwide Poles CC*[179] largely rejected such interpretation. The reason is, probably, because besides validating the role and position of small businesses, the manner in which section 2(e) is couched frames it as an ideal rather than an obligation.

5.80 Because of the expressly stated requirement to consider the weight of the effect of the business conduct of dominant firms in relation to a clearly defined market, it clearly appears that any recognition of the role and position of copyright owners as small businesses as object of competition scrutiny is secondary to the recognition of the effect on competition in the relevant market as the object of competition enquiry. The result is that the available competition law remedies to enforce the recognition are limited to usage solely by the proof of significant anticompetitive effect as the metric for competitiveness. Indeed, this eventuality is confirmed by several commentators, who have lamented the limited impact of the Act's recognition of small businesses in moving the competition law trajectory in South African competition law beyond the traditional

174 Këllezi 2008 supra at p. 62.

175 See Ginsburg 2017 supra at 81–84.

176 So-called relative dominance. See Bakhoum 2017 supra at 21.

177 See s 2(e) of the South African Competition Act 1998. See also Chabane 2003 supra at 4–5; Hartzenberg 2005 supra at 667.

178 See Fox 2000 supra at 586; Chabane 2003 supra at 4.

179 (49/CAC/Apr05) [2005] ZACAC 5 (13 December 2005).

difficulties related to market definition and anticompetitive effect.[180] For similar reasons, there have been suggestions that new competition law jurisdictions should forgo the economic model of market definition in assessing dominance and its abuse.[181]

5.81 However, the combination of the approach embodied in section 8(c) of the Act and the clear objective in section 2(e) of the Act appears to suggest that the South African approach is more enlightened than its Nigerian counterpart (discussed below), particularly as there is room to apply the provisions of the Act in such a manner as to enhance the opportunities for small businesses to compete. It is, however, questionable whether the application of the Act can ever transcend the market identification and anticompetitive effect approach, as the competition enforcers continue to interpret effects in relation to a clearly defined market, and there are no interpretative mechanisms, which can be resorted to for the benefit of the specific transactions in the event of an abusive conduct.[182] The inability of this enforcement approach in South Africa to break away completely from that requirement to evaluate competitiveness from a defined market structural perspective remains a concern.[183]

5.82 Nevertheless, it may be argued that the fact that there is room to even consider the interests of SMEs (of which a significant number of copyright owners in South Africa are) may yield results that enhance the position of copyright owners. As noted by one practitioner:

> Some of the Commission's interventions in this regard have had a positive impact on smaller businesses. For example, following complaints received related to exclusionary conduct by Sasol Nitro, a division of Sasol Chemical Industries (Pty) Ltd (Sasol Nitro) as well as collusive conduct with other participants in the fertiliser industry, the Commission uncovered various anticompetitive practices that were impeding the competitiveness and growth of South Africa's fertiliser industry. Following the Commission's investigation, Sasol Nitro reached a settlement with the Commission, and as part of the conditions to the settlement the firm was requested to divest its fertiliser blending facilities located in Durban, Bellville, Potchefstroom, Endicott and Kimberley. Subsequent research has shown that this is likely to have led to significant entry by several smaller players at the blending level of the fertiliser industry post the Commission's intervention.[184]

180 See Du Plessis 2015 supra at 8.

181 See, for example, Al-Ameen A (2015), *Application of abuse of dominance in new competition regimes: Unconscionability as a stabilising tool at time of indecision*. Available at http://ascola-tokyo-conference-2015.meiji.jp/pdf/ConferencePapers/General%20Session%204/Abayomi%20Al-Ameen_competition%20and%20unconscionability%201%20(1).pdf (accessed 7 March 2017).

182 Ibid.

183 See Roberts S, Tapia J and Ybar M (2013). *The Same and the other: A comparative study of abuses of dominance in Chile and South Africa*. CCRED Working Paper 2; Roberts S and Tapia J, 'Abuses of dominance in developing countries: a view from the south, with an eye on telecommunications', in Gal M, Bakhoum M, Drexl J, Fox E and Gerber D (eds), *The Economic Characteristics of Developing Jurisdictions: Their Implications for Competition Law* (Edward Elgar 2015), p. 357.

184 See Makhaya T (2011), *The interface between competition policy and entrepreneurship*. Compcom.co.za. Available at www.compcom.co.za/wp-content/uploads/2014/09/Competition-News-Edition-41-Dec-2011.pdf, 17 (accessed 6 February 2017).

5.83 The practitioner observes that

> Though the Tribunal did not succeed in its particular use of the public interest arguments in favour of small business in Nationwide Poles (where it was arguing for a different standard of showing substantiality where a small business is harmed), its remarks about the potential of competition law to contribute to an enabling environment for small business development have merit.[185]

5.84 Notwithstanding the probable implication of the acceptance that the Act provides mechanisms for small business to challenge business conduct that affect them and their enterprises, the question of whether such mechanism is efficacious or efficient in addressing the ability of those small business to stay competitive, remains. It appears that so long as any possible remedy is still linked to the conventional competition law proposition, which associates the harm to competition exclusively with harm to a clearly defined market and harm to efficient market processes, the application of the Act may not even take off in the first place. This leads to the unavoidable conclusion that regardless of the recognition of the contractual position of small businesses, section 8 is still inextricably intertwined with the traditional competition law proposition which reserves competition law remedies to cases where competition (in the form of efficient market processes) in a clearly defined market has been harmed. The inapplicability of the Act may foreclose the benefits of competition law enforcement which include the threat of exorbitant fines as a compelling force that may shape the conduct of platform firms.[186] As exemplified in the European Commission's complaint against Google with respect to the Android operating system, Google made voluntary commitments to rectify the anticompetitive conduct rather than go through the hog of trial.[187] Through the formal step of sending a Statement of Objections, the European Commission informs the firms subject to an investigation of the objections raised against them. Sending a Statement of Objections does not prejudge the final outcome, as the Commission may still decide to close proceedings without a formal decision. In some cases, sending a Statement of Objections may result in the offending firm making voluntary commitments to rectify the alleged anticompetitive conduct.

5.85 Business practices that affect competition in a relevant market are subject of clear rules, which the courts and competition enforcers apply to resolve such matters.[188] These matters are decided by a definition of a market in terms of geographical location and in terms of products and services that are substitutable by consumers in such geographical location. The effect of the business practice

185 Ibid. According to Makhaya, the Competition Appeal Court was careful to make it clear that its decision did not seek to diminish the ability of small and medium businesses to 'use the Act to protect their ability to compete freely and fairly' (case number 49CACAPRIL05).

186 For instance, see s 69 of the Act. Penalties for contravention of the Act may be up to 10% of the offending firm's annual turnover. See also s 74(2) of the Federal Competition and Consumer Protection Act 2019.

187 See Google Android Statement supra.

188 Hughes 2009 supra at 389–392.

on such defined market is what invites antitrust scrutiny.[189] Business practices that concern economic or contractual inequalities are somewhat more problematic.[190] It involves evaluating the objectives of competition law to ascertain whether it should be concerned with economic imbalances that may exist in contractual relationships.[191] The application of competition law to the contractual terms as used in relation to copyright-protected music content on multi-sided music platforms and the likely abuses that may arise from the economic dependences that they create, is difficult because there is a presumption regarding the existence of competition. This presumption relates to the efficiency in the distribution of the music content and the achievement of consumer welfare in that the consumer's need for access to music content is met at no monetary costs to the consumer.[192] It therefore seems unlikely that South African competition enforcers would find contravention of the Competition Act in the copyright terms as used in multi-sided music platforms simply on the basis that the ability of copyright owners to continue in business is hampered by the copyright terms set by the platform firms as part of their economic activities.

5.86 However, there may be hope for the 'small business' argument under the newly enacted Competition Amendment Act 2018. Specifically, section 1(c) of the South African Competition Amendment Act 2018 has expanded the definition of 'exclusionary act' to include an act that impedes or prevents a firm from 'participating in' a market. It is submitted that this provision may put the position of copyright owners as described earlier in context. However, the Competition Amendment Act 2018 is not yet in force, as it is currently awaiting the president's proclamation.[193]

Nigeria

5.87 As indicated in Chapter 1, Nigeria's competition statute was just recently (2019) enacted. Section 72(1) of the Federal Competition and Consumer Protection Act, 2019, provides for the prohibition against abuse of dominant position similar to the position in South Africa and in the EU.

5.88 The criteria for ascribing dominance to any undertaking are stated in general terms. Section 70(1) provides that a firm is 'considered to be in a dominant position if it is able to act without taking account of the reaction of its customers, consumers or competitors'. It seems that similar to the South African approach, this criterion does not exclude the possibility of recognising the dominant position of the platform firm in relation to the copyright owner. In addition to the general criteria for assessing dominance, the Federal Competition and Consumer Protection Act admits other criteria for assessing dominance. Such

189 See, e.g., Lamadrid de Pablo A, 'The double duality of two-sided markets' [2015] *Competition Law Journal*, 7; Alexiadis 2017 supra at 92–94.

190 Bakhoum 2017 supra at 9.

191 Ibid.

192 Bakhoum 2017 supra at 9; Boy 2006 supra at 220.

193 Section 46 of the Competition Amendment Act, 2018.

criteria as stated in section 72(3)(a) to (h) of the bill include the alleged dominant firm's links with other firms, legal barriers to market entry experienced by other firms and even the ability of 'opposite markets' to shift to other firms. Again, it is possible to consider platform firms in the context of multi-sided music platforms as being in a dominant position in view of their effect on the ability of copyright owners to shift to other platform firms. This consideration may be extended to the financial power of the platform firms who control the revenue system under the licensing terms. The language of section 72(3)(b) to (h) of the Act seems to suggest that the prohibition against abuse of dominance under the Act may apply to the copyright terms as used in multi-sided music platforms especially where the terms affect competition as protected by the Copyright Act.[194]

5.89 In delineating what conduct may amount to an abuse of dominant position, the Act is similar to South Africa and differs from the EU, which employs an open-ended approach that accepts the possibility of recognising different forms of abusive conduct.[195] Accordingly, the implementation of the copyright terms may only be considered as abusive if it falls within the conduct listed in section 72(2) of the Act.

5.90 Furthermore, the requirement of dominance on the part of the platform firm is to be assessed in relation to a relevant market. For the purpose of identifying the relevant market, the Act stipulates criteria such as geography, demand-side substitutability[196] and supply-side substitutability.[197] Section 71 of the Act which lists these criteria, employs the expression 'include', suggesting that other criteria outside those listed in the section may be considered in delineating the relevant market.[198] In this regard, it is argued that the production and distribution of music content in the context of multi-sided music platforms may be considered a relevant market in which the platform firm may be dominant. Similarly, the relationship between the platform firm and the copyright owner in the case of the *gratis* licensing term may, even though non-monetary, constitute a relevant market. The fact that a product or service is provided for free does not preclude the assumption of a market.[199]

5.91 In terms of the applicable prohibited conduct in relation to multi-sided music platform, section 72(2)(c) of the Act is most similar to its South African counterpart. Section 72(2) of the Act prohibits the conduct of engaging in an 'exclusionary act . . . if the anti-competitive effect of that act outweighs its

194 Section 72(3)(f) considers 'actual or potential competition by undertakings established within or outside the scope of application of' the Act.

195 See *British Airways v Commission* supra at paras 57–59.

196 Demand-side substitutability relates to the extent consumers are able to substitute the demand for goods and services provided by other firms for those provided by another firm. See Regulation 19(2)(b) of the Competition Practices Regulations 2007.

197 See s 71 of the Act. Supply-side substitutability deals with the extent to which suppliers are able to supply goods and services that provide an alternative to consumers. See Regulation 19(2)(c) of the Competition Practices Regulations 2007.

198 See s 71 of the Act. It provides that 'for the purpose of delineating the relevant market under this Act, the criteria that shall be taken into account include'.

199 See Gal and Rubinfeld 2015 supra at 3.

technological efficiency and other pro-competitive gains'. It seems from the wording of section 72(2)(c) that like its South African counterpart, the onus lies on the copyright owner to show that the anti-competitive effect of such exclusion outweighs its technological, efficiency or other pro-competitive gain. By extension, it may be difficult to discharge that burden of proof in the circumstances of the multi-sided music platforms.

5.92 Indeed, section 73(3) will not consider conduct that may have efficiency and/or technological benefits as prohibited abusive conduct. Nor will conduct that does not lead to substantial elimination of competition be considered as abusive. By excusing conduct that 'contributes to the improvement of production or distribution of goods or services or the promotion of technological or economic progress, while allowing consumers a fair share of the resulting benefit'[200] and prohibiting conduct that 'impede the transfer or dissemination of technology',[201] the Act seems to provide an indication of what it considers 'anti-competitive effect'. This provision is quite similar to the position in the case of section 8(c) of the South African Competition Act, as both provisions require a weighing of pro-competitive and anti-competitive effect. The existing competition framework in Nigeria's telecommunications sector as evident from the Competition Practices Regulations, 2007, lend credence to this position.[202] The application of the 'jurisprudence' available from the Competition Practices Regulations, 2007 (the 'Regulations') suggests that Nigeria may lean towards the EU and South African approach to enforcing competition law on multi-sided music platforms,[203] the Regulations define dominance in terms of a relevant market clearly stipulating that 'the evaluation of dominant position shall begin with the definition of the relevant communications market or markets'. Also, similar to the position in South Africa, it is required that the alleged conduct must affect competition in terms of efficiency before it falls within the prohibited conduct.[204] Accordingly, the difficulties and opportunities applicable in the South African context may be experienced in the case of Nigeria.

5.93 This notwithstanding, it is not certain how this provision may be applied in practical terms. Having been quite recently enacted (2019), the Federal Competition and Consumer Protection Act makes Nigeria a young, amateur competition law jurisdiction, which would require guidance and flexibilities to properly apply and enforce the law.[205]

200 Section 73(3).

201 Section 73(4).

202 While the provisions of the Competition Practices Regulations, 2007 do not apply to markets outside the telecommunications sector; they may have some practical application. See Nigerian Communications Commission (2009). *Consultation paper on dominance in selected communications markets*. Abuja. See *Emerging Markets Telecommunication Service Limited v MTN Nigeria Communications Limited and Visafone Communications Limited*, Suit nos. FHC/L/CS/130/2016 (unreported).

203 Section 7 of the South African Competition Act clearly defines 'dominant firm' in relation to power and/or share in a clearly defined market.

204 See s 73(3).

205 See Okorie C, 'An analysis of the IP-related provisions of the Nigerian Federal Competition and Consumer Protection Act 2019' [2019] *Journal of Intellectual Property Law & Practice*, https://

Privacy terms

5.94 The same considerations as discussed earlier in relation to the copyright terms apply *mutatis mutandis* to the privacy terms as implemented in multi-sided music platforms. While there may be anti-competitive conduct relating to the processing of personal information and by extension, the rights of data subjects, competition law will be applied based on the provisions of the statute and using criteria available under the statute to assess such conduct. Basically, the refusal of access to data will not necessarily contravene the Competition Act in the absence of market definition, dominance in that market and anti-competitive effects in terms of the Act. As shown in the previous section, analysis of potential anti-competitive effects can be quite complex.[206]

5.95 Further, the chances of claiming that data is an essential facility such that refusal of access to copyright owners and uploaders would offend section 8(b) of the Competition Act in the case of South Africa or section 72(2)(b) of the Federal Competition and Consumer Protection Act in the case of Nigeria is quite slim. In the case of South Africa, the difficulty arises from the fact that section 1 defines essential facility as an infrastructure or resource that cannot be easily replicated and one, which without access, a firm would not reasonably be able to provide goods and services. So, merely thwarting efforts to obtain access or the existence of difficulties in duplicating the data analytics is unlikely to suffice.[207]

Conclusion

5.96 In this chapter, it has been shown that there are specific problems in applying competition law on platform firms that rely on copyright-protected music content and personal data to provide their services to a specific customer segment. Platform firms are 'content-oriented' rather than based on trading (in the e-commerce sense) per se. Many of the applicable competition law rules are inferred from section 8 of the South African Competition Act, which in many respects is similar to section 72(2) of the Nigerian Federal Competition and Consumer Protection Act. These statutory provisions prohibit abuse of dominant position. They require the erring firm to be dominant in a relevant market and more significantly, for their conduct to have a high degree of anticompetitive effect. Where the conduct of the allegedly erring firm only leads to the exit of a small firm, the prohibition may not apply.

5.97 In South Africa, the lack of decided cases upholding such weaker firms' interests in antitrust interventions bears testimony to the apparent disregard of the

doi.org/10.1093/jiplp/jpz064; Ani L 'Rethinking competition law and policy: building a framework for implementation in Nigeria' [2012] *NIALS Journal of Business Law*, Maiden Edition, 1.

206 Sutherland P and Kemp K, *Competition Law of South Africa* (Service Issue 21, LexisNexis Butterworths 2017) 5–91 to 5–93.

207 Okorie C, 'An analysis of the IP-related provisions of the Nigerian Federal Competition and Consumer Protection Act 2019' [2019] *Journal of Intellectual Property Law & Practice*, https://doi.org/10.1093/jiplp/jpz064.

enforcers in favour of the continued application of the 'anticompetitive effect' approach. It has also been shown that the institutionalisation of similar requirement by Part II of the Nigerian Competition Practices Regulations of 2007, following the liberalisation of the telecommunication sector, may put Nigeria on the same pane as its South African counterpart, since it points the way for future competition law enforcement. In terms of differences between South Africa's position and the Nigerian position considered in this chapter, what is clearly lacking in the case of Nigeria, but which is clearly present under section 2(e) of the South African Competition Act, 1998, is the stated objective that considers the continued ability of small businesses to participate in the economy.[208]

5.98 Yet, this chapter has also demonstrated that competition is affected in the implementation of the copyright and privacy terms in the context of multi-sided music platforms, as the implementation create economic dependences that threaten the freedom to compete of the copyright owners. In this regard, because platform firms control the revenue flow and revenue share and may exercise termination rights without justification, the contractual terms set by these platform firms may adversely affect competition in the marketplace for the distribution of music content and may lead to decreased incentive to produce. The current approach that considers only harm to consumer welfare or harm to competition in terms of market efficiency may result in the unhealthy assumption that the copyright market is competitive when the reverse may well be the case. In these circumstances, it is argued that there is a need for prohibition of abusive conduct for non-dominant platform firms and in cases where the freedom to compete or participate in a market is unduly fettered. This is especially so when the protection sought for the freedom of the copyright owners to compete is not a protection of their right to profit. Rather, the competition law scrutiny is expected to ensure that protection is guaranteed for efficient, competitive copyright owners who can compete effectively in the market and whose freedom are restricted by dominant platform firms.[209] Under such regulatory framework, the implementation of the copyright and privacy terms in multi-sided music platforms is expected to promote the freedom of the copyright owners to compete. As such, platform firms will be prevented from abusing their superior position as firms upon whom copyright owners are dependent. Indeed, there can be no competition without competitors.[210] In the context of multi-sided music platforms where copyright owners are akin to both suppliers and customers, protection of the competition process would allow them to avoid exploitative as well as exclusionary practices that originate from dominant or relatively dominant firms.[211] Their protection as market participants in this case may be more important than their protection as

208 Brassey M and others. *Competition Law* (Juta 2002) 2.

209 Bakhoum 2017 supra at 22.

210 Behrens and Fox 2006 supra at 228.

211 Fox 2006 supra at 237; Drexl J, 'Consumer welfare and consumer harm: adjusting competition law and policies to the needs of developing jurisdictions', in Gal M, Bakhoum M, Drexl J, Fox E and Gerber D (eds), *The economic characteristics of developing jurisdictions: Their implications for competition law* (Edward Elgar 2015), 289–290.

end consumers.[212] Protecting the competition process guarantees the protection of all actors, be they big or small.

5.99 In the circumstances, the presumption that in providing wider access to music content, the copyright terms used in multi-sided music platforms offer a competitive and efficient market for those music content, may be problematic. Corollary to the foregoing, the argument is that there is no need to bring the business practices related to the platforms under competition law scrutiny or to enquire if those practices achieve the cardinal purposes (encouraging the creation *and* distribution of copyright works) of copyright law. Such presumption, it is argued, does not take cognizance of the effect that the implementation of the copyright terms may have on the market for music content, that is the position of and the interaction between the various market participants.

212 See Drexl 2015 supra at 289; Evenett 2015 supra at 28–30.

CHAPTER 6

Regulatory and advisory directions

Introduction

6.1 This chapter aims at proposing ways in which South Africa and Nigeria may apply copyright law, privacy law and the complementary legal framework of competition law to regulate the activities of multi-sided music platforms. The manner in which copyright-protected music content and personal data are used in multi-sided music platforms and the implications of such uses from the context of copyright, competition and privacy laws have been discussed in the preceding chapters. Understanding the foregoing is crucial to the copyright law framework, which protects the music content used in multi-sided music platforms; privacy protection, which protects the privacy interests of natural and legal persons; and the application of competition law, which regulates the economic activities of firms.

6.2 Difficulties involving legislative and interpretative gaps in copyright, privacy and competition statutes have been identified in earlier chapters. Therefore, this chapter offers recommendations and suggestions as to how these difficulties may be addressed.

Regulatory and advisory directions

6.3 In view of the challenges posed by the implementation of the copyright and privacy terms in the context of multi-sided music platforms and the present inadequacies of the regulatory framework, it is imperative to consider how South Africa and Nigeria may apply copyright law, privacy law and competition law towards regulating the use of protected music content and personal data. Three possibilities arise here: legislative changes, regulatory cooperation and appropriate judicial interpretation of the legislative framework. Each solution is discussed below.

Law reform suggestions

6.4 It is important to consider legislative reforms within the copyright, privacy and competition law framework that may make these regulatory frameworks amenable to appropriately regulating the activities of multi-sided music platforms. Three key possibilities arise here:

- The introduction of a duly clarified exclusive right of communication to the public within the current copyright protection system;
- The expansion of the current bouquet of copyright limitations and exceptions;
- Provision for addressing anti-competitive effects of relative dominance within the competition framework in South Africa and Nigeria.

Each of these options is surveyed below.

Clarified right of communication to the public

6.5 As stated earlier, one of the copyright challenges in regulating multi-sided music platforms is closely related to the exclusive rights underlying the copyright terms. The understanding or the perspective taken regarding the regulatory framework may either encourage or discourage platform firms from adopting problematic copyright terms. Therefore, to address the highlighted concerns, it becomes imperative to provide a robust copyright regulatory framework that may serve as an *ex ante* tool for the regulation of multi-sided music platforms.

6.6 Besides the much debated value gap proposal and the calls for the reform of the safe harbour–based regime as it pertains to the platform firms, the literature makes subtle mention of a third option that may provide an avenue for the application of copyright law in regulating multi-sided music platforms. This framework is based on the clarification of the right of communication to the public as part of the copyright system in South Africa and Nigeria. As established in Chapter 3 of this book, the expression, 'communication to the public' is capable of expansive and restrictive definitions as to require clarification, but there is no provision in the copyright legislation of South Africa and Nigeria explicitly defining the scope of the right.[1] The CJEU jurisprudence on the definition of the contours of the right of communication to the public offers a foundational basis for the formulation of this framework.[2] According to this framework, platform firms in using the music content to generate revenue from advertising may be making a 'communication to the public' and would, therefore, be obliged to agree licensing terms with the relevant copyright owners of the music content being communicated. Such use, as described in Chapter 3,[3] includes the tagging, optimisation, advertising and other conduct of the platform firm in the context of the licensing terms with multi-sided music platforms.[4] Clarification of the right of communication to the public along these lines will particularly influence the

1 See paras 3.74, 3.81–3.82.
2 See paras 3.62–3.67.
3 For example, para. 3.92.
4 See Rosati 2017 supra at 15.

copyright terms in a multi-sided music platform environment.[5] Apart from the fact that this proposal avoids many of the concerns raised with respect to the value gap proposal and the related safe harbour regime, it has other significant advantages.[6]

6.7 First, such approach to the right of communication to the public is more likely to overcome the focus on the right of reproduction associated with the value gap proposal and safe harbour regime. Because of the focus on the reproduction right, platform firms have been able to take benefit of the music content without being obligated to share revenue or enter into appropriate licensing arrangements. Further, the focus on reproduction right continues a history of copyright owners expecting revenue from commercial, non-commercial and incidental uses of their works. The provision for and/or clarification of the right of communication to the public in South African and Nigerian respective copyright systems would eliminate these issues, as the recommendation focuses on uses of music content in the business model context. By specifically clarifying the scope of the act of communication to include the activities of the platform firms in the context of multi-sided music platforms, copyright law may be applied to regulate the uses of music content in that environment.

6.8 Secondly, a system based on a clarified right of communication to the public would seldom raise concerns about potential copyright infringement or anticompetitive usage or algorithmic restraints.[7] Due to the certainties provided by such system, platform firms would be even less likely to risk being involved in copyright infringement suits on account of what serves as the hub of their business model.[8] As evidenced by revenue-based licensing arrangements, many platform firms have elected to enter into duly negotiated licensing arrangements with some copyright owners, particularly in Europe and in the US. For instance, after the *PRS v SoundCloud* suit, SoundCloud has become licensed with major copyright owners.[9] Similarly, YouTube negotiated licensing arrangements with Viacom and GEMA after their respective suits. In this regard, the platform firms undertake to account for advertising revenue received in respect of the copyright-protected content owned by selected copyright owners and to share the revenue with them based on an agreed sharing formula. Although these arrangements have met with criticisms regarding the pre-selection criteria, which results in the exclusion of most copyright owners in South Africa and Nigeria who are small businesses/SMEs as highlighted in Chapters 3 and 5 of this book,[10] the basis for pre-selection itself and the revenue-sharing formula, they may also be interpreted as important steps towards the recognition and adoption of copyright terms based on the right of communication to the public.

5 Rosati 2017 supra at 11–12; Angelopoulos 2016 supra at 14.

6 See paras 3.111–3.140.

7 See Litman J, 'Fetishizing copies', in Okediji R (ed), *Copyright Law in an Age of Limitations and Exceptions* (Cambridge University Press 2017), 111; Stadler 2007 supra at 958–959.

8 Ibid.

9 See IFPI 2017 supra.

10 Paras 3.102 and 5.69.

6.9 Thirdly, the proposal to clarify the boundaries of the exclusive rights to recognise the conduct of the platform firms as falling within the communication to the public right should be beneficial towards ensuring continued participation by platform firms. Already, licensing arrangements in the US and EU with major labels and right holders show that these platform firms are cottoning on to the idea that value should flow to copyright owners when the platforms derive financial benefit from their copyright-protected music content. Encouraging the continued deployment of multi-sided music platform is particularly crucial when it is considered that non-continuation may considerably reduce the viability of the music copyright industry. Indeed, as was made clear in Chapter 2, dissemination of copyright works is crucial to a competitive copyright industry. By providing legal certainty (through a clearly defined bouquet of rights), the risks of non-participation and abuses would be substantially reduced.

6.10 The dividends of the suggested framework make even more sense when the *PRS v SoundCloud* suit and the subsequent out-of-court settlement are considered. The claims made by the PRS have been shown to be of global application. Having the suggested framework in place would mean that platform firms would be unlikely to deploy multi-sided music platforms without considering the economic interests of the copyright owners. Rather, they would have been compelled to conclude licensing arrangements that ensured the continuation of their business activities. Furthermore, by clarifying the boundaries of the exclusive rights, policymakers and lawmakers would better position the music copyright industry for more economic growth. Consequently, platform firms would not be virtually left to their devices at the risk of growth in the music copyright industry.

6.11 Fourthly, due to its focus on the very activities of the platform firms (as against the activities of the users of the platform) and its consideration of the profit-making nature of the activities, a duly clarified communication to the public regime may be potentially easier to enforce before a court than an undefined copyright usage framework or one which broadly interprets the reproduction right. It would also minimise or remove the focus on reproduction right as the source of value or revenue for copyright owners.[11]

6.12 Finally, the described regulatory framework would ensure that both copyright owners and platform firms capture value from the deployment of multi-sided music platforms. This would hold true from an *ex ante* perspective, in the first place. It would also hold true *ex post*, since copyright and ancillary frameworks may both have roles to play in ensuring protection against market-wide harm resulting from contravening the regulatory provisions. Copyright infringement suits may be instituted on the basis of such clarified right of communication to the public, where appropriate.

6.13 It must be pointed out that the communication to the public approach may be in theory criticised, due to the allegation that it represents yet another

11 See, e.g., paras 3.112–3.114.

attempt to widen the scope of copyright protection in the face of digital advancements.[12] The criticism lies in the fact that the components of the new definition may not take cognisance of the import of the copyright terms relating to usage as discussed in Chapter 3.[13] Nevertheless, this appears to be a minor issue, especially when compared with the concerns raised regarding the EU value gap proposal and the focus on the safe harbour regime and given that this right already exists in international copyright treaties.[14] As identified in Chapters 2 and 3, there is ample indication that both South Africa and Nigeria as signatories to the international copyright treaties have the legislative leeway to apply this option. Indeed, in the case of South Africa, the Copyright Review Commission Report recommends this approach.[15] Calls for more detailed regulation of the area have been persistent in the relevant consultations and scholarly output. As mentioned in Chapter 1 and considered in Chapter 3, in January 2015, in their respective government communications, both South Africa and Nigeria commenced steps to amend their respective copyright law to make it fit for the digital age. While the process is still ongoing even at the time of writing this book, vigorous engagements from both government and industry stakeholders indicate the existence of higher chances that the result of the amendment process may well provide some relevant solutions to the application of copyright law to regulate the use of protected content in multi-sided music platforms. In all these, care must be taken to ensure that delineation of the parameters of the exclusive rights does not end up over-expanding the scope of the relevant rights. As argued earlier, setting the right of communication to the public squarely in the business model context and excluding personal use and/or mere reproduction may resolve the issue. Moreover, by providing for revenue share only in the case of the business model, copyright law may be more suitably applied in the regulation of copyright use in multi-sided music platforms as no one could successfully argue that the copyright terms restricts creativity, access or usage.

Practical enforcement of a clarified right of communication to the public

6.14 Having highlighted the advantages of the communication to the public regime and rebutted likely criticism of the approach, it is necessary to evaluate its practical enforcement, the issue of implementation being up to the platform firms. Ideally, the codification of an appropriately clarified right of communication to the public will provide a copyright regulatory framework that may engender more acceptable copyright terms for multi-sided music platforms. However, bearing in mind that the law does not set or design business models for firms but rather provides an over-arching framework within which business models

12 Katz 2013 supra at 216–217; Samuelson 2017 supra at 22–23.

13 See paras 3.24–3.28.

14 Paras 3.52–3.61.

15 See Copyright Review Commission (2011). *Copyright Review Commission Report*. Department of Trade and Industry, para. 4.8.2. Available at www.gov.za/sites/www.gov.za/files/CRC%20 REPORT.pdf (accessed 7 January 2018).

may be established, it is pertinent to consider how the suggested model may be enforced. The premise here is that platform firms may, if unchecked, still be able to work around those frameworks to thwart their principles. While the modification of the access and usage terms within the context of the suggested framework may be an easy pill for platform firms to swallow, it is likely that the modification of the licensing terms to permit a paid licensing regime may not enjoy a similar easy ride. As demonstrated in Chapter 3 using the *German Press Publishers* case, the creation or clarification of a new right may be inadequate. In that chapter, it was shown that in Italy, Spain and Germany, creating a new Press Publishers right did not result in the licensing revenue sought for the Press Publishers, as they were compelled to either license for free or risk the freemium service being discontinued in the territory.[16]

6.15 Therefore, it is suggested that a middle ground may be to express the right of communication to the public in terms of copyright limitation imposed by a statutory or compulsory licence as discussed in the next paragraphs. As the next paragraph shows, this suggestion is influenced by a consideration of the tests proposed in the EU cases of *Magill, IMS Health* and *Microsoft*, respectively, discussed in Chapter 5 of this book.[17]

Expanding the scope of limitations and exceptions

6.16 Providing for and/or clarifying the right of communication to the public mechanism alone would be of limited help in applying copyright law and competition law to regulate the use of protected content in multi-sided music platforms. To apply copyright law to regulate such use, it is also crucial to deal with the issue identified in Chapter 3 regarding the role of copyright limitations and exceptions in delineating rights of copyright users.[18] This addresses the issues regarding whether the platform firms' use of the music content and their activities qualify as permissible uses of copyright-protected content.

6.17 From the arguments developed in the previous chapters, it is to be noted that the activities of the platform firms in deploying the platform and in using the music content result in the free distribution and access to music content. Accordingly, given the objective of copyright and competition law in promoting wider dissemination of copyright products to consumers, there is need for caution in circumscribing the activities of the platform firms. However, given the profit-making intention of the platform firms in implementing the copyright terms, there is need for balance in addressing these two significant interests. In this regard, the bouquet of limitations and exceptions may, as highlighted in Chapter 3, play a role in regulating the uses.

6.18 Rather than leave the regulation of the use of music content in multi-sided music platform solely to the clarification of the right of communication to the

16 See para. 3.84.
17 See paras 3.19–3.24.
18 See para. 3.141.

public, it is suggested that the canopy of copyright limitations and exceptions be applied to the activities of the platform firms and by extension, the implementation of the copyright terms. Specifically, the use of music content in multi-sided music platforms should be considered as falling within the scope of the right of communication to the public but such right should be limited by permitting its exploitation upon the payment of an established licensing rate. Under this scheme, platform firms would be obligated to pay established licensing rates to copyright owners when they deploy the platform for use of music content. Further, copyright owners will be unable to hold platform firms to ransom under this scheme. This serves the benefit of providing the platform firms as copyright users with the clear legitimacy needed to make use of the music content in the business model context. It also continues the platform's 'legacy' of providing music content to consumers free of charge.[19]

6.19 As pointed out in Chapter 3 of this book, the Nigerian Copyright Bill 2015 provides for a compulsory licensing scheme for copyright users that exercise the right of communication to the public in certain instances.[20] However, this is limited to producers and performers of sound recording. The suggestion is that the licensing scheme should be extended to other categories of authors and copyright owners with respect to music content. Further, rather than have the collecting societies set the rates with the attendant issues (already highlighted in Chapter 3) regarding the monopoly of collecting societies and its abuse,[21] it may be best to set the rates through a rate-setting tribunal established by statute.[22]

6.20 It is proposed that South Africa and Nigeria applying copyright law in this manner to regulate the use of protected content in multi-sided music platforms would ensure that the law does not preclude the establishment and continuity of business activities that make innovative uses of copyright content. The law will also not preclude increased access to music content afforded by the internet through a restrictive application of the exclusive rights framework. Even though the *Magill, IMS Health* and *Microsoft* cases discussed in Chapter 5 were based on competition law, it is argued that the suggestion of adopting a compulsory licence approach to the use of protected content in multi-sided music platforms, aligns with the tests proposed in those cases.[23]

6.21 The 'innovation balance test' which seeks to balance the copyright owner's incentives to create with the level of innovation in a given industry may be applied in considering the copyright owners' interests vis-à-vis the creativity represented in the use of music content in the context of multi-sided music platforms. In line with those EU cases, the need to protect the copyright owner's incentives to create should not constitute an objective justification to the issuance

19 Samuelson 2017 supra at 35–71.

20 See para. 3.84.

21 Ibid.

22 Daly P, 'Courts and copyright: some thoughts on standard of review', in *The Copyright Pentalogy: How the Supreme Court of Canada Shook the Foundations of Canadian Copyright Law*, 51–54 (University of Ottawa Press 2012).

23 See paras 5.19–5.24.

of the compulsory licence.[24] Similarly, it is argued that the 'new product test', which supports the issuance of a compulsory licence where the refusal to license by a copyright owner may prevent the appearance of a new product for which there is consumer demand, equally supports a compulsory licence under copyright law.

6.22 Accordingly, the 'new product' and 'innovation balance' tests have been adapted to support a 'competition impact' approach to the application of copyright law in regulating the use of protected content in multi-sided music platforms.

Addressing the effects of relative dominance

6.23 From the arguments proffered in Chapters 2 and 5 of this book, the application of competition law rules prohibiting both restrictive agreements and unilateral abuse of market power can complement the copyright law regime in the achievement of its objectives.

6.24 As already discussed in Chapter 5, the relative dominance of platform firms may affect the individual freedom of copyright owners, in the case of multi-sided music platforms where the copyright owner as a supplier or a customer depends 'exclusively' on the platform firms as a distributor or a buyer and does not have equivalent alternatives in the 'world of platforms'.[25] Such dependence may also affect the freedom or ability of the copyright owner and other platform firms to compete in the distribution of music content. In such cases, the individual economic freedoms of the copyright owner where it is a firm may be restricted. Indeed, access to the services of the platform firm may be a prerequisite for effective competition in the market for the provision of music content in Nigeria and South Africa. In such a situation, there is evidently cause for worry for competition in such copyright markets. To address the identified effects of the undue exercise of the relative dominance and apply competition law towards the regulation of the use of protected content on multi-sided music platforms, it is suggested to conceptualise the competition concerns as a situation of economic dependence whose abuse is prohibited. Accordingly, statutory provisions should be adopted against abuse of economic dependence either as a separate prohibition or where the statute adopts an open approach to prohibition of unilateral abusive conduct, within the prohibition against abuse of dominance. The work of the ICN in the approach to and implementation of prohibitions against abuse of economic dependence may be helpful in this regard.[26]

6.25 The concept of economic dependence and its abuse is a creation of competition law in several jurisdictions.[27] Specific statutory provision is present in

---

24 McMahon K, 'Interoperability: indispensability and "special responsibility" in high technology markets' [2007] *Tul J Tech & Intell Prop*, 9, 123.

25 See para. 5.69.

26 See InternationalCompetitionNetwork.org (2009). *International Competition Network*. Available at www.internationalcompetitionnetwork.org (accessed 22 May 2018); ICN Report 2008 supra.

27 See ICN Report 2008 supra; Bakhoum 2017 supra at 9–11; Këllezi 2008 supra at 61–68.

Germany[28] and France.[29] In some other jurisdictions, the notion is represented in the interpretation of abuse of dominance provisions within competition law or in the provisions prohibiting unfair business practices or contractual arrangements.[30] The availability of diverse legal instruments for the regulation of economic dependence and its abuse highlights divergences in domestic legislative approaches to the recognised criteria for the conduct, recognised effects of the conduct and available remedies.[31] However, for the present purposes, the recommendation is based on the prevalent general criteria of a situation of economic dependence.

6.26 The major prerequisite for a finding of the existence of economic dependence is the absence or costs, for the dependent firm, of alternative firms or solutions to sell or to purchase its products or services in the market.[32] In such cases, the economic dependence stems either from the fact that the market is highly concentrated or from the nature of the relationship between the dependent firm and the independent firm.[33] A firm (dependent firm) is said to be economically dependent on another (independent firm) if the dependent firm is reasonably unable to or lacks sufficient means of switching to other firms, in order to continue its business.[34] In fact, whereas the independent firm can end the relationship without incurring a loss, such can engender significant economic damage for the dependent firm.[35]

6.27 Such inability to switch may be present when the dependent firm:

(a) is a small or medium size enterprise and regularly obtains from the dependent firm, 'in addition to discounts customary in the trade or other remuneration, special benefits which are not granted to similar purchasers';[36]
(b) is a retailer of branded or high-quality products produced by the independent firm and the former cannot afford not to have and sell the items in its shops;
(c) is in a 'long-standing relations' with the independent firm who is largely its major or only other business partner;
(d) is involved in the distribution, purchase or sale of a product that is usually scarce;
(e) is dependent on the independent firm for specific technical products.

28 See Act Against Restraints of Competition in the version published on 26 June 2013 (Bundesgesetzblatt (Federal Law Gazette) I, 2013, p. 1750, 3245), as last amended by Art. 5 of the law of 21 July 2014 (BGBl. I p. 1066).

29 See Art L 420–2 of the Commercial Code.

30 See ICN Report 2008 supra at 13–14; Bakhoum 2017 supra at 2.

31 See Bakhoum 2017 supra at 10–11.

32 See Këllezi 2008 supra at 69; Bakhoum 2017 supra.

33 See Këllezi 2008 supra at 69.

34 Ibid. at 64–65, 70.

35 See Këllezi 2008 supra at 65.

36 Section 20(1) of the German Act against Restraints of Competition. See also Këllezi 2008 supra at 61.

6.28 The rationale underlying the prohibition against the abuse of economic dependence was the belief that the structure of the market and competition therein may be protected by providing protection to efficient[37] but smaller (weaker) market operators from the incidence of dependence on bigger (stronger) operators.[38] In this regard, an abuse of economic dependence occurs when a business operator upon which another operator depends, applies that dependence in a transaction or transactions to the detriment of the continued operation or existence of the dependent party.[39]

6.29 The implementation of copyright terms in the context of multi-sided music platforms clearly provides a market for the distribution of music content. However, for copyright owners of the music content, the copyright terms may limit their freedom to compete in that market to the detriment of the continued operation or existence of the copyright owner.[40] Therefore, it is worth considering avenues to apply competition law in regulating the use of protected content in multi-sided music platforms. The copyright terms operate in such manner as to 'exploit' the copyright-protected music content while only offering revenue for a select few chosen based on criteria set by the platform firms. It is suggested that the delineation of copyright terms with no revenue share attached to it despite use of copyright content to generate revenue can fall under the provision relating to abuse of economic dependence through a contextualised definition of the notion of dependence.

6.30 In neglecting to clarify the scope of the exclusive rights generally and, to explicitly involve financial benefit, lawmakers have provided leeway for the platform firms to use copyright content in deploying business models without needing to pay corresponding revenue to the copyright owners, thus promoting the dissemination of copyright products at the expense of other market participants such as the copyright owner. Conceiving of such scenario as creating a form of economic dependence would solve this problem and regulate the business model, at least in part, because it would focus the inquiry on the marketplace (that is where the money flows) and all market participants rather than on the act of reproduction which with digital technology is par for the course. More importantly, the rule against abuse of economic dependence would assist in addressing *ex ante* the issue of the creation of economic dependence, typically arising under the copyright terms. The remedies applicable to a finding of abuse of economic dependence will involve a positive order to stop the abuse as well as directives regarding what the abusive firm is required to do.[41]

6.31 An additional consideration in the notion of economic dependence concerns the question of appropriate approach or enforcement test. Again, different

37 See Këllezi 2008 supra at 67.

38 See Këllezi 2008 supra at 61; Bakhoum 2017 supra at 14.

39 For example, see French Competition Council, Decision 04-D-26 of 30 June 2004 in *SARL Reims Bio*. This decision was upheld by the Paris Court of Appeal, Decision of 25 January 2005, and the French Supreme Court, Decision of 28 February 2006.

40 See paras 5.34 to 5.43. See Këllezi 2008 supra at 84–85.

41 See Këllezi 2008 supra at 87.

jurisdictions apply different tests, which may, in some cases, lead to a finding of no abuse, even when a situation of economic dependence exists and has adverse effects. For instance, under the French Commercial Code, a finding of abuse of economic dependence may only be made where, in addition to the requirement of absence of alternative solution, there is an adverse effect on the relevant market. This enforcement test (also known as 'equally efficient competitor test')[42] will only classify exclusionary conduct as abusive and prohibited if such conduct can exclude an equally efficient competitor in the same market rather than or in addition to an efficient market participant who may not necessarily be a competitor.[43] In applying the test, there is a comparison between the efficiency of the independent firm and that of the alleged dependent firm.

6.32 Such tests fall into the same difficulties as that experienced within 'efficiency-based' competition rules highlighted in Chapter 4 of this book. Accordingly, it will be difficult to apply such test to the copyright terms in the context of multi-sided music platforms, which involves vertically related firms (copyright owners and platform firms), which operate in different market levels. Bakhoum explains the requirement of this test and its inherent difficulties:[44]

> This requirement goes beyond the vertical relationships to consider the horizontal effect of a situation of economic dependence in a given market, from a horizontal and macroeconomic perspective. This combination of contractual (analysis of the dependence from the bilateral point of view) and competition (taking the market as a benchmark for a finding of abuse) related requirements made difficult the enforcement of the provision in practice. . . . Such requirement expresses the difficulties in dealing with abuse of economic dependence with the traditional competition law approach, which requires that the market be affected.

6.33 Such a test is however, not of universal application as exemplified in the case of countries such as Germany, Italy and Japan, which do not require the market be affected or compare efficiencies of competitors in such market for a finding of an abuse of economic dependence. In these jurisdictions, a finding of abuse of economic dependence may be made where the freedom of choice of markets participants is unduly circumscribed because of the dependence of such participant on an economically stronger market participant. In such cases, the law is applied to restore the economic freedom of such economically weaker firms and protect the competition process.[45] For this reason, this enforcement criterion is suggested as better suited to the regulation of the use of protected content in multi-sided music platforms in the South African and Nigerian context.

6.34 Corollary to the foregoing is the issue of how the prohibition against abuse of economic dependence may become part of the law in South Africa and

---

42 Ibid. at 86.

43 See European Commission (2005). *DG Competition discussion paper on the application of Article 82 of the Treaty to exclusionary abuses*. Available at http://ec.europa.eu/comm/competition/antitrust/art82/discpaper2005.pdf, para. 63 (accessed 21 February 2017).

44 See Bakhoum 2017 supra at 15. See also Këllezi 2008 supra at 86.

45 See Bakhoum 2017 supra at 26–27 arguing particularly for the adoption of such perspective within competition law and particularly in developing countries. See also Këllezi 2008 supra at 85.

Nigeria. For South Africa, it is suggested that the formulation and implementation of guidelines as to assessment under the Competition Amendment Act 2018 provide ample opportunity to recognise the notion of abuse of economic dependence. Indeed, it is argued that the notion of abuse of economic dependence may provide the much-sought balance between protecting the interests of small businesses and protecting the interests of platform firms as investors and innovators. As highlighted in previous chapters of this book, platform firms make significant investments in designing the platforms, algorithms and 'advertisement-enabling' features.[46]

6.35 The South African competition enforcers have been quite insistent on applying the market-efficiency test in competition law enforcement and have resisted the recognition of conduct similar to the abuse of economic dependence described earlier, within the list of recognised competition law infractions. However, the Copyright Amendment Act 2018 can provide an avenue for a dual approach to competition law regulation, which may apply to the use of protected content in multi-sided music platforms. Indeed, given that the same conduct may in some cases amount to both abuse of economic dependence and abuse of dominance (as exemplified in *Attrakt v Google*), such dual approach is to be recommended.[47]

6.36 In the case of Nigeria, the notion of economic dependence and prohibition against its abuse may be incorporated within the competition law framework through a combination of legislative (in the form of regulations made by the Federal Competition and Consumer Protection Commission pursuant to its powers under section 18 of the Act) and public enforcement of the statutory provisions. As scholars such as Al Ameen suggest, competition law in developing countries and young competition law jurisdictions may be better served by the more appropriate abuse of economic dependence principles than by the prevalent 'effects-based' competition law approach.[48]

6.37 Regulating the use of protected content in multi-sided music platforms through the competition law notion of restriction of abuse of economic dependence also has the benefit of engendering soft law initiatives such as an industry code of practice involving relevant stakeholders. Such code of practice may require that access terms should explain or delineate procedures for denial/refusal of access to platforms. For instance, platform firms may suspend the counting of views but retain previous view count by showing still images of such music content with the most recent view count. Given the present feature of permitting partners to mute videos containing their copyright-protected music content, there is a strong possibility that this option is feasible. Such procedure may enable the

46 For example, see para. 3.124.

47 See *Attrakt v Google* supra; ICN Report 2008 supra at 20–22.

48 See Al-Ameen A (2015), *Application of abuse of dominance in new competition regimes: Unconscionability as a Stabilising Tool at Time of Indecision*. Available at http://ascola-tokyo-conference-2015.meiji.jp/pdf/ConferencePapers/General%20Session%204/Abayomi%20Al-Ameen_competition%20and%20unconscionability%201%20(1).pdf (accessed 7 March 2017).

copyright owners continue to 'trade' on their publicity through view counts and ensuing social media and brand ambassador relationship, even when their music content no longer has access to the platform.[49]

6.38 The provision for the notion of abuse of economic dependence can also engender stakeholder dialogues to define best practices for matters such as content recognition technologies. These standards or code of practice may contain:

(a) Certifiable popularity index – Platform firms may be required to issue copyright owners with a document or 'badge' that provide an accurate and verifiable record of matters such as view counts, number of 'likes', number of 'followers' and the like.[50]

(b) Requirement of payment of undisputed sums prior to termination or takedown – Platform firms may be required under the code to adopt contractual provisions that ensure that they pay copyright owners all undisputed sums accumulated on the platform in the event that the platform firm intends to terminate its agreement with the copyright owner.

6.39 Such code of practice may eventually become a regional or international standard if properly drafted. The premise for this suggestion is that such industry code only addresses the pertinent areas of use of protected content on multi-sided music platforms that have been shown to be unaligned with competition law goals, while leaving problem-free areas to market forces.

Regulatory cooperation

6.40 Given the possibility of anti-competitive conduct relating to the processing of personal information and the rights of data subjects, and the fact that competition law will only assess such conduct using criteria available under the competition statute, it is not only likely that different outcomes would result but also, the same conduct may be assessed by both competition and data protection enforcers. For these reasons, it is submitted that the suggestions in the literature that there should be cooperation (formal and informal) between competition and data protection regulators should be implemented.[51]

6.41 In the case of South Africa, this is more easily achieved, as section 21(1)(h) of its Competition Act allows the Competition Commission to negotiate agreements with other regulatory bodies for the purpose of harmonising regulatory

49 The significance of the view count as a value metric was explained in Chapter 3, para. 3.128, and Chapter 5, para. 5.39.

50 YouTube already does this on some level to recognise specified milestones in the number of subscribers. See 'Verification Badges on Channels – YouTube Help' (Support.google.com, 2019), https://support.google.com/youtube/answer/3046484?hl=en (accessed 4 July 2019).

51 Koornhof P and Pistorius T, 'Convergence between competition and data protection law: A South African perspective' [2018] 8(3) *International Data Privacy Law*, 277–283 (Koornhof and Pistorius 2018); Lynskey O, 'At the crossroads of data protection and competition law: time to take stock' [2018] 8(3) *International Data Privacy Law*, 179–180 (Lynskey 2018).

jurisdiction over competition matters. Also, as noted in Chapter 4,[52] the Protection of Personal Information Act permit the Regulator to refer complaints to other regulatory bodies where it is ascertained that such regulatory body is more suited to deal with the subject matter of a given complaint.[53] It is submitted that a combined reading of these provisions provides strong foundation for effective cooperation between the regulatory bodies.

6.42 Nigeria may not be so straightforward. While the Federal Competition and Consumer Protection Commission has concurrent jurisdiction in matters of competition and consumer protection with the regulatory authorities in charge of other sectors, there is no specific provision that mandates or provides imperative for co-operation agreements. This is because section 105(2) of the Act stipulates that the Competition Commission will have precedence over the sector regulators.[54]

6.43 Apart from cooperation between competition and privacy protection regulatory bodies, competition enforcers may also exercise the powers under section 43A of the South African Competition Act and Part X of the Federal Competition and Consumer Protection Act to conduct a formal inquiry into the state of competition in the market for data and/or music content. Such inquiry may lead to positive results such as recommendation for new or amended policy, legislation and even initiation of complaints against erring firms.[55]

Application of judicial mechanisms

6.44 As a further alternative, the courts are not left out. Judicial interpretation, which takes cognisance of the identified effects of the copyright terms used in multi-sided music platforms and their underlying causes, would boost the implementation of the suggested regulatory approach. This also has the advantage of applying regulation only in those particularly problematic areas where it is most needed (such cases naturally being more likely to make it before the court), while avoiding pushing the issue too aggressively in individual transactions.

6.45 If statutory provision is not made for defining the scope of the exclusive rights or expanding the limitations and exceptions, it is still open to courts to use their discretion to delineate such clarification as to regulate the use of music content in multi-sided music platforms. In this regard, an interpretation that fits with the reality of the value metric in the digital copyright market will offer a better approach to applying copyright and competition law in regulating the use of protected content in multi-sided music platforms. As demonstrated in Chapters 3 and 4, the new value metric of access to consumer and consumer's data,

52 See Chapter 4, para. 4.76.

53 Section 78 of the Protection of Personal Information Act.

54 Okorie C, 'An analysis of the IP-related provisions of the Nigerian Federal Competition and Consumer Protection Act 2019' [2019] *Journal of Intellectual Property Law & Practice*, https://doi.org/10.1093/jiplp/jpz064.

55 See s 43C(1) and 43C(3) in the case of South Africa's Competition Act and Part X in the case of Nigeria's Federal Competition and Consumer Protection Act.

including advertisement-based revenue can be understood as a call to approach the perception of the copyright terms used in multi-sided music platforms. Similarly, competition enforcers may interpret the effects of the copyright terms as an abuse of dominance in appropriate circumstances using the 'unconscionability' test as opposed to the efficiency-based approach currently applied at least in South Africa.[56]

6.46 Speedy judicial enforcement of the suggestions made in this chapter may be aided by the use of a small claims court and/or copyright tribunals such as are already provided for under the existing respective copyright laws of South Africa and Nigeria. The proposed amendments to the copyright laws in both South Africa and Nigeria, have further expanded the utility of copyright tribunals in this regard.[57] In this regard, the criticisms regarding the expansion of the scope of the jurisdiction of the Tribunal under the Amendment may be addressed by providing an appropriate review system within the courts and/or strengthening the constitution of the tribunals by appointing copyright experts as members.[58]

6.47 Of course, there is the risk that judicial interpretation may not provide the expected relief while it would also possibly result in precedents that perpetuates the status quo.[59] However, such risks are minimal particularly in the face of explicitly stated rules and enforcement approaches. More significantly, it is to be noted that very few copyright cases make it to court and the suggested regulatory approach will require litigation in order to activate judicial action.

6.48 In the case of competition law regulation, the commencement of investigation by the relevant competition enforcer may be all that is required to engender proper conduct by the platform firm. As highlighted in Chapter 5, the threat of exorbitant fines may cause the platform firm to enter into commitments that will rectify the anticompetitive conduct.[60]

56 Al-Ameen supra at 11–12.

57 See the proposed Section 29A inserted by Clause 30 of the Copyright Amendment Bill 2017 in the case of South Africa. See Riby-Smith 2017 supra at 221.

58 Daly 2012 supra at 51–54.

59 Court actions are instituted in the hope that the Judge will interpret the law in line with the plaintiff's arguments. But that may not be so. Indeed, the judgment in the cases of *Viacom v YouTube* supra, *GEMA v YouTube* supra were not quite what was expected.

60 See Chapter 5, para. 5.84; Google/Android Statement supra.

CHAPTER 7

Conclusion

> Attempting to impose rules which clash with strongly established norms, or making law in such detail that the . . . user is not able to understand or comply with it, are not the only ways in which laws can be rendered meaningless. Law needs to regulate the reality which is faced by those who are subject to the law.[1]

Copyright serves the purpose of promoting competition. Properly applied, copyright protection provides the competitive environment required to enable firms to profit from their creative works. This encourages innovation effort and improves dynamic efficiency, to the ultimate benefit of consumer and societal welfare. Thus, copyright laws should be seen as encouraging firms to engage in competition, and in particular competition that involves risks and long-term investments. Corollary to the foregoing, it seems imperative that business models and activities, which are founded on (dynamic) uses of copyright-protected content, take cognisance of this competition-based objective. Indeed, any copy right-based terms used in business activities that fail to measure up to this objective are likely to affect the (music) copyright industry adversely. At the same time, any form of regulation of such copyright-based terms should recognise the ways in which the copyright-protected content is used and preserve the firms' incentives to invest in the market. The imperative is to ensure that businesses operate in a manner as to benefit the society. To this end, South Africa and Nigeria should enforce a legal regime that ensures that commercial users of copy right-protected content work within the objectives of the copyright regime and the complementary competition law regime.

By the same token, privacy protection aims at securing the privacy and individual liberties of data subjects – natural and legal persons whose data may be processed. The aim is to ensure that firms who process personal data do not undertake such activities to the detriment of the data subjects. The internet and innovations in technology have combined to expand the uses to which personal data may be put.

This being premised, the activities of multi-sided music platforms clearly represents a context where the use of copyright-protected content and personal

1 Reed 2013 supra at 151.

data of copyright owners and uploaders may preclude competition in the copyright market. Abuse of economic dependence represents the most serious risk for copyright owners in the context of multi-sided music platforms, and offers a solid basis for concerns regarding competition in the music copyright industry. This opportunistic conduct may lead platform firms to gain undue economic advantages, at the expense of the copyright owners and the copyright system. The cause of the problem must be identified in the copyright and privacy terms widely adopted so far by multi-sided music platforms. Such copyright terms raise several questions as to the best approach to reducing the risks to competition in the copyright industry whilst ensuring continued dissemination of music content. By the same token, privacy terms raise questions regarding the best way to interpret the rights of data subjects to protect competition in the music industry.

South Africa and Nigeria are representative of developing countries in Africa in this regard given their unique economic positions. South Africa possess significant elements of both developed and developing economies while Nigeria has striking features of both developing and least-developed economies. Both countries' music copyright industry is rife with copyright owners who as independent record companies and publishers qualify as small businesses/SMEs requiring the protection of competition to ensure a viable music copyright industry. In an industry characterised by 'ubiquitous intermediation'[2] and prevalence of user-upload digital distribution platforms, where platform firms are crucial to ensuring that music content owned or produced by small businesses/SMEs reach consumers, where access to the consumer is the new way to monetise copyright and where platform firms are also equipped with more far-reaching technical powers in comparison to their older, analogue counterparts, it is imperative to secure the fate of the music copyright industry.

This book has made clear that, to apply copyright, privacy and competition laws to regulate the relevant activities of multi-sided music platforms, an improved legal regime should be put in place. Such a regime should be based on the *ex ante* clarification of the parameters of the relevant exclusive rights under copyright law and a balancing expansion of the scope of limitations and exceptions. Further rules on reducing and/or eradicating abuse of economic dependence should be included, as a means of influencing the implementation of the copyright terms used in multi-sided music platforms. Influencing the implementation of copyright terms, however, also means that undue restrictions on platform firms should be eschewed. Consequently, platform firms need not feel constrained in the manner they deploy their business model, particularly when this would lead to weaken or even destroy their business. The adoption of an improved legal regime based on protecting economic dependencies may also prove effective when considered from an *ex post* standpoint. A regime focused on addressing business practices, indeed, would better regulate business/economic activities in the event of any opportunistic conduct. In this regard, Chapter 6 of this book developed an

2 Angelopoulos 2016 supra at 335.

in-depth examination of the different approaches to copyright, privacy and competition law regulation, which could be potentially applied. Relief against abuse of economic dependence is possibly one effective regulatory approach.

Present and future challenges call for a deeper reflection on the scope and the role of multi-sided music platforms in the emerging global context. As the business models of these platforms become the go-to business model in the music copyright industry and their activities are increasingly global, both copyright owners and platform firms will need to pay more attention to the legal frameworks and enforcement systems that may apply to them. This book has developed a thorough examination of the main risks to competition in the copyright industry arising in the context of the use of protected content and personal data in multi-sided music platforms. The path proposed to apply copyright, privacy and competition laws to regulate the implementation of its current copyright-based and privacy-related terms and protect competition will hopefully help the music copyright industry to navigate through this new approach to using protected content.

APPENDIX I

PRS v SoundCloud

Claim no HC-2015-003033

IN THE HIGH COURT OF JUSTICE

CHANCERY DIVISION

INTELLECTUAL PROPERTY

BETWEEN:

PERFORMING RIGHT SOCIETY LIMITED

Claimant

-and-

SOUNDCLOUD LIMITED

Defendant

PARTICULARS OF CLAIM

The Claimant

1. The Claimant ("PRS") is a collecting society whose members comprise writers, composers and publishers of musical works (which expression includes the lyrics to be used with any musical works). It is the assignee from its members of the performing right in such works and grants licences for the use of such right. The performing right includes the right to communicate the works to the public as that expression is used in section 20 of the Copyright, Designs and Patents Act 1988 ("**the CDPA**").

2. PRS is the owner of the performing right in more than 6 million musical works over a wide variety of musical genres ("**the PRS Repertoire**"). Through arrangements with its sister collecting societies in other jurisdictions, PRS controls the rights to license more than 8 million further musical works in the United Kingdom. PRS owns or controls the performing right in the vast majority of musical works embodied on commercially released sound recordings.

3. The PRS Repertoire includes, in particular, the musical works that are listed in **Annex 1** ("**the Sample Works**") in which PRS is the owner of the right to communicate the works to the public. The full list of the PRS Repertoire is available for inspection on reasonable notice.

The Defendant and its service

APPENDIX I

4. Since its incorporation in 2007, the Defendant has been, and is now, the owner and operator of a website currently located at soundcloud.com and m.soundcloud.com ("the SoundCloud Website"), and related mobile and desktop applications which have been launched by the Defendant at various times since 2007, including services integrated into other services or platforms, such as Sonos (together with the SoundCloud Website, "the SoundCloud Services").

5. The SoundCloud Services provide, and are intended by the Defendant to provide, an online and mobile music service whereby members of the public are able to download or stream recordings, the overwhelming majority of which are recordings of musical works. As described in the Defendant's marketing materials:

"SoundCloud lets you hear more music & audio. Find new and trending music. Collect tracks and playlists. Follow friends and artists. Discover podcasts, comedy and news.

KEY FEATURES

- *Enjoy the tracks you liked and the playlists you created*
- *Hear your stream and enjoy what the friends and artists you follow have shared*
- *Explore Trending Music and Trending Audio feeds*
- *Search directly for tracks, artists and other users"*

6. The SoundCloud Services, and the Defendant's operation thereof, include the following features:

6.1. Registered users of the SoundCloud Services are able to upload recordings to the SoundCloud Website. Certain mandatory fields must be completed by the user during the upload process. In particular, the title of the content must be provided and a 'tag' (selected from a drop down list) included. The 'tag' is designed and intended by the Defendant to make it easier for users to find the content through the search facilities provided by the Defendant.

6.2. Uploaders must also select: the type of licence they wish to grant to the Defendant (namely "All Rights Reserved" or "Creative Commons"); whether they want the uploaded content to be private or publicly available; and whether download of the content should be enabled. Where upload is via the "Classic Uploader" function, the user may provide additional information, such as record label information, the release catalogue number and the International Standard Recording Code (ISRC).

6.3. The content can be uploaded in a number of file formats, including MP3 and WAVE, and is converted by the Defendant into a different file format before it is made available to users.

6.4. Users of the SoundCloud Services are able to listen to the content that has been uploaded by streaming it to their computers or mobile devices or via other services or platforms such as Sonos and/or (where downloading of the content has been enabled) by downloading it.

6.5. A free text search facility is provided, which invites and enables users to search for music content by artist, band or track.

6.6. The 'Explore' section of the SoundCloud Website provides a comprehensive listing of "*what's up-and-coming on SoundCloud*". The 'Explore' section is highly structured so as to provide users with a convenient means of identifying the most popular music content. It enables users to browse (and consume) "trending" music. As explained on the SoundCloud Website: "*'Explore' ranks trending tracks by how much engagement (plays, likes, reposts) they have received over the past two weeks and favours the newest tracks by their upload date.*" Alternatively, users may browse popular music content that has been categorised into one of 30 music genres.

6.7. Users are able to 'like' and repost available tracks. The latter is described on the SoundCloud Website as the "*fastest way to share your favourite new discoveries on SoundCloud*". Facilities are also provided to enable users to share music on social media, including via Facebook and Twitter.

6.8. Users are able to 'follow' other users of the SoundCloud Services who have uploaded content.

6.9. Users are able to create and to share playlists of tracks.

6.10. The Defendant provides music recommendations to users of content that may be of interest to a particular user based on that user's usage of the SoundCloud Services to date (i.e., the type of music that has been consumed or liked by that user). Examples of recommendations of the Sample Works are at **Annex 2** hereto.

6.11. The Defendant provides recommended music 'playlists' (i.e., playlists available on the SoundCloud Services which feature tracks that have been accessed by the particular user).

6.12. The Defendant enables users to like, share, re-post and/or add either a listed track or a complete existing playlist to their own playlist(s).

6.13. The Defendant provides recommendations of other users/artists to follow. These recommendations are based on content that the particular user has accessed using the SoundCloud Services and are updated as the user accesses more/different content.

6.14. The Defendant provides what is effectively an interactive webcasting service. The SoundCloud Services allow users to listen to a continuous music-based webcast. Once the user has selected one track, the SoundCloud Services automatically select the next track to be streamed (and the one after that and so on). The contents of the webcast are based on tracks that have been recommended to the user by the SoundCloud Services. The user can pause and skip tracks as desired. Effectively, the SoundCloud Services 'push' content to the user based on the user's musical taste as identified by the user's SoundCloud usage history. In addition, tracks listed within each content genre in the 'Explore' section can be listened to by users as a continuous stream.

6.15. The Defendant provides information that is indicative of the popularity of each listed track (including the number of plays, 'likes' and reposts received).

6.16. The Defendant provides statistical information to uploaders of tracks to the SoundCloud Services. As stated in the "Help / Stats" section of the SoundCloud Website: *"When you share your tracks on SoundCloud and across the web, it is great to know who, where, when and how often your tracks have been listened to. With SoundCloud stats, you can view in-depth information about your sounds. We have recently redesigned our stats to show how often your tracks have been Played, Liked, Commented on, Reposted and Downloaded. You can also go into more detail; discovering new fans by viewing location, top listeners, apps and sources."* The extent of the data that is available to the user depends on whether the user has paid for a "Pro" or "Pro Unlimited" membership. Users can view their SoundCloud statistics on a per track basis and/or in relation to a selected date range.

6.17. Users are able to post comments in respect of particular tracks and against specific points in the track.

6.18. The Defendant promotes specific content via, and in connection with, the SoundCloud Services. By way of example only:

6.18.1. The Defendant sends marketing emails to registered users of the SoundCloud Services suggesting available playlists based on tracks that have been liked by that user and encouraging the recipient user to consume further music using the SoundCloud Services: see for instance the email at **Annex 3** hereto with the subject heading "*... we found some playlists for you*", which states: "*You recently liked "Sam Smith x Nile Rodgers x Disclosure x Jimmy Napes – Together", which was also added to the following playlists. Check them out!*"

6.18.2. The Defendant selects and promotes a 'SoundClouder of the Day'. The 'SoundClouder of the Day' is typically a song writer, musician or band selected by "*a member of the SoundCloud staff*" and featured on the SoundCloud Services, Twitter and Facebook. Examples (at **Annex 4** hereto) of instances in which PRS members have been selected and promoted as SoundClouders of the Day include:

"*With hints of Bright Eyes and Jenny Lewis, today's SoundClouder of the Day is Annie Dressner*" (10 January 2013)

"*Get swept away by Nicholas Stevenson's dulcet lo-fi folk jams. He's our SoundClouder of the Day*" (26 April 2013)

6.18.3. Previous SoundClouders of the Day are collated in a moderated group, enabling users to browse and stream associated tracks: "*A curated group of handpicked SoundClouder Of the Day. By the SoundCloud staff*" ... "*We'll collect all previous SCOTD'ers in this moderated group so browse around and we hope you find something you like or find interesting.*"

6.18.4. The Defendant publishes posts on its Facebook page and sends promotional messages directly to registered users. Examples (at **Annex 5** hereto) include:

"Heard Ninja Tune Official on SoundCloud before? Well if you are a fan and following, you get access to NEXT SoundCloud. If you are not, start listening and following by midnightPST to get access?" (8 November 2012)

"Hear an exclusive live recording of jazz legend Donald Byrt at 1973's Montreux Jazz Festival, via Blue Note Records: http://snd.sc/Wcq9Nx" (26 February 2013)

"Hear more at home! Now you can play SoundCloud tracks and playlists on your Sonos speakers, thanks to our new partnership: http://bit.ly/1roZVX2" (10 July 2014)

"Over 500k hours of new music uploaded to SoundCloud this month" (1 July 2015)

6.18.5. The Defendant publishes tweets and retweets on the Twitter social media service concerning music that is available via the SoundCloud Services and/or encouraging user engagement with the SoundCloud Services. Examples (at **Annex 6** hereto) include:

"Hear Céret, France-based singer-songwriter Freddy Garcia's jazz influenced song "Bluesville by the Sea" (5 June 2015)

"Hear the beautiful vocals of #SCOTD acoustic singer-songwriter Louise Bruce in the heartfelt song, "Half Light" (6 June 2015)

"More #techno? More #country? More #house? More #powerpop? What do you want to #HearMore of? (24 June 2015)

"BLACK SUN" available now: soundcloud.com/deathcabforcut...
Black Sun is the first single off Death Cab for Cutie's upcoming album Kintsugi, Out March 31st Follow Death Cab for Cutie Online" (26 January)

6.18.6. The Defendant promotes music available on the SoundCloud Services and/or refers to promotional activities through the SoundCloud Newsletter. See for example (at **Annex 7** hereto):

"*Moby has been embracing various social applications for the release of his latest album 'Wait for Me'. He's using the SoundCloud player widget for his clever Facebook app and there's a nice integration with Twitter that lets you tweet your album review before downloading the track for free. All of this is very well executed and we're thrilled to be part of it. Listen to his new record on SoundCloud.*" (Newsletter dated 13 August 2009)

"*Pro Partner update*

Look out for Pro Partner: now in beta, we're working with selected partners including Sleigh Bells, The Guardian, Two Doors Cinema Club and Chromeo to experiment with new visual elements.

We'll be integrating the best new features in to the full SoundCloud experience." (Newsletter dated 18 September 2013)

6.18.7. The Defendant coordinates and runs various promotions which market and link to specific musical works available via the SoundCloud Services. Examples (at **Annex 8** hereof) include:

"*Heads up producers and remixers!*

Esteemed composer Junkie XL, the man behind the music for 300: Rise of an Empire, wants to hear your take on his music behind the movie:

Get the full details and enter here: http://goo.gl/wx8YUS" (19 March 2014)

"*US folks: remember to vote for your favorite original track from the 10 semi-finalists who entered Green Label Sound: Open Call by 1/30.*

The prize offer includes a $50K grant to record an EP, a music video and more!

Vote here: http://bit.ly/glsopencall" (29 January 2015)

6.18.8. The Defendant promotes new services and available content through posts published on its Blog (to which SoundCloud users can subscribe for free). By way of example, a Blog post published on 15 December 2014 (at Annex 9 hereto) promoted 'Collection', a service designed to encourage further user consumption of music via the SoundCloud Services:

"Introducing Collection, your new SoundCloud home on the web

We designed Collection to make it easy for you to build your own home on the web for your favorite music & audio. Follow artists, like tracks and playlists, build your own playlists of favorite tracks, and be the first to hear what's new from your favorite creators. Whether you're using SoundCloud on web or on iPhone, you'll find everything you love in your personal, private Collection (we'll be bringing it to you on Android in 2015).

You can play your liked tracks in the order that you've added them, or mix it up with the Likes shuffle. Get to your Collection on the web by logging in and clicking https://soundcloud.com/you/collection. We hope you'll settle in, hit play and enjoy — with your Collection, you'll hear all your favorites for hours with just one click."

6.19. The Defendant is able to exercise control over the content that is uploaded to the SoundCloud Services and, in particular, is able to block, remove or delete any such content and to limit or restrict access to any such content.

7. The SoundCloud Services make available very large numbers of recordings to very large numbers of users. According to a blog post published by the Defendant on 4 June 2015:

7.1. 100 million tracks have been uploaded to the SoundCloud Website.

7.2. The SoundCloud Services have 175 million monthly users.

8. The primary purpose of the SoundCloud Services is to enable users to access and consume music. The SoundCloud Services provide a sophisticated and user-friendly service that enables users to access and consume the vast amount of music that the Defendant thereby makes available. Furthermore, the Defendant controls and curates the content made available on the SoundCloud Services, in particular by:

8.1. Providing that the content is categorised and easily searchable;

8.2. Making recommendations to users;

8.3. Pushing particular content to users;

8.4. Promoting particular content; and

8.5. Providing facilities for users to follow, 'like' and share particular content.

9. The Defendant provides the SoundCloud Services with a view to making profit.

10. A very substantial number of the recordings made available on the SoundCloud Services are recordings which embody musical works (or substantial parts thereof) which have been commercially released (including original studio recordings, recordings of live performances and cover versions). It is to be inferred that, in respect of such recordings, the Defendant knows that (a) the commission of acts restricted by UK copyright requires the licence of the copyright owner of the musical works embodied on such recordings and (b) the UK performing right in relation to the large majority of such musical works is very likely to be owned or controlled by PRS.

11. Furthermore, the Defendant has entered into licences with the owners of the copyrights in sound recordings which are made available on the SoundCloud Services in the UK. Pending disclosure herein, PRS does not know the identities of all such licensors or the terms of the licences but understands that the licensors include the Warner Music Group and Merlin, a global rights agency for the independent music sector. Furthermore, the Defendant has entered into licences for the territory of the United States with the owners of copyrights in musical works embodied in recordings which are made available on the SoundCloud Services in the UK. Pending disclosure herein, PRS does not know the identities of all such licensors or the terms of the licences but understands that the licensors include the National Music Publishers' Association, Sony/ATV and Warner Chappell. By reason of the foregoing, it is to be inferred that:

11.1. The Defendant has knowledge of the sound recordings in respect of which it has obtained licences.

11.2. The Defendant has knowledge of the fact that it has no licence in respect of the copyright in the musical works embodied on those sound recordings.

11.3. The Defendant has knowledge of the musical works in respect of which it has obtained licences for the territory of the United States.

11.4. The Defendant has knowledge of the fact that it has no licence in respect of the copyright in those musical works in the UK.

11.5. The Defendant has knowledge of the fact that the performing right in the UK in respect of musical works which have been commercially released is very likely to be owned or controlled by PRS.

The Defendant's infringement of copyright

12. The content made available on the SoundCloud Services includes:

12.1. Recordings (including recordings by the original artists as set out in Annex 1) of the Sample Works.

12.2. Recordings of very substantial numbers of other musical works which form part of the PRS Repertoire. PRS has conducted a limited, non-exhaustive analysis of a sample of musical works owned or controlled by PRS and identified more than 4,400 such musical works that are made available on the SoundCloud Services.

13. In the premises, the Defendant has infringed, and continues to infringe, copyright in the Sample Works and in other works which form part of the PRS Repertoire as follows:

13.1. By communicating those works to the public within the meaning of section 20 of the CDPA without the licence of PRS. In particular:

13.1.1. By its provision and operation of the SoundCloud Services as set out above, the Defendant intervenes in a material way and in full knowledge of the consequences of its actions to give access to such works to users of the SoundCloud Services.

13.1.2. The Defendant thereby makes those works available to the public by electronic transmission in such a way that members of the public may access them from a place and at a time individually chosen by them.

13.1.3. The works are made available from the UK and/or are targeted at members of the public in the UK.

13.1.4. The communication of the works is not a communication which does not use a different technical means to that of an original communication. If, contrary to the foregoing, the communication is a communication which does not use a different technical means to that of an original communication, it is a communication to a public which was not considered by the copyright owner when any such original communication was authorised.

13.2. Furthermore or in the alternative, by authorising its registered users to communicate those works to the public within the meaning of section 20 of the CDPA without the licence of the PRS. In particular:

13.2.1. By uploading such works to the SoundCloud Services, the registered users intervene in a material way and in full knowledge of the consequences of their actions to give access to such works to users of the SoundCloud Services.

13.2.2. Those registered users thereby make those works available to the public by electronic transmission in such a way that members of the public may access them from a place and at a time individually chosen by them.

13.2.3. The works are made available from the UK and/or are targeted at members of the public in the UK.

13.2.4. The communication of the works is not a communication which does not use a different technical means to that of an original communication. If, contrary to the foregoing, the communication is a communication which does not use a different technical means to that of an original communication, it is a communication to a public which was not considered by the copyright owner when any such original communication was authorised.

13.2.5. By its provision and operation of the SoundCloud Services as set out above, the Defendant provides the means whereby its registered users infringe copyright and it facilitates and encourages them to do so. It provides facilities and assistance and promotion which make it simple for registered users to upload works and which are designed and intended by the Defendant to provide those registered users with the widest possible public access to the works uploaded by them. Infringement of copyright is the inevitable consequence of the uploading of works by registered users when the licence of the owner of the copyright in the underlying musical work has not been obtained. The Defendant has control over the content uploaded to the SoundCloud Services. The Defendant is required to prove the steps which it takes to prevent infringement of copyright but, without prejudice thereto, it is averred that such steps are inadequate to prevent the widespread infringements of PRS's copyrights which are committed through the SoundCloud Services.

13.3. Furthermore or in the alternative, the Defendant is a joint tortfeasor with its registered users in respect of their said infringements of copyright in such works. In particular:

13.3.1. The registered users have committed and continue to commit acts of infringement as set out above.

13.3.2. In the premises, by its provision and operation of the SoundCloud Services as set out above, the Defendant has induced, incited or persuaded to commit those acts. The very purpose of providing the SoundCloud Services is to cause or procure acts which will amount in law to infringement of copyright.

13.3.3. Furthermore or alternatively, in the premises, by its provision and operation of the SoundCloud Services as set out above, the Defendant has assisted its registered users in their infringements of copyright and has so involved itself in those infringements as to have been engaged in a common design or concerted action to commit those acts.

Safe Harbours

14. The Defendant has asserted that it is not liable for copyright infringement and does not require the licence of PRS in order to make available musical works which form part of the PRS Repertoire on the grounds that it is entitled to the protection from liability for copyright infringement afforded by Regulations 17, 18 and/or 19 of the Electronic Commerce (EC Directive) Regulations 2002 ("the Regulations") (implementing Articles 12, 13 and 14 of Directive 2000/31/EC ("the E-Commerce Directive"). As to that (and without the assumption of the burden of proof, which rests on the Defendant, and without prejudice to PRS's Reply):

14.1. The Defendant is required to prove that it is an information society service within the meaning of the Regulations and the E-Commerce Directive.

14.2. So far as Regulation 17 (Article 12 of the Directive) is concerned:

14.2.1. The SoundCloud Services do not consist of the transmission in a communication network of information provided by a recipient of the service or the provision of access to a communication network. To the extent that the Defendant stores information, that storage is not automatic, intermediate and transient storage taking place for the sole purpose of carrying out a transmission in a communication network and is not limited to a period no longer than is reasonably necessary for a transmission.

14.2.2. Furthermore as set out above, the SoundCloud Services involve the selection and modification by the Defendant of the information that is transmitted to its users. In particular, the Defendant is involved in the selection of the content that is pushed to its users and in the modification of the information by the conversion of its file formats.

14.2.3. Furthermore, as set out below, in its provision and operation of the SoundCloud Services, the Defendant's activity is not of a mere technical, automatic and passive nature; the Defendant has knowledge of and control over the information which is transmitted.

14.3. So far as Regulation 18 (Article 13 of the Directive) is concerned:

14.3.1. The SoundCloud Services do not consist of the transmission in a communication network of information provided by a recipient of the service. To the extent that the Defendant stores information, that storage is not automatic, intermediate and temporary storage and is not for the sole purpose of making more efficient onward transmission of the information to other recipients of the service upon their request.

14.3.2. Furthermore as set out above, the SoundCloud Services involve the modification by the Defendant of the information that is transmitted to its users by its conversion of the file formats.

14.3.3. Furthermore, as set out below, in its provision and operation of the SoundCloud Services, the Defendant's activity is not of a mere technical, automatic and passive nature; the Defendant has knowledge of and control over the information which is transmitted.

14.4. So far as Regulation 19 (Article 14 of the Directive) is concerned:

14.4.1. The SoundCloud Services do not consist of the storage of Information provided by a recipient of the service. In its provision and operation of the SoundCloud Services, the Defendant's activity is not of a mere technical, automatic and passive nature; the Defendant has knowledge of and control over the information which is stored.

14.4.2. In support of the foregoing, PRS will rely on the matters set out at paragraphs 5 to 11 above.

14.4.3. In the premises, it is averred that the Defendant's activity is not that of a neutral host but it takes an active role in:

14.4.3.1. The conversion of file formats;

14.4.3.2. The encouragement and facilitation of access to content;

14.4.3.3. The provision of assistance in the optimisation of the presentation of content;

14.4.3.4. The promotion and recommendation of content;

14.4.3.5. The selection of content which is pushed to users;

14.4.3.6. The collection and provision of data usage statistics to its registered users.

14.4.4. Furthermore, it takes such an active role in the knowledge that a very substantial proportion of the content embodies musical works which are protected by UK copyright, and whose communication to the public requires the licence of the relevant copyright owner, who is, in very many instances, PRS.

14.4.5. Furthermore or in the alternative, it is averred that the Defendant has actual knowledge of unlawful activity or information and is aware of facts or circumstances from which it would have been apparent to the Defendant that the activity or information was unlawful and, upon obtaining such knowledge or awareness, it has failed to act expeditiously to remove or to disable access to the information. In support of the foregoing, PRS will rely on the following:

14.4.5.1. Paragraphs 10 and 11 above are repeated.

14.4.5.2. Since, at the latest 2010, PRS has informed the Defendant that there were substantial numbers of musical works being made available on the SoundCloud Services in infringement of PRS's copyright.

14.4.5.3. In the circumstances, the illegal activity would have been apparent to a diligent economic operator in the Defendant's position.

14.4.5.4. Furthermore, by letter dated 20 July 2015, PRS's solicitors provided the Defendant with a list of over 4,400 musical works in which the performing right was owned or controlled by PRS and which were then being made available on the SoundCloud Services. The Defendant has not acted expeditiously to remove or disable access to those works.

The Relief Sought

15. PRS seeks declarations that:

15.1. The Defendant has infringed PRS's copyright in the Sample Works and the other works that form part of the PRS Repertoire and have been made available on the SoundCloud Services.

15.2. The Defendant is not entitled to the protection of Regulations 17, 18 or 19 of the Regulations.

16. By reason of the Defendant's infringement of copyright, PRS has suffered loss and damage equal to the reasonable licence fee that would have been agreed between a willing licensor and willing licensee in respect of the Defendant's activities. PRS is entitled to an enquiry to determine the full extent of the Defendant's infringement of copyright in the PRS Repertoire. Furthermore, having regard to the flagrancy of the Defendant's continued and continuing infringements despite its knowledge thereof and having regard to the benefit accruing to the Defendant, which has thereby been able to develop the SoundCloud Services into one of the UK's most popular online music services, PRS claims additional damages pursuant to section 97(2) of the CDPA.

17. In the alternative to the foregoing, and at PRS's election, PRS is entitled to an account of profits from the Defendant.

18. Furthermore, and in any event, the Defendant threatens that, unless restrained by the Court, it will continue to infringe PRS's copyright in the Sample Works and other musical works which form part of the PRS Repertoire. PRS is entitled to an injunction aimed at prohibiting the continuation of such infringement in accordance with Article 11 of Directive 2004/48/EC ("the Enforcement Directive").

19. PRS is entitled to an order in accordance with Article 15 of the Enforcement Directive for appropriate measures, at the Defendant's expenses, for the dissemination of the information concerning the decision in these proceedings, including displaying the decision and publishing it in full or in part.

20. In the alternative to paragraphs 18 and 19 above, PRS is entitled to an injunction pursuant to section 97A of the CDPA on the footing that (as set out above) the Defendant is a service provider whose service is being used by its registered users to infringe copyright and who has actual knowledge of that fact.

21. PRS claims interest pursuant to section 35A of the Senior Courts Act 1981 on such sum and at such rate and from such date as the Court thinks fit.

AND THE CLAIMANT CLAIMS:

1. Declarations that:

   1.1. The Defendant has infringed PRS's copyright in the Sample Works and the other works that form part of the PRS Repertoire and have been made available on the SoundCloud Services.

   1.2. The Defendant is not entitled to the protection of Regulations 17, 18 or 19 of the Regulations.

2. An enquiry to determine the full extent of the Defendant's infringement of copyright in the PRS Repertoire and the damages resulting therefrom.

3. Additional damages pursuant to section 97(2) of the CDPA.

4. Alternatively, at PRS's election, an account of profits.

5. An injunction restraining the Defendant (by itself or its employees, officers or agents, and whether alone or jointly with others) from communicating to the public or authorising the communication to the public without the licence of PRS of musical works which form part of the PRS Repertoire (as notified to the Defendant by PRS from time to time).

6. Alternatively such other injunction as may be effective, proportionate and dissuasive for the purpose of enforcing and protecting PRS's rights.

7. An order for dissemination and publication of the judgment.

8. All such other accounts and enquiries and further or other relief as may be necessary or appropriate.

9. Interest pursuant to section 35A of the Senior Courts Act 1981 on such sum and at such rate and from such date as the Court thinks fit.

10. Costs.

Statement of truth

The Claimant believes that the facts stated in these Particulars of Claim are true. I am duly authorised by the Claimant to sign this statement of truth.

Signed: ....

Name: ....S.J. BAGGS,..............

Served on 28 August 2015 by Wiggin LLP of 10th Floor, Met Building, Percy Street, London W1T 2BU, Solicitors for the Claimant

IN THE HIGH COURT OF JUSTICE

Claim no HC-2015-003033

CHANCERY DIVISION

INTELLECTUAL PROPERTY

BETWEEN:

PERFORMING RIGHT SOCIETY LIMITED

Claimant

-and-

SOUNDCLOUD LIMITED

Defendant

PARTICULARS OF CLAIM

Wiggin LLP
10th Floor
Met Building
22 Percy Street
London
W1T 2BU
Ref: SJB/RA/NR

APPENDIX I

Claim No HC-2015-003033

IN THE HIGH COURT OF JUSTICE
CHANCERY DIVISION
INTELLECTUAL PROPERTY

BETWEEN:

PERFORMING RIGHT SOCIETY LIMITED

Claimant

- and -

SOUNDCLOUD LIMITED

Defendant

DEFENCE

---

1 In this Defence, unless otherwise indicated:

1.1 paragraph numbers refer to paragraphs of the Particulars of Claim;

1.2 defined terms have the same meanings as those specified in the Particulars of Claim, without admission; and

1.3 the Defendant denies all allegations made in the Particulars of Claim, save as admitted below.

2 The Defendant ("**SoundCloud**") operates an internet platform accessible at http://soundcloud.com/ which provides facilities by which audio content may be uploaded and stored by users of the platform and transmitted to other users ("**SoundCloud Platform**"), as further particularised below.

3 The SoundCloud Platform is a hub of creativity, innovation and culture. Approximately 110 million sounds have been uploaded to the SoundCloud Platform by 163.5 million registered users, including universities, political parties, radio stations, journalists, and broadcasters. It is also used by composers, performers, publishers and record labels lawfully to host and promote their own music. Insofar as SoundCloud is aware of specific content on the SoundCloud Platform, it is lawful on its face and appears to have been uploaded by its author or licensee.

4 SoundCloud takes all reasonable steps to prevent infringement of copyright from occurring by means of the SoundCloud Platform. For example, it operates a notice-and-takedown policy in accordance with industry best practices, educates users about

their copyright obligations, uses innovative audio fingerprinting technology automatically to detect potentially infringing uploads, and operates a repeat infringer policy, as further particularised at paragraphs 56 to 63 below.

5 For the reasons explained at paragraphs 90 to 104 below, SoundCloud is an information society service provider that is entitled to the benefit of the hosting and mere conduit safe harbours in respect of the entirety of the acts alleged in the Particulars of Claim, insofar as any of those acts would otherwise be capable of giving rise to liability.

6 Where SoundCloud is properly notified of allegedly infringing material, its practice is expeditiously to take steps to remove or disable access to such material. For the reasons explained at paragraphs 105 to 118 below, PRS has not properly notified SoundCloud of the locations of any material about which it complains.

7 Without prejudice to that contention, SoundCloud denies that it would be liable for any of the acts alleged in the Particulars of Claim, for the reasons explained at paragraphs 76 to 89 below. SoundCloud merely supplies facilities which may be used by third parties, and neither authorises infringement nor is jointly liable for infringements committed by registered users of the SoundCloud Platform.

The Claimant and its alleged rights

8 As to paragraph 1:

8.1 The first sentence of paragraph 1 is admitted. SoundCloud is not aware of which particular writers, composers or publishers of musical works are members of PRS.

8.2 The second sentence of paragraph 1 is not admitted. SoundCloud does not know the basis upon which PRS claims to own the "performing right" of the copyrights of its members. SoundCloud has no knowledge of the scope of the assignment alleged or the nature of any arrangements between PRS and collecting societies in other jurisdictions.

8.3 It is denied (insofar as it is alleged) that PRS owns or controls the right to copy any musical work within the PRS Repertoire.

8.4 The third sentence of paragraph 1 is denied. The "performing right" referred to in that sentence is not understood. To perform, show or play a work in public, is an act restricted by the copyright in a work within the meaning of sections 16(1)(c) and 19 of the *Copyright, Designs and Patents Act 1988* ("1988 Act"), and the right to control this restricted act is the "performing right" in a work. The right to control the restricted act of communicating a work to the public by electronic transmission as defined by sections 16(1)(d) and 20 of the 1998 Act is a distinct right and not part of the "performing right" in a work.

9 Paragraphs 2 and 3 are outside SoundCloud's knowledge and are not admitted. Further:

9.1 As to the Sample Works relied upon by PRS, SoundCloud has no knowledge of the subsistence and ownership of copyright in those musical works and PRS is put to proof of the subsistence of such copyright and its rights to the same.

9.2 As to the more than 6 million musical works referred to in paragraph 2 and described as the PRS Repertoire, SoundCloud has no knowledge of the subsistence and ownership of copyright in those musical works and, insofar as such works are relied upon by PRS, PRS is put to proof of the same.

9.3 Where PRS controls the rights to license musical works through arrangements with other collecting societies, SoundCloud has no knowledge of the nature of those arrangements and, in particular, whether the authors of such works have assigned or licensed their copyrights. Insofar as such works are relied upon by PRS, PRS is put to proof of the same.

The Defendant and its platform

10 The SoundCloud Platform comprises:

10.1 a number of databases which store information about users, uploaded sounds, interactions with sounds, statistics and other data ("**SoundCloud Databases**");

10.2 a number of virtual and physical servers on which uploaded sound files, media and other user data are stored, along with the SoundCloud Databases and SoundCloud Website ("**SoundCloud Servers**");

10.3 a website interface which retrieves and displays information from the SoundCloud Databases to members of the public, and which provides an interface for registered users to upload material to the SoundCloud Servers ("**SoundCloud Website**"); and

10.4 an alternative interface allowing registered users to access audio content and other data hosted on the SoundCloud Platform from compatible mobile devices using mobile applications ("**SoundCloud App**").

11 Each of the components of the SoundCloud Platform operates in a technical, automatic and passive manner. In particular:

11.1 The SoundCloud Databases automatically store information that is added to them by users of the SoundCloud Platform at their request.

11.2 The SoundCloud Servers automatically store the files that are uploaded to them by such users at their request. Uploaded files are automatically processed and may be converted into a permitted file format using the automated technical means described at paragraph 36 below.

11.3 The SoundCloud Website automatically displays information which is retrieved from storage in the contents of the SoundCloud Databases and the SoundCloud Servers and at the selection of users of the SoundCloud Platform.

11.4 The SoundCloud App automatically displays information which is retrieved from storage in the contents of the SoundCloud Databases and the SoundCloud Servers and at the selection of a user of the SoundCloud App.

12 The SoundCloud Servers which host audio content are located in the United States and cached in content distribution networks operated by third parties. SoundCloud also operates servers in The Netherlands, but these servers relate to customer and usage data and do not host any audio content. None of the servers that are under SoundCloud's control are located in the United Kingdom.

13 As to paragraph 4:

13.1 It is admitted that SoundCloud was incorporated in 2007, and that SoundCloud has since 2008 owned and operated a website at http://soundcloud.com/.

13.2 It is denied that paragraph 4 sets out an accurate or complete description of the SoundCloud Platform. Paragraphs 10 and 11 above are repeated and are further particularised below.

13.3 It is admitted that on 8 February 2010 SoundCloud launched the SoundCloud App for iOS devices, and on 27 November 2011 launched the SoundCloud App for Android devices. These applications may be downloaded from the iTunes App Store and Google Play Store onto any compatible smartphone.

13.4 It is denied that SoundCloud owns or operates any other services or platforms. Sonos is a service operated by Sonos Inc, an American manufacturer of audio hardware, and is separate from SoundCloud. SoundCloud has developed various Application Programming Interfaces ("APIs") which allow software developers to interconnect their own products and services with the SoundCloud Platform, but SoundCloud does not operate such services, and such services do not form part of the SoundCloud Platform.

14 Paragraph 5 is denied insofar as it seeks to characterise the SoundCloud Platform as a service whereby SoundCloud provides and intends to provide recordings of musical works to members of the public, and otherwise admitted.

15 SoundCloud operates a weblog which contains postings about the SoundCloud Platform and is accessible at http://blog.soundcloud.com/ ("**SoundCloud Blog**"). The SoundCloud Blog is powered by standard blogging software known as WordPress, which is licensed from and hosted by a third party. The SoundCloud Blog is a separate website, uses distinct technology and does not form part of the SoundCloud Platform.

16 SoundCloud also maintains various social media accounts, including on Facebook, Twitter, Tumblr and other platforms. Those platforms are operated by third parties and do not form part of the SoundCloud Platform. Employees of SoundCloud are responsible for posting information to these social media accounts. The social media accounts do not form part of the SoundCloud Platform.

17 The SoundCloud Platform hosts approximately 110 million audio content files. These files are uploaded and made available by users of SoundCloud, not by SoundCloud. Paragraph 7 is denied to this extent, and otherwise admitted.

18 The SoundCloud Platform stores audio content which has been uploaded by its registered users. SoundCloud merely provides technical facilities by means of which members of the public may access such content if and to the extent they are permitted to do so by the person who uploaded the content. The facilities provided include the following:

User registration

19 A member of the public may choose to register as a user of the SoundCloud Platform by completing the SoundCloud registration form, which requires the prospective user to agree to the SoundCloud Terms of Use and Privacy Policy.

20 A copy of the Terms of Use (as last amended on 12 March 2013) is at **Annex 1** of this defence ("**Terms of Use**"). A copy of the Privacy Policy (as last amended on 10 June 2015) is at **Annex 2** of this defence ("**Privacy Policy**"). The Terms of Use include warranties and indemnities relating to the rights of the user to upload their audio content to the SoundCloud Platform.

Uploading of audio content

21 Any registered user may upload audio content to the SoundCloud Platform using an automated software tool known as an "**uploader**". Uploaded content is stored on the SoundCloud Servers by a technical and automatic process and at the request of the relevant user.

22 As at August 2015, approximately 12.9 hours of audio content were being uploaded to the SoundCloud Platform every minute by registered users.

23 At the time of uploading audio content, or afterwards, the uploader may provide certain information they wish to be associated with their content (known as "**File Metadata**"), as follows:

23.1 The user may "tag" their content by typing text of their own choosing (each word known as a "tag") or may select from an automatically generated drop-down list of tags commonly selected by other users.

23.2 Tagging may be undertaken solely by the uploader of audio content to the SoundCloud Platform. It is not performed by SoundCloud or by non-uploading users of SoundCloud, though if the uploader begins to type a part of a tag, an automatic completion algorithm will suggest matching words based on existing data in the SoundCloud Databases. Tags are stored automatically in the SoundCloud Databases and associated with the content specified by the user.

23.3 The purpose of tagging is to facilitate content creators to guide new fans to their content. However, SoundCloud does not itself create or modify tags. Tagging is a normal feature of any modern internet platform.

23.4 Paragraph 6.1 is otherwise admitted save as stated above.

24 File Metadata that is provided by an uploader is automatically stored in the SoundCloud Databases and associated with the relevant audio content.

25 The uploader may optionally input additional File Metadata into text fields visible in the uploading interface. The fields available in the default uploader are: "buy link", "record label", and "original release date". The "buy link" field allows the uploader to direct users to an external website of their choice from which copies of the audio content may be lawfully purchased. Additional fields may be optionally enabled, including the International Standard Recording Code ("**ISRC**"), which uniquely identifies a sound recording. Statistical analysis of the SoundCloud Databases indicates that 0.3% of uploaded audio content has an associated ISRC and 2.98% has an associated record label specified in their File Metadata.

26 Before any audio content may be uploaded, the uploader is required to warrant that they have the necessary rights to upload their audio content to the SoundCloud Platform, and is directed to the Terms of Use and copyright education material.

27 Before uploaded audio content is added to the SoundCloud Platform, it must pass an automated surveillance procedure, the aim of which is to prevent the upload of content containing unlicensed copyright works. Details of that procedure are set out at paragraphs 57 to 59 below.

Licensing of uploaded content by users

28 At the time of uploading audio content to the SoundCloud Platform, or afterwards, the uploader may select the terms under which they make it available to third parties. If an uploader does not select such terms, the default terms will apply to the uploaded audio content. The uploader has sole control over if, when and how their content is made accessible by members of the public using the facilities provided. SoundCloud does not exercise any control over these decisions.

29 Among the options available to the uploader are to permit streaming or downloading of audio content, or both. However, that choice is made by the uploader and SoundCloud will not intervene, except to remove or disable access to the content in the circumstances described in paragraphs 56 to 69 below.

30 SoundCloud does not grant, and is not entitled to grant, any licence to third parties with respect to uploaded audio content. Any such licence is granted directly by the uploader to the relevant third parties in terms determined solely by the uploader. Paragraph 6.2 is denied if and insofar as it alleges otherwise.

31 Uploaders grant a separate licence to SoundCloud to the extent necessary for SoundCloud to provide hosting services for each item of audio content and to carry out the automated processes directed by users with respect to the content. Paragraph 6.2 is otherwise admitted save as stated above.

Nature of audio content hosted on SoundCloud

32 SoundCloud does not know the details of the individual items of audio content that have been uploaded to the SoundCloud Platform by registered users. However, SoundCloud is aware of the existence of very substantial audio content other than music which is hosted by SoundCloud, including:

32.1 educational material uploaded by universities, such as the University of Cambridge (595,000 followers), University College London (534,000 followers), London School of Economics (246,000 followers), Yale University (616,000 followers), and the National Gallery of Art (708,000 followers);

32.2 political announcements uploaded by the White House (115,000 followers) and the Labour Party;

32.3 scientific material uploaded by NASA (76,600 followers);

32.4 news coverage and original programming uploaded by *The Guardian*, *The Times*, *The Mirror*, BBC Radio 4, BBC World Service, and Huffington Post;

32.5 coverage of civil unrest in Burundi uploaded by local journalists after the local government shut down national radio broadcasters;

32.6 evidence of political corruption in Turkey uploaded by whistle-blowers; and

32.7 sports coverage uploaded by Arsenal Football Club (713,000 followers).

33 Examples of audio content uploaded by SoundCloud users which are not commercially released musical works are attached as **Annex 3** to this Defence.

34 In the premises, the SoundCloud Platform hosts a wide variety of audio content, including both musical and non-musical content.

Transcoding of uploaded content

35 Audio content which is stored digitally must be encoded into a particular file format. The SoundCloud Platform is capable of storing audio files in file formats including AIFF, WAV, FLAC, ALAC, OGG, MP2, MP3, AAC, AMR and WMA. The available file formats are neutral as to nature of the audio content.

36 All uploaded content must be converted into a common file format for streaming. This is done automatically by the SoundCloud Servers according to a technical process known as "**transcoding**". The original file is also stored in its native format, and may be downloaded by a third party only if the uploader has chosen to make the content available for download. Paragraph 6.3 is admitted, save as stated above.

Listening facilities

37 Users of the SoundCloud Platform are able to listen to audio content insofar as this is permitted by the uploader, by using the facilities provided by the SoundCloud Website, the SoundCloud App, or a service operated by a third party (such as Sonos) using the SoundCloud API.

38 The available listening facilities depend on the permissions which have been specified by an uploader with respect to a particular item of audio content. The SoundCloud Platform will permit access to stored content where it has been instructed to do so by

the uploader, and upon the request of a user. The listening facilities comprise the following:

38.1 Where the uploader has specified that audio content is able to be downloaded, and such content is requested by a user for download, the original file uploaded by the uploader is transmitted automatically from its storage location on the SoundCloud Servers to the downloader at his or her request.

38.2 Where the uploader has specified that audio content is able to be streamed, and such content is requested by a user for streaming, the transcoded file (which was converted by the SoundCloud Servers at the request of the uploader) is transmitted sequentially and automatically from its storage location on the SoundCloud Servers to the streaming user at his or her request.

39 SoundCloud does not intervene in the process of downloading or streaming audio content. The retrieval of stored audio content is fully automated on the SoundCloud Platform and is configured to answer the request of a user only in accordance with the instructions provided by the uploader. Paragraph 6.4 is admitted, save as stated above.

Indexing and search facilities

40 Like any modern website, SoundCloud includes a text search facility by means of which users may search the SoundCloud Databases for hosted content. The search facility is not directed or restricted to music content or to artists or bands. Users may search for particular uploaders by their username, and may search for playlists and groups.

41 The search facility is fully automated and operates analogously to the Google search engine. It operates as follows:

41.1 All public audio content and user information on the SoundCloud Servers is "indexed" automatically according to algorithms developed by third parties and licensed by SoundCloud.

41.2 When a user carries out a search, the text of their query is supplied to the relevant SoundCloud Database and search results are ranked in order of relevance according to a proprietary algorithm.

41.3 The ranking is applied to all audio content in the same way.

41.4 Ranking is an automatic technical process that results in the search index being stored on the SoundCloud Servers, and search results being delivered to the user in order of relevance.

42 SoundCloud does not play any role in formulating search terms chosen by users. When search results are displayed to users, this occurs without any manual intervention by SoundCloud and without any optimisation of the presentation of audio content. Paragraph 6.5 is admitted, save as stated above.

Browsing and interacting with audio content

43 Users may browse the SoundCloud Platform by means of the SoundCloud Website or SoundCloud App. SoundCloud does not normally intervene in the presentation of particular audio content to users. Page elements are generated as follows:

43.1 Certain areas of the SoundCloud Website and SoundCloud App contain static text content (for example, the Terms of Use) which has been authored by one or more employees of SoundCloud.

43.2 Each page or screen has a standard appearance and formatting (including a header and footer, toolbar and navigation menu) that has been determined by SoundCloud.

43.3 Some employees of SoundCloud may also be registered users of SoundCloud. It is possible that such persons have themselves uploaded audio content, or commented on or interacted with audio content. If they have done so using a personal account, that is in their personal capacity and without the authority or direction of SoundCloud.

43.4 Save as stated in paragraphs 43.1, 43.2 and 43.3 above, all accessible page elements consist of content that has been supplied by users of the SoundCloud Platform. Such content has been stored automatically on the SoundCloud Servers at the time of its creation, and is retrieved from storage automatically when it is requested by a user who accesses the SoundCloud Website or SoundCloud App.

44 Paragraph 6.6 is therefore denied insofar as it alleges that the "Explore" section of the SoundCloud Website is deliberately or manually structured by SoundCloud, or that music content has been categorised by SoundCloud or its employees. Insofar as music genres are concerned, the contents of the "Explore" section are wholly generated by a computer algorithm stored on the SoundCloud Servers. Audio content is classified automatically into a number of standard genres (the names of which were initially specified by SoundCloud) using File Metadata and artificial intelligence.

45 Audio content is classified as "trending" based on a computer algorithm which operates on statistical data contained in the SoundCloud Databases to determine how frequently, and how recently, users have interacted with the content. SoundCloud does not manually intervene to classify or rank particular music content.

46 A user may interact with audio content on SoundCloud by liking it, commenting on it, following the person who uploaded it, adding it to a playlist of their own creation, reposting it to their own profile, or sharing it on social media. These and related features are common among modern internet platforms. All interactions are performed by users and not by SoundCloud. SoundCloud does not have knowledge of or control over the interactions performed by users. Paragraphs 6.7, 6.8, 6.9, 6.12 and 6.17 are admitted.

Automated content recommendations

47 Paragraphs 6.10, 6.11 and 6.13 are denied insofar as they allege that SoundCloud intervenes to provide music or playlist recommendations for particular audio content. It does no such thing. These features operate as follows:

47.1 A computer algorithm identifies related audio content that has been stored on the SoundCloud Servers based on its similarity to an item of audio content chosen by the user. Similarity is assessed based on how users have interacted with content in the pas' SoundCloud does not manually intervene to recommend audio content, and the similarity algorithm is applied neutrally across the entire SoundCloud Platform.

47.2 When a user requests the "related tracks" for an item of audio content, the algorithm is applied and the best matches are automatically displayed. SoundCloud does not have any knowledge of or control over the input to this algorithm or the results it displays.

47.3 When a user requests the "in playlists" for an item of audio content, a database query is performed to retrieve a stored list of playlists in which the content appears. Every user will see the same list.

47.4 When a user browses the SoundCloud Website or SoundCloud App, certain behavioural signals are automatically stored in the SoundCloud Databases based on their activity, such as the tracks they have favourited or reposted, and the users they have followed.

48 Paragraph 6.14 is denied insofar as it alleges that the SoundCloud Platform is an interactive webcasting service. The SoundCloud Platform merely provides facilities for uploaders to make available their audio content and for other users to access it upon their request. This includes a facility that allows users to listen to audio content on a

continuous basis, but this requires users first to request a particular item of content that is hosted on the SoundCloud Servers. A sequence of further hosted audio content is then generated automatically using the content recommendation algorithm mentioned at paragraph 47.1 above. Content is automatically included in the sequence based on its similarity to the most recent item listened to by that user. Only a user who has requested that item will receive such content.

Audio content statistics

49 The SoundCloud Platform automatically records basic statistical information, including the number of times a piece of audio content is played and when, the number of likes and shares, and who interacts with the content. Such information is stored in the SoundCloud Databases.

50 Basic statistic information is displayed to users adjacent to audio content. More detailed information is displayed to the uploader of the content. SoundCloud does not monitor or curate these statistics, which are produced automatically and without intervention. Paragraphs 6.15 and 6.16 are admitted, save as stated above.

Alleged promotion of audio content

51 It is admitted that SoundCloud has taken certain steps to promote the SoundCloud Platform among its users and to third parties, as it is entitled to do. However, save as set out below, it is not admitted that SoundCloud has intervened to promote any audio content that relates to PRS members.

52 As to the particulars to paragraph 6.18:

52.1 Users receive notifications of activity on the SoundCloud Platform in accordance with their communication preferences. Such notifications may consist of emails or push notifications on the SoundCloud App:

(a) Some notifications are general marketing communications which advertise the SoundCloud Platform as a whole and do not relate to specific audio content.

(b) On other occasions, notifications may promote a particular uploader or event which is accessible on the SoundCloud Platform, but do not relate to specific audio content.

(c) Email notifications which relate to specific audio content are not normally authored by employees of SoundCloud, but are automatically generated from users' data stored in the SoundCloud Databases and snippets of pre-determined text. Any audio content mentioned in such notifications has not been selected by SoundCloud but rather is based on the user's activity on the SoundCloud Platform.

52.2 The "SoundClouder of the Day" was manually selected by an employee of SoundCloud until June 2014 and published to social media websites and the SoundCloud Blog. Since then it has not formed part of any communications by SoundCloud. When such communications were made, it is admitted that they were intended to promote specific audio content and to benefit the creators of that content, but it is denied that any audio content was thereby selected, optimised or promoted other than as expressly mentioned in the communications.

52.3 It is not admitted that any of the previously featured SoundClouders of the Day have been PRS members at the material time or that any of the audio content they uploaded embodies the Sample Works. In any event, SoundCloud was entitled to, and did, rely on the representations made by each featured SoundClouder of the Day when they uploaded their audio content to the SoundCloud Servers.

52.4 It is admitted that in or around October 2010 SoundCloud created a "group" (a collection of sounds) for the purpose of showcasing previous SoundClouders of the Day. Links were progressively added to this group which directed users to 202 audio files which had been uploaded by third parties. Users who chose to access this group would be shown an automatically-generated index of this audio content. It is admitted that SoundCloud exercises control over the inclusion of tracks in this group, but not admitted that the tracks contained in the group include any PRS Repertoire or Sample Works. SoundCloud has not added any audio content to this group for 3 years.

52.5 SoundCloud has made various postings on social media, including those mentioned at paragraphs 6.18.4 and 6.18.5. Save where a posting mentions a specific track by name, or links to specific audio content, the purpose of these postings is to promote the SoundCloud Platform as a whole. Paragraph 16 above is repeated.

52.6 SoundCloud has sent a newsletter periodically to its registered users. The contents of the newsletter are authored by employees of SoundCloud and do not form part of the SoundCloud Platform. Their purpose is to promote the SoundCloud Platform as a whole. Paragraph 6.18.6 is admitted save as stated.

52.7 It is denied that SoundCloud has conducted the promotions mentioned at paragraphs 6.18.7. Those promotions were operated by third parties such as

Warner Bros and PepsiCo, who are users of the SoundCloud Platform. It is further not admitted that such promotions were targeted at users anywhere other than in the United States.

52.8 SoundCloud operates the SoundCloud Blog, which does not form part of the SoundCloud Platform and contains communications of a general and marketing nature. Paragraph 15 above is repeated.

Monitoring of audio content

53 SoundCloud does not actively monitor or review the material uploaded by registered users to the SoundCloud Platform, unless it has been notified of a specific instance of audio content requiring manual review. Even in the case of the automated technical surveillance described at paragraphs 57 to 59 below, an employee of SoundCloud does not manually intervene or examine any material that is in the process of being uploaded.

Alleged control over audio content

54 SoundCloud is unable to exercise control over the audio content that is uploaded to the SoundCloud Platform by users of SoundCloud. In particular:

54.1 SoundCloud cannot select audio content before it is uploaded by a user. SoundCloud exercises no control over the content that the user chooses to upload. SoundCloud only controls the Terms of Use.

54.2 SoundCloud cannot pre-emptively review audio content after it is uploaded by a user before it is stored on the SoundCloud Servers. That is because uploaded content appears automatically on the SoundCloud Platform after it has been uploaded (in accordance with the uploader's instructions), if it passes the surveillance mechanisms described below. It would also be impracticable to do so given the volume of uploaded material. Paragraph 22 above is repeated.

54.3 SoundCloud cannot practicably review audio content after it has been uploaded and stored at the direction of the uploader, save in cases where harmful or unlawful content is reported by a user, where a valid take-down request is received, for technical troubleshooting, or in other isolated cases. Automated technical surveillance processes are carried out periodically, as described at paragraph 58 below.

55 SoundCloud does exercise administrative and technical control over the SoundCloud Servers, and so is able to intervene in particular cases, and upon being properly notified, to remove files and database entries associated with audio content, or to

disable access to audio content in particular territories or worldwide. However, it is denied that this amounts to control over all content uploaded to the SoundCloud Platform. Save as stated above, paragraph 6.19 is denied.

Steps taken to prevent copyright infringement

56 At all material times, SoundCloud has adopted a range of measures with the intention of avoiding or minimising the risk of copyright infringement on the SoundCloud Platform. These measures include the following:

Content Identification System

57 Since 2010, SoundCloud has operated an automated technical surveillance system whose aim is to prevent audio content from being uploaded to the SoundCloud Platform which consists of, or incorporates, copyright works. The system is known as the "Content Identification System" ("**CIS**") and currently operates as follows:

57.1 When an audio content file is uploaded by a user, it is transmitted automatically to two "fingerprint" services (known as "Audible Magic" and "Drakkar") which compare the contents of the file against their reference database of known sound recordings. Audible Magic is a third party service which is used by many leading record labels, broadcasters and movie studios. Drakkar is a proprietary tool developed by SoundCloud.

57.2 If either fingerprint service returns a match, CIS takes action specified by the right-holder who supplied the matching reference work (for example, removing the upload), unless the uploader or audio content has been added to a "whitelist" of authorised users and files (such as verified record labels), normally at the request of a right-holder via Deck The process is designed to accommodate all file formats in which audio may be uploaded to the SoundCloud Platform.

57.3 CIS is fully automatic and does not rely upon human intervention. Even the act of adding sound recordings to the matching database is automated and carried out solely by participating right-holders.

57.4 Audible Magic's reference database comprises over 15 million files, which are delivered directly to Audible Magic by record companies and other right-holders. The Drakkar reference database currently contains over 11.7 million files. A participating right-holder may add new reference works to the database at any time. It is open to PRS to participate in CIS and provide reference works, but so far it has chosen not to do so.

58 CIS is applied multiple times to all uploads: once at the time of upload, again after 40 hours, and again after 14 days. In addition, CIS is periodically re-applied to all audio content files stored on the SoundCloud Servers on an ongoing basis at least every 85 days. To date CIS has identified and removed more than 13.2 million audio content files in total.

59 CIS has been voluntarily developed by SoundCloud as part of its commitment to preventing and combatting copyright infringement on the SoundCloud Platform. SoundCloud has invested approximately £4 million in building and developing CIS, in addition to the cost of employing a team of 6 full time software engineers and product managers whose sole job is to maintain and improve CIS.

User education

60 SoundCloud has published a range of materials intended to educate users of the SoundCloud Platform in copyright matters. The SoundCloud Website includes a dedicated copyright section, which explains the basics of copyright, provides a copyright checklist to prospective uploaders, and links to third party resources. The SoundCloud Help Centre also includes a dedicated copyright section. Copies of selected educational materials are at **Annex 4.**

Notice-and-takedown

61 At all material times, SoundCloud has operated a rapid and effective procedure by which unauthorised copyright material may be reported. Any interested person can notify SoundCloud of the URL of any audio content which has been uploaded by a user to the SoundCloud Platform which the person alleges infringes copyright. Notifications can be made via an online form, to the SoundCloud nominated copyright agent, or by email to copyrights@soundcloud.com. Copies of these notification materials are at **Annex 5**.

62 Additionally, the page for every audio file uploaded to the SoundCloud Platform contains a prominent "Report Copyright Infringement" button. Copyright reports may be sent by any member of the public who clicks this button.

63 No copyright reports have been received by SoundCloud via this procedure from PRS.

Copyright support team

64 Since 2012, SoundCloud has employed a dedicated "Copyright Support Team" which aims to act on all copyright reports within 24 hours, and normally responds much sooner. The team comprises 5 full time employees and is split across 2 locations, 9 time zones apart, to provide maximum responsiveness.

65 Since December 2014, a member of the Copyright Support Team has been on call at all times to respond to emergency reports of leaked pre-release audio content. Certain right-holders are able to report such content via a dedicated reporting channel.

Copyright portal

66 SoundCloud provides selected copyright owners with access to a dedicated copyright portal known as "**Deck**". Among other things, Deck enables these right-holders to remove unauthorised content from the SoundCloud Platform directly without the need to report it to SoundCloud. Removal via "Deck" adds the fingerprint of the audio content to a blacklist which prevents any users from uploading matching audio content to the SoundCloud Platform in the future.

67 Deck is used by a number of record labels, publishers, and industry bodies, including IFPI and the RIAA. PRS is aware of the existence of the Deck but to date PRS has chosen not to avail themselves of it.

SoundCloud's conduct overall

68 SoundCloud has acted as a reasonable economic operator would in seeking to implement and operate the measures referred to in paragraphs 56 to 67 above.

69 In the premises, SoundCloud has taken all reasonable steps within its power:

69.1 to prevent the infringement of copyright, including copyrights which PRS claims to own, from occurring using the facilities provided by the SoundCloud Platform;

69.2 to cease any infringements that are brought to its attention; and

69.3 to prevent future infringements of the same rights.

70 As to paragraph 8:

70.1 It is admitted that the SoundCloud Platform is sophisticated, popular and user-friendly.

70.2 Insofar as relevant, the primary purpose of the SoundCloud Platform is to allow content creators to connect with their fans and audiences by means of the diverse technical facilities outlined above. Uploaders are solely responsible for determining what is uploaded, to whom that content is accessible and on what terms, and how that content may be shared.

70.3 It is denied that it is thereby SoundCloud who makes available audio content that has been uploaded to the SoundCloud Platform by users.

70.4 It is admitted that audio content is indexed, classified and searchable. Such processes are technical and automatic. Paragraphs 40 to 42 above are repeated.

71 Save as stated otherwise in this Defence, paragraph 8 is admitted.

72 Paragraph 9 is admitted.

73 The first sentence of paragraph 10 is not admitted. Inference (a) is denied because:

73.1 SoundCloud does not monitor the contents of the SoundCloud Platform. Paragraph 53 above is repeated.

73.2 SoundCloud relies, and is entitled to rely, upon the representations and contractual warranties supplied by uploaders that they are entitled to communicate the audio content they upload.

73.3 Save as set out below, SoundCloud is not aware of any specific instance in which a particular audio content file stored on the SoundCloud Servers embodies any of the Sample Works and/or PRS Repertoire.

74 Inference (b) is not understood and is embarrassing for want of particularity. It is denied that SoundCloud has knowledge as alleged in the second sentence of paragraph 10(a) or (b).

75 Paragraph 11 is denied and its relevance is not understood. SoundCloud has made content licensing arrangements in connection with the launch of a new service in the United States but that service is not provided in the United Kingdom.

Allegations of copyright infringement

76 It is denied that SoundCloud has engaged in any act restricted by the copyright with respect to the Sample Works and/or PRS Repertoire. Paragraph 13 is therefore denied for the reasons set out below.

The Sample Works

77 SoundCloud does not have, and has never had, actual knowledge that recordings of the Sample Works or any of them are stored on the SoundCloud Servers and/or are accessible from a location on the SoundCloud Platform. Paragraph 12.1 is not admitted.

78 Paragraph 12.2 is vague and unparticularised. PRS claims to be the owner or licensee of copyright in unspecified musical works in the PRS Repertoire. SoundCloud cannot plead to this allegation. As to the second sentence of paragraph 12.2, it is specifically

denied that PRS has identified where and how any particular musical work is being made available on the SoundCloud Platform. To avoid doubt, it is not admitted that PRS possesses any relevant rights with respect to any particular work. Paragraph 9 above is repeated.

79 The following paragraphs are without prejudice to SoundCloud's contention that there is no evidence that any of the Sample Works are or have ever been made available on the SoundCloud Platform and, in the absence of such evidence, its non-admission of that allegation.

Primary liability

80 It is denied that SoundCloud has engaged in any act of communication to the public of any musical work owned or controlled by PRS which is embodied in audio content, whether by making available any such work by electronic transmission in such a way that members of the public may access it from a place and at a time individually chosen by them or otherwise.

81 It is admitted that an act of making available occurs when audio content is uploaded by a user to the SoundCloud Platform such that it has passed the CIS upload checks mentioned in paragraph 57 above and has been stored on the SoundCloud Servers, and in circumstances where that user has specified that members of the public may access the file by streaming and/or downloading it. However, the relevant act of making available is committed by the user who uploaded the content in question to the SoundCloud Platform. In particular:

81.1 SoundCloud merely provides physical facilities, namely the SoundCloud Servers, for enabling the making of a communication by users of the SoundCloud Platform. The resulting acts of communication are performed by the SoundCloud users, not by SoundCloud.

81.2 SoundCloud does not itself engage in any act when a user uploads an item of audio content to the SoundCloud Servers. The SoundCloud Platform stores the content on the SoundCloud Server and records its associated File Metadata in the SoundCloud Databases.

81.3 SoundCloud does not itself engage in any act when a member of the public accesses audio content by means of the SoundCloud Website or the SoundCloud App and such content is electronically transmitted at the request of that user. SoundCloud does not control the content of the matter communicated and does not control the decision by the user to allow it to be communicated. It is obvious to users of the SoundCloud Platform that audio content with which they interact has been uploaded and made available by another user of the Platform, and not by SoundCloud.

81.4 SoundCloud does not intervene in transmissions of audio content. Any audio content that has been uploaded by users of SoundCloud is duly stored and transmitted solely in accordance with the instructions of the uploader, and the SoundCloud Platform is a mere amanuensis as regards the storage and execution of such instructions.

82 In the premises, it is registered users of the SoundCloud Platform who communicate sounds to the public using the facilities provided by that Platform, and not SoundCloud.

83 Further or alternatively, it is denied that any act of communication of the Sample Works is an act taking place in the United Kingdom. Paragraph 12 above is repeated. SoundCloud will aver that:

83.1 The mere accessibility of the SoundCloud Platform to users in the United Kingdom is insufficient for it to be targeted there.

83.2 Whether a particular audio content file is targeted to a particular territory depends on the objective intention of the person who uploaded that file to the SoundCloud Platform. PRS has not identified any particular uploaders of audio content, so SoundCloud is unable to plead to this allegation. In any case, such intention would be outside the knowledge of SoundCloud in any particular case.

83.3 It is admitted that SoundCloud allows premium subscription services to be paid for by content creators in pounds sterling. However, such services are optional and do not form part of the SoundCloud Platform that is offered to all users.

84 In the premises, if (contrary to SoundCloud's case) any act of communication to the public of a Sample Work has occurred for which it is responsible, such act has not taken place in the United Kingdom because it has not been targeted to that territory.

85 Paragraph 13.1 is accordingly denied.

Authorisation liability

86 SoundCloud has neither granted nor purported to grant to its registered users the right to do any of the acts complained of by PRS. In particular:

86.1 SoundCloud has deployed every measure reasonably within its power to prevent such acts from occurring. Paragraphs 56 to 69 above are repeated.

86.2 No reasonable registered user who uploads an audio file could deduce that SoundCloud possessed or purported to possess the authority to grant permission to exploit copyright works embodied in that audio file. This is clear *inter alia* from the educational material displayed to uploaders and other users.

86.3 The SoundCloud Platform has substantial and well-known non-infringing uses. Paragraphs 3 and 32 to 34 above are repeated.

86.4 It is specifically denied that SoundCloud has encouraged users to infringe copyright. Paragraph 60 above is repeated.

86.5 SoundCloud has an arms-length relationship with users of the SoundCloud Platform, save as indicated below. That relationship is regulated by the Terms of Use but SoundCloud otherwise possesses no direct control over the behaviour of registered users. Paragraph 54 above is repeated.

86.6 SoundCloud imposes all necessary and appropriate contractual restrictions on the use of third parties' copyright material by means of the Terms of Use. Those terms are not mere window dressing and are enforced against alleged infringers.

86.7 SoundCloud has no actual knowledge that a particular audio content file uploaded to the SoundCloud Platform infringes PRS's copyrights. Paragraphs 105 to 115 below are repeated.

87 In the premises, if any infringement occurs, the provision of facilities by SoundCloud goes no further than mere enablement or inadvertent assistance. Paragraph 13.2 is accordingly denied.

Joint liability

88 SoundCloud has neither procured infringement of, nor joined in a common design with registered users, to infringe PRS's alleged copyright in the Sample Works. In particular:

88.1 SoundCloud has not induced, incited or persuaded registered users to upload audio content to which they do not possess the relevant copyrights. It is specifically denied that the purpose of providing the facilities comprising the SoundCloud Platform is to cause or procure infringements of copyright.

88.2 SoundCloud has not formed any common design or agreement with registered users to infringe copyright. The full extent of SoundCloud's agreement with users is embodied in the Terms of Use, which expressly prohibit infringement. Paragraphs 20 and 54 above are repeated.

88.3 Paragraph 87 above is repeated. Mere assistance is insufficient and the relevance of paragraph 13.3.3 is not understood.

89 Paragraph 13.3 is accordingly denied.

Safe harbours

90 The SoundCloud Platform provides an information society service or services. In particular:

90.1 Paragraphs 12 to 58 above are repeated.

90.2 The SoundCloud Platform provides services normally provided for remuneration.

90.3 The SoundCloud Platform provides its services at a distance.

90.4 The SoundCloud Platform provides its services by electronic means.

90.5 The SoundCloud Platform's services are provided at the individual request of a recipient of the services.

91 SoundCloud is a service provider who provides an information society service within the meaning of regulation 2 of the Regulations and Article 2 of the E-Commerce Directive.

Hosting

92 If and to the extent that a Sample Work (or other work upon which PRS relies) has been stored on the SoundCloud Servers as a result of having been uploaded by a registered user of the SoundCloud Platform:

92.1 PRS does not possess any relevant rights with respect to the copying of musical works within the PRS Repertoire, including the Sample Works. In the premises, PRS lacks standing to bring proceedings for copying of the Sample Works arising from their reproduction and storage in the SoundCloud Servers. The following sub-paragraphs are without prejudice to that contention.

92.2 Such activity consists of the storage of information.

92.3 That information was provided by a recipient of the service, namely the uploading user.

92.4 SoundCloud does not have, and at all material times has not had, actual knowledge of unlawful activity or information in respect of such stored information for the reasons set out below in paragraphs 106 to 115 below, save in respect of the works identified in paragraph 116 below.

92.5 Further, SoundCloud is not, and at all material times has not been, aware of facts or circumstances from which it would have been apparent to SoundCloud, or a diligent economic operator in the position of SoundCloud, that the activity or information was unlawful. Paragraphs 32 and 53 to 55 above are repeated.

92.6 Alternatively, upon obtaining such knowledge or awareness, SoundCloud has acted, or will act, expeditiously to remove and/or to disable access to the information for the reasons set out below in paragraphs 111 to 116 below.

93 Further, in respect of the storage of information uploaded to the SoundCloud Servers by registered users of the SoundCloud Platform:

93.1 such activity is of a technical, automatic and passive nature; and

93.2 SoundCloud has neither knowledge of nor control over the information which is stored.

94 Paragraph 14.4 is accordingly denied.

95 Alternatively, if and to the extent that SoundCloud is found not to have acted passively and neutrally with respect to any audio content stored on the SoundCloud Servers, SoundCloud will rely on the hosting safe harbour in respect of all remaining content which is so stored.

96 The matters alleged at paragraph 14.4.3 are not relevant to the question of whether SoundCloud has acted neutrally and passively. As to its subparagraphs:

96.1 Denied. Transcoding is an automated technical process undertaken at the request of an uploading user. Paragraphs 35 and 36 above are repeated.

96.2 Denied. Save as set out above, SoundCloud has not knowingly encouraged or facilitated access to particular audio content, and/or has not done so in relation to the Sample Works.

96.3 Denied. SoundCloud does not assist users to optimise the presentation of particular audio content, which is displayed in a standard format and at their request, save in particular instances. Paragraphs 43 to 46 above are repeated.

96.4 Denied. Save as set out in paragraph 100 below, content recommendations occur as part of an automated technical process undertaken by computer algorithms resident on the SoundCloud Servers. Paragraph 47 above is repeated.

96.5 Denied. No content is "pushed" to users. All content is transmitted at the request of an individual recipient of the SoundCloud Platform, namely the requesting user. Paragraph 48 above is repeated.

96.6 Denied. Statistics are collated automatically as part of the normal technical operation of the SoundCloud Databases. Paragraphs 49 and 50 above are repeated.

97 Paragraph 14.4.4 is vague and unparticularised. SoundCloud is unable to plead to the allegation that PRS is "in very many instances" the owner of copyright in unspecified musical works which are said to be protected by copyright in the United Kingdom.

98 Further, paragraph 14.4.4 is based on an apparent misapprehension as to the knowledge possessed by SoundCloud in relation to specific audio content uploaded to the SoundCloud Platform. Paragraph 21, 53 and 54 above are repeated. In the premises, paragraph 14.4.4 is denied.

99 In respect of the storage and transmission of information from the SoundCloud Platform to users of the Platform:

99.1 any activity of SoundCloud is limited to the technical process of operating and/or giving access to the transmission network; and

99.2 such activity is of a technical, automatic and passive nature;

99.3 SoundCloud has neither knowledge of nor control over the information which is transmitted or stored.

100 Insofar as SoundCloud has linked to specific audio content hosted on the SoundCloud Platform, it is admitted that SoundCloud has intervened to promote that specific audio content and will thereby have selected the information contained in the transmission of the linked page on the SoundCloud Website. However, it is not admitted that SoundCloud will have selected the content of any subsequent transmission of the audio content if a user later requests to stream or download the audio content mentioned on that page.

101 In the premises, SoundCloud cannot be liable for damages or for any other pecuniary remedy in respect of liability arising from the storage of the Sample Works on the

SoundCloud Servers. The hosting safe harbour provides a complete defence to any liability arising from the copying or transmission of PRS's alleged copyright works.

102 Paragraph 14.2 is accordingly denied.

Mere conduit

103 Further or alternatively, if and to the extent that a Sample Work has been transmitted from the SoundCloud Servers to a recipient of the SoundCloud Platform, SoundCloud will rely upon the mere conduit safe harbour in respect of such activities insofar as they consist of transmission in a communication network of information provided by a user of the SoundCloud Platform. Paragraph 14.3 is otherwise denied.

104 In the premises, SoundCloud cannot be liable for damages or for any other pecuniary remedy in respect of liability arising from the transmission of the Sample Works from the SoundCloud Platform to users of the Platform. The mere conduit safe harbour provides a complete defence to any liability arising from the electronic transmission of PRS's copyright works to the public.

Allegations of actual knowledge

105 It is denied that SoundCloud has actual knowledge of unlawful activity or information on the SoundCloud Platform in respect of the Sample Works or at all. Paragraphs 79 to 89 above are repeated.

106 Further, it is denied that SoundCloud is aware of facts or circumstances from which it would have been apparent to SoundCloud that such activity or information was unlawful. In particular, where a registered user has uploaded audio content to the SoundCloud Servers which has passed the CIS upload checks mentioned in paragraph 57 above:

106.1 SoundCloud is not aware of whether or not the uploader is a PRS member.

106.2 SoundCloud is not aware of whether or not the uploader is a member of a collecting society in another territory from whom PRS licenses rights. In such a case, SoundCloud is also not aware of whether the uploader is lawfully entitled to grant licences under the work. Paragraph 9.3 above is repeated.

106.3 SoundCloud is not aware of whether or not the uploaded audio content embodies PRS Repertoire or is a commercially released sound recording.

107 At no time has PRS given SoundCloud any proper or effective notice of unlawful activity or information hosted on the SoundCloud Platform which is sufficient to confer actual knowledge of the same.

108 Further or alternatively, it is denied that SoundCloud has failed to act expeditiously to remove or to disable access to such information.

109 It is admitted that PRS's solicitors sent a letter of claim to SoundCloud's solicitors on 20 July 2015 (after commencing this action), and without prior warning ("20 July Letter"). The letter attached a table listing some 4475 examples of PRS Repertoire identified by *inter alia* its track title, artist, album and ISRC, and made the allegation that these works were being made available on the SoundCloud Platform, but did not include any details of where on the SoundCloud Platform the said works were alleged to be located. None of the notified tracks were Sample Works. Paragraph 14.4.5.4 is admitted to this extent.

110 The 20 July Letter was deficient *inter alia* for the following reasons:

110.1 It did not set out details of the location of the information in question on the SoundCloud Platform.

110.2 It did not set out details of the unlawful nature of the information in question.

110.3 It was not sent to SoundCloud by means of any of the advertised channels for reporting allegations of copyright infringement.

110.4 It did not include any of the Sample Works among the list of 4475 works referred to in the letter.

111 Despite SoundCloud's repeated requests, PRS has refused to provide any, or any adequate, details of the alleged infringements:

111.1 On 23 July 2015, SoundCloud's solicitors wrote to point out the deficiency of the 20 July Letter and to request the details needed to remove or disable access to the works.

111.2 On 28 July 2015, PRS's solicitors wrote to SoundCloud's solicitors refusing to provide the requested details. This meant *inter alia* that SoundCloud could not identify or remove the works mentioned in the 20 July Letter.

111.3 On 31 July 2015, SoundCloud's solicitors again wrote to request proper details of the allegedly infringing material (including its URL), PRS's rights to it, and its unlawful nature, and to give details of the material which SoundCloud had been able to identify from the 20 July Letter.

111.4 On 6 August 2015, PRS's solicitors wrote to SoundCloud's solicitors refusing to provide the requested details, and refusing to clarify the nature and scope of its rights in relation to the works notified in the 20 July Notice.

111.5 A period of without prejudice discussions in relation to the claim concluded on or around 28 August 2015.

111.6 On 28 August 2015, SoundCloud applied for an order that PRS provide the requested details of the alleged infringements.

112 Copies of the relevant correspondence relating to the 20 July Letter are at **Annex 6** to this Defence.

113 In the premises, the 20 July Letter was ineffective to confer actual knowledge upon SoundCloud of the allegedly unlawful information in relation to the Sample Works and/or the PRS Repertoire.

114 Further, service of the Particulars of Claim was ineffective to confer actual knowledge upon SoundCloud of the allegedly unlawful information in relation to the Sample Works. Sub-paragraphs 110.1 to 110.3 above are repeated.

115 Save as stated above, paragraph 14.4.5 is denied.

116 Notwithstanding this, on or around 31 July 2015, SoundCloud developed a means of searching the SoundCloud Databases for File Metadata which matched the ISRCs supplied by PRS. This allowed it to identify approximately 250 files which were said by their uploaders to embody musical works which PRS had notified. On the same day, SoundCloud took steps to disable access to all the identified URLs. It also sent warning notices to the relevant uploaders of these works in accordance with its repeat infringer policy. A list of this audio content and its URLs is at **Annex 7** to this Defence.

117 Following the disabling of access to these 251 URLs, SoundCloud has received complaints from registered users who assert that their audio content was wrongfully removed from the SoundCloud Platform. For example, on 12 August 2015, SoundCloud was contacted by a registered user who represented an independent music publisher, and claimed that uploads of the publisher's sound recordings had been incorrectly removed. SoundCloud referred the individual to PRS. A copy of this correspondence is at **Annex 8**

118 It is neither possible nor appropriate for SoundCloud to be put in a position whereby it must adjudicate a dispute between PRS and its own members, or its affiliates' members, concerning their ability to license and digitally exploit their own musical works. SoundCloud is faced with competing claims from PRS and certain of those members, and is unable to determine who is correct in any particular case. In the premises, SoundCloud does not have actual knowledge of unlawful activity or information uploaded by such a member. PRS is put to strict proof that, in each and every such instance: (1) the claim made by the member concerned that it is lawfully

entitled to upload content onto the SoundCloud Platform is wrong, and (2) that SoundCloud is aware of this alleged fact.

No general monitoring duty

119 Further or alternatively, to impose any form of liability on the basis of Sample Works and/or PRS Repertoire which has been uploaded to the SoundCloud Platform without the knowledge of SoundCloud, and in circumstances where the details of those uploads have not been notified, or properly notified, to SoundCloud by PRS, would amount to the imposition of a general monitoring duty upon SoundCloud. This would be contrary to Article 15(1) of the E-Commerce Directive.

120 In the premises, the Court may not impose, and SoundCloud cannot be liable for, damages or any other pecuniary remedy, or any injunctive remedy, in respect of any duty the discharge of which would require SoundCloud to monitor unspecified audio content in order to avoid liability.

The relief sought

121 It is denied that the Claimant is entitled to the relief claimed in paragraphs 15 to 21, or to any relief.

122 As to paragraph 15:

122.1 SoundCloud has not infringed PRS's copyright in the Sample Works or the other works that form part of the PRS Repertoire.

122.2 Alternatively, no case is properly pleaded with respect to the PRS Repertoire and it would be inappropriate to grant declaratory or other relief in respect of such unspecified works.

122.3 SoundCloud is entitled to the protection of at least regulations 17 and 19 of the Regulations, and Article 15(1) of the E-Commerce Directive, for the reasons set out above.

123 As to paragraph 16, it is not admitted that PRS has suffered loss and damage. It is denied that PRS is entitled to additional or any damages. Paragraph 9 above is repeated.

124 As to paragraph 17, it is denied that SoundCloud has received any profits that are attributable to the upload of Sample Works to the SoundCloud Platform.

125 SoundCloud admits and avers that it will continue to operate the SoundCloud Platform as set out above. SoundCloud further admits that it will owe an equitable duty to take reasonable and proportionate steps intended to avoid facilitating an act of infringement

of PRS's copyright that has been properly notified to it in a manner sufficient to confer actual knowledge of that infringement. SoundCloud stands ready to discharge that duty to the extent that any such notification is received from PRS in the future.

126 In the premises, it is denied that PRS is entitled to an injunction under Article 11 of the Enforcement Directive. Save as stated, paragraph 18 is denied.

127 Paragraph 19 is not admitted.

128 Paragraph 20 is denied. Neither upon receipt of the 20 July Notice nor upon service of the claim form and Particulars of Claim has SoundCloud obtained actual knowledge of its service being used to infringe PRS's copyright in the Sample Works or at all. Further or alternatively:

128.1 A service provider injunction would be disproportionate having regard to the substantial volume of non-infringing material hosted on the SoundCloud Platform. Paragraphs 32 to 34 above are repeated.

128.2 A service provider injunction would lack clarity unless it specified the URLs of each individual item of audio content on the SoundCloud Platform to which access must be disabled. Such an injunction would not be necessary in circumstances where SoundCloud has already volunteered to remove or disable access to any infringing audio content at its source which is properly notified to it. Paragraph 125 above is repeated.

129 Paragraph 21 is admitted insofar as PRS is entitled to any pecuniary remedy (which is denied).

130 If it is concluded that SoundCloud has not infringed any right belonging to PRS, but PRS is nonetheless entitled to injunctive relief, SoundCloud will aver that it is entitled to its costs of the action and the cost of implementing any order that the Court may make.

MARTIN HOWE QC
JAANI RIORDAN

DATED this 2 October 2015

STATEMENT OF TRUTH

The Defendant believes that the facts stated in this Defence are true.

I am duly authorised by the Defendant to sign this statement.

Full name: Gregor Pryor

Signed: ....

Position or office held: Partner, Reed Smith LLP

Address for receiving documents:
Reed Smith LLP
The Broadgate Tower
20 Primrose Street
London EC2A 2RS

Filed and served on 2 October 2015 by Reed Smith LLP, The Broadgate Tower, 20 Primrose Street, London EC2A 2RS, solicitors for the Defendant

30

APPENDIX I

IN THE HIGH COURT OF JUSTICE
CHANCERY DIVISION
INTELLECTUAL PROPERTY

Claim No HC-2015-003033

PERFORMING RIGHT SOCIETY LIMITED

Claimant

- and -

SOUNDCLOUD LIMITED

Defendant

DEFENCE

Reed Smith LLP
The Broadgate Tower
20 Primrose Street
London EC2A 2RS
Phone: +44 20 3116 3000
DX 1066 City / DX18 London

Ref: SPMS/GJP/SP/766897.6

Solicitors for the Defendant

Claim no HC-2015-003033

IN THE HIGH COURT OF JUSTICE

CHANCERY DIVISION

INTELLECTUAL PROPERTY

BETWEEN:

PERFORMING RIGHT SOCIETY LIMITED

Claimant

-and-

SOOUNDCLOUD LIMITED

Defendant

REPLY

---

1. In this Reply:

   1.1. PRS adopts the same definitions and abbreviations as are employed in the Particulars of Claim and the Defence.

   1.2. Save where the contrary appears, references to paragraph numbers are references to the corresponding paragraph in the Defence.

   1.3. PRS joins issue with the Defendant on its Defence, save insofar as it consists of admissions or is admitted below.

2. As to paragraph 8:

   2.1. Under the Articles of Association of PRS:

      2.1.1. By Article 7(a), every member shall, on election or at any time thereafter if requested by PRS, assign or cause to be assigned to PRS all rights to be administered on his behalf by PRS in accordance with the provisions of the Article.

2.1.2. By Article 7(c), the rights to be administered by PRS on behalf of a member include the "performing right".

2.1.3. The "performing right" is defined as meaning, in respect of any work, among other things, the right to communicate the work to the public, all rights in the nature of that right, including any extension or modification of that right which by virtue of any present or future enactment exist or may exist and such corresponding rights as may exist under the laws relating to copyright in all other countries in the world as in force from time to time.

2.2. As set out in the Particulars of Claim, it is the right to communicate to the public which the Defendant has infringed and continues to infringe. The Defendant well knows that that is an aspect of the performing right which is administered by PRS on behalf of its members because this fact is common knowledge and because PRS has informed the Defendant of this fact.

3. Paragraph 9.2 is noted. For the avoidance of doubt, it is PRS's contention that, as a matter of proportionate and cost-effective case management, the Court should determine first whether the Defendant, by its operation of the SoundCloud Services, has committed the act of communication to the public and whether the Defendant is entitled to the benefit of Regulations 17 or 19 of the Regulations. It would not be proportionate and cost-effective for the Court, in determining those issues, to be required to make findings as to (i) PRS's ownership of copyright in relation to each and every work within the PRS Repertoire and (ii) each and every act of infringement in relation to each and every such work. Insofar as it is necessary, the determination of the extent of the infringing acts committed by the Defendant should form part of the inquiry to be conducted after determination of the issues referred to above. PRS will seek directions from the Court accordingly.

4. As to paragraph 11, it is averred that:

4.1. All of the components of the SoundCloud Services are designed and implemented by, or at the direction of, the Defendant.

4.2. Those components are intended by the Defendant:

4.2.1. To enable it to provide the SoundCloud Services and the features and functionality that form part of those services and

4.2.2. To give the Defendant the knowledge and control over the uploaded content that enable it to provide the SoundCloud Services and the features and functionality that form part of those services.

4.3. The operation of those components is not neutral and is not technical, automatic and passive but are designed and intended to enable the Defendant to provide a sophisticated and user-friendly music-streaming and download service which competes with similar licensed services. By way of example, in relation to the matters referred to in paragraph 11:

4.3.1. The Defendant dictates the nature of the information that is provided by users. In particular, it is responsible for and controls the drop down list of 'tags' from which users must select in order to facilitate the identification of the content by other users.

4.3.2. The Defendant is responsible for and controls the conversion of files into a format permitted by the Defendant in order to facilitate the transmission of the content to other users.

4.3.3. The Defendant is responsible for and controls the choice of the information that is retrieved and displayed to users.

5. Paragraph 20 is noted. It is denied, if it be so alleged, that the Terms of Use are the only terms which govern the Defendant's storage and transmission of content. Pending disclosure herein, PRS repeats paragraph 11 of the Particulars of Claim.

6. As to paragraph 28, it is admitted that the uploader may select whether they want the uploaded content to be private or publicly available and whether it should be available to download. However, the default terms (as dictated and set by the Defendant) provide that the uploaded content will be publicly available (but not available for download).

7. As to paragraphs 23.2, 41, 44, 45, 47 and 48, to the extent that the operation of the SoundCloud Services involves the use and application of algorithms (which, for the avoidance of doubt, the Defendant is required to prove), it is averred that:

7.1. All such algorithms are designed and written by or at the direction of the Defendant.

7.2. They are designed and intended by the Defendant to achieve their specific purposes, including, on the Defendant's case, the provision of matching words for 'tags' (paragraph 23.2), the indexing of, and search for, content (paragraph 41), the selection of content for the "Explore" section of the SoundCloud Website (paragraph 44), the selection of "trending" content (paragraph 45), the selection of content to be recommended to users (paragraph 47) and the selection of content to be 'pushed' to users (paragraph 48).

7.3. It is denied, insofar as it be alleged, that the use of algorithms renders the Defendant neutral and passive in relation to the information provided and the content made available as a result of that use.

7.4. The Defendant could, if it chose to do so, not provide the functionality in relation to which it claims to use algorithms. The Defendant could, for example, choose not to 'push' content to users or to supply selections of content to be recommended to users. When it does 'push' such content and supply such selections, those acts, including the selection of the content that is 'pushed' and/or recommended, are not the acts of any uploader or user. They are the acts of the Defendant and are within the knowledge and control of the Defendant.

7.5. Furthermore, to the extent that the Defendant has chosen to provide such functionality and to use algorithms in relation to it, pending disclosure of the materials relevant to the algorithms relied upon by the Defendant and technical analysis of their design, it is averred that:

7.5.1. The use of algorithms does not entail that the Defendant does not have knowledge and control over the results of such use. The algorithms are the means by which the Defendant obtains and utilises its knowledge and exercises its control in relation to the content that is uploaded.

7.5.2. The way in which the algorithms operate and, thus, the results of that operation are entirely within the knowledge and control of the Defendant.

7.5.3. The Defendant is able to direct and control the operation of the algorithms so that they produce results in accordance with criteria set and dictated by the Defendant.

7.5.4. Pending disclosure, it is to be inferred that the Defendant has set criteria and designed algorithms in order to produce the results which are in fact produced. They are designed and intended by the Defendant to encourage and facilitate the upload and consumption of content.

7.5.5. The Defendant has the power to set different criteria and/or to design and implement algorithms which would produce different results.

7.5.6. Where, for example, particular content is 'pushed' to a user or is included in a selection of recommendations to a user, that is a result of the decisions made and implemented by the Defendant as to (i) the criteria according to which the algorithms are to operate and (ii) the design and operation of those algorithms.

7.5.7. The selection of the content that is 'pushed' and/or recommended is not made by any uploader or user. It is made by the Defendant and is within the knowledge and control of the Defendant.

8. As to paragraph 30, according to the Defendant's Terms of Use, those terms are not intended to give rights to anyone except the uploader and the Defendant. It is to be inferred that users of the SoundCloud Services are impliedly licensed by the Defendant in respect of their use of the content on the SoundCloud Services.

9. As to paragraph 32, it is admitted that there is a relatively small amount of non-music content made available via the SoundCloud Services. On the basis of a random sampling exercise carried out on behalf of PRS in November 2015:

9.1. 92.1% of files were music content.

9.2. 7.7% of files were non-music content.

9.3. 0.2% of files were of indeterminate content because the relevant link was not operational.

10. As to paragraph 43, it is averred that the Defendant's operation of the SoundCloud Services constitutes intervention in the presentation of all the audio content that is thereby made available to users. Without prejudice to the generality of the foregoing:

APPENDIX I

10.1. The Defendant has its own SoundCloud account accessible at https://soundcloud.com/soundcloud, to which content is uploaded.

10.2. Content uploaded onto that account includes recordings of works written or co-written by members of PRS, the performing right in which is owned by PRS as follows:

10.2.1. "I Have Been A Fire" – Luke Sital Singh: https://soundcloud.com/soundcloud/sets/creator-clubhouse

10.2.2. "The Guilty One" - Marina Florance (and Julie Allen Fox as additional writer): https://soundcloud.com/soundcloud/sets/international-womens-day-2014.

10.3. It is to be inferred that these works were uploaded by employees of the Defendant in the course of their employment.

11. As to paragraph 52.1(c):

11.1. It is noted that email notifications are not normally authored by employees of the Defendant. It is inferred that the Defendant sends out email notifications which are so authored. It is to be inferred that the employees who author such communications have knowledge of the content made available on the SoundCloud Services.

11.2. To the extent that it is alleged that the email notifications are automatically generated with snippets of pre-determined text (which, for the avoidance of doubt, the Defendant is required to prove), it is averred that:

11.2.1. The means by which such notifications are generated and sent are designed and written by or at the direction of the Defendant.

11.2.2. The content of such notifications and the selection of users to whom they are sent is controlled and dictated by the Defendant.

11.2.3. It is denied, insofar as it be alleged, that the fact (to the extent that it is a fact) that the Defendant uses automated means to generate and send such notifications renders the Defendant neutral and passive in relation to them or their content.

11.2.4. The Defendant could, if it chose to do so, not provide such notifications.

11.2.5. Furthermore, to the extent that the Defendant has chosen to provide such notifications, and to use automated means in relation to them, pending disclosure of the materials relevant to those means relied upon by the Defendant and technical analysis of their design, it is averred that:

11.2.5.1. The use of such means does not entail that the Defendant does not have knowledge and control over the results of such use.

11.2.5.2. The way in which the automated means operate and, thus, the results of that operation are entirely within the knowledge and control of the Defendant.

11.2.5.3. The Defendant is able to direct and control the operation of the automated means so that the notifications that are thereby generated and sent are in accordance with the Defendant's intentions.

11.2.5.4. Pending disclosure, it is to be inferred that the Defendant has given instructions to procure that the automated means result in email notifications being generated and sent to those to whom the Defendant intends them to be sent and with the content which the Defendant intends to be included.

11.2.5.5. The Defendant has the power to procure that the automated means operate in a different way and produce different email notifications.

12. As to paragraph 52.6, the Defendant's newsletters promote particular music content. It is admitted that they also (and thereby) operate to promote the SoundCloud Services generally. The Defendant's averment that that is their purpose and the Defendant uses specific content uploaded by users for the purpose of promoting the SoundCloud Services as a whole is noted and adopted.

13. As to paragraph 57:

13.1. It is admitted that Audible Magic is a service used by rightsholders and licensors. It is offered in various versions with differing degrees of effectiveness. The Defendant is put to proof of the version it uses. Audible Magic anyway only operates by reference to "fingerprints" of sound recordings. It does not operate to identify musical works embodied in sound recordings (and PRS does not, in any event, have "fingerprints" for musical works within its repertoire).

13.2. Accordingly, even if implemented and operating efficiently and comprehensively, Audible Magic will only identify works within the PRS Repertoire to the extent that the owner of a sound recording embodying such works has provided a "fingerprint". Audible Magic will not be effective to identify, e.g., cover versions and remixes of works within the PRS Repertoire.

13.3. As PRS understands it, the Drakkar tool is similarly inappropriate and ineffective to identify works within the PRS Repertoire.

13.4. Even in respect of sound recordings which are identified, the Defendant will not block access to the sound recording (and the musical work embodied therein), unless the owner of the sound recording requires this. Furthermore, the Defendant will not block access to the sound recording (and the musical work embodied therein) where, for example, the uploader (including "verified record labels") has "whitelisted" the sound recording to be made available on the uploader's SoundCloud "channel". This is despite the fact that:

13.4.1. the Defendant knows (because it is common knowledge) that a musical work embodied in a sound recording will have a separate copyright from the sound recording and that the licence of the owner of both copyrights is required in order for the sound recording to be made available without infringement of copyright;

13.4.2. the Defendant knows that it does not have the licence from the owner of the relevant copyright in the musical work embodied in the sound recording; alternatively the Defendant has no reason to believe that it does have such licence. In particular, where, as paragraph 57.2 impliedly asserts, the Defendant has made special arrangements for "verified record labels", the Defendant knows that those record labels do not own the copyright in the musical works embodied in the sound recordings of those "verified record labels" and that a further licence is required from the owner of such copyright.

14. As to paragraph 66, the management of content via the Back-portal requires an effective ability to identify sound recordings by reference to "fingerprints". It is inappropriate and ineffective to enable identification and blocking of works within the PRS Repertoire.

15. As to paragraph 73.2 (and generally in relation to the Defence), to the extent that the Defendant claims to rely upon any representations or contractual warranties supplied by uploaders, it is denied that the existence of such representations and contractual warranties are relevant, save insofar as they may provide the Defendant with rights to be indemnified by uploaders in the event that they were untrue. Furthermore, it is denied that the Defendant does so rely and/or that any such reliance is reasonable. In support thereof, PRS will rely on the following:

15.1. it is in practice unlikely that uploaders read the Defendant's Terms of Service;

15.2. as the Defendant knows, inter alia from the operation of CIS:

15.2.1. The uploading of unauthorised and unlicensed content to the SoundCloud Services is commonplace;

15.2.2. The uploading of commercially released content, in respect of which a user other than a record label does not have any appropriate licence or authorisation, is commonplace;

15.3. the Defendant has entered into licensing agreements with record companies and publishing companies and organisations which would have been unnecessary if the uploaders' representations and warranties were true and/or if the Defendant believed them to be true and relied upon them;

15.4. the matters set out in paragraphs 10, 11 and 14.4.5 of the Particulars of Claim and paragraph 13.4 above.

16. As to paragraph 75, the relevance of paragraph 11 of the Particulars of Claim is as set out therein. Without prejudice thereto, and pending disclosure of the licence agreements entered into by the Defendant:

16.1. as PRS understands it, the Defendant has entered into licensing arrangements with rightsholders in relation to the US in respect of sound recordings and musical works.

Those licences extend to cover sound recordings which embody works within the PRS Repertoire;

16.2. to the extent that the licences relate to sound recordings, the Defendant knows (because it is common knowledge) that a musical work embodied in a sound recording will have a separate copyright from the sound recording and that the licence of the owner of both copyrights is required in order for the sound recording to be made available without infringement of copyright;

16.3. it is to be inferred from the fact that the Defendant has entered into these licences that, contrary to the position adopted in the Defence, it has sufficient knowledge and control over the content uploaded to the SoundCloud Services to recognise that it needed to enter into licences with the licensors. Furthermore, by entering into those licences, the Defendant acquired knowledge and control over the rights thereby licensed;

16.4. in recognising the need for those licences and in entering into those licences, it is to be inferred that the Defendant was at the same time aware of:

16.4.1. the fact that there were rights in the musical works embodied in the licensed sound recordings, in respect of which the Defendant was not being, and has never been, granted a licence, and

16.4.2. the fact that any licence in relation to musical works was territorially limited to the US.

16.5. as PRS understands it, the Defendant's purported justification for this is that the licensing arrangements in the US relate to the launch of a new service in the US, which the Defendant plans to subsequently launch in the UK. The Defendant is required to prove that the relevant licences in relation to any sound recordings are in fact territorially limited to the US. Furthermore, the Defendant is required to prove what material distinction exists between the new service and the service currently provided in the UK. In particular, the Defendant is required to prove that there is any distinction which would justify a conclusion that the Defendant has less knowledge and control over the content uploaded to the SoundCloud Services as they are made available to users in the UK as compared with the new service.

16.6. Furthermore, and in any event, the content that is made available in the US pursuant to the licences entered into by the Defendant is, or includes, content that is also made available in the UK in circumstances where, it is to be inferred, the Defendant knows that it is licensed (as to the rights granted by the relevant licences) in the US but not elsewhere.

17. As to paragraph 77, as at the date hereof, the Sample Works continue to be made available on the SoundCloud Services, including the content identified in the screenshots of recommendations at Annex 2 to the Particulars of Claim. Despite service of the Particulars of Claim and annexes on the Defendant on 28 August 2015, the Defendant has taken no steps to remove that content or any other content embodying the Sample Works (further instances of which are provided by way of the Reply to the Request for Further Information served herewith). It is to be inferred that the Defendant has taken no steps to send any warning to, or to suspend or terminate the account of, the users who uploaded this content.

18. As to paragraph 83:

18.1. It is averred that the SoundCloud Services are targeted at the public in the UK. Pending disclosure, PRS will rely on the following:

18.1.1. the Defendant is an English company;

18.1.2. the SoundCloud Services are presented in English;

18.1.3. subscriptions for the Defendant's Pro and Pro Unlimited plans are priced in £ sterling (for UK users). Those plans are optional but they are offered to all users of the SoundCloud Services. If the Defendant did not intend to target members of the public in the UK, it would not offer those plans in £ sterling;

18.1.4. the popularity of the SoundCloud Services in the UK;

18.1.5. the fact that the Defendant accepts uploads from, and makes content available to, users in the UK;

18.1.6. the fact that the Defendant collects and processes data from, users in the UK (in relation to, e.g., their listening history, "likes", etc);

18.1.7. the fact that the Defendant describes the SoundCloud Services as *"the world's leading social sound platform where anyone can create sounds and share them everywhere"*. It is to be inferred that members of the public in the UK are within the class of *"anyone"* at whom the service is targeted and that the UK is within *"everywhere"* where the Defendant intends the service to be used.

18.2. To the extent that, contrary to PRS's principal case, the intention of uploaders as to the targeting of any communication to the public is relevant, it is to be inferred that by using the SoundCloud Services for the purposes of their communication to the public uploaders must intend to target all those at whom the SoundCloud Services are targeted, which, as set out above, includes members of the public in the UK.

19. As to paragraph 119, Article 15(1) of the E-Commerce Directive only applies to providers when providing the services covered by Articles 12, 13 and 14 of the E-Commerce Directive. In its Defence, the Defendant does not claim to be providing services covered by Article 13 of the E-Commerce Directive. For the reasons set out in the Particulars of Claim and herein, the Defendant is not providing a service covered by Articles 12 or 14 of the E-Commerce Directive.

EDMUND CULLEN QC

<u>Statement of Truth</u>

The Claimant believes that the facts stated in this Reply are true. I am duly authorised by the Claimant to sign this statement of truth.

Signed: ....

Name: S.J. BAGGS

Served on 1 December 2015 by Wiggin LLP of 10th Floor, Met Building, Percy Street, London W1T 2BU (Solicitors for the Claimant)

IN THE HIGH COURT OF JUSTICE

Claim no HC-2015-003033

CHANCERY DIVISION

INTELLECTUAL PROPERTY

BETWEEN:

PERFORMING RIGHT SOCIETY LIMITED

Claimant

-and-

SOUNDCLOUD LIMITED

Defendant

REPLY

Wiggin LLP
10th Floor
Met Building
22 Percy Street
London
W1T 2BU
Ref: SJB/RA/NR

APPENDIX II

Attrakt v Google

07638–2016

Gen. Case List no. 86198/2013

Judgment no. 7638/2016 published on 17/06/2016

Gen. Case List no. 86198/2013

Register no. 6111/2016 dated 17/06/2016

(*rectangular stamp*)
SCHETTINO, LAWYER
COURT OF MILAN
THE COURT OFFICER
28TH JUNE 2016
APPLICATION No.: 2 LEVIES OF EXECUTION IN FAVOUR OF THE PLAINTIFF CERTIFIED COPY
URGENCY OF MATTER CONFIRMED
REVENUE STAMPS AFFIXED IN PAYMENT OF FEES
EURO 2 X 15.38

Signed by: MARINA ANNA TAVASSI Issued by: POSTECOM CA3 Serial # 10fd82 – Signed by: SILVIA GIANI Issued by: POSTECOM CA3 Serial #: d1cf9 Signed by: CARMELO GAROFALO Issued by: POSTECOM CA3 Serial #: deeee

REPUBLIC OF ITALY
IN THE NAME OF THE ITALIAN PEOPLE
COURT OF MILAN

SECTION SPECIALISING IN BUSINESS MATTERS – A -

The Court, sitting as a panel, is composed of the following Judges:

Her Hon. Marina Anna Tavassi	Presiding Judge
Her Hon. Silvia Giani	Drafting Judge
Her Hon. Alima Zana	Judge

passed the following

JUDGMENT

in the civil action at first instance entered under General Case List no. **86198/2013** brought by: **ATTRAKT S.R.L.**, acting through its duly authorised representative, represented and defended by the lawyer EUGENIO KRAUSS and by the lawyer SIMONE SCHETTINO, by virtue of due powers of attorney set out at the foot of the writ of summons, with address for service elected in MILAN, VIA VITTORIO VENETO, 24, at the office of defence counsel, Mr. SCHETTINO;

PLAINTIFF

against

GOOGLE IRELAND LTD., acting through its duly authorised representative, represented and defended by the lawyers MARIO SIRAGUSA, FERDINANDO EMANUELE, CARLO SANTORO, SAVERO VALENTINO and ROBERTO ARGERI, by virtue of due power of attorney dated 17th February 2014, attachment A to the set out at the foot of the appearance, with address for service elected in MILAN, VIA SAN PAOLO, 7, at the office of defence counsel, Mr. SANTORO

DEFENDANT

RE: Antitrust law/Abuse of economic dependence/Unfair competition

PLEADINGS

For the Plaintiff:

On the merits, as a substantive ruling:

May the Court

- dismiss the counterclaim made by the defendant, as unfounded on the facts and as a matter of law;
- make a finding of and declare the breach of contract on the part of Google and, as a result, declare the AdSense and AdWords Contracts currently in force with Attrakt to be terminated. through the fault and negligence of the said Google.

Also on the merits, in any event

Make a finding of and declare: (i) the abuse of economic dependence committed by Google to the detriment of Attrakt; (ii) the abuse of a dominant position committed by Google; (iii) the acts of unfair competition committed by Google to the detriment of the plaintiff.

As a result, may the Court declare null and void and/or having no legally binding effect the clauses in the AdSense Contract that grant Google the right to withdraw *ad nutum* (exercisable with immediate effect), and limit the liability of

Google to 125% of the amount paid over the last 12 months prior to the date on which liability arose in the manner envisaged in art. 9 of Law no. 192 dated 18th June 1998 and articles 1431 and 1342 of the Italian Civil Code.

Also on the merits, in any event

Order that compensation be paid of all damage incurred by Attrakt, as systematically listed and provisionally quantified in the paragraph in the writ of summons headed "REGARDING THE QUANTIFICATION OF THE DAMAGE", or for the lesser or greater amount that may be deemed fair in the light of the results of the examination, or, if the case, on an equitable basis, the amount indicated provisionally as €9,673,810.00 (nine million, six hundred and seventy-three thousand, eight hundred and ten), together with interest and monetary revaluation, as well as any further damage, as envisaged in art. 1224, paragraph II, of the Italian Civil Code.

As a subordinate ruling:

In the unlikely event that the Court finds that invalid "clicks" were made on the AdSense announcements published on the Attrakt site, may it re-establish the amount of the fee, excluding only the fees relating to individual clicks actually demonstrated as being invalid.

In any event

with award of costs, duties and legal fees.

By way of preliminary enquiries

The plaintiff insists in its request for the admission of testimonial proof, as formulated in the pleadings pursuant to art. 183, paragraph VI, no. 2) and 3), of the Italian Code of Civil Procedure.

It insists in its request that the Court order an expert witness report in order to assess the value of the Plaintiff Company at the time at which relations with Google were interrupted, as well as the potential future economic development of the company, in order to assess the damage incurred as a result of the defendant's conduct, ascertaining also the defendant's market shares in on-line advertising.

On behalf of the Defendant:

May the Court, having dismissed any other application, motion, plea or brief to the contrary, make rulings to this effect:

1 As a preliminary ruling, to dismiss the requests made by Attrakt S.r.l. in liquidation in their entirety, as unfounded on the facts and as a matter of law;
2 As an alternative ruling, having made a finding that Attrakt S.r.l. in liquidation committed a breach of its obligations envisaged in the AdSense Contract (as defined during the action), to terminate the agreement pursuant to art. 1453 of the Italian Civil Code, through the fault and negligence of the said Attrakt S.r.l. in liquidation and, as a result, dismiss the requests made by it in their entirety.

3 In any event, as a counterclaim:

(i) having made a finding that Attrakt S.r.l. in liquidation committed a breach of its obligations envisaged in the AdSense Contract (as defined during the action), to order it to return to Google Ireland Ltd. (if the case, also as compensation of damage) the amounts unduly received since September 2011, amounting to a total of Euro **1,955,114.62**, or the lesser or greater amount ascertained during proceedings or deemed fair (together with interest and revaluation);

(ii) to make a finding that Google Ireland Ltd. is owed the sum of USD **20,212.28** (Euro 18,532 at the exchange rate applying on 2nd February 2016) on the basis of the AdWords Contract (as defined during the action), and, as a result, order it to pay the sum to Google Ireland Ltd. (together with interest pursuant to Legislative Decree no. 231/2002, from the due dates indicated in the invoices up to the date of settlement); (iii) to order Attrakt in liquidation to pay compensation for further damage at the rate ascertained during the proceedings or deemed fair;

4 to order Attrakt in liquidation to reimburse the expenses, fees and cost of this action (together with VAT and Lawyers' social security fund contribution (CPA) as envisaged by law).

***

GROUNDS

1 *The plaintiffs requests*. In a writ served on 26th November 2013, the plaintiff company brought a civil action against the company Google, requesting that a finding be made that the defendant had committed breaches of its contractual obligations, that the said defendant was responsible for the abuse of a dominant position and/or of economic dependence, as well as acts of unfair competition and that as a result, it order compensation to be paid for the damage incurred by the Plaintiff. It put forward that:

- Attrakt operated in the design, development and sale of online advertising, the creation and running of websites; it was the owner of the search engine ATTRAKT.COM, benefitting from its own software for the indexation of the contents. This search engine had been on line since September 2011 and recorded around 15,000 registered users in December 2012; the site had a daily average of 1,700,000 individual visitors originating from all over the world.
- Attrakt had entered into two separate contracts with Google: Google AdSense in July 2011 and Google AdWords in September 2011. The AdWords service allowed the subject purchasing determined keywords (in this case Attrakt) to appear on top of the Google search engine at the moment a user had entered the keywords in question.

- By operation of the AdSense Contract, on the other hand, Attrakt made available certain advertising spaces on its web pages for Google's benefit, the latter acting as intermediary, on the one hand paying Attrakt for the space allocated on its website and, at the same time, selling these spaces to advertisers; the process of selecting the announcements to be included at every instance according to the type of visitor was dealt with exclusively by Google, incorporating a code which could not be modified by the host site; the remuneration due depended on the number of clicks and views.
- Attrakt, on the one hand, attracted users onto its website by means of the AdWords programme, paying large amounts to Google in order to appear in the top positions, and on the other, was paid by Google for advertising in favour of third parties on its site.
- The investment made by Attrakt in AdWords increased from 40,000.00 $ in September 2011 to 160,000.00 at the beginning of 2012 and Attrakt was inserted in the list of the "*Top Partners of Google AdWords*" and was invited, on 27th September 2012, to an event organised by the former.
- Google assisted Attrakt in the running of the pages, suggesting excellent implementations necessary to increase revenues and, in particular, urged the plaintiff to invest in AdWords so that it could earn more from adverts inserted using AdSense; the earnings with AdSense in fact increased considerably, rising from 76,000.00 $ in September 2011 up to 317,715.00 $ in November 2012.
- On 11th January 2013 however, Google notified Attrakt of a breach of the AdSense policy, inviting it to make modifications to its site and detecting connections to sites for adults. The managers at Attrakt then contacted the accounts manager at Google, informing him of the counter-measures that had been taken in the meantime; on 16th January 2013 however, Attrakt's AdSense account was definitively disabled, preventing the plaintiff from gaining access to the AdSense accounts and detaining the amounts owed to Attrakt for the months of December 2012 and January 2013, amounting to a total of Euros 503,400.95 (of which 334,700.95 related to the payments for the month of December and 168,700.00 to the month of January).
- The defendant Google exercised its right of withdrawal, envisaged in the contract entered into by the parties, alleging that it had recorded "an invalid click activity", whilst several months later, in July 2013, Attrakt decided to rescind also the second AdWords contract, still in force between the parties.
- Google had acted solely for the purpose of eliminating the plaintiff company from the market, due to its strong, rapid growth over a period of only a few years, inventing a "breach of AdSense policy", which, in truth, had never occurred.

2 *The arguments put forward by the defendant.* In its appearance filed on 25th June 2014, the defendant Google requested that the plaintiff s requests be dismissed, making a counterclaim directed at obtaining a finding that Attrakt had committed a breach of the AdSense contract and an order for the return of the sums unduly received. It also requested that the plaintiff be ordered to pay the fees outstanding relating to the AdWords contract and put forward that:

- Attrakt had created a system designed to generate huge profits "at practically zero cost" and in breach of various contractual clauses; it had designed a mechanism that allowed it, via the Google AdWords service, to attract users to its site, who then generated larger gains from the advertising announcements handled by Google AdSense;
- Attrakt had supplied partial information. On 11th January 2013, Google had challenged the presence of AdSense announcements "on pages whose contents were intended for an adult public". Attrakt used the Google AdWords service to acquire keywords "at low prices and to advertise them on its website"; the pages on the plaintiff s site to which the users were attracted contained Google AdSense announcements disguised as search results.
- The right of withdrawal from the AdSense contract had been exercised legitimately by Google, which then returned to the advertisers the sums which Attrakt alleged were owed to it.
- Google had not abused its alleged dominant position, nor Attrakt's non-existent economic dependence; far from acting in "bad faith", Google had exercised its fully legitimate power-conferring right, attributed to both parties; a choice that it was forced to make in the interests of its advertisers and internet users.
- As regards the counter-claim, Google requested that Attrakt return the sums it had unlawfully obtained through the "invalid click" system, calculated at Euros 1,955,114.62, together with the outstanding fee payable under the AdWords Contract, taking into account the sum already withheld from the deposit paid by Attrakt, amounting to Euros 100,000.00.

3 *The course of proceedings.* Having designated the terms referred to in art. 183, paragraph 6, of the Italian Code of Civil Procedure, having heard the parties' explanations regarding the functioning of the programmes under examination, the Judge considered the action to have reached the stage for a ruling to be made and fixed a hearing for the submission of pleadings on 2nd February 2016, and, having set the legal terms for the filing of the written pleadings, assigned the action for a ruling by the court sitting as a panel.

4 *The jurisdiction of the Court, Section specialising in business matters.* The alleged abuse of a dominant position by Google is adequate to establish the functional jurisdiction of this Section specialising in business matters (Section A) by operation of the exclusive jurisdiction assigned to it by art. 3 of Legislative Decree 168/03, as replaced by art. 2, paragraph 1, letter d),

of Legislative Decree no. 1/12, for all antitrust offences, whether having a Community dimension or founded on national legislation.

5 *The reconstruction of the facts of the action.* In order to make a ruling on the requests put forward by the parties and, more specifically, to ascertain whether the withdrawal *ad nutum* by the defendant Google constitutes an abuse – qualified alternatively as a breach of contract, an abuse of a dominant position, an abuse of economic dependence and acts of unfair competition – the relevant facts, verified with reference to supporting documentation, should be reconstructed.

Firstly, it should be made clear that the first objection received by Attrakt on 11th January 2013 from Google, which was prior to the withdrawal, related to the existence of connections on its page to sites for adults. In its e-mail dated 11th January 2013, Google merely asked Attrakt to "*bring its AdSense account into line with the standards regulating the programme . . . making modifications to the site within 72 hours*" and describing the breach as the "*publication of Google announcements on pages that have contents intended for an adult public.*"

After the plaintiff satisfied the requests made by Google, the company nevertheless decided to block the AdSense service with effect from 16th January 2013.

The defendant, on its part, has recognised during the course of the action, that Attrakt had eliminated the connections to its sites for adults, in response to the invitation made by Google itself, but it also claimed in the action, that the termination of the agreement was also justified by other contractual breaches on Attrakt's part, in truth not specifically challenged on the date of the withdrawal (transcript dated 14th April 2016).

These are therefore the relevant facts reconstructed in chronological order:

- *11th January 2013:* Google challenged Attrakt for breach of contract consisting of permitting the existence of links to sites for adults, asking it "*to make modifications to the site within 72 hours*". Attrakt took action immediately over the next few days, remedying the breach (plaintiff's doc. 19).
- *16th January 2013:* Google informed Attrakt that it had deactivated the Google AdSense account, merely stating that it had "*detected invalid activities*", without specifying what the breach consisted of and limiting itself to pointing out the possibility of making an internal complaint to resolve the problem (defendant's doc. 10). From that moment, Attrakt was unable to gain access to the AdSense programme, and not even to view insertions from third parties on its site or control payments owed to it. From that date Google had also blocked payments due for the months of December and January, of the large sums of Euros 334,700.95 and Euros 168,700.00 respectively.
- *17th January – 4th February 2013:* Attrakt immediately began to ask its contacts at Google the reasons for blocking the programme, at first imagining that it concerned a breach connected with that dating back to 11th January and then, taking action and reaffirming to Google all the measures

it had taken: in an e-mail dated 17th January Attrakt stated (verbatim) "*being unaware of the ground for the deactivation, the only sensible thing we can do is to attribute the reason to the mail sent to us last Friday by AdSense in which attention was drawn to the contents intended for an adult public on a page of results, and I am writing to describe the counter measures we have taken*" (plaintiff s docs. 18–2 and 18 3). It then made numerous requests for help and information, pointing out the enormous difficulties encountered as a result of Google's incomprehensible conduct. Reference is made to the e-mails dated 24th January 2013 (doc. 18–4), dated 22nd January 2013 (doc. 5) and 31st January 2013 (doc. 18–6), in which Attrakt repeatedly pointed out that "*the situation is creating serious problems*" and again "*after 15 days of unjustified deactivation of our AdSense account, I kindly ask you once again for your comments. Our AdSense account does not reply and we have at no point been given any notification whatsoever. We have informed you on more than one occasion that we need to discuss the matter by phone, but this has always been denied. We cannot explain this total refusal to communicate on your part and it seems to us that Google is not aware of how serious the situation has become.*" As result of Google's silence, on 1st February 2013, Attrakt asked once again for replies and explanations, not knowing what to do. It stated that it had not yet been paid around 330 thousand Euros for December and expressed "*the extreme difficulty*" in which it now found itself; it continually asked how AdSense intended to proceed with regard to its future contractual dealings with Attrakt and the outstanding payments; in particular, it asked whether payment would be received from AdSense in the near future, whether AdSense intended to break off relations definitively with Attrakt and even, how it could "*fail to reply or to give reasons for its decision*".

On 4th February 2013, still unaware of the reason for the deactivation, it asked for help in drawing up an internal complaint, since "*any activity and implementation carried out or made on the site is known to Google, agreed with and approved by it*" (plaintiff s doc. 18–8).

- *10th February 2013*: Google replied with an e-mail to Attrakt, after the latter had proposed making an internal complaint, informing it that it "*confirmed the definitive closure of the AdSense Account*" for breaches of the contractual conditions ("*for violation of our terms and conditions*"). It then added: "*Accounts disabled for invalid click activity will receive no further payment nor any reissue of previous payments. Your outstanding balance and Google's share of the revenue will both be fully refunded back to the affected advertisers. Thank you for your understanding in this matter. We understand that you may want more information about your account activity. However, because we have a need to protect our proprietary detection system, we're unable to provide our publishers with any details about their account activity*".

Finally, it retained the sums due for the months of December 2012 and January 2013 (defendant's doc. 11).

6 *Contractual relations between Google and Attrakt.* Having reconstructed the facts, the two contracts entered into between Attrakt and Google, relating to the AdSense and AdWords programme, in July and September 2011 respectively, must be examined. The AdWords service allowed the subject who acquired determined keywords from Google, namely Attrakt, to appear on Google's search engine at the moment the user inserted the keywords in question.

By operation of the AdSense contract, on the other hand, the plaintiff Attrakt made available to Google a number of advertising spaces on its website pages and Google, on the one part, paid Attrakt for the allocated space and, on the other, sold these spaces to advertisers. The process of selecting the announcements to be included at every instance according to the type of visitor was dealt with exclusively by Google, incorporating a code that could not be modified by the host site; the remuneration due depended on the number of clicks and views. Attrakt, on the one hand, therefore attracted users onto its website by means of the AdWords programme, paying large amounts to Google in order to appear in the top positions; on the other, the plaintiff was paid by Google for the adverts of third party advertisers appearing on its website, which were viewed by users who, as each case arose, visited the Attrakt page(AdSense contract).

Attrakt earned its profits, though fairly modest during the first few months, exclusively on the difference between the income received through the AdSense contract, that is, the share of fees paid by Google in the performance of its contractual obligations imposed under that agreement, and the large amounts paid by it to Google as the fee for the obligations agreed in the AdWords contract. Attrakt's entire turnover was therefore represented by income stemming from the AdSense contract, bearing in mind also the contractual restrictions against displaying, on the Attrakt website page, advertising announcements other than Google. Reference is made to clause 3.6 of the AdSense contract, which provided that Attrakt "*could not display advertisements or contents that could be confused or otherwise associated with Google*".

Far from generating profits at "zero cost", as repeatedly claimed by Google in its defence, Attrakt earned its profits by incurring enormous costs to Google's advantage. One need simply point out that, as emerges from the plaintiff's table no. 23, which sets out the accounting entries of the parties on the basis of estimates made by Google, on the date when activities commenced, in November 2011, Attrakt paid Google, in order to acquire the aforementioned keywords, in consideration of the share of fees, amounting to Euros 52,082.00 received from Google under the AdSense contract, sums totalling Euros 43,524.00; in December 2011, in consideration of the fees received amounting to Euros 76,350.00, it had paid Google, on the same basis, the sum of Euro 61,602.00, with a rising trend, that reached a peak in the month of December 2012, when Google withdrew from the contract.

It is therefore apparent at this point that, since the plaintiff s turnover was made up exclusively of activities stemming from the AdSense contract with Google, the profits made by Attrakt were modest, bearing in mind the heavy costs incurred to acquire the AdWords advertising campaigns, campaigns promoted by Google itself (see financial statement relating to the year 2012, which records a profit figure of only Euros 37,627.00).

6.1. *The AdSense Contract.* The AdSense contract, stipulated on 29th July 2011 (doc. 6) is a standard form drawn up by Google, which when read, reveals the clear position of strength held by Google and the weakness of the other contracting party, subject to all kinds of directives, and subject to Google's right to withdraw from or terminate the contact. For example, attention is drawn to clauses 3.1, 3.2, 3.3, 3.6, 6.2, 11 and 12, which reveal far-reaching controlling, monitoring and directive powers imposed on Attrakt, which, on its part, had to *follow instructions given from time to time by Google, to permit it to control the announcements, links, search results, etc.; to display a Google search field on the Property; to position the announcements; to implement the keys.* Attrakt was subject to restrictions on its ability *to display on its web pages advertising announcements other than Google's.* Considering payments, in particular, the contract provided that Google's share of profits on advertising announcements of third party advertisers would be established by Google "*at its discretion*" and that payment would be calculated "*exclusively on the basis of registers kept by Google*". It also provided, in clause 11, for limited liability on Google's part, a clause which will be considered in greater detail below.

6.2. An examination of the contracts and correspondence exchanged by the parties to the action reveals a decidedly unbalanced picture in favour of the defendant Google, which, from the setting-up of the contractual relationship until its conclusion, dictated the conditions, time schedule and modifications to be implemented on the site owned by Attrakt. It continually made demands of Attrakt of all kinds, aimed basically at monitoring developments in the contractual relations and the possibility of growth on the part of Attrakt.

The continual requests for information, the directives and controls constitute clear evidence of the fact that, apart from a business form, unbalanced in favour of the defendant, who decided the fees to be paid and the shares, on the other hand, to which it was entitled for intermediation activities, the Google company was aware of the operations carried out by Attrakt, and hence no increase or anomalous development in the advertising displayed could escape it, unless it was permitted by the company or, even encouraged. The increase in turnover stemming from the contracts was always observed with interest by Google, which, on its part, encouraged the AdWords campaign and received punctual, immediate replies from Attrakt – as it acknowledged itself in the correspondence – on the operating methods used to earn profits, with regard to the interdependent relationship between the two AdWords and AdSense contracts, as well as the technical aspects with which users were redirected to the

Attrakt landing-page. Attrakt had in fact also sent the defendant, on more than one occasion, numerous examples of landing pages, in response to express requests from Google account managers, so that the characteristics could be verified and modifications suggested. As documented in the correspondence between the parties (doc. 11) Google was aware that most of the traffic on the Attrakt engine originated from AdWords campaigns; in fact, the AdWords campaigns and markets targeted by Attrakt were monitored and even encouraged by Google, to the point that Attrakt was forced to ask for help from Google when completing the internal complaint form, seeing that "*any activity carried out or implementation made on the site were known to you, agreed with and approved by you*".

Google could therefore certainly not complain that the Attrakt traffic derived to a large extent from the acquisition from Google campaigns, as it has in fact done in this action, in which it claimed that Attrakt "*acquired keywords on AdWords which had nothing to do with it and that cost little*", being familiar with the mechanism with which Attrakt operated and having itself encouraged the acquisition of AdWords campaigns.

The defendant was therefore familiar with the Attrakt business, and the increased number of clicks that had alternated with time through the AdWords advertising campaigns, which it had itself encouraged, also in connection with more than one Country. Evidence of the developments taking place in the contractual relations can be found, for example, in doc. 11.1, an e-mail dated 24th January 2012 in which reference is made to the implementation of AdWords campaigns to increase the number of clicks. Also, the dispatch of the landing-page, the supply of all the information required to verify, examine and control the functioning of the system and theme adopted to display the "user side" pages.

The replies given by Attrakt were always prompt, immediate and comprehensive, with regard to all the profiles requested, indicating the AdWords campaigns and markets on which it was mainly concentrating. It complied with requests and recommendations made, see doc. 11.3 dated 22nd October 2012, giving continuous notification of AdWords campaigns that had contributed towards a further increase in the number of clicks and views.

Finally, the documented picture has revealed, not only a position of strength and an imbalance to Attrakt's detriment – as well as the profile of a real economic dependence which will be further examined below -, but the performance of a contract in good faith on the part of Attrakt, active and collaborative under the most varied profiles, throughout the term of the contractual agreement.

7 *The abusive withdrawal by Google from the AdSense contract.* Having reconstructed the nature of the respective business activities and the concrete methods adopted, relevant in order to bring Google's actions within the definition of unlawful conduct contrary to the principle of good faith, the methods used to exercise the right of withdrawal on its part at the beginning of 2013 must now be examined.

7.1 Art. 7 of the AdSense contract, headed "*Termination; Cancellation*", provides for the right, conferred upon both parties, to terminate the contractual relationship on any ground and without prior notice. More precisely, the partner contracting the service (in this case, Attrakt) was entitled to terminate the agreement sending notice to the address adsense-it@google.com. with effect ten days after the notice in question was dispatched. As regards Google, it "*may, at any time, terminate all or part of the programme, terminate this Contract and suspend or terminate* the *participation of any Property in the Programme, either in whole or in part*".

In the light of these facts emerging, taking into account the position of strength held by Google and the methods it adopted to withdraw from the contract, Google's conduct during the execution of the contract may be defined as contrary to the principles of good faith, as well as unlawful within the meaning envisaged in art. 9 of Law no. 192/1998.

It is certainly true that in fixed term contracts, withdrawal is permitted, in order to reflect the need to avoid an obligatory binding agreement from persisting perpetually, but this is not crucial in order to rule out the unlawful nature of conduct, if the withdrawal is not in keeping with the principles of good faith, by virtue of the methods adopted to carry it out. What is however decisive in this judgment is not to establish whether withdrawal was permitted, but whether the withdrawal was exercised in keeping with the principles of good faith, seeing that good faith must preside over every stage of the contract, accompanying it throughout its execution, from the moment it is set up, to its performance and its termination.

7.2. *The nullity, pursuant to art. 1341 of the Italian Civil Code, of the contractual clause relating to withdrawal ad nutum.* As regards the invoked nullity, pursuant to art. 1341 of the Italian Civil Code, since the contractual clause provided for withdrawal *ad nutum* in favour of both parties, specific approval is not required pursuant to art. 1341 of the Italian Civil Code (Supreme Court, 6314/2006).

7.3. *Abuse of the right.* As repeatedly confirmed by the Supreme Court, good faith is an expression of the duty of solidarity based on art. 2 of the Italian Constitution, which obliges each of the parties to the binding agreement to act in such a way as to maintain an equilibrium between their mutual interests, regardless of whether specific contractual obligations or specific regulations exist. A violation of this principle therefore constitutes a breach in itself and may oblige the party at fault to compensate for damage stemming from it (see also Joint Court Sections no. 23726 dated 15.11.2007; Supreme Court no. 1618 dated 22.1.2009; Supreme Court no. 21250 dated 6.6.2008; Supreme Court no. 23273 dated 27.10.2006; Supreme Court no. 13345 dated 7.6.2006; Supreme Court no. 264 dated 11.1.2006).

The criterion of good faith provides the judge with a fundamental tool when controlling – also for the purpose of making amendments or additions – the contractual document; and this offers a means of guaranteeing the reconciliation of opposing interests (see Joint Court Sections no. 23726 dated 15.11.2007). The principles of business propriety and good faith in the performance and interpretation of contracts, referred to in arts. 1175, 1366 and 1375 of the Italian Civil Code, are relevant both when identifying contractual obligations and when balancing the opposing interests of the parties; taking the first aspect, they compel the parties to perform their obligations, even if not expressly envisaged in the contract or by the law, when this is necessary in order to preserve the interests of the other party; taking the second aspect, they allow the court to intervene, also by making amendments or additions to the contents of the contract, whenever this is necessary in order to guarantee that the interests of the parties are reconciled and to prevent or repress the abuse of this right (Supreme Court 20106/2009; 13580/2015).

In the event, therefore, of proven disparity between the strengths of the contracting parties, an assessment by the court as to whether or not the withdrawal was abusive must be wider and more rigorous, and may be made regardless of whether negligence or specific intent to harm are involved ((Supreme Court 13580/2015).

The withdrawal *ad nutum* by Google without specifically challenging Attrakt in any way, and without even giving prior notice or justification, bearing in mind the position of strength held by Google and the economic dependence of Attrakt, is considered illegitimate, having violated the most fundamental rules of propriety in dealings between private individuals. Google withdrew *ad nutum* without giving any explanation, without allowing a fair period of time to seek out new working partners in the market and, even, and this must be stressed, unlawfully retaining a large sum and thereby exercising a form of private self-protection, which is not envisaged by the law and, in fact prevented Attrakt from continuing to operate. Google abused its position of strength, forcing the other party to make disproportionate sacrifices and acted arbitrarily.

This conduct, consisting not only of the withdrawal, but also the withholding of amounts essential for the survival of Attrakt, is particularly serious and constitutes an abuse of a right. "*A right is abused when the holder of a subjective right, though establishing no formal prohibitions, exercises that right in a manner that is unnecessary and not in keeping with the principles of propriety and good faith, demanding a disproportionate, unjustified sacrifice from the other party to the contract, for the purpose of obtaining results that differ from and go beyond those for which those powers or rights were conferred. If these underlying conditions are met, the Court making a ruling on the merits is permitted to judge and declare actions taken in violation of the prohibition against abuse of right to be ineffective, or to order the subject abusing his right to compensate the other contracting party for damage, regardless of whether there was any specific intention to harm and without necessarily interfering with the economic choices of the individual or entrepreneur, seeing that what is prohibited in these circumstances is not the action taken with negotiating autonomy, but the abuse of that autonomy*" (Supreme Court, 18/09/2009).

To this it must be added, as already mentioned, that such a sudden interruption of relations with a subject "functionally dependent" upon it, without any justification, should have been considered carefully by the defendant, who, in keeping with the principles of propriety and good faith, could have limited the destructive effects that a decision of this kind would have on the plaintiff s core business.

It is therefore by causing an unjustified, disproportionate sacrifice on the part of the other contracting party, certainly foreseeable by Google, that the abusive exercise of its right takes place, particularly when considering the actual methods with which the power of withdrawal was exercised.

The requisites for the abuse of a right are satisfied here: 1) the holding of a subjective right by a subject; 2) the possibility that the right in question can actually be exercised in a number of different ways which are not rigidly pre-set; 3) the fact that this actual exercise, even if formally in keeping with the framework attributing the right in question, involves methods that may be rebuked when assessed either in or out of court; 4) the fact that, due to the method adopted to exercise the right, there is an unjustified imbalance between the benefit to the holder of the right and the sacrifice that must be made by the other party (Supreme Court, ref. above).

7.5 *Arguments in Google's defence.* Google claimed, in its defence, the withdrawal was exercised with just cause as, in its opinion, Attrakt had committed a series of contractual breaches, regarding the connection with sites for adults and invalid clicks.

As regards the challenge made by Google in relation to the contents for adults, it has already been seen that, as emerges from an overall examination of the e-mails exchanged dating back to January 2013, this was of no significance, seeing that when requested by the defendant to remedy the situation, the plaintiff satisfied all the requests made of its with great rapidity. This fact was also admitted during the course of proceedings, when the defendant referred to a second letter (doc. 10) in order to identify the reason for the withdrawal.

Reading a few passages from the e-mail in question, it is in fact apparent that Google did not provide any particular reason, limiting itself generally to invalid stereotypical formulas and generic indications of actions: "[...] *we have detected invalid activities on your site and your account has been deactivated. There is a limit to the amount of information that we can provide on the specific breach arising in your case* [...]" and also "we *are making efforts to create an online ecosystem that is advantageous to the publisher, the advertisers and users. For this reason, at times we are forced to take action against accounts that demonstrate an approach towards users or advertisers that may have a negative effect on the overall perception of the ecosystem"*.

It also emerges from the correspondence, that Attrakt had continued for several days to ask for information and explanations, without being given any reason, apart from the fact that such information could not be given on company policy grounds, but being advised that an internal complaint could be made, and only after this, an application to the Google legal office.

The outcome of the complaint, however, made no difference, as the notice closing the procedure (defendant's doc. 11) did not even provide any valid reasons, nor was Attrakt given the opportunity to take steps or comply with presumed, unclear rules of conduct.

The overall picture leaves no doubt that the conduct on Google's part was far from transparent, and certainly contrary to the general principles laid down by our legislation, which negotiating autonomy cannot overlook.

It was only during the course of the action that Google claimed a breach of rules, defined by the same "arbitration", attributing Attrakt with conduct consisting of generating a large part of its traffic through "*the acquisition of keywords on AdWords that cost little*" – facts of which Google was well aware and in fact encouraged – and then directing users onto its page, where the AdSense adverts were already shown.

The defendant was well aware of the exact *modus operandi* adopted by the defendant and evidence of this can be found in numerous e-mails between attract and Google staff, in which the former's way of doing business was acknowledged and in which landing pages that Attrakt had proposed to its users were transmitted.

The revenues produced by the execution of the AdSense contract represented the only source of profit for Attrakt.

Google therefore withdrew without just cause, without giving any reason, and being aware of the relationship of strength and survival created with Attrakt and, what is worse, withholding large sums, essential to Attrakt if it were to continue to operate.

Its abusive conduct, contrary to the principle of good faith was exacerbated considerably by the fact that it retained, totally at its own discretion and without any justification whatsoever, large sums relating to the monthly payments for December 2012 and January 2013.

In addition, the amounts, due as monthly payments prior to the arbitrary termination of the agreement, had been estimated by Google itself, who during the course of the action, though alleging the existence of invalid clicks, at no point specifically challenged the amount it had quantified.

Finally, the claim on the part of Google that it had returned amounts to the advertisers, apart from failing to justify its decision to withhold them arbitrarily at Attrakt's expense, is not even proven, the document produced for this purpose (doc. 26) certainly not constituting satisfactory evidence.

8 *The abuse of economic dependence*. Even though the conduct on the part of Google, when it withdrew from the contract, constitutes the abuse of a power-conferring right exercised beyond the limitations and protection afforded by national legislation, the case in question also amounts to a "textbook" example of abuse of economic dependence within the meaning envisaged in art. 9 of Law 192/1998, particularly where it refers to "*the refusal to sell or the refusal to purchase and the arbitrary interruption of business dealings underway*".

According to art. 9 of the aforementioned enactment, which is the epitome of a good faith clause, the situation in which an undertaking is capable of bringing about, in its business dealings with another undertaking, an excessive imbalance of rights and obligations, is considered economic dependence. The position of dependence is assessed by also taking into account the real possibility that the party subjected to abuse has to find satisfactory alternatives in the market. The position of dominance is not sanctioned in itself, but only if it is transformed into an excessive imbalance of rights and obligations weighing upon the weaker party.

The abuse of economic dependence envisaged in art. 9 referred to, though falling within the context of provisions regulating sub-supplies, expresses the principle of good faith and applies to all relations between enterprises (Supreme Court no. 24906/2011). It presupposes a situation of economic dependence of a customer company on its supplier and the abuse of this position, creating a significant disparity in rights and obligations.

In the case under examination, Attrakt found itself in a position of total economic dependence on Google, as evidenced by the imbalance of rights and obligation in Google's favour, resulting from the contents of the contractual provisions as well as the correspondence, the exclusive nature of Attrakt's relationship with Google, the breakdown of the turnover and the income deriving exclusively from Google, to the point of being eradicated after Google's withdrawal (see financial statement 2012).

Google abused this dependence, imposing burdensome conditions, arbitrarily interrupting contractual relations underway and even retaining amounts due that it should have paid as fees; amounts which were not only objectively substantial, but also of fundamental importance to Attrakt for the continuation of its business activities.

The termination, in such an abrupt manner, adopting the methods used, together with the failure to pay the fees owed to it, prevents Attrakt from finding satisfactory alternatives on the market in time.

9 *Alleged abuse of dominant position.* Finally, as to the plaintiff s allegation that an antitrust offence was committed, the Court believes that the abuse of a dominant position is covered entirely by the various considerations of the offence already acknowledged and the findings described above.

10 *Order against Google to return the amounts retained.* Having found that the relationship was terminated in an arbitrary manner, and that an abuse of economic dependence took place, and having also made a finding that Google committed a breach of contract when failing to pay Attrakt as fees, amounts envisaged in the contract as monthly payments prior to the termination of the agreement, Google is ordered, on this basis, to pay Attrakt the sums of Euros 334,700.95 and Euros 168,700.00, making a total sum of Euros 503,400.95, together with interest pursuant to Legislative Decree no. 231/2002, commencing on the respective due dates up to the date of settlement (December 2012 and January 2013).

As already mentioned, the amounts were calculated by Google itself, exercising the discretional powers conferred upon it by art. 12 of the contract. Google's claim in its defence that it cannot pay the sum to Attrakt as it has been returned in its entirety to the advertisers, is of no significance, not only because this fact has not been proven, but also because it would, in any event, be irrelevant, failing to rule out the illegitimate nature of the actions taken by arbitrarily retaining the sums to Attrakt's detriment.

11 *General order against Google to compensate damage caused by the arbitrary interruption of the AdSense contract.* Having made a finding that the AdSense was interrupted arbitrarily, abusing the dependent economic position held by Attrakt, and that the conduct engaged in breached the good faith clause, exacerbated by the fact that large sums, of fundamental importance to Attrakt's future business activities, were retained, Google is obliged to compensate the damage it caused and it will therefore be necessary, for this purpose, that an expert witness report be drawn up, in fact already requested by the plaintiff in the action; this damage will be quantified later on in the proceedings, by operation of a separate order to adjourn the action (see Supreme Court, 9404/2011; supreme Court 15686/2005).

12 *Counterclaim by Google relating to the AdSense contract.* As regards the counterclaim made by Google relating to the return of the amounts received by Attrakt over previous years, this matter may be considered as already covered by the considerations made above, regarding the arbitrary interruption of business relations, abuse of economic dependence and, more generally, conduct contrary to the principle of good faith engaged in by Google during the execution and termination of the agreement and the request must therefore be dismissed.

Furthermore, it also pointed out that the nature of the legal relationship, if continuing to be performed, would have prevented the counterclaim, even if it were admitted, from having any retroactive effect.

13 *The nullity of the contractual clause relating to limited liability on the part of Google.* Clause 11.3 of the AdSense contract provides that Google's liability cannot "*exceed 125% of the net amount paid by Google to Attrakt over the last 12 months immediately prior to the moment at which liability first arose*".

13.1 The clause is null and void as it provides in favour of the party the draw up the contractual conditions a limitation of liability without specific approval in writing in the manner envisaged in art. 1341, second paragraph, of the Italian Civil Code. As already noted, the contracts under examination were in fact drawn up on forms already prepared by Google in order to standardise particular contractual dealings, which are covered by the provisions contained in articles 1341 and 1342 of the Italian Civil Code. The clause in the AdSense contract, concerning the limitation of liability, is oppressive and, not having been specifically signed, is therefore null and void.

13.2 The plea put forward by the defendant that the request that the contractual clause be found null and void is inadmissible is not founded.

It is true that the request for a finding of nullity was put forward by the plaintiff for the first time with its pleading submitted pursuant to art. 183, paragraph six, no. 1, of the Italian Code of Civil Procedure, that is, within the term permitted to amend the requests made. In the case under examination, there is no point in debating whether the *mutatio libelli* (modification of the complaint) is prohibited or the *emendatio* (amendment) is permitted, as the request for a finding of nullity is also admissible after assertion, and also investigation, procedures have been precluded, as the nullity of the contract can be raised by the court of its own motion. The Joint Court Sections have settled the legal conflict regarding the ability of the court to raise of its own motion the nullity of a contract during an action brought to obtain the termination of the agreement in question, confirming the power of the court to raise of its own motion, on the basis of the facts alleged and proven or, in any event, emerging during the course of proceedings, any form of nullity of the contract for which termination has been requested (Supreme Court, Joint Court Sections, 12–12–2014, no. 26242; Supreme Court, 7th February 2011, no. 2956; Supreme Court 20th August 2009. No. 18540; Supreme Court 15th September 2008, no. 23674).

This informal power satisfies the need to safeguard the general interests of a determined class of subjects and also interests coinciding with values of constitutional relevance, such as the proper functioning of the market (art. 41 of the Italian Constitution) and the substantial equality between contracting parties in an asymmetric position (art. 3 of the Italian Constitution).The only limitation to the exercise of this power to raise nullity of its own motion is found in the obligation on the part of the Judge to inform the parties, after raising the issue, of the ground for the nullity of the contract, instituting due process to discuss the matter throughout the proceedings (articles 111, 2nd paragraph, of the Italian Constitution, 101, 2nd paragraph and 183, paragraph 4, of the Italian Code of Civil procedure).

Returning therefore to the case in question, the nullity is not impeded by the preclusive limitations imposed on the activities in question, but can also be raised at any stage of proceedings of the court's own motion and was discussed during the due process.

14 *Counterclaim by Google relating to the AdWords contract.* Taking the AdWords contract, the counterclaim made by Google relating to the return of the sum of US$ 20,212.28 for the execution of the AdWords contract should be admitted. Though it is true to say that it was the plaintiff's intention that the two contracts operate interdependently, after the AdSense contract was suspended, Attrakt had decided to continue to execute the contract until July 2013, even though it could have withdrawn from the AdWords agreement, and so it must therefore be ordered to pay the amounts still outstanding.

As is made apparent during the action, Google had already retained a part of the amount owed to it as a security deposit paid by Attrakt when the contract was entered into, following an express request to set off the amount deposited against the residual debt (defendant's doc. 13), the plaintiff Attrakt must be ordered to return the remaining amount, calculated by Google at US$ 20,212.28 at the exchange rate applying on the date of actual payment, together with interest pursuant to Legislative Decree no. 231/2002 from the due date in the invoices up to the date of settlement.

15 *The request made by Attrakt for the deposit paid under the AdWords contract to be returned.* The considerations set out above determine the dismissal of Attrakt's request that the security deposit be returned, since: 1) the AdWords contract has continued as expressly desired by Attrakt, who could have withdrawn but chose not to, but proceeded to receive Google advertising via the AdWords service. 2) The amount given by Attrakt as a security deposit was retained by Google at Attrakt's express request, having asked, as backed up by documentary evidence, that "the credit kept on deposit by Google be used to pay a number of the invoices" (see defendants' doc. 13).

16 *Regarding the adjournment of the action.* Having made a finding that Google is liable under contract for a breach of its obligations to act in good faith and for abuse of economic dependence and ordered to compensate damage (see *above no. 11*), the action is adjourned, to be dealt with in a separate order, making it necessary for an expert witness report to be drawn up (see Supreme Court 9404/2011).

17 *Costs of the action.* As the judgment given is not final, the costs of this action will be paid when judgment on the merits has been given (see Supreme Court 28467/2013; Supreme Court Joint Sections 711/1999; Supreme Court Joint Sections 9441/2011).

UPON THESE GROUNDS

The Court of Milan, Section specialising in business matters – A – not making a final ruling on the requests made by **ATTRAKT S.R.L.** against **GOOGLE IRELAND LTD**. and the counterclaim made by Google against Attrakt, provides as follows:

- having made a finding relating to the breach of contract on the part of Google in relation to the AdSense contract, Google is ordered to pay Attrakt the sum of Euros 503,400.95, together with interest pursuant to Legislative Decree no. 231/2002 commencing on the respective due dates for the respective payments of Euros 334,700.95 and Euros 168,700.00, up to the date of settlement;
- a finding is made relating to the nullity of clause 11.3 of the AdSense contract that provides for the limitation of liability in favour of Google;

- having made a finding relating to the contractual liability for a breach of its obligations to act in good faith and for abuse of economic dependence, Google is ordered to compensate damage to be quantified later in the proceedings, in a separate order adjourning the action;
- admitting the counterclaim made by Google that the court admit the right to the fee relating to the AdWords contract, Attrakt is ordered to pay Google the sum of US$ 20,212.28 at the exchange rate applying on the date of actual payment, together with interest pursuant to Legislative Decree no. 231/2002 from the due date in the invoices up to the date of settlement;
- dismisses the further counterclaims made by Google;
- adjourns the action, to be dealt with in a separate order,
- costs to be dealt with in the final judgement.

So ruled in Milan, in Counsel Chambers on 5th May 2016.

The Drafting Judge	The Presiding Judge
Her Honour Silvia Giani	Her Honour Marina Anna Tavassi

(*Stamps*)

Copying fees of € 15.38 paid by
applying revenue stamps on the original
pursuant to art. 285 of Pres.Decree 115/2002
Milan, 28.06.16
THE CLERK OF THE COURT (*signature illegible*)

REPUBLIC OF ITALY – In the name of the law – Ordering all the Court Officers who are requested to do so and anyone else responsible for doing so, to execute this authority, the Public Prosecutor to lend his or her assistance and the Officers of the Pubic forces to make their contribution when legally required to do so.

This first copy of the authority to execute is a certified copy of the original and is issued in favour of the Plaintiff.

Milan, 4th July 2016 THE CLERK OF THE COURT Signed by the COURT OFFICER Michele LENTINI
(*round stamps*)
ORDINARY COURT OF MILAN

Following due examination for service of documents purposes

Milan, 4th July 2016
THE COURT OFFICER
THE COURT OFFICER
Michele LENTINI
(*signature illegible*)

REFERENCES

Abor J and Quartey P, 'Issues in SME development in Ghana and South Africa' [2010] 39(6) *International Research Journal of Finance and Economics* 223.

Adler MD, 'Regulatory theory', in Patterson D (ed), *A Companion to Philosophy of Law and Legal Theory* (John Wiley & Sons 2009).

Aganga O, *The Indirect Liability of Mobile Service Providers in South Africa: A Comparative Study* (Masters, University of Pretoria 2013).

Aitman D and Jones A, 'Competition law and copyright: has the copyright owner lost the ability to control his copyright?' [2004] 26(3) *European Intellectual Property Review* 137.

Akester P, 'The new challenges of striking the right balance between copyright protection and access to knowledge, information and culture' [2010] 32(8) *European Intellectual Property Review* 375.

Al-Ameen A, 'Application of Abuse of Dominance in New Competition Regimes: Unconscionability as a Stabilising Tool at Time of Indecision' (*Ascola-tokyo-conference-2015.meiji.jp*, 2015), http://ascola-tokyo-conference-2015.meiji.jp/pdf/ConferencePapers/General%20Session%204/Abayomi%20Al-Ameen_competition%20and%20unconscionability%201%20(1).pdf (accessed 7 March 2017).

Alberts W, 'A tale of two remedies in competition and intellectual property law' [2006] 14(2) *Juta's Business Law* 44.

Alexiadis P, 'Forging a European competition policy response to online platforms' [2017] 18(2) *Business Law International* 91.

Allen Consulting Group, 'Economic Perspectives on Copyright Law' (*Copyright.com.au*, 2003), http://copyright.com.au/wp-content/uploads/2015/08/CentreCopyrightStudies_AllenGroup-EconomicPerspectivesonCopyrightLaw.pdf (accessed 13 September 2016).

Alvesson M and Sandberg J, 'Generating research questions through problematization' [2011] 36(2) *Academy of Management Review* 247.

Anderman S, 'Does the Microsoft case offer a new paradigm for the "exceptional circumstances" test and compulsory copyright licenses under EC competition law?' [2004] 1(2) *Competition Law Review* 7.

Andersen B, Kozul-Wright Z and Kozul-Wright R, 'Copyrights, Competition and Development' (No. 145 UNCTAD Discussion Paper 2005).

Anderson R, 'Competition policy and intellectual property in the WTO: More guidance needed?', in J. Drexl (ed), *Research Handbook on Intellectual Property and Competition Law* (Edward Elgar 2008).

Anderson T, *Popular Music in a Digital Music Economy: Problems and Practices for an Emerging Service Industry* (Taylor & Francis 2014).

Andrews DC, 'Ownership-usage dichotomy and the human element in Newman's free economy' [2013] 66 *Vanderbilt Law Review En Banc* 179.

Angelopoulos C, 'Creative Commons and related rights in sound recordings: are the two systems compatible?' in L Guibault and C Angelopoulos (eds.), *Open Content Licensing: From Theory to Practice* (Amsterdam University Press 2011).

Angelopoulos C, *European Intermediary Liability in Copyright: A Tort-Based Analysis* (PhD, Institute for Information Law (IViR) 2016).

Ani L, 'Rethinking competition law and policy: Building a framework for implementation in Nigeria' [2012] Maiden Edition *NIALS Journal of Business Law* 1.

Asien JO, *Nigerian Copyright: Law and Practice* (2nd edn, Books and Gavel 2012).

Aufderheide P and Jaszi P, *Untold Stories: Creative Consequences of the Rights Clearance Culture for Documentary Filmmakers* (Center for Social Media 2004).

Australian Law Reform Commission, *Copyright and the Digital Economy* (Australian Law Reform Commission 2013).

Baden-Powell E and Duboff A, 'IFPI Digital Music Report 2010 – a heady brew' [2010] 21(4) *Entertainment Law Review* 160.

Bakhoum M, 'A dual language in modern competition law? Efficiency approach versus development approach and implications for developing countries' [2011] 34(3) *World Competition* 495.

Bakhoum M, 'Abuse without dominance in competition law: abuse of economic dependence and its interface with abuse of dominance', in Nihoul P (ed), *Abuse Regulation in Competition Law: Past, Present and Future* (Edward Elgar 2017).

Balganesh S, 'Rethinking copyright: property through the lenses of unjust enrichment and unfair competition' [2007] 156 *University of Pennsylvania Law Review PENNumbra* 345.

Balkin JM, 'Digital speech and democratic culture: a theory of freedom of expression for the information society' [2004] 79 *New York University Law Review* 1.

Barnet RD and Burriss LL, *Controversies of the Music Industry* (Greenwood Publishing Group 2011).

Barrett BT, (2015). *Modernizing Copyright for Equitable Treatment in the Streaming Age* (Doctoral dissertation, Florida Atlantic University Boca Raton 2015).

Bartholomew M and McArdle PF, 'Causing infringement' [2011] 64 *Vanderbilt Law Review* 675.

Bartholomew M and Tehranian J, 'The secret life of legal doctrine: the divergent evolution of secondary liability in trademark and copyright law' [2006] *Berkeley Technology Law Journal* 1363.

Batchelor B, 'Antitrust challenges to cross-border content licensing: the European Commission investigations of collecting societies and iTunes' [2007] 13(8) *Computer and Telecommunications Law Review* 217.

Bechtold S, 'Digital rights management in the United States and Europe' [2004] 52(2) *American Journal of Comparative Law* 323.

Bechtold S, 'Directive on the harmonisation of certain aspects of copyright and related rights in the information society', in Dreier T and Hugenholtz PB (eds), *Concise European Copyright Law* (Vol. 2, Kluwer Law 2006).

Behrens P and Fox E, 'Abuse of market power: controlling dominance or protecting competition?' in Ullrich H (ed), *The Evolution of European Competition Law: Whose Regulation, Which Competition?* (Edward Elgar 2006).

Bekkelund K, 'Succeeding with freemium: exploring why companies have succeeded and failed with freemium' [2011] *Innovation and Entrepreneurship, Specialization Project* 4350.

Bently L and Sherman B, *Intellectual Property Law* (Oxford University Press 2014).

Berger B, Matt C, Steininger D and Hess T, 'It is not just about competition with "free": differences between content formats in consumer preferences and willingness to pay' [2015] 32(3) *Journal of Management Information Systems* 105.

Bermann GA, Glenn P, Scheppele KL and Shalakany A, 'Comparative law: problems and prospects' [2010] 26 *American University International Law Review* 935.

Bertholdsson S and Dahir J, *Consumers' Perception of Freemium Services* (Master of Science in Business and Economics (Civilekonom) Business and Economics, Luleå University of Technology 2015).

Boldrin M and Levine D, *Growth and Intellectual Property* (No. W12769 National Bureau of Economic Research 2006).

Boldrin M and Levine D, 'The case against intellectual property' [2002] 92(2) *American Economic Review* 209.

Booth N and Matic JA, 'Mapping and leveraging influencers in social media to shape corporate brand perceptions' [2011] 16(3) *Corporate Communications: An International Journal* 184.

Bourreau M, Gensollen M and Moreau F (2008). '*The Digitization of the Recorded Music Industry: Impact on Business Models and Scenarios of Evolution* (Department of Economics and Social Sciences Telecom Paris 2008). Available at https://ssrn.com/abstract=1092138 (accessed 25 November 2016).

Boy L, 'Abuse of market power: controlling dominance or protecting competition?' in Ullrich H (ed), *The Evolution of European Competition Law: Whose Regulation, Which Competition?* (Edward Elgar 2006).

Brand J, 'Intellectual property and the abuse of dominant position in South African competition law' [2005] 122 *South African Law Journal* 907.

Brassey M et al. *Competition Law* (Juta 2002), 2.

Breyer S, 'The uneasy case for copyright: A study of copyright in books, photocopies, and computer programs' [1970] *Harvard Law Review* 281.

Brinker I and Holzmüller T, 'Competition law and copyright – observations from the world of collecting societies' [2010] *European Intellectual Property Review* 553.

Brochu E, De Freitas N and Bao K, 'The sound of an album cover: Probabilistic multimedia and information retrieval' [2003] *Artificial Intelligence and Statistics (AISTATS)*.

Brodley JF, 'Economic goals of antitrust: efficiency, consumer welfare, and technological progress' [1987] 62 *New York University Law Review* 1020.

Brown CS, 'Copyleft, the disguised copyright: why legislative reform is superior to Copyleft licenses' [2010] 78 *University of Missouri Kansas City Law Review* 749.

Browning D, Chang LC, Forberg J, Fox M, Hsiao PH, Sutton T and Vandervlugt C, 'Legal implications arising from the changing face of music retailing' [2006] 17(6) *Entertainment Law Review* 167.

Burk DL, 'The creating around paradox: responding to Joseph P. Fishman, *Creating around Copyright*' [2014] 128 *Harvard Law Review* 118.

Burton D (ed), 'Using literature to support research', in *Research Training for Social Scientists: A Handbook for Postgraduate Researchers* (Sage 2000), 137.

Cadwalladr C, 'Google, democracy and the truth about internet search' [2016] 4(12) *Guardian* 2016.

Cardoso R and Ren Y, 'European Commission – PRESS RELEASES – Press Release – Antitrust: Commission Sends Statement of Objections to Google on Android Operating System and Applications – Factsheet' (*Europa.eu*, 2016), http://europa.eu/rapid/press-release_MEMO-16-1484_en.htm (accessed 7 March 2017).

Carroll M, 'Creative Commons and the new intermediaries' [2006] 45 *Michigan State Law Review* 2005.

Carroll M, 'Creative Commons as conversational copyright', In P Yu (ed), *Intellectual Property and Information Wealth: Issues and Practices in the Digital Age* (Praeger 2007).

Carroll MW, 'Creative commons as conversational copyright' [2007] *Public Policy Research Paper* 445.

Cernat L and Holmes P, 'Competition, competitiveness and development: lessons from developing countries' (United Nations Conference on Trade and Development United Nations Publication Symbol No. UNCTAD/DITC/CLP/2004/1 2004).

Chabane N, 'An Evaluation of the Influence of BEE on the Application of Competition Policy in South Africa' (Trade and Industrial Policy Strategies Annual Forum, Johannesburg, 2003).

Cheliotis G, 'From open source to open content: Organization, licensing and decision processes in open cultural production' [2009] 47(3) *Decision Support Systems* 229.

Chesbrough H, *Open innovation: The new imperative for creating and profiting from technology* (Harvard Business Press 2006).

Chesbrough H, 'The era of open innovation' [2006] 127(3) *Managing innovation and change* 34.

Chesbrough H, 'The logic of open innovation: managing intellectual property [2003] 45(3) *California Management Review* 33.

Chesbrough H, 'Why companies should have open business models' [2007] 48(2) *MIT Sloan Management Review* 22.

Chesbrough H, *Open Business Models: How to Thrive in the New Innovation Landscape* (Harvard Business School Press 2006).

Chin YW, 'What role for abuse of superior bargaining position laws?' [2016] 256(3) *New York Law Journal.*

Chynoweth P, 'Legal research', in Knight A and Ruddock L (eds), *Advanced Research Methods in the Built Environment* (Wiley-Blackwell 2008).

Clark D, 'Revocation and the unilateral contract: A reappraisal' [2000] 17 *New Zealand Law Review* 35.

Clark T, '*Google v. Commissioner*: A comparison of European Union and United States antitrust law' [2016] 47 *Seton Hall Law Review* 1021.

Coetzer BL, *A Business Model for the Digital Distribution of Music in the South African Context* (Masters dissertation, University of Pretoria, 2009).

Cohen JE, Loren LP, Okediji RL and O'Rourke MA, *Copyright in a Global Information Economy* (Wolters Kluwer Law & Business 2015).

Colston C and Galloway J, *Modern Intellectual Property Law* (Taylor & Francis 2010).

Commission Notice, 'Guidelines on the Application of Article 101 of the Treaty on the Functioning of the European Union to Technology Transfer Agreements OJ No. 2014/C 89/03' (European Union 2014).

Commission Notice, 'Guidelines on the Application of Article 81 of the EC Treaty to Technology Transfer Agreements OJ No. 2004/C 101/02' (European Union 2004).

Comninos A, 'Intermediary liability in South Africa' [2012] *Association for Progressive Communications, Intermediary Liability in Africa Research Papers* 3.

Consumer Focus, 'Competition, copyright and collective rights management: A consultation on growth and innovation in the creative and digital technology industries' (Consumer Focus 2011).

Cooke C, 'Dissecting the Digital Dollar (Part One). How Streaming Services Are Licensed and the Challenges Artists Now Face', *London: Music Managers Forum* (2015).

Copyright Bill 2015 available at http://reform.copyright.gov.ng/images/COPYRIGHTBILLCIRCULATIONCOPY02112015.pdf (accessed 9 December 2015).

Copyright Review Commission (2011). *Copyright Review Commission Report*. Department of Trade and Industry, para. 4.8.2. Available at www.gov.za/sites/www.gov.za/files/CRC%20REPORT.pdf (accessed 7 January 2018).

Corbett S, 'Creative Commons licences, the copyright regime and the online community: is there a fatal disconnect?' [2011] 74(4) *Modern Law Review* 503.

Cornish J, 'Sound recordings and copyright' [1993] 24 *International Review of Intellectual Property and Competition Law* 306.

Correa C, 'Intellectual property and competition law: exploration of some issues of relevance to developing countries' [2007] 21 *ICTSD IPRs and Sustainable Development Programme Issue Paper*.

Cotter TF, 'The procompetitive interest in intellectual property law' [2006] 48 *William & Mary Law Review* 483.

Craig CJ, 'Locke, labour, and limiting the author's right: a warning against a Lockean approach to copyright law' [2002] 28(1) *Queen's Law Journal* 1.

Cross JT and Yu PK, 'Competition law and copyright misuse' [2007] 56 *Drake Law Review* 427.

Culture Arts and Jobs, 'The Creative Industries in South Africa' (Department of Labour South Africa 2007).

D'Agostino G, *Copyright, Contracts, Creators: New Media, New Rules* (Edward Elgar 2010).

Dale S, 'Case Study: South Africa – Equal Opportunity to Compete' (*IDRC – International Development Research Centre*, 2016), www.idrc.ca/en/article/case-study-south-africa-equal-opportunity-compete (accessed 25 November 2016).

Daly P, 'Courts and copyright: some thoughts on standard of review', in Geist M (ed), *The Copyright Pentalogy: How the Supreme Court of Canada Shook the Foundations of Canadian Copyright Law* (University of Ottawa Press 2012).

Davies G, *Copyright and the Public Interest* (2nd edn, Sweet & Maxwell 2012).

Davies N, 'The digital music revolution: how will traditional rights operate in the on-line music world?' [2005] 16(6) *Entertainment Law Review* 137.

De Beer J, Armstrong C, Oguamanam C and Schönwetter T, *Innovation & Intellectual Property – Innovation & Intellectual Property Collaborative Dynamics in Africa* (UCT Press 2014).

Dean OH, *Handbook of South African Copyright Law, Loose-Leaf Updates* (Juta 2006).

Deazley R, *Rethinking Copyright: History, Theory, Language* (Edward Elgar 2006).

Defeo M, 'Unlocking the iPhone: how antitrust law can save consumers from the inadequacies of copyright law' [2008] 49 *Boston College Law Review* 1037.

Dehin V, 'The future of legal online music services in the European Union: a review of the EU Commission's recent initiatives in cross-border copyright management' [2010] 32(5) *European Intellectual Property Review* 220.

Deloumeaux L, 'The Globalisation of Cultural Trade: A Shift in Consumption International flows of cultural goods and services 2004–2013' (UNESCO Institute for Statistics 2016).

Depreeuw S, *The Variable Scope of the Exclusive Economic Rights in Copyright* (Wolters Kluwer 2014).

Derclaye E and Favale M, 'Copyright and contract law: regulating user contracts: the state of the art and a research agenda' [2010] 18 *Journal of Intellectual Property Law* 65.

Dimgba N, 'Introduction to Competition Law: A Sine Qua Non to a Liberalised Economy' (Rules Watch: Competition Legislation & the New World Order, 2016).

Dobusch, L, and Quack, S, 'The Copyright Dispute: A Transnational Regulatory Struggle', in Hemmungs Wirtén E, and Ryman M (eds.), *Mashing-up Culture: The Rise of User-generated Content* (Counter 2009), 140–161.

Dobusch L, 'The digital public domain: relevance and regulation' [2012] 21(2) *Information & Communications Technology Law* 179.

Doerr J, Benlian A, Vetter J and Hess T, 'Pricing of content services: an empirical investigation of music as a service' [2014] *Sustainable E-business Management* 13.

Domb Krauskopf AE, *'Fire, Lights, Everything!' Exploring Symbolic Capital in the Tecnobrega Dance Scene* (Master of Science in Comparative Media Studies, Massachusetts Institute of Technology 2009).

Dörr L, Wagner T, Benlian A and Hess T, 'Music as a service as an alternative to music piracy?' [2013] 5(6) *Bus Inf Syst Eng* 383.

Doyle G, 'Television and the development of the data economy: Data analysis, power and the public interest' (2018) 9 *International Journal of Digital Television* 56–58.

Doyle G, 'Television production: Configuring for sustainability in the digital era' (2017) 40 *Media, Culture & Society* 285–295.

Drahos P and Braithwaite J, *Information Feudalism* (Earthscan 2002).

Drassinower A, 'A note on incentives, rights, and the public domain in copyright law' [2011] 86(5) *Notre Dame Law Review* 1869.

Drassinower A, 'A rights-based view of the idea/expression dichotomy in copyright law' [2013] 16 *Canadian Journal of Law and Jurisprudence*.

Dreier T, 'Berne Convention for the protection of literary and artistic works', in Dreier T and Hugenholtz PB (eds), *Concise European Copyright Law* (Vol. 2, Kluwer Law 2006).

Dreier T, 'Contracting out of copyright in the information society: The impact on freedom of expression', in Griffiths J and Suthersanen U (eds), *Copyright and Free Speech: Comparative and International Analyses* (Oxford University Press, 2005).

Drexl J (ed), *Research Handbook on Intellectual Property and Competition Law* (Edward Elgar 2010).

Drexl J, 'Competition law as part of the European Constitution', in *Principles of European Constitutional Law* (Hart 2010).

Drexl J, 'Consumer welfare and consumer harm: adjusting competition law and policies to the needs of developing jurisdictions', in Gal M, Bakhoum M, Drexl J, Fox E and Gerber D (eds), *The Economic Characteristics of Developing Jurisdictions: Their Implications for Competition Law* (Edward Elgar 2015).

Drexl J, 'Copyright, Competition and Development' (*Wipo.int*, 2015), www.wipo.int/export/sites/www/ip-competition/en/studies/copyright_competition_development.pdf (accessed 10 November 2015).

Drexl J, 'The relationship between the legal exclusivity and economic market power. Links and limits', in Govaere I and Ullrich H (eds), *Intellectual Property, Market Power and the Public Interest* (Lang 2008).

Du Plessis L, 'How Does Competition Law Enforcement Benefit Small Business' (*Compcom.co.za*, 2015), www.compcom.co.za/wp-content/uploads/2015/03/Competition-Commision-September-Newsletter.pdf (accessed 5 March 2017).

Duke A and Richardson M, 'Music markets and bad actors in copyright and competition law' [2008] 16(2) *Competition and Consumer Law Journal* 203.

Dusollier S, 'The master's tools v. the master's house: Creative Commons v. copyright' [2006] 29 *Columbia Journal of Law & Arts* 271.

Edwards L, 'Role and Responsibility of the Internet Intermediaries in the Field of Copyright and Related Right' (*Wipo.int*, 2011), www.wipo.int/export/sites/www/copyright/

en/doc/role_and_responsibility_of_the_internet_intermediaries_final.pdf (accessed 31 January 2017).

Eisenhardt K and Graebner M, 'Theory building from cases: opportunities and challenges' [2007] 50(1) *Academy of Management Journal* 25.

Ekpa F and Kure B, 'Fair dealing as an exception to the infringement of copyright: an obstacle to the effective enforcement of copyright claims in Nigeria' [2015] 2 *Idah Bar Journal of Contemporary Legal Issues* 245.

Elkin-Koren N, 'After twenty years: copyright liability of online intermediaries', in Frankel S and Gervais DJ (eds), *The Evolution and Equilibrium of Copyright in the Digital Age* (Cambridge University Press 2014).

Elkin-Koren N, 'Copyright in a digital ecosystem: A user rights approach', in R. Okediji (ed), *Copyright Law in an Age of Limitations and Exceptions* (Cambridge University Press 2017).

Elkin-Koren N, 'Copyright policy and the limits of freedom of contract' [1997] 12(1) *Berkeley Technology Law Journal* 106.

Elkin-Koren N, 'Exploring Creative Commons: a skeptical view of a worthy pursuit', in Guibault L and Hugenholtz P (eds), *The Future of the Public Domain: Identifying the Commons in Information Law* (Kluwer Law 2006).

Elkin-Koren N, 'Tailoring copyright to social production' [2011] 12(1) *Theoretical Inquiries in Law* 309.

Elkin-Koren N, 'The new frontiers of user rights' [2016] 32 *American University International Law Review* 1.

Elkin-Koren N, 'User-generated platforms', in Dreyfuss RC, Zimmerman DL and First H (eds), *Working within the Boundaries of Intellectual Property* (Oxford University Press 2010).

Elkin-Koren N, 'What contracts cannot do: the limits of private ordering in facilitating a creative commons' [2005] 74(2) *Fordham Law Review* 375.

Erickson K and Kretschmer M, 'Research perspectives on the public domain: digital conference proceedings' [2014] 3 *Research Perspectives on the Public Domain: Digital Conference Proceedings (CREATe Working Paper)*.

Erickson K and others, 'Copyright and the Value of the Public Domain' (*Gov.uk*, 2015), www.gov.uk/government/uploads/system/uploads/attachment_data/file/561543/Copyright-and-the-public-domain.pdf (accessed 11 November 2016).

European Commission (2005). *DG Competition Discussion Paper on the Application of Article 82 of the Treaty to Exclusionary Abuses*. Available at http://ec.europa.eu/comm/competition/antitrust/art82/discpaper2005.pdf, para 63.

Evans DS, 'Multisided platforms, dynamic competition and the assessment of market power for internet-based firms' [2016] 10(2) *Competition Policy International Journal* 1.

Evenett SJ, 'Competition law and the economic characteristics of developing countries', in Gal M, Bakhoum M, Drexl J, Fox E and Gerber D (eds), *The Economic Characteristics of Developing Jurisdictions: Their Implications for Competition Law* (Edward Elgar 2015).

Fagin M, Pasquale F and Weatherall K, 'Beyond Napster: using antitrust law to advance and enhance online music distribution' [2002] 8 *Boston University Journal of Science & Technology Law* 451.

Farrand B, 'The digital agenda for Europe, the economy and its impact upon the development of EU copyright policy', in Stamatoudi I and Torremans P (eds), *EU Copyright Law: A Commentary* (Edward Elgar 2014).

Fasan O, 'Compliance with WTO law in developing countries: A study of South Africa and Nigeria' (PhD, London School of Economics and Political Science United Kingdom 2007).

Faturoti B, 'Re-importing the concept of 'authorisation' of copyright infringement to Nigeria from the UK and Australia' [2017] 31(1) *International Review of Law, Computers & Technology* 4.

Favale M, 'Fine-tuning European copyright law to strike a balance between the rights of owners and users' [2008] 33 *European Law Review*. Available at https://ssrn.com/abstract=2613454 (accessed 4 September 2016).

Federal Government of Nigeria, *Draft Competition and Consumer Protection Policy* (2014).

Ficsor M, 'Guide to the copyright and related rights treaties administered by WIPO: And glossary of copyright and related rights and terms' (WIPO 2003), 275.

First H and Waller S, 'Antitrust's democracy deficit' [2013] 81 *Fordham Law Review* 3.

First H, 'Controlling the intellectual property grab: protect innovation, not innovators' [2007] 38 *Rutgers Law Journal*.

Fisher W, 'Theories of intellectual property', in Munzer SR (ed), *New Essays in the Legal and Political Theory of Property* (Cambridge University Press 2001).

Fishman JP, 'Creating around copyright' [2014] 128 *Harvard Law Review* 1333.

FitzPatrick M, '*United Brands Company v. Commission of the European Communities*: window to price discrimination law in the European Economic Community' [1979] 1 *Northwestern Journal of International Law & Business* 338.

Flew T, 'Creative Commons and the creative industries' [2005] 10(4) *Media and Arts Law Review* 257.

Fouché JA, *Crafting the Commons: Modern Approaches to Music as Product* (Masters in music technology dissertation, University of Cape Town 2015).

Fox E and Trebilcock M (eds), *The Design of Competition Law Institutions: Global Norms, Local Choices* (Oxford University Press 2012).

Fox E, 'Equality, discrimination, and competition law: lessons from and for South Africa and Indonesia' [2000] 41 *Harvard International Law Journal* 579.

Fox E, 'We protect competition, you protect competitors' [2003] 26(2) *World Competition* 149.

Fox E, 'What is harm to competition? Exclusionary practices and anticompetitive effect' [2002] 70(2) *Antitrust Law Journal* 371.

Fox, E. 'Comment: abuse of a dominant position: the Americanization of European competition law? The critical role of perspective', in Ullrich H (ed), *The Evolution of European Competition Law: Whose Regulation, Which Competition?* (Edward Elgar 2006).

Frabboni MM, 'IFPI 07 digital music report: consumers call the tune' [2007] 18(4) *Entertainment Law Review* 138.

Frosio G, 'Open access publishing: A literature review' [2014] *Centre for Copyright and New Business Models in the Creative Economy (CREATe)* 1.

Gal MS and Fox EM, 'Drafting competition law for developing jurisdictions: learning from experience', in Gal M, Bakhoum M, Drexl J, Fox E and Gerber D (eds), *The Economic Characteristics of Developing Jurisdictions: Their Implications for Competition Law* (Edward Elgar 2015).

Gal MS and Rubinfeld DL, 'The hidden costs of free goods: implications for antitrust enforcement' [2016] 80(3) *Antitrust Law Journal* 521.

Gallaugher J, Auger P and BarNir A, 'Revenue streams and digital content providers: an empirical investigation' [2001] 38(7) *Information & Management* 473.

Galuszka P, 'Report on the Functioning of the Digital Music Market in Poland' [2013] *SSRN Electronic Journal*. Available at http://ssrn.com/abstract=2391954 (accessed 27 June 2015).

Galuszka P, 'The rise of the nonprofit popular music sector – the case of netlabels', in Karja A, Marshall L and Brusila J (eds), *Helsinki Music, Business and Law. Essays on Contemporary Trends in the Music Industry* (IASPM Norden & Turku: International Institute for Popular Culture 2012).

Garcelon M, 'An information commons? Creative Commons and public access to cultural creations' [2009] 11(8) *New Media & Society* 1307.

Garcia KA, 'Penalty default licenses: A case for uncertainty' [2014] 89 *New York University Law Review* 1117.

Gateau T, 'The role of open licences and free music in value co-creation: the case of Misteur Valaire' [2014] 16(3) *International Journal of Arts Management* 49.

Geiger C, 'Rethinking copyright limitations in the information society: The Swiss Supreme Court leads the way' [2008] 39(8) *The International Review of Intellectual Property and Competition Law* 943.

Geist M (ed), 'Fairness found: How Canada quietly shifted from fair dealing to fair use', in *The Copyright Pentalogy: How the Supreme Court of Canada Shook the Foundations of Canadian Copyright Law* (University of Ottawa Press 2013).

Geist M (ed), *The Copyright Pentalogy: How the Supreme Court of Canada Shook the Foundations of Canadian Copyright Law* (University of Ottawa Press 2013).

Gerber D, *Law and Competition in Twentieth Century Europe* (Clarendon Press 2003).

Ghaziani A and Ventresca M, 'Keywords and cultural change: Frame analysis of business model public talk, 1975–2000' [2005] 20(4) *Sociological Forum Springer Netherlands* 523.

Ghosemajumder S, *Advanced Peer-Based Technology Business Models* (MBA Master's Thesis, Massachusetts Institute of Technology, Sloan School of Management, Cambridge 2002).

Giblin, R and Weatherall K, 'If we redesigned copyright from scratch, what might it look like?' in Giblin R and Weatherall K (eds), *What If We Could Reimagine Copyright?* (Australia National University Press 2017).

Gibson J, 'Risk aversion and rights accretion in intellectual property law' [2006] 116 *Yale Law Journal* 882.

Gilliéron P, 'Collecting societies and the digital environment' [2006] 37(8) *International Review of Industrial Property and Copyright Law* 939.

Ginsburg J, 'Creation and commercial value: copyright protection of works of information' [1990] 90(7) *Columbia Law Review* 1865.

Ginsburg J, 'Separating the Sony sheep from the Grokster goats: reckoning the future business plans of copyright-dependent technology entrepreneurs' [2008] 50 *Ariz L Rev* 577.

Ginsburg J, 'The author's place in the future of copyright' [2008] 45 *Willamette L Rev* 381.

Ginsburg J, 'The role of the author in copyright', in R. Okediji (ed), *Copyright Law in an Age of Limitations and Exceptions* (Cambridge University Press 2017).

Gitonga R, *Social and Political Goals of Mergers in Competition Law: Comparative Analysis of the Efficiency and Public Interest Provisions in Kenya and South Africa* (Masters, University of Cape Town 2015).

Glendon M, Carozza P and Picker C, *Comparative Legal Traditions* (Thomson West 2007).

Goldfein S and Keyte J, 'Big data, web 'scraping' and competition law: the debate continues' [2017] 258(49) *New York Law Journal* 1.

Goldstein P, *International Copyright: Principles, Law, and Practice* (Oxford University Press 2001).

Goyanes M, 'An empirical study of factors that influence the willingness to pay for online news' [2014] 8(6) *Journalism Practice* 742.

Greenleaf G, 'China – from Warring States to Convergence?', in *Asian Data Privacy Laws: Trade and Human Rights Perspectives* (Oxford University Press 2014).

Greenleaf G, 'Global data privacy laws 2019: 132 national laws and many bills' [2019] 157 *Privacy Laws & Business International Report*, 14–18.

Greenleaf G, 'Global Tables of Data Privacy Laws and Bills (5th Ed 2017)' [2017] 145 *Privacy Laws & Business International Report* 14–26.

Greenleaf G, 'Sheherezade and the 101 data privacy laws: origins, significance and global trajectories' [2014] 23 *Journal of Law, Information & Science* 4.

Greenleaf G, 'The influence of European data privacy standards outside Europe: Implications for globalisation of Convention 108' [2012] 2(2) *International Data Privacy Law* 68–92.

Greenleaf G, 'Global data privacy laws 2015: 109 countries, with European laws now a minority' [2015] 133 *Privacy Laws & Business International Report.*

Greenleaf G and Bond C, 'Public rights in copyright: what makes up Australia's public domain' [2013] 23 *Australian Intellectual Property Journal* 111.

Greenstein N, 'Striking the right chord: a theoretical approach to balancing artists' intellectual property rights on remix audio-sharing platforms' [2016] 102 *Cornell Law Review* 211.

Groenewald L, *Legal Analysis of Fair Dealing Relating to Music Works in the Digital Environment* (LLM, University of South Africa 2011).

Grondal L, 'DRM and contract terms' (2006) 2 *Indicare* 3.

Gürel B, 'An external method for establishing the balance in intellectual property rights' scope: Article 102 of the TFEU' [2009] 10 *Global Antitrust Review* 50.

Gürkaynak G, İnanılır O, Diniz S and Yaşar A, 'Multisided markets and the challenge of incorporating multisided considerations into competition law analysis' [2017] 5(1) *Journal of Antitrust Enforcement* 100.

Gutteridge HC, *Comparative Law: An Introduction to the Comparative Method of Legal Study and Research* (Vol 1, Cambridge University Press 2015).

Halmenschlager C and Waelbroeck P, 'Fighting free with free: freemium vs. piracy' [2014] *SSRN Electronic Journal.* Available at https://ssrn.com/abstract=2475641 (accessed 7 August 2016).

Halsbury's *Laws of England* (Vol. 9, 4th edn, Butterworths 1998).

Handke C, *Economic Effect of Copyright: The Empirical Evidence So Far* (National Academy of Sciences 2011).

Handke C, Balazs B and Vallbé J, 'Going means trouble and staying makes it double: the value of licensing recorded music online' [2015] *Journal of Cultural Economics* 1.

Handke C, Stepan P and Towse R, 'Development of the economics of copyright', in Drexl J (ed), *Research Handbook on Intellectual Property and Competition Law* (Edward Elgar Publishing 2008).

Hargreaves I, *Digital Opportunity: A Review of Intellectual Property and Growth* (Intellectual Property Office 2010).

Harms, LTC, *The Enforcement of Intellectual Property Rights: A Case Book* (3rd edn, World Intellectual Property Organisation 2012).

Harris D, 'Time to reboot: DMCA 2.0' [2015] 47 *Ariz St LJ* 801.

Harrison JL, 'Online music: antitrust and copyright perspectives' [2002] 47 *Antitrust Bull* 465.

Hartzenberg T, 'Competition policy and practice in South Africa: promoting competition for development' [2005] 26 *Northwestern Journal of International Law & Business* 667.

Haunss S, 'The changing role of collecting societies in the internet' [2013] 2(3) *Internet Policy Review* 1.

Hawthorne R, 'Has the conduct-based approach to competition law in South Africa led to consistent interpretations of harm to competition?' [2008] 11(3) *South African Journal of Economic and Management Sciences* 292.

Heald PJ, 'How copyright keeps works disappeared' [2014] 11(4) *Journal of Empirical Legal Studies* 829.

Heald PJ, 'How notice-and-takedown regimes create markets for music on YouTube: an empirical study' [2014] 83 *UMKC Law Review* 313.

Heimler A, 'Competition law enforcement and intellectual property rights' [2008] *SSRN Electronic Journal*. Available at https://ssrn.com/abstract=1105326 (accessed 6 September 2016).

Heinemann A, 'The contestability of IP-protected markets', in Drexl J (ed), *Research Handbook on Intellectual Property and Competition Law* (Edward Elgar 2010).

Herberg J, *Injunctive Relief for Wrongful Termination of Employment* (DPhil thesis, University of Oxford 1989).

Hiyashi S, 'The goals of Japanese competition law', in Drexl J, Idot L and Monéger J (eds), *Economic Theory and Competition Law* (Edward Elgar 2009).

Hodge J, S Goga and T Moahloli, 'Public Interest Provisions In The South African Competition Act: A Critical Review' (Competition Policy, Law and Economics Conference, 2009).

Högberg SK, 'The search for intent-based doctrines of secondary liability in copyright law' [2006] *Columbia Law Review* 909.

Hooper R, *Rights and Wrongs: Is Copyright Licensing Fit for Purpose for the Digital Age? The First Report of the Digital Copyright Exchange Feasibility Study* (Intellectual Property Office 2012).

Hope S, *An Investigation of the Effect That the Availability of Legitimate Channels for Acquiring Digital Music Has on Piracy in South Africa* (Masters dissertation, University of Cape Town 2014).

Höppner T, 'EU copyright reform: the case for a related right for press publishers' [2017] *CREATe Working Paper 2017/08*.

Hugenholtz PB, Van Eechoud M, Gompel SV and Helberger N, *The Recasting of Copyright & Related Rights for the Knowledge Economy* (Vancouver 2012).

Hugenholtz PGB, 'International copyright', in *Principles, Law, and Practice* (3rd edn, Oxford University Press 2013).

Hughes P, 'Business strategy and EC competition law: two systems separated by a common language' [2009] 11 *International Company and Commercial Law Review* 387.

Hutchinson T and Duncan N, 'Defining and describing what we do: doctrinal legal research' [2012] 17 *Deakin Law Review* 83.

Hviid M, Schroff S, and Street J, Regulating collective management organizations by competition: an incomplete answer to the licensing problem' [2016] 7 *Journal of Intellectual Property, Information Technology and Electronic Commerce Law* 256.

Ibáñez Colomo P and Lamadrid de Pablo A, 'On the notion of restriction of competition: what we know and what we don't know we know', in Gerard D, Merola M and Meyring B (eds), *The Notion of Restriction of Competition: Revisiting the Foundations of Antitrust Enforcement in Europe* (Bruylant 2017).

International Federation of the Phonographic Industry (IFPI), 'Global Music Report 2017: Annual State of the Industry' (International Federation of the Phonographic Industry (IFPI) 2017).

International Bureau of WIPO, 'WIPO National Seminar on Digital Technology and the New WIPO Treaties (WIPO/CNR/SEL/97/1)' (WIPO 1997).

International Competition Network (ICN), 'Report on Abuse of Superior Bargaining Position' (ICN 2008), www.internationalcompetitionnetwork.org/uploads/library/doc386.pdf (accessed 9 March 2017).

International Federation of the Phonographic Industry (IFPI), 'Digital Music Report: Lighting up New Markets' (International Federation of the Phonographic Industry (IFPI) 2014).

International Federation of the Phonographic Industry (IFPI), 'Digital Music Report: Charting the Path to Sustainable Growth' (International Federation of the Phonographic Industry (IFPI) 2015).

International Federation of the Phonographic Industry (IFPI), 'Global Music Report: Music Consumption Exploding Worldwide' (International Federation of the Phonographic Industry (IFPI) 2016).

Jiang F and Gervais D, 'Collective management organizations in china: practice, problems and possible solutions' [2012] 15(3) *Journal of World Intellectual Property* 221.

Jing-jing Y, 'Review of the 8th Amendment of the German Copyright Act: ancillary copyright for press publishers: a backward legislation step in the era of the internet?' [2015] 2 *Journal of Science, Technology and Law* 5.

Jockers M, Sag M and Schultz J, 'Digital archives: Don't let copyright block data mining' [2012] 490(7418) *Nature* 29.

Jonathan D, Wagner T, Hess T and Benlian A, 'Music as a service as an alternative to music piracy? – an empirical investigation of the intention to use music streaming services' [2013] 5(6) *Business & Information Systems Engineering* 383.

Kamba W, 'Comparative law: A theoretical framework' [1974] *International and Comparative Law Quarterly* 485.

Kampel K, 'Competition law and SMEs: Exploring the competitor/competition debate in a developing democracy' (No. 30655 University of Manchester, Institute for Development Policy and Management (IDPM) 2005).

Katz A and Veel P, 'Beyond refusal to deal: a cross-Atlantic view of copyright, competition, and innovation policies' [2013] 79(1) *Antitrust Law Journal* 139.

Katz A, 'A network effects perspective on software piracy' [2005] 55(2) *University of Toronto Law Journal* 155.

Katz A, 'Commentary: is collective administration of copyrights justified by the economic literature?' In Boyer M, Trebilcock M and Vaver D (eds), *Competition Policy and Intellectual Property* (Irwin Law 2009).

Katz A, 'Copyright and competition policy', in Towse R and Handke C (eds), *Handbook on the Digital Creative Economy* (Edward Elgar 2013).

Katz A, 'Copyright collectives: good solution but for which problem?' in First H, Dreyfuss RC and Zimmerman DL (eds), *Working within the Boundaries of Intellectual Property: Innovation Policy for the Knowledge Society* (Oxford University Press 2009).

Katz A, 'Fair use 2.0: the rebirth of fair dealing in Canada', in Geist M (ed), *The Copyright Pentalogy: How the Supreme Court of Canada Shook the Foundations of Canadian Copyright Law* (University of Ottawa Press 2013).

Katz A, 'Making sense of nonsense: intellectual property, antitrust, and market power' [2007] 49 *Arizona Law Review* 837.

Katz A, 'Substitution and Schumpeterian effects over the life cycle of copyrighted works' [2009] *Jurimetrics* 113.

Katz A, 'The potential demise of another natural monopoly: new technologies and the administration of performing rights' [2006] 2(2) *Journal of Competition Law and Economics* 245.

Katz A, 'The potential demise of another natural monopoly: rethinking the collective administration of performing rights' [2005] 1(3) *Journal of Competition Law and Economics* 541.

Katz A, 'What Antitrust Law Can (And Cannot) Teach About The First Sale Doctrine' [2012] https://doi.org/10.2139/ssrn.1845842.

KEA European Affairs, (2012). Licensing music works and transaction costs in Europe. Available at www.keanet.eu/docs/music%20licensing%20and%20transaction%20costs%20-%20full.pdf (accessed 10 July 2015).

Këllezi P, 'Abuse below the threshold of dominance? Market power, market dominance, and abuse of economic dependence', in *Abuse of Dominant Position: New Interpretation, New Enforcement Mechanisms?* (Springer 2008).

Kemp D, 'Copyright on steroids: in search of an end to over-protection' [2009] 41 *McGeorge Law Review* 795.

Kim M, 'The Creative Commons and copyright protection in the digital era: uses of Creative Commons licenses' [2007] 13(1) *Journal of Computer-Mediated Communication* 187.

Klebanow A, 'Is music the next eBooks? An antitrust analysis of Apple's conduct in the music industry' [2015] 39 *Columbia Journal of Law & the Arts* 119.

Koelman K and Hugenholtz P, 'Online Service Provider Liability for Copyright Infringement, Workshop on Service Provider Liability' (*Pure.uva.nl*, 1999), https://pure.uva.nl/ws/files/3363649/6027_wipo99.pdf (accessed 8 February 2015).

Koelman K, 'Liability for on-line intermediaries' (Imprimatur/Institute for Information Law 1997).

Kolstad O, 'Competition law and intellectual property rights – outline of an economics-based approach', in Drexl J (ed), *Research Handbook on Intellectual Property and Competition Law* (Edward Elgar 2010).

Koornhof P and Pistorius T, 'Convergence between competition and data protection law: a South African perspective' [2018] 8(3) *International Data Privacy Law*, 277–283.

Kopp S and Suter T, 'Developments in copyright policy and network technologies: the first generation' [1998] *Journal of Public Policy & Marketing* 306.

Koscik M and Savelka J, 'Dangers of over-enthusiasm in licensing under Creative Commons, [2013] 7 *Masaryk University Journal of Law and Technology* 201.

Kovacic W, 'The importance of history to the design of competition policy strategy: The Federal Trade Commission and intellectual property' [2006] 30 *Seattle University Law Review* 319.

Krcmar H and others, 'Innovation, Society and Business: Internet-Based Business Models and Their Implications', *1st Berlin Symposium on Internet and Society* (2011), www.hiig.de/wp-content/uploads/2012/04/Business-Models-Paper.pdf (accessed 30 June 2015).

Kretschmer M, 'Access and Reward in the Information Society: Regulating the Collective Management of Copyright' (*Eprints.bournemouth.ac.uk*, 2007), http://eprints.bournemouth.ac.uk/3695/1/CollSoc07.pdf (accessed 30 June 2015).

Kretschmer M, 'Artists' earnings and copyright: A review of British and German music industry data in the context of digital technologies' [2005] 10(1) *First Monday*.

Kretschmer M, 'Regulating creator contracts' [2010] 18 *Journal of Intellectual Property Law* 144.

Kretschmer M, 'The failure of property rules in collective administration: Rethinking copyright societies as regulatory instruments' [2002] 24(3) *European Intellectual Property Review* 126.

Kretschmer M, Klimis G and Wallis R, 'Music in electronic markets: an empirical study' [2001] 3(4) *New Media & Society* 417.

Kumaraguru P, Cranor L., Lobo J and Calo S. 'A survey of privacy policy languages', in *Workshop on Usable IT Security Management (USM 07): Proceedings of the 3rd Symposium on Usable Privacy and Security, ACM* (2007).

Kur A, 'Limiting IP protection for competition policy reasons: a case study based on the EU spare-parts design discussion', in Drexl J (ed), *Research Handbook on Intellectual Property and Competition Law* (Edward Elgar 2008).

Lamadrid de Pablo A, 'The double duality of two-sided markets' [2015] *Competition Law Journal* 7.

Landes W and Posner R, 'An economic analysis of copyright law' [1989] 18(2) *Journal of Legal Studies* 325.

Larkin B, 'Degraded images, distorted sounds: Nigerian video and the infrastructure of piracy' [2004] 16(2) *Public Culture* 289.

Lee Y, 'Copyright and Freedom of Expression: A Literature Review' (*Zenodo.org*, 2015), https://zenodo.org/record/18132/files/CREATe-Working-Paper-2015-04.pdf (accessed 21 October 2016).

Lee, C, Kumar, V and Gupta, S (2013). Designing freemium: a model of consumer usage, upgrade, and referral dynamics. Available at www.people.hbs.edu/vkumar/research/DesigningFreemium.pdf (accessed 15 January 2016).

Lemley M and McGowan D, 'Legal implications of network economic effects' [1998] 86 *California Law Review* 479.

Lemley M and Reese R, 'Reducing digital copyright infringement without restricting innovation' [2004] 56(6) *Stanford Law Review* 1345.

Leonard P, 'Safe harbors in choppy waters: building a sensible approach to liability of internet intermediaries in Australia' [2010] 3 *Journal of International Media & Entertainment Law* 221.

Lessig L, 'Creative Commons' [2003] 55 *Florida Law Review* 763.

Lessig L, 'Re-crafting a public domain' [2006] 18 *Yale Journal of Law & the Humanities* 56.

Lessig L, *Remix: Making Art and Commerce Thrive in the Hybrid Economy* (Bloomsbury 2008).

Li Z and Cheng Y, 'From free to fee: exploring the antecedents of consumer intention to switch to paid online content' [2014] 15(4) *Journal of Electronic Commerce Research* 281.

Li Z, 'Legal Boundaries of Competition in the Era of the Internet: Challenges and Judicial Responses' [2016] *Internet Competition & Regulation Of Online Platforms* 143. Available at www.competitionpolicyinternational.com/wp-content/uploads/2016/05/INTERNET-COMPETITION-LIBRO.pdf (accessed 3 February 2017).

Liang L, 'Copyright, cultural production and open-content licensing' [2005] 1 *Indian Journal of Law and Technology* 96.

Lianos I, 'A Regulatory Theory of IP: Implications for Competition Law' (*Centre for Law, Economics and Society*, 2008), www.ucl.ac.uk/cles/research-paper-series/research-papers/cles-1-2008 (accessed 28 September 2016).

Lianos I, 'Competition law and intellectual property rights: is the property rights' approach right?' [2006] 8 *Cambridge Yearbook of European Legal Studies* 153.

Lincoff B, 'Collecting societies in the digital environment' [2006] 91(4) *International Intellectual Property Law and Policy* 1.

Lippman A, 'Cannibalizing copyright? Vernacularizing open intellectual property in Brazil' [2014] 30(5) *Anthropology Today* 11.

Lipton J, *Rethinking Cyberlaw: A New Vision for Internet Law* (Edward Elgar 2015).

Lister B, 'Competition – it is not just about the Act' [2005] 13(3) *Juta's Business Law* 115.

Litman, J, 'Fetishizing copies', in Okediji R (ed), *Copyright Law in an Age of Limitations and Exceptions* (Cambridge University Press, 2017).

Liu C, Au Y and Choi H, 'Effects of freemium strategy in the mobile app market: an empirical study of Google Play' [2014] 31(3) *Journal of Management Information Systems* 326.

Llewelyn D, 'Intellectual property liability of consumers, facilitators and intermediaries: concepts under common law', in Kamperman Sanders A and Heath C (eds), *Intellectual Property Liability of Consumers, Facilitators and Intermediaries* (Kluwer Law 2012).

Lopez-Galdos M, 'Antitrust policy tools and IP rights: US, transatlantic and international effects' [2016] 15 *Chicago-Kent Journal of Intellectual Property* 441.

Ludington S, 'Reining in the data traders: a tort for the misuse of personal information' (2006) 66 *Maryland Law Review* 140.

Lynskey O, 'At the crossroads of data protection and competition law: time to take stock' (2018) 8(3) *International Data Privacy Law*, 179–180.

Mackenrodt M, 'Assessing the effects of intellectual property rights in network standards', in Drexl J (ed), *Research Handbook on Intellectual Property and Competition Law* (Edward Elgar 2010).

Magretta J, 'Why business models matter' [2002] 80(5) *Harvard Business Review* 87.

Mahrt, Merja, and Michael Scharkow. 'The value of big data in digital media research' [2013] 57(1) *Journal of Broadcasting & Electronic Media* 20–33.

Makhaya T, 'The Interface between Competition Policy and Entrepreneurship' (*Compcom.co.za*, 2011), www.compcom.co.za/wp-content/uploads/2014/09/Competition-News-Edition-41-Dec-2011.pdf (accessed 6 February 2017).

Makino S, Beamish P and Zhao NB, 'The characteristics and performance of Japanese FDI in less developed and developed countries' [2004] 39(4) *Journal of World Business* 377.

Maliszewska-Nienartowicz J, 'The abuse of the dominant position within the internal market of the European Community: from theoretical assumptions to practice' [2007] 3 *Interdisciplinary Management Research* 429.

Mandrescu D, 'Applying EU competition law to online platforms: the road ahead – Part 2' [2017] 28(9) *European Competition Law Review* 410.

Maskus K and Lahouel M, 'Competition policy and intellectual property rights in developing countries' [2000] 23(4) *World Economy* 595.

Matzukis N, *South African music law, contracts and business* (3rd edn, Academy of Sound Engineering 2013).

Maximillian N. Volmar and Katharina O. Helmdach, 'Protecting consumers and their data through competition law? Rethinking abuse of dominance in light of the Federal Cartel Office's Facebook investigation' [2018] 14(2–3) *European Competition Journal* 195–215.

Mercedes Frabboni M, 'From copyright collectives to exclusive "clubs": the changing faces of music rights administration in Europe' [2008] 19(5) *Entertainment Law Review* 100.

Mhlambi T, '"Kwaitofabulous": The study of a South African urban genre' [2004] 1(1) *Journal of Musical Arts in Africa* 116.

Michaels R, 'The functional method of comparative law', in Reimann M and Zimmermann R (eds) *The Oxford Handbook of Comparative Law* (Oxford University Press 2006).

Mizukami PN and Lemos R, 'From free software to free culture: the emergence of open business', in Shaver L (ed), *Access to Knowledge in Brazil: New Research on Intellectual Property, Innovation and Development* (Bloomsbury 2010).

Moffat V, 'Super-copyright: contracts, preemption, and the structure of copyright policymaking' [2007] 41 *UC Davis Law Review* 55.

Montagnani M and Borghi M, 'Positive copyright and open content licenses: how to make a marriage work by empowering authors to disseminate their works' [2008] 12 *International Journal of Communication Law & Policy* 244.

Mounier P, 'Freemium as a sustainable economic model for open access electronic publishing in humanities and social sciences' [2011] 31(3–4) *Information Services & Use* 225.

Mudau S, *The Copyright Protection of Online User Generated Content* (Doctoral dissertation, University of Cape Town 2014).

Mueller-Langer F and Scheufen M, 'Academic publishing and open access', in Towse R and Handke C (eds), *Handbook on the Digital Creative Economy* (Edward Elgar 2013).

Müller R, Kijl B and Martens JK, 'A comparison of inter-organizational business models of mobile app stores: there is more than open vs. closed' [2011] 6(2) *Journal of Theoretical and Applied Electronic Commerce Research* 63.

Newman JM, 'Copyright freeconomics' [2013] 66 *Vanderbilt Law Review* 1407.

Nigerian Communications Commission, 'Consultation Paper on Dominance in Selected Communications Markets' (Abuja 2009).

Noguchi Y, 'Freedom override by digital rights management technologies: Causes in market mechanisms and possible legal options to keep a better balance' [2006] 11 *Intellectual Property Law Bulletin* 1.

Nwogu M, 'Copyright law and the menace of piracy in Nigeria' [2015] 34 *Journal of Law, Policy and Globalization* 113.

O'Dair, M (2012). 'Collaborative, Co-operative and Collective Business Models in the 'New' Music Industries: A Literature Review'. Available at www.nemode.ac.uk/wp-content/uploads/2012/12/ODair-2015-Collaborative-cooperative-and-collective.pdf (accessed 18 November 2017).

O'Sullivan A and Sheffrin S, *Economics* (Prentice Hall 2003).

Oestreicher-Singer G and Zalmanson L, 'Content or Community? A Digital Business Strategy for Content Providers in the Social Age' (2012).

Ohm P, 'Broken promises of privacy: responding to the surprising failure of anonymization' [2009] 57 *UCLA Law Review* 1701.

Okediji RL (ed), *Copyright Law in an Age of Limitations and Exceptions* (Cambridge University Press 2017).

Okoeguale H, 'Strengthening legislative controls over delegated legislation in Nigeria' (2019) 10(2) *Nnamdi Azikiwe University Journal of International Law and Jurisprudence* 35–41.

Okoli C and Carillo K, 'Beyond Open Source Software: A Framework, Implications, and Directions for Researching Open Content' [2013] Available at https://ssrn.com/abstract=1954869 (accessed 3 March 2015).

Okorie C, 'An analysis of the IP-related provisions of the Nigerian Federal Competition and Consumer Protection Act 2019' [2019] *Journal of Intellectual Property Law & Practice*, https://doi.org/10.1093/jiplp/jpz064

Okorie C, 'Nigerian Supreme Court issues guidance on locus standi of collecting societies' [2018] 13(12) *Journal of Intellectual Property Law & Practice* 931–933.

Okorie C, *Use of Music Aggregation in the UK and Nigeria* (Masters, University of Strathclyde 2014).

Okpara JO, 'Factors constraining the growth and survival of SMEs in Nigeria: implications for poverty alleviation' [2011] 34(2) *Management Research Review* 156.

Ola K, 'Evolution and future trends of copyright in Nigeria' [2014] 2(1) *Journal of Open Access to Law* 1.

Ola K, 'Evolution and future trends of copyright in Nigeria', in Fitzgerald B and Gilchrist J (eds), *Copyright Perspectives* (Springer 2015).

Oliveira G and Fujiwara T, 'Intellectual Property and Competition as Complementary Policies: A Test Using an Ordered Probit Model' (*Bibliotecadigital.fgv.br*, 2006), http://bibliotecadigital.fgv.br/dspace/handle/10438/1884

Oliver J, 'Copyright in the WTO: the panel decision on the three-step test' [2001] 25 *Columbia Journal of Law & the Arts*, 119.

Olubiyi IA, 'A comparative analysis of copyright enforcement provisions in Nigeria: maximising the current legal regime' [2014] 5 *Nnamdi Azikiwe University Journal of International Law and Jurisprudence* 89.

Oriakhogba D and Erhagbe E, 'How the Nigerian Supreme Court finally resolved the copyright collective management organizations' *locus standi* conundrum' [2019] *Journal of Intellectual Property Law & Practice*.

Oriakhogba D, 'Copyright collective management organizations in Nigeria: the *locus standi* conundrum resolved?' [2018] 14(2) *Journal of Intellectual Property Law & Practice* 127–135.

Osterwalder A and Pigneur Y, *Business Model Generation: A Handbook for Visionaries, Game Changers, and Challengers* (John Wiley & Sons 2010).

Otegui Nieto J, 'Apple and Spotify, a competition law song?' [2015] 36 *ECLR* 436. Available at https://ssrn.com/abstract=2628051 (accessed 11 October 2016).

Ouma M, 'Copyright and the music industry in Africa' [2004] 7(6) *Journal of World Intellectual Property* 920.

Oyewunmi A and Sanni A, 'Challenges for the development of unfair contract terms law in Nigeria' [2013] 37 *University of Western Australia Law Review* 86.

Pager SA, 'Accentuating the positive: building capacity for creative industries into the development agenda for global intellectual property law' [2012] 28 *American University International Law Review* 223.

Park JH, *Patents and Industry Standards* (Edward Elgar 2010).

Parker N, *Music Business: Infrastructure, Practice and Law* (Sweet & Maxwell 2004).

Pateli A and Giaglis G, 'A Framework for Understanding and Analysing Ebusiness Models' (*Domino.fov.uni-mb.si*, 2003), https://domino.fov.uni-mb.si/proceedings.nsf/Proceedings/4C84233423603AD0C1256EA1002D1A29/$File/25Pateli.pdf (accessed 19 November 2017).

Patterson LR, *Copyright in Historical Perspective* (Vanderbilt University Press 1968).

Patterson MR, 'Must licenses be contracts – consent and notice in intellectual property' [2012] 40 *Florida State University Law Review* 105.

Perel M and Elkin-Koren N, 'Accountability in algorithmic copyright enforcement' [2015] 19 *Stanford Technology Law Review* 473.

Peukert A, 'A bipolar copyright system for the digital network environment' [2005] 28 *Hastings Communications and Entertainment Law Journal* 1.

Picker R, 'Copyright as entry policy: the case of digital distribution' [2002] 47(2–3) *Antitrust Bulletin* 423.

Poel M, Renda A and Ballon P, 'Business model analysis as a new tool for policy evaluation: policies for digital content platforms' [2007] 9(5) *Info-The journal of policy, regulation and strategy for telecommunications* 86.

Pollack W, 'Tuning in: The future of copyright protection for online music in the digital millennium' [1999] 68 *Fordham Law Review* 2445.

Polverino F, 'Hunting the wild geese: competition analysis in a world of "free" ' [2012] *Concorrenza e Mercato* 1.

Posse RI, 'The legal status of copyleft before the Spanish courts [2009] 4(11) *Journal of Intellectual Property Law & Practice* 815.

Preston M and Zurer R, 'Open Content and the Search for a Better Intellectual Property Model: Lessons from Open Source' [2003]. Available at www.cs.duke.edu/courses/cps182s/spring05/assign/project/fall03/raz3_1/opencontent.pdf (accessed 15 November 2015).

Priest E, 'Copyright and free expression in China's film industry' [2015] 26 *Fordham Intellectual Property, Media and Entertainment Law Journal* 1.

Prins D and Koornhof P, 'Assessing the nature of competition law enforcement in South Africa' [2014] 18 *Law, Democracy and Development* 136.

Pujol N, 'Freemium: Attributes of an Emerging Business Model' (2010), https://doi.org/10.2139/ssrn.1718663 (accessed 19 July 2016).

Quinn A, 'Are online music platforms undermining the principles of copyright law?' [2017] 13(1) *Journal of Intellectual Property Law & Practice* 49.

Quintais JP, 'Proposal for a Directive on collective rights management and (some) multi-territorial licensing' [2013] 35(2) *European Intellectual Property Review* 65.

Rae-Hunter C, 'Better mousetraps: licensing, access, and innovation in the new music marketplace' [2012] 7 *Journal of Business & Technology Law* 35.

Rajan M, 'Creative Commons: America's moral rights' [2010] 21 *Fordham Intellectual Property, Media and Entertainment Law Journal* 905.

Raju KD, 'The inevitable connection between intellectual property and competition law: emerging jurisprudence and lessons for India' [2013] 18 *Journal of Intellectual Property Rights* 111.

Reed C, *Making Laws for Cyberspace* (Oxford University Press 2013).

Reid L, 'The judge as law maker' [1972] 12 *Journal of the Society of Public Teachers of Law (New Series)* 22.

Reime EV, *Exploring the Freemium Business Model* (Master's thesis, Centre for Entrepreneurship, University of Oslo, Norway 2011).

Reitz JC, 'How to do comparative law' [1998] 46(4) *American Journal of Comparative Law* 617.

Resnikoff P, 'Sony Forces The Verge To Remove Its Spotify Contract . . . – Digital Music News' (*Digital Music News*, 2015), www.digitalmusicnews.com/2015/05/21/breaking-spotify-forces-the-verge-to-remove-its-sony-contract/ (accessed 13 November 2017).

Rethink Music, 'Fair Music: Transparency and Payment Flows in the Music Industry' (*Berklee.edu*, 2015), www.berklee.edu/sites/default/files/Fair%20Music%20-%20Transparency%20and%20Payment%20Flows%20in%20the%20Music%20Industry.pdf (accessed 13 November 2017).

Riby-Smith M, 'South African copyright law – the good, the bad and the Copyright Amendment Bill' [2017] 12(3) *Journal of Intellectual Property Law & Practice* 216.

Richardson J, 'The Spotify paradox: how the creation of a compulsory license scheme for streaming on-demand music platforms can save the music industry' [2014] 22 *UCLA Entertainment Law Review* 45.

Ricolfi M, 'Consume and Share: Making Copyright Fit for the Digital Agenda' (The Digital Public Domain: Foundations for an Open Culture 2012).

Rimmer M, 'The grey album: copyright law and digital sampling' [2005] 114(1) *Media International Australia Incorporating Culture and Policy* 40.

Rimmer M, *Digital Copyright and the Consumer Revolution: Hands Off My iPod* (Edward Elgar 2007).

Riordan J, *The Liability of Internet Intermediaries* (Oxford University Press 2016).

Ritala S, 'Pandora and Spotify: legal issues and licensing requirements for interactive and non-interactive internet radio broadcasters' [2013] 54 *IDEA: The Law Review of the Franklin Pierce Center for Intellectual Property* 23.

Rizk N, 'From de facto commons to digital commons? The case of Egypt's independent music industry', in De Beer J, Armstrong C, Oguamanam C and Schönwetter T (eds), *Innovation & Intellectual Property: Collaborative Dynamics in Africa* (UCT Press 2014).

Rizk N, 'Notes from Egypt's alternative music scene: business models, commons and copyright' [2010] 13(3) *Journal of World Intellectual Property* 474.

Rizk N, 'Stories from Egypt's music industry: de facto commons as alternatives to copyright', in Rizk N and Shaver L (eds), *Access to Knowledge in Egypt: New Research on Intellectual Property, Innovation and Development* (Bloomsbury 2010).

Rizk N and Shaver L, *Access to Knowledge in Egypt* (London: Bloomsbury Academic 2010).

Robbins I, 'What is the meaning of "like": the First Amendment implications of social media expression' [2014] 7 *Federal Courts Law Review* 123.

Roberts S and Tapia J, 'Abuses of dominance in developing countries: a view from the south, with an eye on telecommunications', in Gal M, Bakhoum M, Drexl J, Fox E and Gerber D (eds), *The Economic Characteristics of Developing Jurisdictions: Their Implications for Competition Law* (Edward Elgar 2015).

Roberts S, 'The role for competition policy in economic development: the South African experience' [2004] 21(1) *Development Southern Africa* 227.

Roberts S, Tapia J and Ybar M, 'The same and the other: A comparative study of abuses of dominance in Chile and South Africa' (CCRED Working Paper 2 2013).

Rosati E, 'Neighbouring rights for publishers: are national and (possible) EU initiatives lawful?' [2016] 47(5) *IIC-International Review of Intellectual Property and Competition Law* 569.

Rosati E, 'The CJEU Pirate Bay judgment and its impact on the liability of online platforms' [2017] *European Intellectual Property Review*. Available at https://ssrn.com/abstract=3006591 (accessed 6 September 2017).

Rosati E, 'Why a Reform of Hosting Providers Safe Harbour is Unnecessary Under EU Copyright Law' (2016), https://ssrn.com/abstract=2830440 (accessed 6 September 2017).

Rose KD, 'Protection from the protectors: does the competition act provide an answer to the misuse of technological protection measures?' [2015] 11(1) *Canadian Journal of Law and Technology* 117.

Rose M, *Authors and Owners: The Invention of Copyright* (Harvard University Press 1993).

Roughton A, 'The interface between intellectual property rights and competition policy' [2008] 3(4) *Journal of Intellectual Property Law & Practice* 270.

Russi G, 'Creative Commons, CC-Plus, and hybrid intermediaries: a stakeholder's perspective' [2011] 7 *Brigham Young University International Law & Management Review* 127.

Sag M, 'Copyright and copy-reliant technology' [2009] 103 *Northwestern University Law Review* 1607.

Sag M, 'Orphan works as grist for the data mill' [2012] *Berkeley Technology Law Journal* 1503.

Salmon R, 'The digital music business: income and royalty payments' [2009] 20(8) *Entertainment Law Review* 278.

Samuelson P, 'Justifications for copyright limitations and exceptions', in Okediji R (ed), *Copyright Law in an Age of Limitations and Exceptions* (Cambridge University Press 2017).

Samuelson P, 'Mapping the digital public domain: threats and opportunities' [2003] 66(1/2) *Law and Contemporary Problems* 147.

Santos A, 'Nurturing creative industries in the developing world: the case of alternative systems of music production and distribution' [2013] 21 *Michigan State University College International Law Review* 601.

Scassa T, 'Acknowledging copyright's illegitimate offspring: user-generated content and Canadian copyright law', in Geist M (ed), *The Copyright Pentalogy: How the Supreme Court of Canada Shook the Foundations of Canadian Copyright Law* (University of Ottawa Press 2013).

Schönwetter T, *Safeguarding a Fair Copyright Balance: Contemporary Challenges in a Changing World: Lessons to Be Learnt from a Developing Country Perspective* (Doctoral dissertation, University of Cape Town 2009).

Schroff S and Street J, 'The politics of the digital single market: culture vs. competition vs. copyright' [2017] *Information, Communication & Society* 1.

Searle N, 'Changing Business Models in the Creative Industries: The Cases of Television, Computer Games and Music' (Intellectual Property Office (IPO) 2011).

Senftleben M, *Copyright, Limitations, and the Three-Step Test: An Analysis of the Three-Step Test in International and EC Copyright Law* (Vol. 13, Kluwer Law 2004).

Sganga C, 'Public e-lending and the CJEU: Chronicle of a missed revolution foretold' [2016] *Opinio Juris in Comparatione* 1.

Shafer S, Smith H and Linder J, 'The power of business models' [2005] 48(3) *Business Horizons* 199.

Shay R, *Users' Entitlements under the Fair Dealing Exceptions to Copyright* (LLM, Stellenbosch University 2012).

Simbro EM, 'Disclosing stored communication data to fight crime: The US and EU approaches to balancing competing privacy and security interests' [2010] 43 *Cornell International Law Journal* 585.

Slater D, Gasser U, Smith M, Bambauer DE and Palfrey JG, 'Content and control: assessing the impact of policy choices on potential online business models in the music and film industries' [2005] 1 *Berkman Publication Series Paper*.

Solo A, 'The role of copyright in an age of online music distribution' [2014] 19 *Media and Arts Law Review* 169.

Sriram S, Manchanda P, Bravo M, Chu J, Ma L, Song M, Shriver S and Subramanian U, 'Platforms: a multiplicity of research opportunities' [2015] 26(2) *Marketing Letters* 141.

Stadler S, 'Copyright as trade regulation' [2007] *University of Pennsylvania Law Review* 899.

Stallman R, *Free Software, Free Society: Selected Essays of Richard M. Stallman* (Free Software Foundation Inc. 2002).

Staples J, Masamba M, 'Fourteen Years Later: An Assessment of the Realisation of the Objectives of the Competition Act 89 of 1998'' (6th annual Competition Commission, Competition Tribunal and Mandela Institute Conference on Competition Law, Economics and Policy in South Africa, Johannesburg, South Africa, 2012).

Stazi A, 'Digital copyright and consumer/user protection: moving toward a new framework?' [2012] 2 *Queen Mary Journal of Intellectual Property* 158.

Sutherland P and Kemp K, *Competition law of South Africa* (Butterworths 2000).

Takigawa, T (2015). Regulating Abuse of Bargaining Position through the Competition Law: Japanese Regulation in Comparison with the EU's Exploitative Abuse Regulation. Available at http://ascola-tokyo-conference-2015.meiji.jp/pdf/Conference Papers/General%20Session% 203/Toshiaki% 20Takigawa_Superi Barg Abuse_Ascola_May2015.pdf (accessed 13 September 2016).

Teague J, 'Saving the Spotify Revolution: Recalibrating the Power Imbalance in Digital Copyright' [2012] *ExpressO*, http://works.bepress.com/jordan_teague/1/ (accessed 4 February 2019).

Teece D, 'Business models, business strategy and innovation' [2010] 43(2) *Long Range Planning* 172.

Török Á, *Competition Policy Reform in South Africa: Towards the Mainstream CP Model for 'Transition' Economies in the Third World* (Mimeo 2005).

Towse R and Handke C, *Handbook on the Digital Creative Economy* (Edward Elgar 2013).

Towse R, 'Copyright and music publishing in the UK', in *The Artful Economist* (Springer 2016), 131.

Towse R, 'Economics of copyright collecting societies and digital rights: is there a case for a centralised digital copyright exchange?' [2012] 9(2) *Review of Economic Research on Copyright Issues* 3.

Towse R, 'Economics of music publishing: copyright and the market' [2017] 41(4) *Journal of Cultural Economics* 403.

Towse R, 'The economic effects of digitization on the administration of musical copyrights' [2013] 10(2) *Review of Economic Research on Copyright Issues* 55.

Towse R, Handke C and Stepan P, 'The economics of copyright law: a stocktake of the literature' [2008] 5(1) *Review of Economic Research on Copyright Issues* 1.

Traphagen M, 'The unfinished business of copyright: a look forward from the Digital Millennium Copyright Act' [2002] 63(7) *International Intellectual Property Law & Policy* 1.

Trott P and Hartmann D, 'Why "open innovation" is old wine in new bottles' [2009] 13(4) *International Journal of Innovation Management* 715.

Troxler P, 'Open content in the creative industries: a source for service innovation?' in Wolf P, Kazi S, Troxler P and Jonischkeit R (eds), *Supporting Service Innovation through Knowledge Management* (KnowledgeBoard and Swiss Knowledge Management Forum 2009).

Tussey D, 'Music at the edge of chaos: a complex systems perspective on file sharing' [2005] 37 *Loyola University Chicago Law Journal* 147.

Tussey D, *Complex Copyright: Mapping the Information Ecosystem* (Ashgate 2012).

UK Competition Commission, 'Merger references: Competition Commission guidelines' (June 2003, CC 2).

UK Department of Trade and Industry, 'Productivity and Enterprise: A World Class Competition Regime' (White Paper section 1.1. 2002).

UNCTAD International Standard Industrial Classification of Economic Activities Revision 4.

United Nations Council on Trade and Development (UNCTAD), 'Creative Economies Report UNCTADIDITC/2008/2' (Geneva, 2008).

United Nations Industrial Development Organization, 'Industrialization in Africa and Least Developed Countries: Boosting Growth, Creating Jobs, Promoting Inclusiveness and Sustainability' (*Unido.org*, 2016), www.unido.org/sites/default/files/2016-09/G20_new_UNIDO_report_industrialization_in_Africa_and_LDCs_0.pdf (accessed 25 September 2017).

United Nations, 'Creative Economy Report' (Geneva, Switzerland: UNCTAD 2008), http://unctad.org/en/docs/ditc20082cer_en.pdf.

Urban JM and Quilter L, 'Efficient process or chilling effects-Takedown notices under Section 512 of the Digital Millennium Copyright Act' [2005] 22 *Santa Clara Computer & High Tech Law Journal* 621.

US Department of Justice and US Federal Trade Commission, 'Antitrust Guidelines for the Licensing of Intellectual Property' (1995).

US Department of Justice and US Federal Trade Commission, 'Antitrust Guidelines for the licensing of intellectual property' (2017).

Van Aswegen PF, 'Right to exclude others from using claimed intellectual property: a perspective from competition law' [2003] 14 *Stellenbosch Law Review* 115.

Van Eechoud MM, *Choice of Law in Copyright and Related Rights: Alternatives to the Lex Protectionis* (Vol. 12, Kluwer Law 2002).

Van Loon S, 'The power of Google: first mover advantage or abuse of a dominant position?' [2012] 22 *Google and the Law: Empirical Approaches to Legal Aspects of Knowledge-Economy Business Models* 9.

Vaver D, 'Some agnostic observations on intellectual property' [1994] 1 *Intellectual Property Rights* 238.

Verhaert J, 'The challenges involved with the application of Article 102 TFEU to the new economy: a case study of Google' [2014] 35(6) *ECLR* 265.

Vesterdorf B, 'The effect of failure to notify the Spanish and German ancillary copyright laws' [2015] 5 *European Intellectual Property Review*. Available at https://ssrn.com/abstract=2558029 (accessed 5 September 2017).

Viswanath, B., Mislove, A., Cha, M. and Gummadi, KP, 'The evolution of user interaction in Facebook' (2nd ACM Workshop on Online Social Networks 2009).

Vlachos P, Vrechopoulos A and Pateli A, 'Drawing emerging business models for the mobile music industry' [2006] 16(2) *Electronic Markets* 154.

Von Lewinski S, 'EU challenges and solutions in the field of collective management of copyright and related rights' [2014] 1 *Social Perspectives - Journal for Legal Theory and Practice* 104.

Waelde C, Kheria S, Cornwell J and Brown A, *Contemporary Intellectual Property: Law and Policy* (4th edn, Oxford University Press 2016).

Wagman S, 'I want my MP3: legal and policy barriers to a legitimate digital music marketplace' [2009] 17 *Journal Intellectual Property Law* 95.

Wagner T, Benlian A and Hess T, 'Converting freemium customers from free to premium: the role of the perceived premium fit in the case of music as a service' [2014] 24(4) *Electronic Markets* 259.

Wagner-von Papp F, 'Unilateral conduct by non-dominant firms: A comparative reappraisal' (ASCOLA Series 2015).

Wakui M and Cheng T, 'Regulating abuse of superior bargaining position under the Japanese competition law: an anomaly or a necessity?' [2015] 3(2) *Journal of Antitrust Enforcement* 302.

Walzel S, 'Competition, Copyright and Collective Rights Management: A Consultation on Growth and Innovation in the Creative and Digital Technology Industries' (Consumer Focus 2011).

Wang J, *Copyright: Rebalancing the Public and Private Interests in the Areas of Education and Research* (Doctoral dissertation, Stellenbosch: Stellenbosch University 2013).

Wang Y, *Fair Use and File Sharing in Research and Education* (Doctoral dissertation, University of Southampton 2009).

Watt R, 'Copyright and contract law: economic theory of copyright contracts' [2010] 18 *Journal of Intellectual Property Law* 173.

Weill P, Malone T and Apel T, 'The business models investors prefer' [2011] 52(4) *MIT Sloan Management Review* 17.

Whish R and Bailey D, *Competition Law* (7th edn, Oxford University Press 2012).

Wise M, 'Competition law and policy in South Africa' [2004] 5(4) *OECD Journal: Competition Law and Policy* 7.

Wu T, 'When code isn't law' [2003] *Virginia Law Review* 679.

Wunsch-Vincent S and Vickery G, *Digital Broadband Content: Music* (OECD 2005).

Yip G, 'Using strategy to change your business model' [2004] 15(2) *London Business School Review* 17.

Zeff RL and Aronson B, *Advertising on the Internet* (John Wiley & Sons 1999).

Zemer L, 'On the value of copyright theory' [2006] 1 *Intellectual Property Quarterly* 55.

Zimmerman D, 'Copyrights as incentives: did we just imagine that?' [2011] 12(1) *Theoretical Inquiries in Law* 29.

Zingales N, 'The Brazilian approach to internet intermediary liability: blueprint for a global regime?' [2015] 4(4) *Internet Policy Review*.

Zott C, Amit R and Massa L, 'The business model: recent developments and future research' [2011] 37(4) *Journal of Management* 1019.

Zweigert K, Kotez H and Weir T, *An Introduction to Comparative Law* (3rd edn, Clarendon Press 1998).

WEBSITES

'Data Noun – Definition, Pictures, Pronunciation And Usage Notes | Oxford Advanced American Dictionary at Oxfordlearnersdictionaries.Com' (Oxfordlearnersdictionaries.com, 2019), www.oxfordlearnersdictionaries.com/definition/american_english/data (accessed 6 July 2019).

(*Eie.ng*, 2019), http://eie.ng/wp-content/uploads/2016/06/Digital-Rights-and-Freedom-Bill-2016.pdf (accessed 8 July 2019).

(*Placng.org*, 2017), http://placng.org/wp/wp-content/uploads/2017/06/Report-on-a-Bill-for-an-Act-to-repeal-the-Consumer-Protection-Act.pdf (accessed 13 November 2017).

(Policies.google.com, 22 January 2019), https://policies.google.com/privacy?hl=en (accessed 5 July 2019).

Abuse of Dominance' | The Competition Commission of South Africa' (*Compcom.co.za*, 2017), www.compcom.co.za/abuse-of-dominance/ (accessed 6 February 2017).

Alexa.com, 'Alexa – Top Sites in South Africa – Alexa' (*Alexa.com*, 2017), www.alexa.com/topsites/countries/ZA (accessed 19 November 2017).

Alfonso Lamadrid, 'More on Google: is scraping anticompetitive?' (*Chillin' Competition*, 14 February 2013), https://chillingcompetition.com/2013/02/14/more-on-google-is-scraping-anticompetitive/ (accessed 22 November 2017).

allAfrica.com, 'Nigeria: Sony Music Entertainment Opens Office in Nigeria' (*AllAfrica-com*, 15 February 2016), https://allafrica.com/stories/201602250349.html (accessed 29 January 2018).

Ana Ramalho, 'EU competence to create a neighbouring right for publishers? The small pieces make up the big picture' (*Kluwer Copyright Blog*, 5 September 2016), http://copyrightblog.kluweriplaw.com/2016/09/05/eu-competence-create-neighbouring-right-publishers-small-pieces-make-big-picture/ (accessed 26 December 2017).

Andrew Rens, 'Department repeats mistakes of others in bid to alter copyright law' (*Business Day*, 13 October 2017), www.businesslive.co.za/bd/national/2017-10-13-department-repeats-mistakes-of-others-in-bid-to-alter-copyright-law/ (accessed 16 October 2017).

Aurelia Schultz, 'IP and African Music Industries: An Interview with Phil Chard – part 4' (*Afro-IP*, 2 September 2016), http://afro-ip.blogspot.com.ng/2016/09/ip-and-african-music-industries_2.html (accessed 20 January 2017).

Bob Aroture, 'Copyright Society of Nigeria welcomes Universal Music Group to Nigeria' (*NLIP Watch*, 19 January 2017), https://nlipw.com/copyright-society-nigeria-welcomes-universal-music-group-nigeria/ (accessed 30 January 2018).

Cherie Hu, 'Understanding A Data-Driven Music Industry Culture – Lessons From Fast Forward' (*Fastforward*, 24 February 2017), www.hypebot.com/hypebot/2017/03/fastforward-understanding-a-data-driven-music-industry-culture.html (accessed 23 November 2017).

Christiana Angelopolous (*Eppgroup.eu*, 2017), www.eppgroup.eu/sites/default/files/event-files/Barbara%20Javornik/201703/17-01-11%20-EPP%20Presentation%20-%20Angelopoulos.pdf (accessed 7 October 2017).

Christina Angelopoulos, 'EU Copyright Reform: Outside the Safe Harbours, Intermediary Liability Capsizes into Incoherence' (*Kluwer Copyright Blog*, 6 October 2016), http://copyrightblog.kluweriplaw.com/2016/10/06/eu-copyright-reform-outside-safe-harbours-intermediary-liability-capsizes-incoherence/ (accessed 26 December 2017).

Copyright Amendment Bill: Draft | South African Government' (*Gov.za*, 2015), www.gov.za/documents/copyright-amendment-bill-comments-invited-27-jul-2015-0000 (accessed 30 August 2015).

Creative Commons, 'What We Do – Creative Commons' (*Creative Commons*, 2017), https://creativecommons.org/about/ (accessed 20 November 2017).

Data Policy' (Facebook, 19 April 2019), www.facebook.com/policy.php (accessed 5 July 2019).

Digital Announce Pan-African Licensing Agreement Through CAPASSO | 7Digital L Global B2B Music Services' (7digital.com, 2015), www.7digital.com/news/7digital-announce-pan-african-licensing-agreement-through-capasso (accessed 2 July 2019).

Divij Joshi, 'You Wouldn't Stream a Car – What Netflix's Refusal to Bow to Pirates Means for Digital Piracy' (*Spicy IP*, 13 May 2017), https://spicyip.com/2017/05/you-wouldnt-stream-a-car-what-netflixs-refusal-to-bow-to-pirates-means-for-digital-piracy.html (accessed 12 July 2017).

Eleonora Rosati, 'Linking for profit, technical means and burden of proof – German BGH applies CJEU case law to Google's Image Search' (*The IPKat*, 18 December 2017), http://ipkitten.blogspot.com.ng/2017/12/linking-for-profit-technical-means-and.html (accessed 23 December 2017).

Eugene Kim, 'More than half of online sales growth in the US came from Amazon last year' (Business Insider, 2 February 2017), www.businessinsider.com/amazon-drives-more-than-half-us-ecommerce-growth-2016-2017-2?IR=T (accessed 6 July 2019).

European commission, 'Antitrust: Commission sends Statement of Objections to Google on Android operating system and applications' (*European Commission-Press Release*, 20 April 2016), http://europa.eu/rapid/press-release_IP-16-1492_en.htm (accessed 6 January 2017).

Facebook.com, 'Copyright Management | Facebook' (*Rightsmanager.fb.com*, 2017), https://rightsmanager.fb.com/ (accessed 23 November 2017).

Facebook.com, 'Terms Of Service' (*Facebook*, 19 April 2018), www.facebook.com/terms.php (accessed 12 June 2019).

Georg Maurer, 'YouTube Business Model' (*Prezi*, 2 June 2015), https://prezi.com/puvz26rl2cbg/youtube-business-model/ (accessed 20 November 2017).

Gnu.org, 'GNU General Public License' (*GNU Operating System*, 29 June 2007), www.gnu.org/licenses/gpl-3.0.en.html (accessed 12 November 2017).

Google, 'How Content ID works' (*YouTube Help*, 2016), https://support.google.com/youtube/answer/2797370?hl=en&ref_topic=2778544 (accessed 14 March 2016).

Google.com, 'Multi-Channel Network (MCN) overview for YouTube Creators' (*YouTube Help*, 2018), https://support.google.com/youtube/answer/2737059?hl=en (accessed 29 January 2018).

Jason Guerrasio, 'Netflix's record-breaking viewership for 'Bird Box' has sparked debate In Hollywood, and some believe the company's lack of transparency hurts filmmakers' (*Business Insider*, 31 December 2018), www.businessinsider.com/

netflix-bird-box-sparks-debate-over-data-in-hollywood-2018-12?IR=T (accessed 8 July 2019).

Joey Akan, 'Private equity investors are making a big bet on afrobeats' rapid rise up the global charts' (*Quartz Africa*, 31 January 2019), https://qz.com/africa/1539118/don-jazzys-mavin-gets-multimillion-dollar-investment/ (accessed 9 July 2019).

Justicia.com, 'Viacom International, Inc et al v YouTube, Inc et al' (*Dockets and Filings* 2017), https://dockets.justia.com/docket/new-york/nysdce/1:2007cv02103/302164 (accessed 29 January 2017).

Libguides: Copyright And Related Issues: Copyright Amendment Bill 2017' (*Libguides.wits.ac.za*, 2017), http://libguides.wits.ac.za/Copyright_and_Related_Issues/SA_Copyright_Amendment_Bill_2017 (accessed 24 November 2017).

Matthew Sag, 'Inside Views: Lessons from South Africa: Protecting Non-Expressive Uses In Copyright Reform' (*Intellectual Property Watch*, 11 July 2017), www.ip-watch.org/2017/07/11/lessons-south-africa-protecting-non-expressive-uses-copyright-reform (accessed 13 November 2017).

Merriam-Webster, 'Definition Of UPLOAD' (*Merriam-webster.com*, 2017), www.merriam-webster.com/dictionary/upload (accessed 11 November 2017).

Money.futureofmusic.org, 'Songwriter and Composer revenue' (*Artist Revenue Streams*, 2017), http://money.futureofmusic.org/wordpress/wp-content/uploads/2012/01/revenue-streams-handoutlist.pdf (accessed 17 November 2017).

NotJustOk.com, 'About NotJustOk' (NotJust*Ok*, 2016), https://notjustok.com/about/ (accessed 14 March 2016).

NotJustOk.com, 'Advertising Opportunities on NotJustOk.com' (NotJust*Ok*, 2016), http://notjustok.com/advertising-opportunities-on-notjustok-com/ (accessed 12 February 2016).

NotJustOk.com, 'Mino' (*My.NotJustOk.com*, 2016), https://my.notjustok.com/login (accessed 14 March 2016).

OECD Guidelines Organisation for Economic Co-operation and Development, '*OECD Guidelines on the Protection of Privacy and Transborder Flows of Personal Data – OECD*' (oecd.org, 2013), www.oecd.org/internet/ieconomy/oecdguidelinesontheprotectionofprivacyandtransborderflowsofpersonaldata.htm (accessed 8 July 2019).

Openmusicarchive.org, 'About Open Music Archive' (*Open Music Archive*, 2017), www.openmusicarchive.org/about.php (accessed 20 November 2017).

Organisation for Economic Co-operation and Development, '*OECD Guidelines on the Protection of Privacy and Transborder Flows of Personal Data – OECD*' (oecd.org, 2013), www.oecd.org/internet/ieconomy/oecdguidelinesontheprotectionofprivacyandtransborderflowsofpersonaldata.htm (accessed 8 July 2019).

Oxford Dictionaries, 'Tag' (*Oxford*, 2017), https://en.oxforddictionaries.com/definition/tag (accessed 22 November 2017).

PabloIbáñez Colomo, 'Android meets Pronuptia, or why software licensing is like a franchising agreement' (*Chillin' Competition*, 25 April 2016), https://chillingcompetition.com/2016/04/25/android-meets-pronuptia-or-why-software-licensing-is-like-a-franchising-agreement/ (accessed 9 March 2017).

Preamble to the Bill (*Eie.ng*, 2019), http://eie.ng/wp-content/uploads/2016/06/Digital-Rights-and-Freedom-Bill-2016.pdf (accessed 8 July 2019).

Prsformusic.com, 'PRS for Music and SoundCloud reach multi-territory licensing agreement' (*PRS for Music*, 21 December 2015), www.prsformusic.com/press/2015/prs-for-music-and-soundcloud-reach-a-multi-territory-licensing-agreement-ending-legal-proceedings (accessed 19 March 2017).

Rosch T, 'Regarding Google's Search Practices – In The Matter Of Google Inc.' (*Ftc.gov*, 2017), www.ftc.gov/sites/default/files/documents/public_statements/concurring-and-dissenting-statement-commissioner-j.thomas-rosch-regarding-googles-search-practices/130103googlesearchstmt.pdf (accessed 22 November 2017).

Sarah Cole, 'Virtual Friend Fires Employee' (*Naked Law*, 1 May 2009), www.nakedlaw.com/2009/05/index.html (accessed 19 November 2009).

SoundCloud.com, 'About SoundCloud' (*SoundCloud*, 2015), https://soundcloud.com/pages/contact (accessed 5 August 2015).

SoundCloud.com, '*Community Guidelines*', https://soundcloud.com/community-guidelines (accessed 14 March 2016).

Spinlet.com, 'Support/FAQ' (*Spinlet*, 2015)' https://spinlet.com/faq-african-musicians-and-moree (accessed 10 July 2015).

Spotify.com, 'About Us' (*Spotify*, 2015)' www.spotify.com/us/about-us/contact/ (accessed 9 June 2015).

Stuart Dredge, 'Taylor Swift still has bad blood with Spotify over streaming music dispute' (*The Guardian*, 4 August 2015)' www.theguardian.com/technology/2015/aug/04/taylor-swift-bad-blood-spotify-streaming-music (accessed 5 August 2015)

The World's Most Valuable Resource Is No Longer Oil, But Data' (The Economist, 6 May 2017), www.economist.com/leaders/2017/05/06/the-worlds-most-valuable-resource-is-no-longer-oil-but-data (accessed 6 July 2019).

TooXclusive.com, 'Advertise' (*TooXclusive*, 2016), http://tooxclusive.com/advertise (accessed 12 February 2016).

TooXclusive.com, 'Contact Us' (*TooXclusive*, 2017), https://tooxclusive.com/contact-us/ (accessed 22 November 2017).

Travis Clark, 'Netflix says a record-breaking 45 Million accounts watched 'Bird Box' in its first week, but we don't know how many finished the movie' (*Business Insider*, 28 December 2018), www.businessinsider.com/netflix-says-45-million-accounts-watched-bird-box-in-first-week-2018-12?IR=T (accessed 8 July 2019).

UNCTAD | Summary Of Adoption Of E-Commerce Legislation Worldwide' (*Unctad.org*, 2019), https://unctad.org/en/Pages/DTL/STI_and_ICTs/ICT4D-Legislation/eCom-Global-Legislation.aspx (accessed 9 July 2019).

Victor Ekwealor, 'Nigeria's President refused to sign its Digital Rights Bill, what happens now?' (*Techpoint.Africa*, 27 March 2019), https://techpoint.africa/2019/03/27/nigerian-president-declines-digital-rights-bill-assent/ (accessed 8 July 2019).

WIPO, 'WIPO Internet Treaties' (*Wipo.int*, 2017), www.wipo.int/copyright/en/activities/internet_treaties.html (accessed 31 January 2017).

WIPO, 'World Intellectual Property Day 2015 – Get up Stand up For music' (*Wipo.int*, 2015), www.wipo.int/ip-outreach/en/ipday/ (accessed 1 May 2015).

Worldbank.org, 'GDP Per Capita (Current US$) | Data' (*Data.worldbank.org*, 2017), https://data.worldbank.org/indicator/NY.GDP.PCAP.CD?locations=ZA&name_desc=false (accessed 12 November 2017).

Yelena Shagall, 'Jacobsen v Katzer: Federal Circuit Affirms Economic Interest of Open Source Copyright Holder' (*Jolt Digest*, 23 August 2008), http://jolt.law.harvard.edu/digest/jacobsen-v-katzer (accessed 23 November 2017).

YouTube.com, 'Terms Of Service – YouTube' (*YouTube.com*, 22 January 2019), www.youtube.com/static?template=terms (accessed 27 June 2019).

INDEX

For Product Safety Concerns and Information please contact our EU representative GPSR@taylorandfrancis.com
Taylor & Francis Verlag GmbH, Kaufingerstraße 24, 80331 München, Germany

www.ingramcontent.com/pod-product-compliance
Lightning Source LLC
LaVergne TN
LVHW011114300926
849160LV00008B/374

9781032086019